# THE SUNDAY TIMES

Book of

# Real Bread

# THE SUNDAY TIMES

Book of

# Real Bread

Michael Bateman & Heather Maisner

Rodale Press Ltd.
Aylesbury

**Editor:** Josie A. Holtom
**Design:** Richard Johnson
**Photography:** Rex Bamber
**Photography for cover and part titles:** Christine Hanscomb
**Illustrations:** Maggie Raynor

*Assistant Editor:* Gillian Andrews. *Picture Research:* Linda Proud. *Index:* Maureen Charters. *Assistant to the Authors:* Sue Ramus. *Editorial and Editorial Research:* Esther Jagger, Sue MacSwiney, Margaret Stevenson. *Administration:* Sue Clack, Nancy Moorcraft. *Recipe Testing and Consultancy:* Dinah Morrison, Judy Lister, Ruth Orme, Sue Ramus. *History Consultants:* Jane Kenrick, Robert Stewart. *Guide to Mills:* Sara Walden.

Campaign Committee for Real Bread

*Chairman:* Michael Bateman. *Health Correspondent:* Dr. Oliver Gillie. *Cookery Correspondent:* Caroline Conran. *Consumer Correspondent:* Richard Milner. *Feature Writer:* Celia Haddon. *Bread Campaign Organiser:* Sue Ramus. *Bread Campaign Advisor:* Susan Campbell.

Photoset by Modern Text Typesetting
Printed in Great Britain by Page Bros. (Norwich) Ltd.

ISBN 0-87857-368-2

2  4  6  8  10  9  7  5  3  1

Picture Credits
Baking Today 40; BBC Hulton Picture Library 11, 14; Steve Benbow 190; Bodleian Library, Oxford 12, 13; Janet and Colin Bord 22; Downfield Windmill 25; Alex Dufort 59, 176; Homepride 287; Flour Advisory Board 285; FMBRA, Chorleywood 38, 42; Stanley Folb *(Here's Health)* 172; Christopher Francis 236; Richard Johnson 27, 304; Mansell Collection 7, 10, 12, 16; John Marks 34-37; Muncaster Mill 24, 25; National Seed Development Organisation Ltd. 30, 31; Barnet Saidman 230, 231; Scala, Florence 10, 284; *Sunday Times* 44; Walsham Mill 26.

# Contents

| | |
|---|---|
| Introduction | 6 |
| The Campaign for Real Bread | 7 |
| The History of Bread | 10 |

# *Part I*
# *The World of Bread*

| | |
|---|---|
| The Organic Farmer | 18 |
| The Miller | 22 |
| The Seed Breeder | 28 |
| The Baker | 32 |
| The Scientist | 38 |
| The Bran Men | 44 |

## Part II
## The People Who Bake—
## And Their Recipes

Elizabeth David                                      50
Jane Grigson                                         55
Caroline Conran                                      59
Doris Grant                                          65
George and Cecilia Scurfield                         74
Maria Johnson                                        83
Renny Harrop and
   The Good Housekeeping Institute                   96
Nina Froud                                          108
Miriam Polunin                                      118
Brian Binns                                         125
Olive Odell and The Women's Institute               136
Elisabeth Lambert Ortiz                             158
Chalice                                             172
Dinah Morrison                                      176
Grodzinski's                                        182
Bobby Freeman                                       190
Ursel Norman                                        198
Adrian Bailey                                       206
Theodora FitzGibbon                                 218
Arabella Boxer                                      222
Marika Hanbury-Tenison                              225
Claudia Roden                                       228
Anton Mosimann                                      230
Alan Long                                           236
Jordan's                                            245
Allinson                                            249
Craig Sams                                          252
Cranks                                              256
Clement Freud                                       258
Len Deighton                                        259
Barbara Ronay                                       261
Fay Maschler                                        262
John Seymour                                        264
Tessa Traeger                                       265
Barbara Cartland                                    266
Stuart Hall                                         268
Fay Godwin                                          270
Jane Asher                                          272

Using up Bread                                      273
A Step-by-step Children's Recipe                    278

## Part III
## All About Bread

How to Bake                                          284

Kneading                                             286

Rising                                              287

Decorating                                          288

Baking                                              288

Cooling, Storing and Freezing                       289

Ingredients:                                        290
   Flours                                           290
   Yeast                                            297
   Liquids                                          298
   Salt                                             299
   Sweeteners                                       299
   Oils and Fats                                    300
   Glazes and Finishes                              300
   Seeds and Garnishes                              301

Equipment                                           302

Where to Buy Good Flour:                            304
   Guide to British Mills                           304
   Retail Outlets Selling Wholemeal Flour           320

Bibliography                                         332

Index                                               332

## Acknowledgements

We would like to thank the writers, cooks and enthusiasts, who so readily agreed to discuss their ideas about bread and gave permission for their recipes to be included in this book. We also wish to acknowledge our indebtedness to the following people and organisations who supplied information for this book or gave support to the Campaign:

Michael Thomas of Avoncroft Museum of Buildings; The Flour Milling and Baking Research Association, Chorleywood; The Plant Breeding Institute, Cambridge; The Flour Advisory Bureau; The National Association of Master Bakers; Booker Health Foods; Dr. Kenneth Barlow and the McCarrison Society; the Vegetarian Society; The Dunn Nutritional Research Institute, Cambridge; The National Federation of Women's Institutes; Howell Roberts, Baking Executive, Allinson; Dr. Kenneth Vickery, Chairman of Council, The Royal Institute of Public Health and Hygiene; MIND typing group, Kensington and Chelsea; Penguin Books Limited for permission to reprint the following recipes from *English Bread and Yeast Cookery:* Barley Bread, a Rye Loaf and Rice Bread (pp 296, 293, 290) © Elizabeth David 1977; and all the many people who contributed to the Campaign for Real Bread—too numerous to mention.

## Introduction

We all have a right to Real Bread, the staple of our diet. At one time it was always baked at home. But the work gradually passed to bakers who could do it more economically, using better ovens, and professional skills.

In our time these bakers have been forced to surrender their individual skills to the cold super-efficiency of factories and machines. In the name of "convenience", bland loaves, sliced and wrapped, have replaced the good old High Street loaf with its tasty, crisp crust.

Now there is a swing against the convenience loaf. The public wants bread which is tastier and healthier; very often the two go together. The modern baker is reviving the old crafts. A top shop like Harrods is suddenly selling more wholemeal and brown bread than white bread.

Above all home bakers are discovering a new convenience, the convenience of baking their own; rediscovering old skills and new pleasures thanks to the efficiency of modern home ovens, and availability of first-class ingredients.

This book is a celebration of the skills of people who have a passionate feeling for quality in bread, and also a real concern for nutrition and health.

A book can only be a key; like everything else practice brings perfection. But bread-making is such a delightful pastime and pleasure, satisfaction comes very quickly. When failures do occur they are inexpensive and are not often repeated.

Making bread is an activity which is rewarding at every level. We hope you will enjoy sharing the experiences of our enthusiastic contributors and have fun with their recipes. Real Bread is in your hands!

Heather Maisner

Michael Bateman

# The Sunday Times Campaign For Real Bread

We deserve better bread. In January 1980 I asked Caroline Conran and Oliver Gillie, *The Sunday Times* cookery and medical correspondents, to help me organise a Campaign for Real Bread for *The Sunday Times* Magazine.

The Campaign for Real Ale had been immensely successful, largely as a result of consumer demands and media pressure. Bread needed help too. High Street customers were being palmed off with just the same factory-made products that beer-drinkers had had to put up with. The plant-baked loaf has many similarities to keg beer. They are convenience products, convenient to the people who sell them.

The Vegetarian Society had started a Campaign for Wholemeal Bread some five years or more earlier. We felt we could endorse their movement, but spread the word wider and include good breads which are not necessarily wholemeal—for example, the breads that used to be baked in every town before the factories assumed their bread monopoly.

Our Campaign began with the introductory pieces by Caroline and Oliver reprinted here. And during the year, in the Magazine, we ran a series of articles, informing people about the merits of different breads and flours.

Our first Campaign Organiser, Susan Campbell, and her successor, Sue Ramus, answered over 5,000 readers' letters between them; most asked how we could help make more wholemeal bread available. Others asked for more nutritional information about fibre and vitamins in wholemeal bread; those who were converted to the idea of healthy bread asked why the government did nothing about it and, in particular, expressed anger that there was no evident control over labelling. Many were indignant that good bread was not available in institutions like hospitals, pubs or canteens.

During the year we published articles about flours (with the help of Justin de Blank, the Queen's Baker); on plant bakers who saw the light and left to restart their own private bakeries; we supplied 5,000 Master Bakers in the country with copies of a poster of British Breads we had specially printed. Richard Milner, *The Sunday Times* consumer correspondent, investigated sliced white bread and showed how it was used as a loss leader in supermarkets, and sold below its "real" price, while wholemeal bread was offered at the full price.

The Campaign won the support of the Minister of Agriculture, Peter Walker, who agreed to tighten up labelling laws, following an inquiry in which our readers took part, showing that a quarter of the loaves sold across the counter as wholemeal were not. In a special article, Celia Haddon unearthed the pioneers of bran, men who risked ridicule in their day to fight and win a scientific case for fibre in the diet. (The interviews are included in the World of Bread section.)

At the end of the year we called a one-day Real Bread Conference at the ICA in London, and government research scientists, experts on nutrition, vegetarians, millers, product managers for supermarkets, bakers, and journalists met to talk about Real Bread; and a few weeks later figures were announced showing that the trend towards wholemeal and brown breads had swung from 15 per cent to 18 per cent in the course of the year. And by January 1981, the plant bakers were producing wrapped wholemeal loaves with a full fibre content to meet the new demand, and consumption continues to grow.

Letters continue to come into the Campaign from people who would like to organise local consumer protection groups. They say they are fed up with being told what bread they are supposed to like; it's their turn now to speak up for themselves.

# The Taste of Real Bread

When you sit down to a meal in Spain, France or Italy, a basket of bread is placed in front of you on the table. While you are waiting for your meal you find that you eat several pieces, and probably ask the waiter to bring more. You enjoy it.

But could you honestly eat your way through a basket of British factory-baked bread? Of course not. In fact, you might be insulted to find it on your table at all, unless you happened to be eating in a motorway service station.

For centuries bread was a proud staple of our diet. Now it appeals less and less. People are not enjoying their bread and, as a result, they are buying less of it. In 1956 the average amount of bread eaten weekly in Great Britain per head was about 3 lb (1.5 kg)—that's about two and a half large loaves. By 1978 we were eating 2 lb (1 kg) per week—equal to two small loaves.

Why are we having to put up with second-rate loaves? The truth is simply that factory-made bread is so much cheaper than real bread. The technological advances of the Sixties and Seventies produced methods which save money.

With the mechanical-chemical process known as CBP (Chorleywood Baking Process) bread rises quickly: cutting the time needed to bake the bread cuts labour costs. In addition, the method enables the baker to use a weaker—and therefore cheaper—flour with more water added.

CBP produces about four per cent more bread from the same materials as traditional methods. It has no crust and not much texture because it has to be under-baked. If it wasn't, the crumbs would jam up the slicing machine. And the consumer wouldn't be able to squeeze the loaf to see if it is "fresh".

The big bakers argue that the British public wants cheap bread. But declining consumption figures show that they don't seem to want it that much, and the giant industries who have taken over from the small bakers are not thriving. As the chairman of one of the Big Three millers (Spillers French, Rank Hovis McDougall, and Associated British Foods) has admitted in a Government report: "We do not see growth in this market; we see only decline."

In England and Wales 70 to 75 per cent of all bread bought is made in factory plants. But in Northern Ireland only 55 to 60 per cent is factory baked. A spokesman for the North of Ireland Bakers, Confectioners and Allied Workers Union, explains exactly why: "In the larger plant bakeries it is a question of quantity, not quality, with a use of more water increasingly in mind to increase the yield. Most master bakers (the bakers who don't work in the bakery plants) give the public what they want. The small bakeries in Northern Ireland use better-quality ingredients than the large plant bakeries, and this is reflected in the increasingly larger share of the market they supply."

The big bakers are now reduced to two. Spillers French pulled out of their big plant-bakery business completely, having lost £28 million in six years on their baking activities. But the other two are still convinced that plant-baked bread is the only thing that the public will buy. Their conviction is that we want a loaf that will keep a week, that is convenient and that we can squeeze through the wrappers.

We believe that a vociferous minority is not easily satisfied, that we care about the standard of our country's bread, and that we would like to be able to buy good bread, knowing what it contains and enjoying it for its character, its value and its daily contribution to our general health and well-being.

*Caroline Conran*

# Our Health

If we want to be healthy, we would do well to eat more bread. Over the last 100 years we have eaten less and less of it: in Britain, bread now provides us with just one-sixth of our energy and protein needs. But our intake of fat and meat has gone up.

At the same time, there has been an increase in the number of people dying from heart disease and an increase in the numbers of women under 30 suffering from breast cancer. Too much animal fat in the diet and too few cereals have been blamed as a cause of these diseases.

Wholemeal bread—made from the whole grain of the wheat—provides extra vitamins, dietary fibre and also, in the wheat germ, substances called essential fatty acids. The importance of these essential fatty acids—also obtained from vegetable oils—is only now beginning to be appreciated. We need a minimum amount of them if the blood is not to become sticky and clot too easily. Essential fatty acids are also necessary for building new cells and new membranes—particularly those lining blood vessels.

Many people don't eat bread on the grounds that it is fattening. But if we get most of our energy from meat and fat we increase the proportions of non-essential fats in our diet. These fats, though a source of energy, are, in excess, fattening. In fact they compete with essential fatty acids in our metabolism and may almost block them out.

The problem is not so much the starches in our diet (such as bread, pasta and potatoes) which are fattening, as the fat which is taken with them. In terms of calories in a given weight of food, bread and other starches are much less fattening than fat or meat. Bread is filling and satisfying and so would serve as a good basis for a slimming diet. This is particularly true of wholemeal bread which contains bran—the fibrous shell surrounding the wheat grain.

Bran is now a major source of fibre in our diet. Until recently this fibre was thought to be indigestible and of no importance. Now it is realised that it plays an important role in providing bulk which softens the food and helps the intestines to operate easily.

The most obvious result of this is to prevent constipation. But it also prevents diverticular disease—a common and serious disorder of the bowel.

Dietary fibre is now widely believed by doctors to prevent many of the diseases of civilisation—such as appendicitis, gallstones, diabetes, varicose veins and piles, as well as heart disease and bowel cancer. These diseases used to be rare before we stopped eating wholemeal bread; they are still rare in native African societies and in parts of Europe where much more dietary fibre is eaten.

Wholemeal bread also contains more B vitamins, more vitamin E and more of the essential trace minerals—copper, manganese, zinc and magnesium. Between 50 and 85 per cent of these minerals are removed with the wheat germ and bran in the manufacture of white flour. Any remaining vitamin E is destroyed when the flour is bleached to make it whiter.

Loss of these vitamins might not matter if a person is eating an otherwise varied diet. However, the long-term effects on health—particularly for those people who are eating a lot of processed foods depleted of vitamins and nutrients—are probably not good.

The research of Professor J.N. Morris at the London School of Hygiene has found that civil servants and bus workers who eat more cereal fibre—whether in bread or breakfast cereals—have fewer attacks of coronary thrombosis.

Oliver Gillie

# The History of Bread

*c.* **3000** BC In Egypt the baking of bread is becoming a sophisticated skill along with the making of beer. All kinds of bread are made (from barley, oats and millet) and the first leavened breads are recorded—in a warm climate wild yeasts are attracted to flour mixtures and bakers are experimenting with the resulting bubbly, leavened doughs. They may even be deliberately adding the yeast from beer mixtures. But the practice of eating leavened bread does not immediately become widespread.

The Egyptians invent a closed oven. Until then the grain mixtures have been cooked on hot stones and in front of open fires.

Throughout the region bread assumes great significance and homage is paid to Osiris, the god of grain. Bread was even used instead of money: the workers who built the great pyramid at Cheops were paid in bread.

*c.* **2300** BC In India grain cultivation begins along the Indus valley.

*c.* **8000** BC Man, who has been predominantly meat-eating, begins to cultivate land and grow simple grass seed, the first wheats. This agricultural revolution begins in the Middle East.

At first grain is crushed by hand with a pestle and mortar. In Egypt they develop a simple saddlestone or quern with a rocking-horse motion.

The first breads bore no relation to the bread we eat today. They were unleavened breads—they had no raising or aerating agent and were made from flours made with a mixed variety of grains. They were a cross between a biscuit and dried-out porridge. The nearest surviving equivalents are flat Indian wheat chappatis or Mexican tortillas.

*c.* **5000** BC Egypt develops grain production along the fertile banks of the River Nile.

*c.* **4500** BC Grain becomes a staple food, and spreads to the Balkans. Gradually, over the next 2,000 years, it spreads throughout Europe.

*c.* **3700** BC The first evidence of grain being cultivated in Britain.

*c.* **3400** BC Wheat has been little more than a skinny grass seed until this time. Now tougher varieties *einkorn* and *emmer* wheat, are evolving. *Emmer* has a tough husk, is strong, enduring, and reliable. It is the mother of modern wheat.

*c.* **1500** BC Horses take over from men who have ploughed by hand. They pull the first iron plough-shares, and so open up heavier soil which could not be cultivated before.

*c.* **1050** BC The south of England becomes a fairly well-established centre of agriculture. Barley and oats are grown freely and by 500 BC wheat is becoming important too.

*c.* **1000** BC In Rome risen, yeasted bread becomes popular.

*c.* **500** BC In Rome grain milling becomes simplified by the invention of the rotary quern: a circular stone wheel turns on another which is fixed—the basis of milling right up to the nineteenth century.

*c.* **450** BC In Greece the watermill is invented: it will eventually provide the power to turn the milling stones to grind wheat, but not for some centuries yet.

*c.* **150** BC In Rome bakers form their first craft guilds and, according to Pliny, the well-to-do Romans insist on the more exclusive and expensive white bread. A preference which will not be shaken for centuries.

*c.* **150** BC Man's first mechanical dough-mixer: Marcus Virgilus Eurysaces invents a mixer, which is powered by horses and donkeys.

*c.*55 BC Roman invasion of Britain. The Romans find the Britons still using simple *emmer* wheat, crushing it by hand, and baking it in small stone-piled "ovens". The Romans introduce more sophisticated techniques including watermills to turn circular stone querns.

*c.* **40** BC Bread and politics. In Rome the authorities decree that bread shall be distributed to adult males — entirely free of charge.

*A rotary corn-mill still in use in the fertile delta region between Alexandria and Cairo.*

*c.* **500** AD Saxons and Danes settle in Britain and introduce rye which endures well in cold Northern climates. Dark rye bread becomes a staple, and remains so until the Middle Ages.

*c.* **550** AD In Europe scratch ploughs are replaced by a Slav invention, a heavyweight plough called a mouldboard which can move the heavy clay soils of Northern Europe. This leads to the introduction of a crop rotation system.

*c.* **600** The Persians are credited with the invention of the windmill. The power generated can be geared to turn heavier circular stone querns for grinding grain. The idea is not exploited in Europe for some 600 years, but they then begin to appear in Western Europe.

*c.* **1066** Introduction of hair sieves, called *temes* or *temses* to sift out bran from flour.

**1086** The Domesday Book. Watermills are shown to be the prime source of milling in Britain. Some 6,000 of them serve a total of 3,000 communities living in lands south of the Trent/Severn.

*c.* **1150** Bakers form themselves into guilds to protect themselves from the powerful manorial barons. In 1155 London bakers form themselves into a brotherhood.

**1191** Windmills come to Britain. The first one recorded is in Bury St. Edmunds, Suffolk.

**1202** The king presents the first laws in Britain to regulate the price of bread and permitted profit.

**1266** The Assize of Bread. This body sits to regulate the weight and price of loaves. The first bread subsidy recorded in Britain is given—12d for eight bushels of wheat made into bread. For breaking the laws, bakers could be consigned to the pillory, or banned from baking for life.

**1307** Bread becomes "big business". White bread has one guild, brown bread another, and this year the London Baker's Company is established. There is a City of London bread market too, in Bread Street, which defends London bread against provincial bread, forcing its rural competitors to sell at uncompetitive prices.

*c.* **1350** Until now windmills have been built around a simple pillar or post—the post mill. Now the tower windmill begins to replace it. Eventually England could boast 10,000 windmills.

*c.* **1400** The Miller's Tale is written. Chaucer pointed to the greedy ways of millers and their suspicious standing in society.

*c.* 1450 It is discovered that growing rye can become infected by a mould which induces terrible madness, hysteria and hallucinations.

1569 Queen Elizabeth I unites the quarrelling white-bread and brown-bread bakers to form the Worshipful Company of Bakers.

*c.* 1620 English settlers in Virginia, USA, establish the first American wheatfields.

1666 The Great Fire of London. London's baking trade is totally destroyed: the mills, granaries, and ovens. Mills and granaries will never flourish to the same degree in the capital again, although baking continues.

*c.* 1700 For the first time in Britain's history wheat begins to overtake rye and barley as the chief bread grain. This is partly due to new agricultural inventions like Jethro Tull's seed-drill.

*c.* 1700 Norfolk farmers introduce a four-year system of crop rotation.

1709 A new act supersedes the Assize of 1266. It empowers magistrates to control the type, weight and price of loaves. Only "white", "wheaten" and "household" bread is permitted, unless a magistrate allows otherwise.

*c.* 1750 Introduction of the "blotting cloth". This allows production of a finer white flour.

1757 A report accuses bakers of adulterating bread by adding alum, lime, chalk and powdered bones to keep it as white as their customers demand. After a searching investigation by a chemist, Henry Jackson, the bakers' reputations are partly cleared, but it is shown that they have indeed been using alum which reacts with protein to toughen the dough.

1757 Parliament bans alum and all other additives to bread, although many bakers ignore the new Act.

1783 First chain of bakery shops in England is set up by Christopher Potter of Westminster. It is the first step to the monopolies which will dominate bakeries 200 years later.

1798 Wheat becomes the predominate grain for baking bread.

1815 The Government passes the Corn Laws to protect British wheat-growers. The duty on imported wheat is raised to a prohibitive level, but at the same time price controls are lifted on bread at home. (Thus undoing the Assize of Bread of 1266—although standard weights for loaves are maintained.) The cost of bread soars.

1822 In the London area the standard weights for loaves are abolished. Bakers must weigh each loaf for the customer in his presence.

1826 Wholemeal bread, as eaten by the military, is recommended as being better for health than the white bread eaten by the aristocracy, following experiments by the French physiologist François Magendie. He reports that a dog fed on fine white bread and water dies after only 50 days; a dog fed on coarse bread "lives and keeps his health".

1834 An experiment in Switzerland which is to change the course of the world's bread-making: the first roller mills go into action. Whereas the stonegrinding mills crush the grain, and distribute

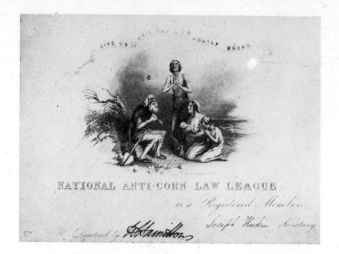

the vitamins and nutrients evenly, the roller mills break open the wheat berry, flattening the nutritious wheat germ so that it can be separated easily from the endosperm. This process quickly and efficiently produces white flour which makes today's mass-produced white loaf. It was not until the 1870s that this process became economic.

**1846** The Corn Laws are repealed, largely as a result of the Irish potato famine, and the duty on imported grain is removed. Hard white flours of strong baking quality are available, setting a national standard for a good-rising white loaf.

**1849** First bakery union founded in Manchester.

**1850** Adulteration of bread continues. *The Lancet,* today an eminent medical journal, risks libel to campaign against illegal additives in bread. The Government responds, and appoints an Analytical and Sanitary Commission which analyses 49 different breads. Not one of them is free of alum.

**1860** Government passes the first Food and Drugs Act, which is designed to ensure that all foods sold are pure.

**1861** Bakery workers extend their union to form the Amalgamated Union of Operative Bakers, Confectioners and Allied Workers.

A revolution in milling. Roller mills come to Britain at last; the first one is at North Shore, Liverpool. Out go the old-fashioned watermills and windmills. Some people still demanded the quality of flour produced by the slower wheat-

crushing processes, but only roller milling could produce the quantity required to feed the rapidly expanding population.

**1887** The Master Bakers and Confectioners organise themselves into a National Association in Birmingham.

**c. 1900** The Master Bakers open Britain's first National Bakery School in London.

**c. 1920** "Ageing" of white flour, which previously occurred during storage, is now achieved by adding agene, or nitrogen trichloride which speeds up the "ageing" of flour as well as making it whiter.

**1923** The British Flour Millers Research Association is formed, with its own laboratory at St. Albans, Hertfordshire.

**c. 1930** Wholemeal flour wins an honourable place in nutrition as scientists identify essential vitamins and minerals.

**1941** Chalk (calcium) is added to bread to prevent rickets (a bone deficiency). This followed an outbreak of the disease in Dublin.

Large factory bakers form their own association, the Federation of Wholesale and Multiple Bakers.

**1942** In order to reduce wheat imports, and essentially because of the shortage of shipping space, the Ministry of Food rules that bread should contain a higher amount of bran and wheat germ, and raises the extraction rate from 70 per cent to 85 per cent. (Extraction rate is the percentage of whole grain recovered as flour.) This becomes known as national flour. The rate does, however, vary during the war according to the exigencies of the blockade.

**1944** Doris Grant publishes *Your Daily Bread,* in which it is explained how home bakers can make wholemeal bread without kneading the dough, and with one rising only.

**1946** The baking industry founds its own research station, known as the British Baking Industries Research Association, at Chorleywood. Later it will be the inventor of a new bread-making process.

**1950** The importance of fibre in diet is suggested by Surgeon-Captain Peter T. L. Cleave. Wholemeal bread has 8.5 per cent dietary fibre, brown bread has 5.1 per cent and white bread has 2.7 per cent.

**1953** The government issues a National Flour Order. Bread with a minimum extraction rate of 80 per cent receives a subsidy, anything with less does not. Even the breads which are not subsidised must have a minimum extraction rate of 72 per cent, and Vitamin B1, nicotinic acid and chalk must be added to enrich them.

**1955** The baking industry chooses chlorine dioxide to replace agene as an improving agent for white flour in Britain and America—although scientists claim that there has never been any evidence of the ill-effects of agene in humans.

**1956** The National Loaf is abandoned. But under the Flour (Composition) Order 1956, all flour which is not 100 per cent wholemeal must contain minimum amounts of chalk (calcium), iron, Vitamin B1, and nicotinic acid.

**1963** Bread and Flour Regulations introduced. These control the basic composition of bread and restrict additives to specified substances.

**1965** The Chorleywood Bread Process, evolved in 1961 by the baking research station, becomes general throughout the country; the slow development of dough is replaced by a few minutes of intense mechanical agitation in high-speed mixers.

**1974** The Food Standards Committee publish a report on bread and flour.

**1976** The Vegetarian Society launches CAMREB, a campaign to promote wholemeal bread.

**1979** Bread strike. This caused an increase in the number of small bakers and the volume of wholemeal bread produced.

**1980** *The Sunday Times* launches its Campaign for Real Bread to promote bread which is tastier and healthier.

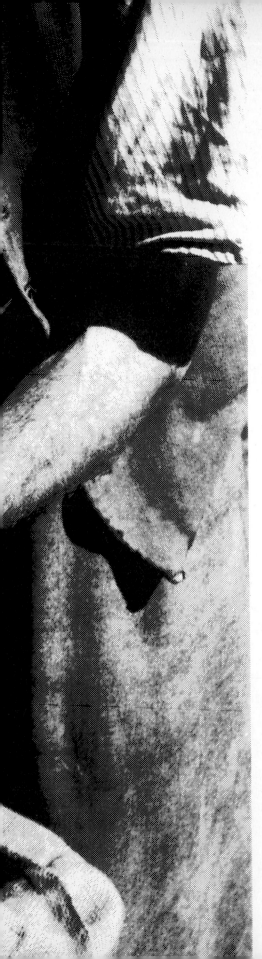

# Part I
# The World of Bread

# The Organic Farmer

*Growing wheat the old way—
without fertilisers or
pesticides.*

THE IRONY OF MODERN life is that if you want something "natural", you will probably have to pay more for it. Food which has been processed, handled in many complex ways, will be cheaper.

There's nothing quite as simple as wholemeal flour. It is simply the whole wheat berries ground up, and sold as such. Yet natural wholemeal flour will cost more than white flour which has been milled and sieved to extract both bran and wheat germ, bolted through fine mesh to sieve it, and bleached, aged and stabilised.

So the organic farmer who puts a spot of farmyard manure on his field is suddenly earning more per ton than the intensive farmer who is buying hugely expensive nitrates (converted from North Sea Oil) and scientifically developed fungicides and insecticides, which are needed to defend the productive but delicate new strains of wheat.

It's an irony which amuses Farmer Bert Capon, a Suffolk farmer who decided ten years ago to reject the apparently huge returns possible with the new crop developments.

"When I became an organic farmer ten years ago, everyone thought I was a crank," he says. Now he finds that everyone wants to get on the band wagon. It's the height of fashion, organic farming. His produce is highly prized, and associated with excellent quality, and therefore commands better prices. He gets 25 per cent more for the wheat he grows without using modern intensive aids.

Unfortunately, in Farmer Capon's view, the organic boom attracts the wrong kind of people suddenly. "Investors. They want to invest in the name *organic*. The words *organic, stoneground,* and even *natural,* appeal to people who want to invest. They recognise that a certain section of the public is gullible enough to pay more for *natural* goods. So you have to pay an exorbitant price for them. Look at the prices in West End wholefood stores. In theory this kind of food should be cheaper, not more expensive."

And so it would be if people came to the farm gate to buy it; if you bought a sack of grain from the farmer. That's the ideal Farmer Capon imagines. "From us you can buy, not three pound and seven pound bags of flour, but 14 lb, 28 lb and 56 lb. You can; and it will store for a couple of months."

Farmers, and consumers, would need to be better organised to bring about his Utopian ideal, although it's simple enough. If you've decided you want the healthier, tastier alternative to the white flour which is sold in the majority of shops, and you don't want to pay high prices for "natural" wholemeal in specialist shops, you should search out a local farmer and buy grain. "Ideally every farmer would have his own small, stoneground mill. I have one. They are not so expensive. You buy the grain from the farmer, and he freshly mills it for you. Or else you buy the grain from him and mill it yourself as you need it, using cheap handmills or small electric mills, or even an attachment to a Kenwood food mixer. Grain will keep for two years, if you keep it in a dry place, so you can have fresh flour every time you bake. If you want a fine unbleached flour, you can sieve it yourself."

Farmer Capon warms to the theme. "You might decide to be even more independent and self-sufficient, and grow your own wheat. You can enjoy the best of modern knowledge with the advantages of traditional practices."

Farmer Capon's ideas are very similar to the philosophy expressed by Dr. Otto Schumaker, whose work he admires, and who wrote the influential book *Small is Beautiful.* He's also a member of The Soil Association, whose members champion the national cause of organic farming, and The Organic Farmers and Growers. The Soil Association's headquarters at Haughley are not many miles from his own farm in the pretty village of Market Weston, close to the Suffolk border, where, a few yards across it into Norfolk, the newly restored Garboldisham Mill mills flour from his grain.

It's a great pleasure to step inside his clean, beautiful farm, with its 350-year-old farmhouse, and its Tudor barns which conceal some surprisingly modern and practical machinery. A flock of black-headed sheep have mown the grass, now cropped like a thick green carpet. He has a dozen Jerseys for milking, 20 head of beef cattle, a dozen pigs and a few sows, 50 Rhode Island Reds, 12 Game Whites, and on the picturesque ponds about 20 ducks. Following old-fashioned farming practice, he seeks a self-supporting balance. From the grain he sells he sieves off each year ten tons of dross and tailings (husks, straw and broken pieces of wheat) and this goes to feed the animals. In the years when he's not growing wheat, he'll maybe have clover or turnips, both animal feeds. Surplus milk from the cows feed the pigs. And the manure from the animals fertilises the land and the pasture in which he grows crops like wheat, barley and oats.

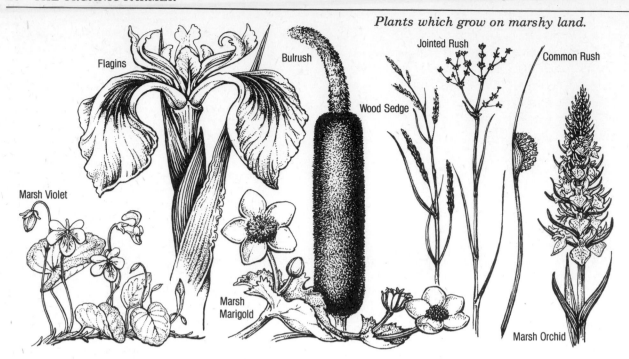

*Plants which grow on marshy land.*

Flagins · Bulrush · Jointed Rush · Common Rush · Wood Sedge · Marsh Violet · Marsh Marigold · Marsh Orchid

This kind of farm has been disappearing fast as monocultures sweep away the elements of traditional mixed farming. Capon would prefer to run a wholly mixed farm, but realises it isn't practical in modern times. So he puts most of his land to crops, but he grows them to the well-tested Norfolk Rotation system to prevent the resources of his land being bankrupted by over-use.

"Wheat is a strong grain and needs clean land and rich soil. So the year before we grow wheat we build up the nitrogen in the soil: we sow beans or clover, or roots, or even leave it fallow. Here is a typical rotation: Year One: Beans or clover (or fallow). Year Two: Wheat. Year Three: Barley or oats. Year Four: Beans or clover (or fallow).

"We don't spray weeds. We even like weeds in the proper place. We let them grow in autumn and plough them into the land. Weeds are only a nuisance in your corn. Land in good heart with good humus gets very few weeds; and the weeds you do get tell you what's wrong. Mayweed is the sign of lack of lime. Watergrass grows where land needs draining."

"I don't spend anything on fertiliser. I don't spend anything on grain, because I keep some back from each year's harvest. I perhaps spend £7 an acre on sending a man round to rogue wild oats—pull out wild oats by hand so that the seeds don't spill—and deal with other weeds. Compare that with the costs of intensive farming. The intensive farmer spends perhaps £55 or more an acre spraying and at least £30 to £40 on fertilisers." Capon knows perfectly well, of course, that the intensive farmer can keep up the performance year in year out, by heavy doses of fertiliser, and he, the organic farmer, must rest the land. But even so, look at the figures.

Capon gets up to £135 a ton for selling his organically-grown wheat to a miller who stone-grinds it. He produces two tons of grain per acre; that earns him a total of £270. Knock off £7 an acre for the cost of hand-weeding and some spot spraying of a mild weedkiller. Profit per acre—around £263.

The intensive farmer gets about £100 a ton, by selling his wheat to the big roller-millers. His yield is three tons an acre, worth £300. Knock off about £55 for spraying insecticides and fungicides, and £35 for fertiliser; £90 altogether. Profit is therefore £210 per acre, £53 less than Farmer Capon.

The intensive farmer can scale up his profits by risking heavier investment in insecticides and fertilisers but Capon doesn't believe they can go on forcing high yields; something will have to give. And farmers who've decided it was a mistake to put all their eggs in one basket will find it too late to turn back the clock. Capon says it takes at least 15 years to turn a farm over to organic principles.

Bert Capon is a lean hawk-eyed man of 56, with long combed grey hair, pipe-smoking, a man who loves to talk. He's been here since he was eight, in

knee pants, when his father rented 200 acres of a large local estate—part of 5,000 acres in all. "We rented the 200 acres at £1 an acre—on strict condition that we didn't pull down hedges, or farm buildings, or uproot woods. Father was a little unhappy; we didn't have the freedom others did. Then the estate was sold, and we were able to buy 200 acres. My father was a conventional farmer, so I don't think he'd have understood why I chose organic farming. He'd have said, "What are you talking about." But I'm thinking of land in the long term. The organic farmer shirks short term profits for long term satisfactions." He's glad they didn't pull down the barns, the hedges and the trees. "Farming is a long term thing, a ten-year thing. You've got to think twice before you pull down a tree."

"I look on life as a whole; I look on myself as the manager of a farm, who is allowed to enjoy it for a while; then I should hand it on in good heart, as it was handed to my father, and from him to me. I'm not depleting, robbing the soil."

But Capon realises that he is privileged among farmers today. It's new to think of farmland as "investment". Capon's father rented it at £1 an acre. By 1966 it was only £2 an acre. Today you buy it—at £2,000 an acre. "We're trying to capitalise the land all the time; in feudal days the only rate charged was a tithe—a tenth. I find it easy to believe in the old feudal system—or at least a romanticised idea of it. It stood for the qualities of life. In the last fifteen years money has been poured into farming, taking away the natural balance. Many farmers are treated like machines and told what to do by the chemical people, the fertiliser people, and ADAS (the government's Agricultural Development Advisory Service). But in the end farming boils down to good husbandry, common sense."

The Capon family enjoy the organic life, with sometimes necessary good humour. When Bert Capon remarks, "Well, we're not in this to make money," his wife replies quickly; "well, we're not."

But they smile; they've produced two grown-up daughters who enjoy the organic life. One, Jane, who works in London, is restoring an old cottage on the farm; the other, Mary, a veterinary nurse, is married to a local farmer, with 1,000 acres.

They all swear by real, home-baked bread made with flour milled from home-grown grain, a sturdy variety called *Maris Widgeon*. Mrs. Capon makes it to Doris Grant's recipe (page 67), cooking it in ceramic pots in the Aga. Mr. Capon eats a loaf a day with cheese. Mrs. Capon says it was due to wholemeal bread that she was able to lose several stone when she went on a crash diet some years ago: a diet which consisted of eating very little besides wholemeal bread, and plain boiled potatoes. "Everybody else cuts out bread and potatoes", she says. "They're wrong." ·

# The Miller

*Stoneground flour—
an old tradition brought
to life with modern technology.*

MICHAEL COOPER owns Walsham Mill, one of the up-and-coming suppliers of organic stone-ground wholemeal flour. He only became a miller five years ago, aiming for the market the big boys miss, the wholefood business. He made such quick strides that wholefood outlets are now only a quarter of his business.

Justin de Blank, the Queen's baker, uses his wholemeal flour. Even his bran is prized. A Birmingham University Hospital dietician tested brans and Cooper's was judged the best. When this was published in an article, a group of Midlands Hospitals ordered regular supplies from him—to keep their patients regular.

Pioneers of the bran movement have had some success helping bed-ridden patients in hospitals; although when Mike Cooper went to his own hospital in Ipswich he found that bran wasn't on the breakfast menu. Nurses told him that they had to go out and buy it for patients, as the hospital quartermaster refused to put it on his food requirements.

Cooper says he's on the quality band wagon: "People want something which is good value for money and nutritionally good. I'm not a health food freak. I think the days of the freaks have gone."

Mike Cooper is the son of an Essex farmer, and a former salesman for an agricultural machinery company. He stumbled on Walsham Mill by chance. The company had asked him to look out for storage space for their machinery. The mill seemed spacious, but the company didn't want it. Suddenly Cooper decided that he did. He was on good terms with enough farmers in East Anglia to go into business, and he knew many of the organic farmers well; he'd always thought they got a poor deal. He decided to mill organic wheats.

"The big millers go for quantity. The crop development people go for quantity too, developing strains with bigger and bigger yields; and you have to use bigger and bigger doses of chemicals and fertilisers to get the yields. I had grown to like the organic farmers, going for smaller yields, but producing beautiful quality. They're the only people growing *Cappelle* now; a lovely grain that makes a lovely flour."

Ten organic farmers provide Cooper with grain. The demands are strict. All wheat goes for laboratory

*Post windmill at Chillenden, Kent.*

analysis to check that no chemical residues from crop sprays and pesticides are present. The tests are so exact, that a field has to be farmed organically for four years before the existing chemicals are leached away, meeting the wholefood demands.

If organic flour is selling in the shops cheaply, says Cooper, darkly, it probably isn't the real thing. "Some unscrupulous people selling organic wheat aren't cleaning their flour, or aren't selling real wheat.

"The farmer growing conventional wheat expects to make up to £220 profit from an acre, based on getting three tons of grain, the magic figure. The organic farmer is lucky if he gets 1½ tons to the acre. To encourage him to grow wheat at all you have to offer him a premium, and we pay them 25 per cent over the rate for ordinary wheat. After that you lose another ten per cent in cleaning it, although we sell that off to animal feed. So organic grain must cost at least 30 per cent more."

Cooper is a big man in his thirties, with a bushy plume of grey hair and half-framed glasses. He dresses all over in warm farmer's brown, and uses a pipe as a prop to emphasise honest points. He obviously enjoys being a miller, and he's growing into the local traditions.

Late into the nineteenth century the eastern counties were landmarked with watermills and windmills. The watermills were older, a fine example being Flatford Mill near Dedham, the mill made famous by the brush of John Constable. Perhaps only a few dozen windmills live on in a decent condition, although preservation societies are active in Norfolk and Suffolk. Mike Cooper is in fact involved in trying to get one back into action in Pakenham, three miles away. The Suffolk Preservation Society has spent £20,000 repairing the outer fabric, and now they hope to install £14,000 worth of milling equipment.

Walsham Mill has a history. There has been a mill on the site since 1577 when John Tyler was the miller. In 1888 there was a historic event in the area, when they bought a new buck—the frame which contains the mechanism which sustains the sails. The buck was dismantled from a mill in Wortham, ten miles north and laid on its side on a huge timber wagon called a drug, and towed by traction engine to Walsham. The journey took a week, partly due to the fact that they had to cut down trees in their path.

Walsham Mill was one of the older kinds of mill, a post mill; the post was a vertical timber, on which the buck revolved. The buck frame was clad with timbers, giving it the name of a smock mill. This kind of mill was less enduring than the large stone and brick tower mills, surmounted by a cap to sustain the sails. They all had a weather-vane, or fantail, to turn the sails into the wind.

All this was gone by the time Cooper arrived. However, the mill house which encased the post still stands, as it usually does: often used as animal shelters or store rooms (there's one which is adapted as a petrol station) and more and more often inventively converted by architects into talking-point dwellings. Cooper's, with a handsome wooden roof, is quite properly his office.

The walls are adorned with notices from the Flour Milling and Baking Research Association. One documents the wide variety of hard British wheats now available: "*Bouquet* and *Flinor*, I use them. *Maris Freeman* and *Maris Widgeon*, good. *Sappo*, good but I don't like it. *Timmo, Waggoner, Sicco*. These are called *A* wheats, large and finely textured. British wheat is as good as anyone else's wheat. I'm biased, but I think it's second to none."

On the far wall is a map of Europe hinting territorial ambitions. "We're selling to Norway," he said. And producing a flour bag printed in Italian: "We started exporting to Italy. But we were squashed by the falling pound."

The visit to see the stonegrinding is an anticlimax. Somehow, having read about craftsmen spending 18 hours at a time "dressing" a pair of large millstones, cutting the radials with a hammer and chisel, you expect something sensational. Suffolk millstones were often made of French burrstone, like five foot wide flat cheeses, weighing a ton or more each, the top one turning slowly on the fixed one below, machinery clanking, the wind sails creaking. The old mills.

Mike Cooper's stone mill wheel is so small you could walk by it. The metal pipe which feeds it with grain from the loft is more prominent; the grinding wheel is held vertically in a metal casing no more than two foot across. As it grinds away, driven by electricity, a pipe with a revolving screw on the Archimedes principle draws the flour up and away, to a weighing and packing unit.

The weigher packer does the job of two people, and although it has cost him £10,000 it will pay for itself in four years. That's the agricultural machine salesman in him talking.

His little mill, which is Danish, pounds out three-quarters of a ton of flour an hour, and soon it will be joined by another, three times as big—and it's British. He thinks it's a model with a future in the export market.

Up in the loft it's very British. Balls of polythene

*John Fairbanks, millwright of Staffordshire, dressing the runner stone of a pair of oatmeal stones at Muncaster Mill, Ravenglass, Cumbria.*

*The milling floor, Muncaster Mill.*

*The ground floor, showing the "jigger box" used for grinding oatmeal, Muncaster Mill.*

*Hopper feeding wheat into grinding stones, Downfield Windmill, Soham, Cambs. Grinding mechanism.*

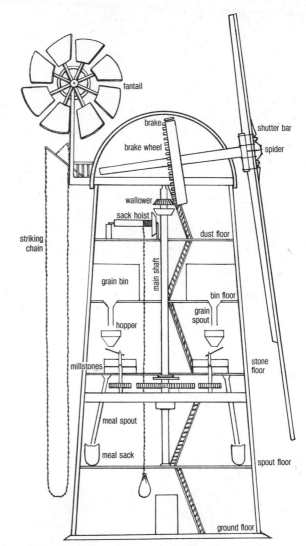

fantail

brake

brake wheel

shutter bar

spider

wallower

sack hoist

dust floor

striking chain

grain bin

main shaft

bin floor

hopper

grain spout

millstones

stone floor

meal spout

meal sack

spout floor

ground floor

*Cross section of a post windmill.*

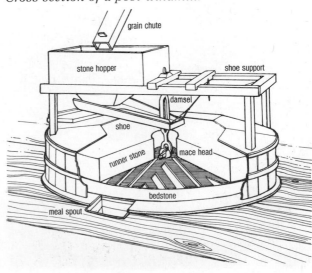

grain chute

stone hopper

shoe support

damsel

shoe

runner stone

mace head

bedstone

meal spout

Top left: *The Boby Wheat Cleaner.*
Below left: *The Juggernaut 36in. stone mill, both at Walsham Mill, Suffolk.*
Above: *Mike Cooper at his desk.*
Below: *Sacks of Walsham Mill wheat grain and flour.*

*The old mill house which encased the post at Walsham Mill, now used as Mike Cooper's office.*

have been unsuccessfully screwed into the eaves to keep out the sparrows; but shreds hang down like playful decorations where the birds have freed them. A brown sparrow swoops under the doorway, and up into a beam. "Free food," growls Cooper.

An ancient machine stands in a corner. It was not obtained from Stowmarket Museum of rural crafts, but it could have been. This machine cleans the wheat; it's a Heath Robinson arrangement of metal sieves in wooden frames. Switch it on and it starts vibrating; the top tray sieves out the larger grains of wheat, and as it is angled, drops its load on to the next shelf, which shakes out the dust and grit (and copious amounts of bird and mice droppings); the third tray is just a flat tin which bounces the grain in front of a fan which plays on it, blowing away husks, bits of fluff and other light matter such as feathers.

Cooper doesn't take any grain until it's four months old. The big steel mills use grain when it's younger, but Cooper prefers mature grain. Once he took a 12 ton load of grain when it was new, to help out a farmer who had nowhere to store it. He stored it in his loft and almost at once it started to heat up. As it became moist Cooper realised it would ruin. "Two of us spent two weeks shovelling it, trying to keep it cool. But it was no good, it went mouldy. It cost me £100 a ton and I managed to sell it for £70, as animal feed."

The worst that can happen is to get an infestation of weevils. "Once we had weevils come in from a farm, and we had to close down for a month to have the place gassed out. Now we have Rentokil come in to dose the place every three months." Chemicals; Cooper squares it in his mind. "You have to have some chemicals."

Cooper works all hours; to the point that sometimes he wishes he had a nine-to-five job. "Farmers are out in the fields all day, so they don't think about ringing you on business till the evening." His wife Carole (who is also mother of two children; they have a boy of 12 and a girl of eight) shares the office chores, but insists they don't talk shop after 5 pm when the mill closes.

Carole bakes her own wholemeal bread from Walsham flour, of course. Her advice. "Leave it to rise for a minimum of five hours. Overnight preferably."

Carole works with a disabled group in the village, and they sell the products at the mill: three legged Suffolk stools and cloth dolls. One thing leads to another, and the Yoxford ladies are making beautiful lemon curd with real butter, so they sell that.

He has family connections in the West Country, and they put him onto a farmer making real farmhouse cheese. "We sell that, too. People try it, and realise it's something different. We sell 2½ tons to 3 tons a month. The farmer used to mature it for a year, but demand is so high, he can only leave it eight months. It's marvellous with our wholemeal bread." A perfect marriage of flavours.

# The Seed Breeder

*The pressure to go for bigger and bigger yields.*

THE SCENE: A LABORATORY in Cambridge. A small room containing miniaturised machinery, modelled on a plant baker's. A tiny impact mixer, a Lilliputian version of the bakery model, pounds up dough in ten minutes instead of three hours. A proving cabinet, regulated by thermostat. An oven, with revolving shelves, which can bake six to eight loaves at a time.

Two research assistants have been baking bread to compare flours grown under the same conditions in the same field. John Bingham, head of the wheat research unit at the Plant Breeding Institute, Cambridge, and colleague John Blackman, wheel in to see four loaves and some piles of brown rolls arranged on a worktop.

One of the loaves stands tall above the others, like a soufflé caught at its highest point. It has a firm crust and is handsomely bronzed. The team prods the sides of it and notes with approval that it gives easily, and then springs back into shape.

"This is the *Bounty?*" says Bingham. They nod, yes. *Bounty* is one of the most successful wheats they have developed here. Two other loaves, 14½ cm and 14 cm high respectively, reach nearly to *Bounty's* shoulders. A fourth, squat and square like the carriage of a tube train, barely reaches *Bounty's* middle.

But *Bounty* is remarkable only in the present company. In all other respects it resembles every other standard white loaf emerging daily from baking factories and sold to the tune of 15 million a day. It tastes as unremarkable as any other plant-baked white loaf. The special quality of this airy beauty is that it is made from refined British wheat. *Bounty* is British. Yet it has the protein quality of Canadian wheat. It mills as well. It absorbs a lot of water which is what the big bakers want.

British wheat, therefore is as suitable for fluffy white bread as costly North American wheats. And fluffy white bread is what the customer wants, the scientists say, and John Bingham and team are botanists, not bakers, or millers, or wholefooders.

They have achieved a measurable scientific breakthrough—there was no British wheat considered good enough for bread-making in this country at the turn of the century. Now they have bred a variety as potent as any we import—and with a yield higher than any in the world.

Organic farmers say plant breeders make a god of quantity. Bingham would not disagree with that.

"Our government has requested us to reduce the level of food imports. Thirty years ago we produced only 2½ million tons of wheat. Today we produce over eight million tons, only two million tons short of our needs. Our only deficiency is in bread-making flour. We produce all the biscuit flour we need, ½ million tons, and all the wheat we need for animal feed for pigs and chickens."

They achieved this growth, doubling yield in 20 years, partly by introducing new varieties, and partly by farming the land more intensively. "We get more out of an acre than anyone else in the world," says Bingham. In Canada they only get ¾ ton an acre, but that's partly because their wheat is spring sown. It could not endure the Canadian winters. And Canadian wheat is given a lower nitrogen feed.

"The average per acre in Britain is nearly 2½ tons, 2.35 tons to be exact. You can't do that with 'muck and magic'. You've got to use artificial fertilisers to get high yields.

"Making bread is just a physical process," says Bingham. "It depends on the protein. The quality of the protein is decided by its genetic make-up." And that's a question of breeding, which is their job. They set out to marry the genes of the best varieties.

Look at *Bounty's* family tree; back at the turn of the century there was no good bread-making wheat in Britain.

The botanists crossed *Browick* and *Red Fife* and produced *Yeoman*, which they launched in 1916.

**Pedigrees of winter wheat varieties with grain quality derived from Red Fife and White Fife**

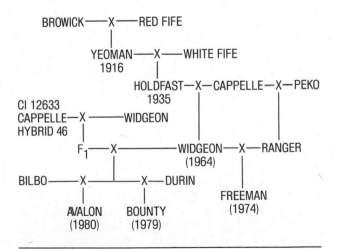

Bounty, *high protein British wheat.*

*Three loaves made from British wheat, from left to right:* Huntsman, Avalon, *and* Bounty.

*Yeoman* was crossed with *White Fife* to produce *Holdfast*, launched in 1935. *Holdfast* was wed to *Cappelle*, a famous French wheat, and produced the now celebrated and sturdy *Maris Widgeon*. And so on. It was a *Widgeon* cross-breed which produced in its turn, in a cross with *Durin*, the famed *Bounty* in 1979 and in 1980 *Avalon*, for which plant breeders forecast an even bigger future than *Bounty*. *Avalon* is marginally preferred by bakers, but millers like its hard milling quality. It is hugely attractive to the farmers as it gives a yield 6 per cent higher than *Bounty*.

*Bounty* was "born" 14 years ago in the lab in Maris Lane, Trumpington, on the south side of Cambridge, where the Plant Breeding Institute stands among 400 acres of farmland. Here they grow experimental crops: wheat, barley, oats and sugar beet, potatoes, red clover, lucerne, kale, field beans, rape-seed for oil.

In 1967 John Bingham and his six-strong team of graduate assistants and researchers, made 200 crosses, using varieties of wheat selected for special genes, like Rht2 which produces short straw. They planted over 2,000 of each, half a million seeds in all.

The target was to produce a wheat with high quality protein, strong resistance to disease, and good lodging (that means short straw, so that it won't be beaten down by wind). It would need early ripening qualities, bearing in mind the erratic British summer. And to make it attractive to farmers, it needed to give a high yield, and therefore respond to large doses of artificial fertiliser. The perfect wheat.

In June the team is out in the fields, examining each of the million specimens to eliminate those which develop brown rust, yellow rust, mildew, spetoria and eyespot. It takes four weeks to check them all. When the ears ripen they make a selection of 45,000, uproot them and thresh them, and almost immediately replant them.

The young plants are treated with diseased spores and examined for their resistance. Of those which survive, the best 3,000 are chosen and the grain replanted. A year later *Bounty* moves through to the last 1,200. Eight years after being planted as a cross, *Bounty* is through to the last 15, and is sent out for official trials with the National Institute of Agricultural Botanists. The grain is now under the scrutiny of the millers—who have their own research station at Chorleywood, Hertfordshire. *Bounty* is tested for its bread-making quality, its protein content, endosperm texture, ease of milling, specific weight and its falling number.

The Hagberg Falling Number test determines the grain's alpha amylase content. Alpha amylase is an enzyme which is stable under heat, and it can become active in baking, turning starch to sugar and giving the bread a sticky crumb. The enzyme becomes particularly active when there is a wet harvest, like 1977. When this occurs the wheat is only suitable for animal feeds.

*Bounty* has a high falling number and it passes all its tests with flying colours. It stands stiffly, and is more resistant to lodging than the popular *Maris Huntsman,* and its straw is shorter. It ripens earlier than *Maris Huntsman* and *Hobbit.* It is particularly resilient against yellow rust and is

*Avalon* loaf and ears of wheat.

tolerant of the chemical sprays to which it will be subjected, such as black grass herbicides like metoxuron and chlortoluron.

The farmers are convinced. Within a year of being launched *Bounty* is growing on 20 per cent of British wheat fields.

If the traditional farmer is puzzled by these new developments, the plant breeders and the National Seed Development Organisation, and the government's Agricultural and Development Advisory Service (ADAS) as well as the chemical companies are all at hand to prompt him to the "right" decisions. And although adopting *Bounty* is a good decision, he may be persuaded that *Avalon* is even better—with its six per cent higher yield.

Once the farmer adopts intensive growing there is a clear—and costly—programme of fertilising and weed prevention laid down. The average farmer probably spends about £90 an acre on this, but the higher the investment, the more tempting the returns. The Institute has documentation on Braiseworth Hall Farm, Tannington, near Framlingham, Suffolk. It is a model of modern farming activity. The national average is 2½ tons an acre and Tannington produced 4½ tons an acre. Although they were not growing a bread wheat, the programme is the same.

For an investment of roughly £150 per acre on fertilisers and pesticides, growing a good new wheat for animal feeds called *Hustler*, they made a profit on paper, of £300 an acre. This was the programme.

September 28. Farmer Bob Harvey and agronomist Edmund Brown sow 270 acres with *Hustler*. The ground has already been enriched with phosphate fertilisers.

October 1. They spray the ground with Tribunil, a herbicide designed to kill broad-leaved grasses before they emerge.

October 2. They spray Avadex, to kill wild oats while they are still seeds.

Throughout the winter, the young leaves sprout, and with no competition from weeds, gain sturdy root-hold.

March 4. The first big boost of fertiliser. They apply 230 lb of nitrates per acre.

March 14. Some weeds like thistles, poppies, chorlock, mayweed, have escaped the October spraying. They now spray with Britox, which kills the broad-leaved weeds.

April 8. The time of rapid spring growth. Heavy boost of nitrogen fertiliser.

April 10. Treatment for possible leaf diseases. Spray with fungicides, like Benlate, which kills eyespot, and Bayleton and Cycocel which are prophylactic and they protect the wheat from yellow rust and brown rust.

May 1. These farmers are out for a record. As the ear of corn emerges, another big application of nitrogen, to make the fertiliser continually available during an important growth stage, because in wet summers, rain can wash out the previous dressing.

May 27. The ear of corn is developing. They spray the fungicide Delsene M and the insecticide Rogor to kill the aphids which thrive at this warm time of the year. (Usually the ladybirds come a week later and gobble up the aphids, but unfortunately this is a week too late for the farmer.)

June 15. A final spraying of Bayleton CF to protect the ears from disease.

August. They harvest over 1,200 tons of wheat, and it is a record.

Four and a half tons an acre might seem the limit for intensive production. John Bingham is sure it is not. "We can go on increasing yields for the next 20 years. The graph will continue to rise steadily."

Will it mean more doses of chemicals on the land? The Plant Breeders say: "Tests are being conducted continually. We don't believe these things are harmful to humans. If you want to eat bread, you have to use them. You can't get the production without them." And higher yields are what most of the farmers are after.

# The Baker

*The skill behind a disappearing craft.*

FASTER AND FASTER. Two pairs of hands, moving like duettists at a piano, fingers stretched out, rotating and undulating. George, in charge, a wiry 61-year-old, and his assistant, John, a reserved and serious Irishman a few years younger, are taking small cubes of dough out to weigh by a machine; with six deft strokes, rolling them forward and back, circling and pressing, they release a pair of perfectly shaped rolls. They roll 2,000. Robots don't work faster.

This is the night shift, George and John make the doughs for the granary loaves, the French sticks, the farmhouse cobs, the knots, rolls and baps; Robert, a young West Indian, stripped to the waist like a boxer, bakes them in the deep ovens. The fourth member of the night team wears an unlikely white trilby, and white coat like a surgeon; Brian, a Welshman, is the stockman, preparing orders for Alex, the delivery man, who will arrive at 6 am.

This is Justin de Blank's bakery, under the railway arches at Vauxhall. Trains thunder busily all night, but outside it is black and dark. If they leave their cars outside a vandal may put a brick through the windscreens. It's happened. Now the cars are drawn up on the inside of the huge wooden doors which seal the arches.

The space opens up like two hangars; the night shift work mostly in the large hangar, baking at three ovens. One is a French-made Guyon Automatic with three decks, gas fired. The other two are newly-built brick ovens; one of them is insulated with 20 tons of sand. They are gas fired too, although the principle is just the same as the old brick ovens which were first heated by burning faggots of wood.

George, who's in charge tonight, worked on such ovens as a child with his father, the village baker in Burnham Beeches, Buckinghamshire. The ovens were fired with beechwood; when times were hard said George, he and his brother were sent out to get some: "From under the bloody hedgerows". His brother is now a successful baker in Bedford.

The ovens create huge pools of heat around them. To bake granary baps they raise the heat to nearly 500°F (260°C). They get a seven or eight minute blast at 490°F (254°C) (when they come out the steam in them softens the crust). Rolls go in at

460°F (238°C) and bake for 10 minutes to develop a hard and crispy crust.

All the ovens have steam jets attached. There's steam and there's wet steam. Wet steam is steam with water added. When the breads go in they give the ovens a 30 second whoosh of wet steam. It softens the surface of the dough, allowing the bread to go on rising evenly in the oven. When the breads are fully risen after 15 minutes, the doors are opened for a minute or two to let in cold air to clear the moisture. Then the crusts can begin to harden and brown.

Everything in the bakery is black or white; flour falls like powdered snow on wooden table surfaces and on the orange floor tiles; black is the scorched colour of the ovens, and the sootblack of encrusted metal baking tins, like barnacles.

Sacks of flour are piled in every corner; wholemeal from Walsham Mill, in Suffolk; "Nice and nutty, the best in the country," says George; Strong white flour from Cranfield, Ipswich, and Spillers (one of the Big Three millers). "The Spillers flour from Tilbury is very good," says George. "The Spillers flour from West Drayton is not. It should be sent back. Tilbury is always good. They have a dedicated miller." George then goes on to complain about some broken flour from Allied Bakeries, another in the Big Three. He suspects it's English wheat. "English wheat dries out, there's little protein." Millers choose not to agree with the bakers about flour quality. Never have, and presumably never will.

A bucket of acetic acid is an unexpected intruder. It's a sentry against the bakers' biggest fear, a fungus known as "rope" which can settle on a batch of wholemeal loaves and turn the inside to goo. Rope develops in wheat which has overheated and starts sprouting. It's like an infectious disease and no-one likes to take the blame. When it happened here they had health inspectors in to play detective. They put the blame fairly and squarely on a consignment of ten tons of sea salt! The bakery was closed and washed down with acetic acid. So now they add a judicious quantity in the dough mix as a precaution.

The machinery of baking is the dough mixer. Round stainless steel containers, three feet wide, are wheeled up to the mixers, and slotted under two dough hooks, which move slowly together like a preying mantis cleaning its paws. Some doughs are mixed for half an hour. Wholemeal bread dough is

Top: *Brioche p.232. Hazelnut Brioche Loaf p.58.*
Right: *Croissants p.106.* Left: *Bagels p.122.*

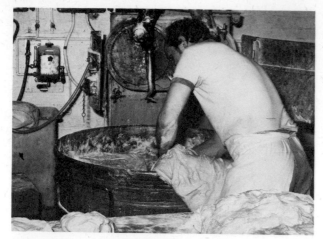

*The soft dough is dragged from the mixing bins.*

*John hacks off units of exactly 1lb 3oz each.*

*The vast ovens swallow another batch of loaves.*

*The 12 ft peel is handled as deftly as a snooker cue.*

mixed for a whole hour. "It's the only way to stretch the gluten," says George. "Otherwise, you get a solid unrisen loaf." Which is how many home bakers' efforts turn out.

A typical "recipe" might be this one for 3,000 milk rolls:

280 lb flour (the baker's sack)
160 lb water
6 lb dried milk
5 lb salt
5 lb yeast
10 lb lard or vegetable fat
10 lb sugar

1. Mix everything together for 25 to 30 minutes.
2. Weigh into chunks: cut into 64 equal pieces on a machine. Feed them into a mangle which first flattens and then rolls them.
3. Put in wooden trays to prove in draught-free zinc cabinets for 45 minutes.
4. Bake at 400°F in brick oven for 10 minutes.

George started the shift at 6.30 pm. The others at 8 pm. They will work through till 6 or 7 am. They are a man short. "Three have left and haven't been replaced. The trade is dying. Men won't come in. Wages are low, and no-one wants to do night work. Men don't see their families. When a man goes out you can't replace him."

Robert the West Indian was young, though. So

*Skilful hands mould the dough into shape.*

*George keeps an eye on the quality of the sticks.*

*Mouth-watering sticks hot from the oven.*

*The perfect results of a hard night's work.*

they were still coming in? Robert spoke with less than enthusiasm. Wearing his hair braided stylishly, listening to Reggae on Capital Radio turned up high, he said it wasn't his idea to become a baker. "My old man told me there was a job here." He started two years ago, and has developed a fine skill. But he has his doubts.

In spite of what he says, Robert works with rapidity and skill; with a scalloped cutting blade he slashes the French loaves quickly at an angle, three or four cuts to each stick; he dips a scrubbing brush in a red plastic bucket to rinse them with egg wash: when baked this gives the effect of varnish.

Like a snooker player cueing a shot, he slides the long willow stem of his 12 foot long peel to the farthest end of the oven, joggling the metal trays

into position. A roll falls off. He jolts the peel, spins the roll, and has it hopping like a tiddleywink back onto the tray. "After a while you get used to these things," he says with a smile.

George remarks to John that Robert is doing a bit of moaning tonight. "Must be the yeast. But he's turning out nice sticks."

They work like navvies. They take no breaks, except to sip cups of tea. Sometimes the tea is undrunk, because a batch of bread has to go into the oven, or come out.

Morale is at its lowest between 2.30 am and 3 am. George has been working for eight hours, and he turns to John: "We're running about half an hour behind schedule." They need more dough to shape. John, a patch of flour appearing on his nose,

quickens his rate of work, hands and elbows pumping. John drags a living lump of soft dough from the bins where it's been mixed: he slaps it down on a floured table, and with a sharp knife hacks off units of exactly 1 lb 3 oz each, tossing them onto scales; two loaves in every three weigh the precise and exact amount; to every third lump he adds a tiny twist of dough, or tears off a shred. The lumps of dough move at unchecked speed, as if on a conveyor belt.

When the bread is baked it will lose two ounces in the oven, and one more ounce as it cools: result a 1 lb loaf.

At the lowest ebb of the night, George vents his anger, and while the loaves unravel under his swift, dexterous hands, he rails at all that's wrong: a poor sack of flour; the yeast which hasn't been turned in rotation in the fridge, and which has been sitting in water. A trolley with a broken wheel feeds his resentment. A shortage of wooden racks, and the tea ration, which has been conspicuously forgotten. This goes very deep. His hands pound the soft dough. If the manager had been a piece of dough, he would be shaped into a monster. By 3 am the mood was so black, it might be better if the manager didn't come in.

There's only one sequel to this burst of anger. Between 3.30 am and 4 am George warms to his favourite theme: his resignation. "This February. You'll see. I've had enough of it. I'm getting tired. And then see what they do without me."

By four o'clock George and John have broken the back of the work. The loaves are stacked in golden beauty, crisp and handsome, in tall wire cooling cages. "This is the first break I've taken all night," says George. He looks at the clock. "Old Joe will be here in a minute. Quarter past four. You can set your watch by him. He's 76, cycles here from Paddington, takes him an hour."

At a quarter past four and certainly not later than 4.17 the bell rings; "Coming Joe." They open part of the huge wooden doors which close the railway arch, and Joe, overcoat collar turned up round his ears, eyes watering, walks in his bike, grinning. Old Joe picks up the loose ends of the shift, starts some of the doughnut, bun and pastry cooking for the next day.

At last George comes off the boil. Stockman Brian comes up asking for a hundred more rolls. "Will you do them?" George: "Yes, I'll do them. (Pause.) Tomorrow night." Brian, trying to check impatience: "But will you do them?" George is in a

mood to go on kidding him. After Brian has gone George says: "The best stockman we've ever had." With resignation he sets off to make yet another batch of dough, a hundred rolls to replace a batch slightly scorched. "Good enough for our ordinary customers," says Brian; "But not for the hotel. They'll complain."

Making and baking another batch of dough could add an hour to the shift. But pros have ways of speeding things up. An extra large slab of yeast goes into the mix with extra sugar, to get the yeast working quickly: after a fast mix, the dough goes through a machine which flattens it into circles, then rolls it into sausage shapes. George arranges them on wooden trays and puts them into a zinc cabinet to prove; free from draughts—or else a skin forms on the dough and stops it rising. Usually dough proves for 45 minutes or more. George is giving these 15 or 20 minutes. "That's fast?" George: "Fast! They're on the motorway."

The rolls are duly baked, 30 minutes in a cooling oven. Out they come, pale biscuit coloured, cos-metically perfect. There's no chance that the hotel will return them. George fingers one: smells it. "Fast dough like this is never any good. The slower you can get it the better." He retrieves one of the darkened rolls which Brian has rejected: "Look at that; a waste of good eating."

The night's work is done, and he sends Robert off home. More of the day shift trickle in to start work; after the buns and pastries some of them will work overtime on biscuits, a special order. They will sell at £3 a pound in pretty tins.

George washes and changes, and looks suddenly years younger, laughing, joking, pulling everyone's leg. He'll wait till the manager comes before he goes home.

This is not the confrontation the mood in the middle of the night promised. The manager comes in from the dark morning into the glare of the bakery lights, blinking behind his glasses.

His Brummagem voice lacks expression, and he seems anxious not to offend, but determined to sustain his own position of authority. But George's eyes are twinkling. He's not going to give his manager a hard time. He runs crisply through the work done during the night.

George retails some of the more concrete complaints. The broken trolley. The shortage of wooden racks. A poor bag of flour. Yeast which wasn't being taken in rotation. The manager nods carefully. Then finally; "There was no tea. I had to give Brian my car, and he went home for some." The manager, like a conjurer, makes a box of teabags materialise. "I hadn't forgotten, George."

George takes the box with satisfaction. He is vindicated. It is in good humour that he drives off, through the lifting dawn, passing the trucks and lorries heading into the city to start their own day's work.

As he drives off he forgets the bakery and its problems. He's thinking of his wife, who is already up, feeding their 48 pedigree miniature sheepdogs. He'll have a light breakfast, and by 10 am will be fast asleep, building up his energy reserves for the next night's shift.

# The Scientist

*The role of the government
research station, which
created the sliced white loaf.*

MOST OF THE COMPLAINTS about modern white bread eventually come to rest at the door of Professor Brian Spencer. He is head of the Flour Milling and Baking Research Association (FMBRA) at Chorleywood, which is funded partly by the government who press them to find ways of making British-grown wheat more acceptable for bread-making, and partly by the baking and milling industry. This is mostly in the hands of three giant companies:

Spillers, who are millers, (they also have interests in poultry, ham, eggs, animal feeds and pet foods); Rank Hovis McDougall, bakers and millers (who are also in canning and animal feeds); and Associated British Foods, millers and bakers (with other interests, including property and finance). Because the Association has divided loyalties, there are sometimes accusations that their research may not always be in the interest of the consumer.

For example: If dietary fibre is important to health, shouldn't they be promoting it? If white bread is tasteless, and white bread sales are falling every year, shouldn't they be teaching bakers to make it better?

The Association is housed in an attractively modern complex of buildings set behind a woody drive near Chorleywood in the quiet Hertfordshire countryside. Professor Spencer leads a team of 130 of the best bread scientists and technicians in the country, probably in the world: scientists whose influence is felt in every seed planted by farmers, every lorry load of grain milled by the millers and every loaf bought by customers across the counter, around 5,000 million a year. Their combined knowledge is immense. Their library alone contains 11,000 reference works on flour and bread. Between them they know the whole A to Z of bread from alpha amylase activity (which jinxes British wheat in wet years and makes it unfit for bread-making)—to the Z-blade Morton mixer (precursor of the high-speed Tweedy fast dough mixer, the process for which Chorleywood is famous).

But with all this knowledge some would say that the scientists can't tell a great loaf from an ordinary one.

A visit to Chorleywood and a chance to hear their side of it. The director, Professor Brian Spencer, is a charming and witty man in his early fifties,

*The Flour Milling and Baking Research Association at Chorleywood, Hertfordshire.*

handsome in an Errol Flynnish way, with a sandy moustache, and smart in a navy pin-stripe suit, with red and black striped tie.

He is a distinguished bio-chemist, and a world authority on enzymes (the key to the behaviour of yeasts); he lectured for 17 years at Trinity College, Dublin, where he became Dean of Science; he has been a visiting professor at Washington University, St. Louis, and at Wisconsin and Harvard; and also spent six months in India with the World Health Organisation.

He took over at Chorleywood from Dr. George Elton, under whom the famous Chorleywood Bread-making Process (CBP) was created, in 1960. CBP utilises a fast dough mixer, and uses much more yeast and higher temperatures than conventional bread-making. It can cut back the first "bulk fermentation" period from three hours to a few minutes.

Gradually, by trial and error they evolved a system which did not depend on the craft of skilled individual bakers. "We were trying to help bakers with tolerance," says Professor Spencer. "A craft baker can still work little tricks, produce a good loaf, but they need tolerance so their bread won't be ruined if they take their eyes off it for four or five minutes." They removed the elements of doubt due to variables like the quality of the flour, weight of yeast, proving temperature, the heat of the oven, and changes caused by adding fat and additives.

Bread technology instead of craft. "What else could we have done?" asks Spencer. "The muffin man doesn't come round any more. Where were people going to buy their bread? In 1918 there were 24,000 independent bakers in Britain. Today there are about 4,500. Without factory bread there wouldn't be enough bread." Four-and-a-half-thousand bakeries can't produce the 15 million loaves which Britons buy each day.

In Professor Spencer's view they managed to produce exactly the bread the customers wanted. "It's not our job to dictate to the public what sort of bread they should buy. We took the advice of marketing people who said that the housewife wanted bread which stayed fresh longer and didn't stale quickly." The CBP method produces a bread with a long life. This suits supermarkets too, giving it a longer shelf life.

"Now there's a swing towards wholemeal and brown and variety breads," says Professor Spencer. "Our people can respond to the swing but they can't

*Professor Brian Spencer.*

dictate it. When Rank Hovis McDougall tried brown bread ten years ago, the public didn't respond. The latest figures show that the demand for wholemeal and brown has risen to 18%. This is due to the publicity the fibre boys have given to wholemeal. You've got a breakthrough. But it's a fad, it's a fashion."

Professor Spencer takes an historic view; the swing will go so far, and then swing back again. This isn't the opinion of Dr. Kenneth Vickery, Chairman of Council, Royal Institute of Public Health and Hygiene, who, speaking at the Sunday Times One-day Real Bread Conference, challenged the Chorleywood representatives: "White bread is on the way out and it will never come back."

Professor Spencer considers the point. "There's a revolt against technology. It's back to the womb, back to the farmhouse. But bread is a matter of history, politics and religion. White bread is partly associated with purity and partly with affluence. We haven't retained rye, which used to be mixed with wheat flour in bread. We don't have sourdough breads like Eastern Europe. We've always been white, like France. Its traditional. It's a result of our stage of development as a nation. We were wealthy in Europe and had access to huge quantities of superb wheat on our doorstep cheaply, Canadian

wheat, which makes a well-risen loaf. In poorer Eastern Europe they were using rye and becoming used to it."

He argues that Britons will go on eating white bread predominantly because socially it is a deeply-rooted custom. "The mood for wholemeal and brown will swing to 25 per cent probably, then stop. But whatever people want to buy, the commercial people will make. Don't underestimate these commercial boys. They are highly competitive. They try to get better bread than the rest. If they can make an honest penny, they will. If they can find a way of selling it, if people want bread which is black, blue with green stripes, they'll make it, if that is what is wanted. Once it was white sliced, now there is a groundswell, and they are feeding it. It's exponential. It will grow."

Lunch. An opportunity to meet some of Professor Spencer's senior colleagues; the director of research, Dr. Douglas Axford; the chief nutritionist, Dr. Nat Fisher; and Dr. Norman Chamberlain, the technical chief who made CBP work in 1960. (The stirring tale of how he did it is recorded in *Breadmaking, The Modern Revolution,* edited by A. Williams; it would make a good movie like a Battle of Britain epic.)

Rolls are served with the lunch: they are Chorleywood-style, light in volume, airy, springy, fluffy, and have no taste at all. What did they say to that? They liked them very much. "Taste is subjective," they say. It didn't seem polite to pursue the question of flavour further but . . .

Hadn't they ever considered asking a cookery writer, like Elizabeth David or a gourmet, or a restaurateur, or hotelier, or an inspector from a food guide to serve on a tasting panel for them, to consider the question of flavour?

Dr. Chamberlain: "No. It's not necessary."

Professor Spencer: "Elizabeth David represents perhaps 0.1 per cent of the population. We're not concerned with such a small minority. Our job is not to cater for tastes which are too bland or too tasty. We try to aim at a middle spectrum. The vast majority of people don't have highly educated, highly sophisticated, very delicately-tuned tastes like Elizabeth David. She's not representative of the bulk of people. She's at the gourmet end."

Dr. Chamberlain: "When Dr. George Elton was director here, we arranged a test for 190 people, in which bread made by CBP was tested against bread made by a longer fermentation process.

## FIG.1: NUTRITIONAL CONTENT OF BREADS PER 100g

| BREAD | CALORIES | PROTEIN g | CARBOHYDRATE g | FAT g | FIBRE g |
|---|---|---|---|---|---|
| RYE | 243 | 9.10 | 52.1 | 1.10 | 0.4 |
| SODA | 264 | 8.0 | 56.3 | 2.3 | 2.3 |
| WHITE | 233 | 7.8 | 49.7 | 1.7 | 2.7 |
| WHOLEMEAL | 216 | 8.8 | 41.8 | 2.7 | 8.5 |

Note: 100g=3½oz approximately
Table compiled from: Geigy Scientific Tables, Allinson, and McCance & Widdowson's *The Composition of Foods,* HMSO 1978

## FIG. 2: VITAMIN CONTENT OF BREADS PER 100g

| BREAD | VIT A µg | THIAMIN mg | RIBOFLAVIN mg | NICOTINIC ACID mg | B6 mg | B12 µg | FOLIC ACID µg | PANTOTHENIC ACID mg | BIOTIN µg | VIT C mg | VIT D µg | VIT E mg |
|---|---|---|---|---|---|---|---|---|---|---|---|---|
| RYE | — | 0.18 | 0.07 | 1.4 | — | — | — | — | — | 0 | 0 | 0 |
| SODA | 20 | (Tr) | 0.06 | 1.3 | 0.09 | 0 | 9 | 0.3 | 1 | 0 | 0.01 | Tr |
| WHITE | 0 | 0.18 | 0.03 | 1.4 | 0.04 | 0 | 27 | 0.3 | 1 | 0 | 0 | Tr |
| WHOLEMEAL | 0 | 0.26 | 0.06 | 3.9 | 0.14 | 0 | 39 | 0.6 | 6 | 0 | 0 | (0.2) |
| STONEGROUND WHOLEMEAL | 0 | 0.20 | 0.10 | 3.50 | 0.30 | 0 | 20 | 0.70 | 2 | 0 | 0 | 1.9 |

Note: 100g=3½oz approximately. 0 means that this vitamin is not present; Tr means a trace is present; figures in parantheses are estimates; a dash indicates that no information is available.
Table compiled from: Geigy Scientific Tables, Allinson, and McCance & Widdowson's *The Composition of Foods,* HMSO 1978.

## FIG. 3: MINERAL CONTENT OF BREAD PER 100g

| BREAD | SODIUM | POTASSIUM | CALCIUM | MAGNESIUM | PHOSPHORUS | IRON | COPPER | ZINC | SULPHUR | CHLORIDE |
|---|---|---|---|---|---|---|---|---|---|---|
| HOVIS | 580 | 210 | 150 | 60 | 190 | 4.5 | 0.18 | — | 88 | 790 |
| RYE | 557 | 145 | 75 | 42 | 147 | 1.6 | 0.28 | — | — | 1025 |
| SODA | 410 | 270 | 150 | 20 | 110 | 1.7 | 0.13 | 0.6 | — | 480 |
| WHITE | 540 | 100 | 100 | 26 | 97 | 1.7 | 0.15 | 0.8 | 79 | 890 |
| WHOLEMEAL | 540 | 220 | 23 | 93 | 230 | 2.5 | 0.27 | 2.0 | 81 | 860 |
| STONEGROUND WHOLEMEAL | 466 | 261 | 26 | 89 | 240 | 3.0 | 0.50 | 2.0 | 81 | 773 |

Note: 100g=3½oz approximately. Dashes mean that no information is available.
Table compiled from: Geigy Scientific Tables, Allinson, and McCance & Widdowson's *The Composition of Foods,* HMSO 1978.

*Tests being carried out on pesticides in the Chorleywood laboratory.*

Many of the audience were bakers and two-thirds couldn't tell the difference." But a third could.

On to health. Bread advertising gives the impression that white bread is especially nutritious. It contains protein, but many nutritionists complain that white bread has had many good things removed from it in milling white flour. The bran is removed, which is dietary fibre, now believed to be not only helpful in countering constipation, but in shielding you from disorders of the colon, like diverticulitis. In addition, the wheat germ is removed in milling, along with essential fatty acids.

Dr. Nat Fisher: "This argument about nutrients is illogical. In our national diet we have a surplus of the nutrients which are in bread. The loss of these few nutrients doesn't matter in a mixed diet. Vitamins which we do need, like Vitamin A, and Vitamin D and C are not in bread." The argument for dietary fibre doesn't touch him. "If people want medicine they can go and take it out of a bottle."

Professor Spencer: "No self-respecting scientist will say the fibre case is proved. They just don't know enough about it. But there's no reason why you shouldn't take bran for your personal convenience, just enough to get your motions right, until you get a nice soft motion."

Although Professor Spencer makes a light-hearted answer, the Association is in the middle of £500,000 worth of government-funded experiments feeding rats with a diet of wholemeal bread, brown bread and white bread.

Dr. Nat Fisher: "If you were in prison, and they fed you on bread and water, it would be difficult to choose between white bread and wholemeal. I don't know which would get you first." Professor Spencer: "I'd be worried for my bones. The phytic acid in wholemeal binds the calcium."

They'd want more evidence before they changed completely from white to wholemeal, said Professor Spencer: "It's very annoying when your friends, who seem to be intelligent in every other way, take the view that white bread's no good. They tell you they've seen a TV report that you'll get cancer of the colon if you don't eat wholemeal bread."

Dr. Chamberlain: "If Burkitt and the fibre boys are believed the present sewage system will be found grossly inadequate."

Why is wholemeal bread more expensive than white? Less is done to it. "If 80 per cent of people ate wholemeal, it would be cheaper," said Dr. Chamberlain.

None of them are against wholemeal. But they are not convinced that it's particularly healthy, and they don't find it particularly palatable, either.

Professor Spencer: "The problem with wholemeal is that you can't get a well-risen loaf. If you use flour of 70 per cent extraction, or 75 or 78, or even 80 per cent extraction, you can get them rising. But after that, no. To make a reasonably expanded loaf you also need a better class wheat. A more expensive wheat. We're not in business to make a new tutti-frutti, but we would be interested in making a good plant-baked wholemeal loaf. It's the bran, or something in the bran that inhibits the rising, and we are trying to find that fraction. The government could help tomorrow by lifting the ban on the use of ascorbic acid in wholemeal. With ascorbic acid (Vitamin C) you can get it to rise more attractively. The law was made to protect those who wanted a completely natural product. It's stopping a lot of people who would like to eat it."

Most of the research work at Chorleywood goes unsung and unpublicised because it isn't put into commercial use by their customers. But they are ready for the day, should the people start clamouring for sourdough breads. Or baguettes. In fact they sent a man to Paris to find out the secret and bring it back.

Professor Spencer: "The hole is the great virtue of French bread. You cut your lip on the crust but it's full of holes which can take a pound of butter. Superb stuff. We sent a researcher to Paris one year, to the Moulin Rouge . . ."

"Le Grand Moulin de Paris . . ." corrected a colleague.

". . . we don't know where he went," says Spencer. "I bet he did go to the Moulin Rouge. We sent a man to discover the secret. The critical thing is to end up with large bubbles. When you're handling the dough you mustn't abuse it or knock air out of it. After you've mixed your dough, long or slow fermentation, you must mould it into a ball and leave it for 10 minutes.

"Then it's carefully rolled into long batons, and exact cuts are made on the top. The cuts are superfine, made at a diagonal, almost horizontally, overlapping by no more than 2 cm. The ratio of crust to crumb is of utmost importance. For the first ten minutes it must be baked with moisture, then finished with a dry bake. The object of the baguette is to finish with a large area of crust. And large bubbles inside."

A poster record of their research into French bread and photographs of experiments are pinned on a lab wall. "It was wonderful to have the bread around while we were making it," says Spencer wistfully. But he says the British will never buy French bread seriously. French bread is made with soft flour and stales quickly. "The English house-wife doesn't want to buy bread twice a day, even supposing there were enough bakers to make it." It's been tried. A year ago they had a French baker come over and bake French bread with French wheat and everyone said how wonderful. "But it only lasted three months."

Besides work on bread and flour, and cakes and biscuits, and pork pies and sausage rolls and Christmas puddings, they have a watchdog role: they are concerned with nutrition, food labelling, food poisons and residues in crops from pesticides and herbicides. They do laboratory tests.

"We're as worried as anyone," says Professor Spencer. "We examine for myco-toxins. We have a very large programme. The question of pesticides accumulating in the wheat is taken into account— the Codex Alimentarius sets down limits. British grain is well below the required safe level and this takes accumulation into account."

FMBRA also acts as an arbiter between farmers and millers. The Common Market sets a basic price for bread wheats. If the millers don't offer a higher market price, the EEC pays the basic rate. It's called "Intervention".

In 1980 the millers didn't offer a higher market price and a lot of farmers thought they'd collect on Intervention. But the FMBRA tests showed that many of the wheats didn't have the necessary machinability of dough. "We tested 1,400 samples," says Professor Spencer, "and two-thirds failed the test. Obviously some people were trying it on."

At a time when the government is trying to encourage farmers to grow bread wheats this can be demoralising. The EEC Intervention tests aren't particularly helpful. "The obvious test for flour is a baking test, but the Common Market partners can't agree on what that might be. So the tests are just machinability tests. Whether you can handle the doughs—if they're sticky or not."

"If a farmer is turned down for Intervention, he can sell his grain for animal feed, more cheaply. But he'll be inclined to grow feed wheat the next year."

So in 1980 the farmer was being offered £104 a ton by the millers. The Intervention rate was £110. If his wheat failed the machinability tests, he had to sell it for feed for £99 odd.

Say a farmer grows 2.4 tons of *Bounty* per acre. If it fails Intervention, he might only get £90 for feed. But he could have grown 2.7 tons of *Maris Huntsman,* the animal feed, and got £90 a ton, and made £27 more per acre. A farmer with 315 acres who fails Intervention is therefore losing £8,500.

It's a gamble like any other in a farmer's life. "The formula is, the farmer gets around 6 per cent less yield for growing bread-making flour, but he is paid 6 per cent more for it."

Allied Bakeries encourage British farmers, and put out 400,000 tons to contract, guaranteeing a price as long as it contains a certain level of protein, around 11 per cent.

The government wants to see Britain self-sufficient in wheat. "But if we left the EEC every baker would go back to strong Canadian wheat in a flash," says Spencer. "Home-grown wheat creates every sort of problem. We grow it in small fields, and quality varies from one field to another. In Canada they grow hundreds of thousands of acres of even quality, and it arrives by the tankerful in even quality." It is hard for Britain to compete.

# The Bran Men

*Three eminent doctors put the case for more bran in our bread and diet.*

Top left: *Dr. Denis Burkitt.*
Left: *Surgeon-Captain Peter Cleave.*
Above: *The Rev. Dr. Hugh Trowell.*

IN THE CAMPAIGN for real bread, three eminent men are championing the cause of bran. They believe if we ate lots of wholemeal bread we would stand a better chance of avoiding such ills as diabetes, varicose veins, peptic ulcers, gallstones, piles and even coronary disease.

Introducing the pioneers: Messrs. Cleave, Burkitt and Trowell.

## Surgeon-Captain Peter Cleave

About 25 years ago, a naval doctor warned that modern man was destroying himself with his appetite. Refined sugar and white flour were wrecking the human body, producing an epidemic of ills. His warning went unheeded.

But today, Surgeon-Captain Peter T. L. Cleave is no longer regarded as a crank. Instead he has been acclaimed as a pioneer whose research may free man from a burden of illness, and he was recently awarded two gold medals for his work. At 73, he no longer practises medicine, though he keeps a watchful eye on current research.

Cleave's interest in diet started in the last war when he was the medical officer on board the battleship *King George V.* To keep his men regular, he put them on a daily dose of bran. After some initial disgust, the ship's company approved, and once when bran supplies ran out, there was a formal request for more.

Over the next 20 years Peter Cleave started to piece together a wide-ranging theory about man and his food, looked at in the light of evolution. For thousands of generations man had been eating wholemeal grains with only fruits for sugar. Yet in the past two centuries, white flour with the bran refined out of it, and masses of refined sugar has been added to our food. Man's body had not had time to adapt, he argued. The sugar and white flour released energy into the bloodstream too quickly, and man ate too much of it for his needs. And the absence of fibre meant the bowels could not work properly. This two-fold disorder produces such ills as ulcers, heart disease and piles.

The first appearance of this theory was in the *Journal of The Naval Medical Service* in 1956. But the medical profession took little notice. The Journal was not widely read, and anyway, who was this naval doctor, Cleave? A less tenacious man might have given up. But he persisted, and penned 10,000 letters to amass evidence. Over the next few years he brought out a series of booklets on different aspects.

In 1962, when he retired, Peter Cleave began working on a book, *The Saccharine Disease*, which would bring together all the aspects of his theory.

"It was the work of a great genius with quite remarkable vision," says Dr. Denis Burkitt, one of his first converts, to whom Cleave was introduced in 1967. "I think the concept is going to do more for medicine than Fleming did with the discovery of penicillin. His book shows just what can be done by deduction."

Burkitt had just retired from his job as a surgeon in Africa. He already knew rural Africans were not prey to many diseases of civilised life; Cleave's theory explained why. Burkitt took up the hypothesis and Cleave's ideas began to reach a wider audience.

By 1973 the American Senate committee on diet asked Cleave to give evidence. He was now known as "the bran man". But his complete theory was still far from accepted. "The second and more important part of my work is still far from being truly appreciated. Sugar is much more dangerous than white flour, because it is eight times more concentrated.

"Any interference with people's eating habits is bound to be unpopular. There's a lot of money at stake. We have to stop children from eating sweets. Of course, wholemeal bread is the first essential . . . I take three heaped dessertspoons of bran a day. You can never suffer from having too much. This is really vitally important. If you just try it, you'll not need a word of recommendation from me. You'll find out for yourself."

## Dr. Denis Burkitt

Dr. Denis Burkitt first met Peter Cleave in 1967. "It was," he says, "one of those serendipitous occasions. I knew intuitively that Cleave was right because of my experience in the Third World."

Up to this moment, Dr. Burkitt had been known only for his work on cancer. As a surgeon in Uganda, he had tracked down a rare form of the disease now called Burkitt's lymphoma. "This meant I was allowed to speak where others weren't.

I also had the unique opportunity to test Cleave's hypothesis." For Burkitt was in touch with some 15 hospitals in developing countries. They had been reporting back to him about cancer, but now he switched his interest to fibre, and asked the hospitals to see if people on a primitive fibre-rich diet suffered from the "civilised" diseases. "If people are looking for something and don't find it, you know it's not there."

With enormous energy, Burkitt started pushing the idea that fibre may protect against disease. He involved Dr. Hugh Trowell in the campaign. The breakthrough came when he was invited to give a memorial lecture in London. "At that time it would have been quite impossible to talk about a whole lot of different diseases in one article. But the *British Medical Journal* asked for my lecture text, and even before they knew what it was about, they said they'd print it."

He wrote an introduction for Cleave's book, edited a further book on the subject with Hugh Trowell, lectured everywhere, and in 1979 produced a book, *Don't Forget the Fibre in Your Diet*. He had made it very hard indeed for doctors to ignore the theory.

He eats what he preaches. Breakfast is a huge plate of bran cereals or porridge with added bran. Lunch is wholemeal bread with peanut butter or honey. At supper there is a little meat and lots of potatoes.

And unexpectedly the bread industry loves him. For while he campaigns for wholemeal bread, he also thinks we should eat a lot more of it. "We should treble our bread intake, and eat something nearer wholemeal. That would be the most important change in our diet."

Burkitt's life has been shaped by Christian faith. Originally he planned to be an engineer, but Christianity turned him towards medicine and work overseas. "It wasn't until I got that sense of direction that I ever won prizes. I was poor clay, but God the potter made something of it."

He is not very happy with the scientific spirit of the day. "We're in an age when people won't believe anything unless it's proved. But that is not a valid approach to life. After all, Captain Cook took vegetables with him on his voyage, though vitamins weren't discovered until the 1930s. If he hadn't his men would have had scurvy." But if man persists in trying to live by bread alone, Dr. Burkitt would at least like it to be wholemeal.

## Reverend Dr. Hugh Trowell

The Reverend Dr. Hugh Trowell has played a major role in the struggle to make people realise the importance of fibre in the diet. Yet his interest in it started only after he had retired from two other careers. Now, aged 76, he had spent the past 11 years lobbying nutritionists, investigating what fibre is, and what it does to the body, and compiling a list of everything written on the topic.

Dr. Trowell's first career was the 30 years he spent as a physician in East Africa, where he helped to identify a protein-deficiency disease known as *kwashiorkor*. "There was very slow recognition of this, though it's now known to be one of the commonest nutritional diseases. There was a lot of opposition to my theories. I was asked for my resignation. It gave me a feeling, 'It's all right, chum, you just go on with it'."

He worked for 10 years as a vicar and hospital chaplain in Salisbury, again showing he had no fear of controversy. He chaired a committee on euthanasia, and wrote a book about it.

"Retirement" in 1969 lasted for about a year. He was invited to Uganda, and there he met an old colleague from his East African days, Dr. Denis Burkitt, who by this time had been converted by Cleave. "Burkitt asked me to find out what dietary fibre was," recalls Trowell, who was himself ripe for conversion to this thesis. When he was still in Africa, Trowell had published a book entitled *Non-infective Diseases in Africa*. It had briefly listed all the problems such as diabetes, coronary disease, piles and bowel troubles that rural Africans did not suffer. Now, he decided to research further.

"When I came back and started researching fibre, I found nothing at all in Lewis's medical Library or in the cumulative Medical Index. Indeed, the Index only started to collect articles on fibre in 1977, but now there are plenty of references."

With the help of Burkitt, Trowell redefined dietary fibre, and then began to compile a bibliography of references. Together they edited a book.

He also started the slow work of lobbying the medical profession in this country, and the slightly faster work of getting the Americans interested. "I think my work on *kwashiorkor* came in useful. I was able to look up nutritionists and to have talks at a high level. I met a certain amount of incredulity, but you sometimes have this streak which makes you go on." Trowell won't give up without a fight.

Trowell has differed from Cleave in placing less emphasis on sugar. By looking at the diabetes death figures for the war years and after, he suggests it is not the rise in sugar consumption which led to more deaths, but the demise of the fibre-rich National Loaf.

Like his fellow campaigners, Dr. Trowell believes the first stage in making people healthier must be the adoption of wholemeal bread. White bread, with added bran, is not a good substitute. "It's to do with eating the starch packaged with the fibre. The mixture slows down absorption and influences digestion. Just adding bran is not the same."

Dr. Trowell and his wife Peggy are not fanatics. They eat wholemeal bread and not too much meat. "I spread my butter thinner than I used to, and I don't take too much milk. I've halved my sugar consumption, but I don't think of it as a terrible evil. I'm too old to save my body or soul."

He does not expect to see rapid changes. "Much of the evidence I've produced is not conclusive. Probably only those who already have the illnesses will be strongly motivated enough to change their diets. But if we can produce cures with diet, then it will start to catch on."

He has now turned his attention to the whole question of the diseases found in Western man but not in developing countries. He has another book to be published later this year. "We hope to produce a new outlook in doctors. Up until now, medical science has concentrated on understanding disease at an almost molecular level, yet they haven't found many causes or cures. We can't cure obesity, for instance." With a nice sense of timing, the Reverend Dr. Hugh Trowell is moving on to a new field of interest for his eighties.

# Part II
# The People Who Bake
# -And Their Recipes

# Elizabeth David

Elizabeth David is a champion of fine bakers and good home-baked bread and the implacable enemy of the factory loaf. She is the most distinguished cookery writer of our time, and her book on bread is one of the most authoritative on the subject.

She was first after the war to speak out against the tyranny of convenience foods. Her classic books on Mediterranean food were published in the Fifties and early Sixties. First French then Italian cooking, and then she came back to English cooking, throwing a bridge across a century of bad habits to revive some of the good, old traditions of earlier times.

She spent five years researching and writing *English Bread and Yeast Cookery* (Penguin £1.95p) published in 1977, a work of considerable scholarship. It immediately won the Glenfiddich Writer of the Year Award. It has been a precious bible for the home baker ever since.

Some of her book is directed against the monopolists who mopped up bakeries and millers in the Fifties and Sixties, only to replace their craft bread with the tasteless pap which is factory bread.

Critics like herself, she says, "are dismissed by the spokesmen and the apologists of the milling-baking industry as emotive, unrealistic, alarmist, mischievous. The bread produced in factories, the milling industry claims, is incontrovertibly what the overwhelming majority wants. They support their claim by telling us that two out of every three loaves bought today by the British housewife are processed by one of the two major combines. When these companies send out their market researchers with questionnaires, what are the reasons given by the housewives for their choice? They are 'availability', 'convenience' (which means, I think, that the slices are the appropriate size for toast and sandwiches) and 'hygiene'. These are reasons which include no mention of anybody buying the bread because they actually like it, and reasons which appear also to imply bored indifference to the bread itself. It happens to be there in the shop, so it is bought. The customers like it being wrapped in paper and they like the shape. Is that choice?"

But her scathing opinion of white sliced bread is only an aside in a book which is otherwise a celebration of a great history of baking; hers is a book to read and enjoy, and a book to use.

Here she answers questions about her own childhood memories of bread, her preferences, and her hope for a better future for the next generation. And we give some of the special recipes for bread enjoyed in Britain some centuries ago, which she has revived for us today.

*What are your childhood memories of bread?*
I remember lovely tall cottage loaves with floury crusts. They looked and tasted home-made, but they weren't, they came from the village bakery. We were given thick slices with butter and home-made jam or jelly for nursery tea. At grown-up teas there was polite thin brown bread and butter.

*When did it dawn on you that British bread was becoming indifferent?*
I don't think that it was until the late Fifties that I realised the extent to which English bread had deteriorated. Until then, in my district of Chelsea, there were about five small bakeries within easy walking distance. I could usually find something acceptable at one or other of them. Then suddenly all those little bakeries began to disappear, until only one was left. When the good baker there—whose baps and French bread I used to buy—retired, I stopped buying bread, except for the occasional rye from a Jewish bakery in Soho. Of course I realised later that the situation was being duplicated all over the country.

*How did you start baking bread?*
I came to bread-making via learning to make pizza and brioche doughs, in the Fifties. At first I baked mostly white bread, then started experimenting with wholemeal, barley flour, rye flour and all sorts of mixtures. Since 1963, about, I have baked my own bread regularly.

*How often do you bake bread?*
Once or twice a week. Might be more. It depends if I'm entertaining or not. I don't bake bread "for pleasure". I bake it because I can't eat bought bread. Not that bread-making isn't a creative and satisfying process which everybody, and I mean everyone, should be taught at school, but it's a tyranny to be *driven* into making bread because what the bakers supply is so awful.

*Which breads do you prefer?*

I still prefer a basic loaf of 85% wholewheat, or my own mix made up of about fifty/fifty unbleached white flour and wholemeal flour. There's an easy rye loaf recipe in my book which I like very much too. Among the surprises when I was experimenting were potato bread and rice bread. They're both delicious. Baps are enormously useful too.

*Could plant bakers bake better bread?*

The Chorleywood Process researchers claim that many breads other than the standard loaves produced by the big combines, the plant bakeries, could be made using their process. But unmatured, over-yeasted dough with the additives demanded by the process will always produce indifferent bread, poor in flavour, crust, texture. Boring bulk.

*Doctors say we need more fibre in our diet but the Chorleywood people say it's not important to get it from wholemeal bread?*

I think it *is* important. I also think it's a terrible mistake to get fanatical about wholemeal bread. It's difficult to make it well and many people do genuinely dislike it, just as others genuinely dislike white bread. (Adherents of the two factions never believe in the honesty of each other's preferences.) People who need extra fibre can always get it via a packet of bran, although it's a rather expensive way of going about it. But you surely know you don't persuade people to eat wholemeal bread by telling them "it's good" for them. Those who switch to it and to other forms of brown bread tend to do so because they prefer the flavours and textures to those of white pap.

I'd be wary of those figures concerning the increased consumption in 1980 of wholemeal and other brown bread being due to medical publicity concerning high fibre. In the first place it takes two years to get properly sifted figures. In the second, an increased consumption of various brown breads could just as easily be due to the massive advertising by Associated British Foods (Garey Weston) for *Sun Bran* loaf, made with a mixture of standard white flour and bran. The name *Sun Bran* must mislead many people. Weston said last summer at their A.G.M. that they were selling ten million pounds worth a year. They also have something called *HiBran,* and Spillers French advertise a mix of white flour and bran for the Chorleywood Process and a second version for less drastic methods. It's called *White'N'Bran.* There's also *Granary,* a proprietary mixture owned by a malting combine, much advertised and very popular. Too sweet for my taste, still I suppose it's quite wholesome.

Of course, so much the better if Associated British Foods and Rank Hovis MacDougall are paying for advertising which the small bakers can't afford. Some of it surely rubs off on them and benefits their sales.

*How can we ensure better bread in the future?*

The only way we'll get better bread is by educating the population to demand it. You have to teach people to *think* about what they're eating, and to distinguish between one kind of bread and butter and another, above all to *want* to know what they're putting in their stomachs, and to take an active pleasure in eating wholesome bread, rather than regarding it merely as packaging for a slice of cheese or ham. If a course of bread-making as mentioned earlier were made compulsory in every school, as it is in Denmark, within a generation there'd be no more mystique in bread-making, at least some of the young would grow up understanding what it's all about and they'd very soon learn to discriminate between good bread and bad.

# An Easy Rye Loaf

*Makes 1 loaf*

THE FLOUR:
*10 oz strong white flour*
*2 oz rye meal or flour*

THE STARTER:
*½ oz fresh yeast or ¼ oz dried yeast*

AND...
*8 fl. oz water*
*½ oz salt*

METRIC EQUIVALENTS:
*300 g strong white flour*
*60 g rye meal or flour*
*15 g fresh yeast or*
*8 g dried yeast*
*250 ml water*
*15 g salt*

NOTE:
*The rye meal I use, when it is obtainable, is Mrs. Horsfield's which is stoneground. Supplies are erratic. A more finely milled, much whiter, rye flour is marketed by Prewett's. This flour has less flavour than Mrs. Horsfield's coarse brown meal, but it is easier to work with. Allow a larger proportion, say 3 to 4 oz (90 to 125 g) of rye flour to 9 to 10 oz (275 to 300 g) of 81% wholewheat flour or wholemeal flour.*

*Rye bread is often made with a leaven or sourdough starter, which gives it a characteristic sour taste, but it is by no means essential. A dough of predominantly white flour with a small proportion of rye is very easy and straightforward. It makes a delicate and delicious bread especially good with smoked fish and white cheeses. It stays moist longer than wholemeal bread, and even when several days old is still good for cutting into thin slices, which makes it welcome to anyone who suffers from weight problems but is reluctant to renounce bread entirely. Quantity for a tin of 1½ to 1¾ pt (1 litre) capacity.*

YEAST STARTER:
Mix the yeast with a little warm water.

THE MIX:
Blend the two flours together. Put the salt into a measuring jug, dissolve it in a little very hot water. Make up to the 8 fl.oz (250 ml) with cold water.

FIRST AND SECOND RISINGS:
Mix the dough and leave to rise as usual, for an hour or a little longer. If you have time, give the dough two risings and breakdowns instead of the usual one before shaping it and putting it in the warmed and greased tin.

FINAL RISING:
With a sharp knife or scissors make an incision the whole length of the loaf, and widen this by pressing into it with the side of your hand. Sprinkle the top with rye flour. Leave the dough to rise to the top of the tin.

PRE-HEAT OVEN
to 450°F (230°C) Gas 8.

BAKING TIME:
Bake for 15 minutes in centre of oven then turn down to 375°F (190°C) Gas 5, for 15 minutes. Turn the loaf out of the tin and give it another 10 minutes with the oven lowered to 325°F (170°C) Gas 3, or even with the oven turned off.

# Rice Bread

*In colour — page 88*

*This is excellent bread for keeping, since the rice remains moist, and the texture is beautifully light and honeycombed. It is also a loaf which is very easy to mix and bake. It is hard to describe the flavour of rice bread; until it has been tried, it is also difficult to believe how delicious it is.*
*Use a sandwich loaf tin of 3 to 3½ pt (1¾ to 2 litre) capacity.*

*Makes 1 large loaf*

THE FLOUR:
*1 lb 2 oz strong white flour*

COOKING THE RICE:
Put the rice in a thick saucepan of 1¾ to 2 pt (1 to 1¼ litres) capacity. cover it with three times its volume of water. Bring to the boil, cover the saucepan, leave the rice to cook steadily until the water is absorbed and little holes have formed all over the surface of the rice. While the rice is cooking, weigh out and prepare all the other ingredients.

THE RICE:
*3 oz rice plus three times its volume of water*

THE STARTER:
*½ oz fresh yeast or ¼ oz dried yeast*

YEAST STARTER:
Cream the yeast with a little warm water.

AND . . .
*½ to ¾ oz salt*
*rather under ½ pt water*

THE MIX:
Put the salt in a measuring jug and dissolve it in ¼ pt (150 ml) of very hot water, then add cold water to make up the correct quantity. When the rice is cooked, and while it is still very warm, amalgamate it very thoroughly with the flour. Now add the yeast, then the salted water, and mix the dough in the usual way. It will be rather soft.

METRIC EQUIVALENTS:
*560 g strong white flour*
*90 g rice, plus three times its volume of water*
*15 g fresh yeast or 8 g dried yeast*
*15 to 20 g salt*
*about 250 ml water*

FIRST RISING:
Cover it and leave it to rise for 1 to 1½ hours until it is at least double in volume, and bubbly. Probably the dough will be too soft to handle very much so it may be necessary to dry it out a little by adding more flour before breaking it down and transferring it—very little kneading is necessary—to a warmed and well greased tin.

NOTES AND VARIATIONS:
*The variety of rice used is not, I think, of great importance. I always have Italian round-grained and Basmati long-grained rice in the house and have used both for bread. Those who habitually use only brown unpolished rice will know that it takes longer to cook and absorbs more water than white rice.*

SECOND RISING:
The dough should fill two-thirds of the tin. Cover it with a cloth or sheet of polythene, and then leave it until it has risen above the top of the tin.

PRE-HEAT OVEN:
to 450°F (230°C) Gas 8.

BAKING TIME:
Bake in centre of oven for 15 minutes, then at 400°F (200°C) Gas 6, for another 15 minutes, before turning the loaf out of its tin and returning it to the oven, on its side, for a final 15 to 20 minutes at the same temperature. If the crust shows signs of baking too hard and taking too much colour, cover the loaf with a large bowl or an inverted oval casserole.

In colour—page 216

*Makes 1 large loaf
    or 2 smaller loaves*

THE FLOUR:
*1 lb strong white flour
4 oz barley flour*

THE STARTER:
*½ oz fresh yeast or ¼ oz dried
    yeast*

AND...
*12 fl. oz tepid water
2 to 3 tablespoons of buttermilk,
    cream or creamy milk*

METRIC EQUIVALENTS:
*500 g strong white flour
125 g barley flour
15 g fresh yeast or 8 g dried
    yeast
350 ml tepid water
2 to 3 tablespoons buttermilk,
    cream or creamy milk*

NOTE:
*The proportions of barley flour to
white flour, 81 or 85%
wholewheat flour which go to
make a good barley loaf can
be varied according to taste. For a
stronger, darker bread, use
12 oz (350 g) of 81% wholewheat
flour to 4 oz (125 g) each of
wholemeal and barley flour,
with other ingredients as
before.
Before we went to press Mrs. David
wrote to say that she now uses a
fairly recent product, Harvest Gold
dried yeast, which is now freely
available: "I find it quick and efficient
and no trouble at all."*

# Mild Barley Bread

*Barley bread is particularly good with English cheeses such as matured Cheddar, Wensleydale and Lancashire—when, and if, such commodities are to be found. Although owing to its greyish crumb, barley bread may not look immediately appetising, those who acquire a taste for it are likely to become addicts. I am one. It is an addiction which is not always easily satisfied. In London, barley flour is difficult to come by. I have found it best to bake barley bread in tins, as opposed to making hand-moulded loaves. Using tins, a moister dough can be made so the bread retains its freshness and its very characteristic aroma and flavour for three or four days, whereas a "crusty" barley loaf bakes rather hard, and dries out quickly. For this mild-flavoured loaf use a sandwich tin of 3½ pt (2 litre) capacity and 4 in (10 cm) deep.*

YEAST STARTER:
Put yeast in a cup and pour enough tepid water over to cover it. Give the yeast a good 10 minutes to return to active life. Mix to a cream.

THE MIX:
Thoroughly mix the two different flours in a bowl. Pour the creamed yeast into the centre of the flour. Add some of the tepid water and stir it round with the yeast using a wooden spoon. Pour in the rest of the water and mix it with your hands. Work a minute or two till it comes away from the sides of the bowl. Form it into a ball, and sprinkle it with flour. Cover with polythene.

FIRST RISING:
Leave 1½ to 2 hours to expand to twice its original volume.

SECOND RISING:
Break it down with a good punch with your fist and knead it two or three times. Put it in a greased tin to rise till it doubles in size.

PRE-HEAT OVEN
to 425°F (220°C) Gas 7.

BAKING TIME:
Bake in centre of oven for 15 minutes, then reduce heat to 400°F (200°C) Gas 6, for next 15 minutes. Shake loaf from tin and return it on its side to the oven, turned down to 350°F (180°C) Gas 4, for a further 15 to 20 minutes. It is baked when the loaf gives out a resonant sound when you tap the sides and the bottom crust with your knuckles. Leave to cool on a rack.

# Jane Grigson

Like many north country women, Jane Grigson's grandmother was a good baker. In a steamy kitchen in South Shields, with its black iron range, she would turn out beautiful loaves, and make dough-boys with currant eyes and currant buttons for her grandchildren.

Jane Grigson grew up in Sunderland during the Depression. Meals were plentiful for her family, but unimaginative. She says she comes from a class whose cooking skills had atrophied. Dishes were necessarily confined to what an able and willing miner's daughter could produce on a temperamental kitchen range. When the war came, cooks, house-maids, and morning women disappeared into munitions factories. Some of their employers, in spite of rationing, were entranced to be allowed the freedom of their own kitchens for the first time. She recalls her mother's delight at making the Doris Grant loaf towards the end of the war. "I remember her excitement. People didn't realise how easy it is to cook with yeast. Elizabeth David makes this point. Yeast is absolutely foolproof."

In 1946 Jane Grigson went up to Cambridge. Fitzbilly Chelsea buns were the height of gas-tronomy in those difficult years, and you queued for them when you had the money, hoping they would not run out before you got into the shop. Her interest in food was not really stimulated until she first went to Florence in 1949, after taking an English degree. Returning to the *pensione* after morning lectures, she walked through the San Lorenzo market that smelled of Parmesan in the midday heat, as people grated cheese for their lunchtime pasta. Being hard up, she discovered tripe with tomato; pasta with raw egg broken into it; eggs baked in olive oil; lovely bread with a washed hard look to the crust.

A year later Elizabeth David published her first book, *Mediterranean Food*. It opened northern tastes to new standards of preparing and enjoying meals. The grey, necessary puritanism of the war seemed at last to be over.

It was also Elizabeth David who recommended Jane Grigson to *The Observer Magazine* in 1968, following her first book *Charcuterie and French Pork Cookery*. It is the best work on the subject in English—and in French. It grew out of ignorance, and slowly, as she talked to charcutiers, found such recipes as she could, tasted what she did not know.

By this time she and her husband, the poet Geoffrey Grigson, had found a small cave house in a village on the Loir, a tributary of the grand Loire, to the north of Touraine. They seemed to eat little but pork for four years.

Other books followed, *Good Things, English Food, The Mushroom Feast, Fish Cookery, Jane Grigson's Vegetable Book* and most recently *Food with the Famous*. At the moment she is writing a book on fruit.

Jane Grigson's favourite breads often have extra things added to them, olives for instance, walnuts, hazelnuts, mushrooms. Nut oils or good green olive oil take the place of butter or lard. She feels bread-making should be quick and simple, not a rite or a cure for bad temper. "As I often make bread three times a week, I don't have much time for pounding dough. *Harvest Gold Fermipan* yeast and a Kenwood chef dough hook are my answer. The bowl is tied into a plastic carrier for the bread to rise. Then it's punched down and shaped, and put back in the carrier to prove. It's so painless, so automatic, that I'd forget all about the dough if it weren't for the kitchen timer. When there are children about, they make the bread. It should be the first thing we all learn to cook. Makes us respect what we put into our mouths. How can you eat trash after making bread?"

# Walnut Granary Bread

*Makes 1 large loaf*

THE FLOUR:
*1 lb 1 oz* Granary *flour*
*5 oz unbleached white flour*

THE STARTER:
*1 packet* Harvest Gold
 (Fermipan) *yeast*

AND . . .
*2 level teaspoons fine sea salt*
*2 tablespoons walnut oil*
*¾ pt warm water (90° to 110°F)*
*4 oz shelled walnuts, coarsely*
 *chopped*

METRIC EQUIVALENTS:
*530 g* Granary *flour*
*150 g unbleached white flour*
*1 packet* Harvest Gold (Fermipan)
 *yeast*
*2 level teaspoons fine sea salt*
*2 tablespoons walnut oil*
*scant ½ litre water at blood heat*
*125 g shelled walnuts, coarsely*
 *chopped*

*For years I made a white loaf with walnuts and onions, in the Burgundy style: now we prefer the more versatile walnut Granary bread, though sometimes I do add a little onion to part of the dough, to serve with soup or for sandwiches.*
*Two level teaspoons of any dried yeast, or ½ oz (15 g) fresh yeast, and your hands can be used instead of Harvest Gold yeast and an electric mixer or food processor.*

THE MIX:
Put the flours, yeast and salt into the mixer bowl or processor. Stir in the walnut oil. Have ready ¾ pt (scant ½ litre) water at blood heat, between 90°F and 110°F, and mix it in slowly stopping when the dough forms a muff round the dough hook(s) or a ball in the processor. Extra flour, up to 2 oz (60 g) can be added, if you overdid the water.

FIRST RISING:
Pour a little walnut oil on the dough. Turn it round in the mixer bowl, or a deep basin, until it and the sides are coated. Tie the bowl into a plastic carrier bag, or secure plastic or cling film across the top of the bowl with an elastic band. Leave in a warm place for an hour—it should roughly double.

SECOND RISING:
Punch down the dough and mix in the walnuts. Shape it into a hump and place on an oiled baking sheet, or divide between loaf tins. Tie again into the plastic carrier, leaving plenty of space so that there's no risk of the dough sticking to it. Put in a warm place for half an hour.

PRE-HEAT OVEN
to 450°F (230°C) Gas 8.

BAKING TIME:
Bake for 30 minutes or until the loaf sounds hollow when you tap the base. Brush over the top with milk and leave to cool slowly in a warm place, on a rack or across the hot tins.

# Cretan Olive and Onion Bread

*This delicious bread is ideal for picnics or snacks. It looks very pretty when cut with the spirals of chopped black olives showing on each slice.*

THE MIX:
Put the flour, yeast and salt into the mixer bowl or processor. Stir in the olive oil. Have ready ¾ pt (scant ½ litre) water at blood heat, between 90°F and 110°F, and mix it slowly stopping when the dough forms a muff round the dough hook(s) or a ball in the processor. Extra flour, up to 2 oz (60 g) can be added, if you overdid the water.

FIRST RISING:
Pour a little olive oil on to the dough. Turn it round in the mixer bowl, or a deep basin, until it and the sides are coated. Tie the bowl into a plastic carrier bag, or secure plastic or cling film across the top of the bowl with an elastic band. Leave in a warm place for an hour—it should roughly double.

THE FILLING:
While the dough rises mix together the black olives, finely chopped onion and dried mint.

SECOND RISING:
Punch down the dough and roll it out on a floured board. Scatter the olive mixture over it. Roll up the dough and leave to rise a second time, for about half an hour.

PRE-HEAT OVEN
to 450°F (230°C) Gas 8.

BAKING TIME
Place on an oiled baking sheet and bake for 30 minutes or until the loaf sounds hollow when you tap the base. Brush over the top with milk and leave to cool slowly in a warm place.

Olive bread makes a good base for *pan bagna,* to take on a picnic. Roll or pat the dough into 3 shallow large rounds and prick the top before baking. Check after 25 minutes to see if the bread is cooked.

*In colour—page 88*

*Makes 1 large loaf*

THE FLOUR:
*1 lb 6 oz unbleached white flour*

THE STARTER:
*1 packet* Harvest Gold (Fermipan) *yeast*

AND...
*2 level teaspoons fine sea salt*
*2 tablespoons olive oil*
*¾ pt warm water (90 to 110°F)*
*8 oz black olives, stoned, chopped coarsely*
*5 oz onion, finely chopped*
*1 dessertspoon dried mint*

METRIC EQUIVALENTS:
*675 g unbleached white flour*
*1 packet* Harvest Gold (Fermipan) *yeast*
*2 level teaspoons fine sea salt*
*2 tablespoons olive oil*
*scant ½ litre water at blood heat*
*250 g black olives, stoned, chopped coarsely*
*150 g onion, finely chopped*
*1 dessertspoon dried mint*

# Hazelnut Brioche Loaf

*Makes 3 loaves*

THE FLOUR:
*14 oz unbleached white flour*

THE STARTER:
*1 packet* Harvest Gold (Fermipan)
*yeast*

AND . . .
*2 large eggs*
*5 tablespoons hazelnut oil*
*2 level teaspoons fine sea salt*
*¼ pt water at blood heat*
*4 oz shelled hazelnuts*

METRIC EQUIVALENTS:
*400 g unbleached white flour*
*1 packet* Harvest Gold (Fermipan)
*yeast*
*2 large eggs*
*5 tablespoons hazelnut oil*
*2 level teaspoons fine sea salt*
*150 ml water at blood heat*
*125 g shelled hazelnuts*

*This bread is closer to the French* pain brioché *than to the richer fluted* brioche. *Hazelnuts and hazelnut oil—from Robin Yapp, The Old Brewery, Mere, Wiltshire, Justin de Blank shops or Taylor and Lake, the wine merchants—give a delightful smell, taste and texture. Use it at breakfast and for toast, as the base for apples, apricots and peaches baked on bread to serve with salads.*
*An enriched dough of this kind needs more yeast, and a lower oven temperature, than the normal bread dough.*

THE MIX:
Put the first five ingredients into the mixer bowl or processor. Have ready ¼ pt (150 ml) water at blood heat (between 90°F and 110°F). Start mixing the dough and, as the eggs break up, begin to add the water. Go slowly as you should not allow the dough to become too sticky. Slight tackiness does not matter, but try to avoid having to add extra flour. Remember that the later addition of ground nuts will have a drying effect.

FIRST RISING:
Oil the mass of dough and the sides of the bowl. Stretch cling film or plastic across the top and tether it with an elastic band. Leave in a warm place for 1 hour to rise.
Meanwhile toast the nuts under the grill or in the oven at 300°F (150°C) Gas 2. Rub away the skins in a cloth. Reduce to a coarse powder in a processor or nut mill: if the texture is uneven, so much the better.

SECOND RISING:
Knock down the dough and mix in the nuts. Warm and oil 3 tall coffee tins of 1¼ pt (750 ml) capacity. Divide the dough between them. Tie into a plastic carrier and leave in a warm place for 30 minutes.

PRE-HEAT OVEN
to 375°F (190°C) Gas 5.

BAKING TIME:
Bake for 35 to 40 minutes. Cool for 2 minutes in the tins, then run a knife round and ease out the loaves. Brush the tops over with milk.

# Caroline Conran

Cookery writer Caroline Conran is an unrelenting critic of plant-baked bread. She believes that Britain is one of the few countries where people have forgotten they have a right to good bread. And it's not as if it's difficult to make. In less developed countries, housewives with the humblest of cooking facilities make their own bread. "They cook it on stones, on slabs, in all sorts of primitive ways. It comes straight off the heat, you eat it at once, and that makes it wonderful."

In the kitchens of the Moti Mahal open-air restaurant in India she watched them make *naan* which is served hot straight from the ovens. "The bakers sit cross-legged on a platform beside the open *tandoors* (pit-ovens). They shape the dough by tossing it up and down, and then slap it down the hole. It cooks on the side of the oven, then they hook it out again. It comes out a flat pear-drop shape." The bakers work all day; making their own dough and cooking it: "It must be hell for them," she says thoughtfully, "but it's so simple, and such marvellous bread."

In India she also tasted Moghul bread—the traditional bread of the courts: "It's made in layers, like flaky pastry. It looks very flat, but it rises as it cooks. They fry it in ghee or oil and it's delicious."

Another delicious loaf, *focaccia,* she ate nearer home, this time at Restaurant Augusti in Rome: "It's a flat loaf, less than an inch thick, soaked with fragrant olive oil and sprinkled with crystals of salt. They make a fresh loaf for every customer."

It's this lovely freshness that Caroline finds lacking in British bread: "Perhaps we try to keep our bread too long. We make it last, and it loses its immediate character. The flavour seems to fade away when the bread has gone cold.

She remembers her mother used to cook a solid worthy loaf. It was fine at first, but the family were made to eat it until it was all used up: "It gradually took on a sad musty flavour as it went stale." In those days of war-time rationing, two events stood out in Caroline's week: the arrival of the Harrod's van every Friday with one "absolutely delicious" wholemeal loaf, and pocket-money day, when she bought hot Bath buns from the local bakery.

Today, she's unhappy if one of her own loaves hangs around too long: "The best thing is if your loaf is eaten straight away." She's now experimenting with an Italian bread that is "quickly made, quickly cooked and quickly eaten". Fresh home-made bread, warm from the oven, gives pleasure to the cook and to the eaters: "People are always pleased if you give them hot bread. It's so absolutely lovely—something special, just for you."

Don't worry about the occasional failures. It may not always be your fault! "I produced a wholemeal loaf with a bitter horrible taste. It was the flour. It had gone rancid."

The quality of flour is vital. "If you haven't got good flour, you can't make good bread." Caroline even tastes the dough before she bakes it, to be sure that it's going to be a good loaf. "Once you've got a feeling for it, you can make bread out of almost anything. You can put in whole grains, seeds and nuts."

A friend of hers makes saffron bread with walnuts and anchovies, or olives and pimentos. Caroline doesn't quite go that far. But she does feel that anyone can bake a loaf—including young children. She gave bread-making classes at the local primary school. "Children love playing with dough. It's far better than plasticine. It's alive and grows beneath their hands. They play with it until they are satisfied with the shapes. Then they cook it and eat it."

Here are her tips for beginners:
*Use fresh yeast, if you can, and not too much of it. Start with brown loaves. They're easier to succeed with and they already have a good flavour. Always use good flour.*

# Cholla

*Makes 2 loaves*

THE FLOUR:
*1¾ lb strong white flour*

THE STARTER:
*1 oz fresh yeast*
*1 teaspoon honey*
*¼ pt warm water*

AND . . .
*2 teaspoons salt*
*about ½ pt warm milk*
*1 egg*
*poppy seeds*

METRIC EQUIVALENTS:
*850 g strong white flour*
*30 g fresh yeast*
*1 teaspoon honey*
*150 ml warm water*
*2 teaspoons salt*
*about 300 ml warm milk*
*1 egg*
*poppy seeds*

*This is a version of the traditional Jewish loaf.*

THE MIX:
Dissolve the yeast and honey in the warm water. Mix the flour and salt in a warm bowl. Make a well in the centre and pour in the yeast mixture. Flick a layer of flour over the top and leave until the yeast froths up and cracks the film of flour. Mix everything together with enough warm milk to make a smooth, firm dough. Knead well for several minutes on a floured board. Form the dough into a ball and place in a bowl.

FIRST RISING:
Cover it with a sheet of polythene and a cloth, and allow to rise in a warm place until doubled in size, about 1½ hours. Knead the dough briefly on a floured board, and divide into two. Cut each half into 3 pieces, and form them into little sausage shapes. Roll each piece into a long, thin snake, and use them to make 2 long, fairly loose plaits. Turn the ends under so that they meet.

SECOND RISING:
Place the plaits on buttered baking sheets and cover lightly. Leave in a warm place to prove until swollen and puffy.

PRE-HEAT OVEN
to 425°F (220°C) Gas 7.

TO BAKE:
Beat the egg with a few drops of water, and brush the surfaces of the loaves. Then sprinkle them very thickly with poppy seeds.

BAKING TIME:
Bake for about 45 minutes. After 15 minutes REDUCE HEAT to 350°F (180°C) Gas 4, covering the loaves very loosely with foil if they seem to be getting too brown. Cool on a rack, and eat warm or cold.

# Pitta Bread

*Makes 8*

THE FLOUR:
*1 lb strong white flour*
*1 lb wholemeal flour*

*Pitta is an excellent Arab bread. It's simple to make and is baked within minutes in a very hot oven. Pitta are hollow in the centre. Traditionally pitta bread is made with all white flour.*

THE STARTER:
*2 oz fresh yeast*

AND . . .
*1 pt warm water*
*1 oz salt*
*5 tablespoons olive oil*

YEAST STARTER:
Dissolve the yeast in a little of the warm water.

THE MIX:
Mix the flours in a warm bowl and make a well in the centre; pour the yeast mixture into the well. Add the remaining warm water, mixed with the salt and olive oil, and make a soft dough.

FIRST RISING:
Knead for 10 minutes, then form into a ball. Smooth all over with a little more oil and allow to rise, well covered and in a warm place, for 1½ hours or until doubled in size.

SECOND RISING:
Knead again briefly, then divide into 8 pieces. Roll each piece into a ball, cover and let it rise once more, for 30 minutes.

PRE-HEAT OVEN
to 475°F (240°C) Gas 9.

THIRD RISING:
Now roll them out flat into ovals about ⅛ in (3 mm) thick, and lay them on well-greased and floured baking sheets. Cover and leave for a further 30 minutes.

BAKING TIME:
Place the baking sheets either on the bottom of the oven or on the lowest rack. Bake for 10 to 15 minutes. Remove from the oven and cover with a cloth so that the bread does not become crisp.

METRIC EQUIVALENTS:
*500 g strong white flour*
*500 g wholemeal flour*
*60 g fresh yeast*
*600 ml warm water*
*30 g salt*
*5 tablespoons olive oil*

# Chappatis

*This unleavened bread is the simplest and most basic form of bread. Serve hot with Indian dishes. Bring to the table stacked in a napkin.*

THE MIX:
Mix the flour and salt in a bowl, then add the water and mix to a dough. Knead thoroughly until it is smooth and malleable. Put it in a bowl, cover it with a damp cloth and leave for 30 minutes.

PRE-HEAT PAN:
Now heat a large, heavy iron frying-pan or griddle over a medium heat. Let it get thoroughly hot while you cut the dough into 12 pieces, shape them into balls, and roll each ball into a very thin disc, using plenty of dry flour.

COOKING TIME:
Place 2 or 3 chappatis in the frying-pan and let them cook until the edges start to curl. Turn them over, and cook a little longer until the chappatis lose their moist look. When they are cooked hold them over a gas flame or very hot electric burner for a few seconds, when they will puff up like balloons.

In colour — page 200

*Makes 12*

THE FLOUR:
*8 oz wholemeal flour or a*
*    mixture of 4 oz 85% wholewheat*
*    flour and 4 oz wholemeal flour*

AND . . .
*4 fl.oz water*
*½ teaspoon salt*

METRIC EQUIVALENTS:
*250 g wholemeal flour or a mixture*
*    of 125 g 85% wholewheat flour*
*    and 125 g wholemeal flour*
*100 ml water*
*½ teaspoon salt*

In colour—page 200

# Naan

*Makes 6*

THE FLOUR:
*8 oz strong white flour*

THE STARTER:
*1 oz fresh yeast*
*5 tablespoons warm water*

AND . . .
*½ teaspoon salt*
*¼ teaspoon black onion seed.*
  *(optional)*
*about 4 fl.oz warm water*

METRIC EQUIVALENTS:
*250 g strong white flour*
*30 g fresh yeast*
*5 tablespoons warm water*
*½ teaspoon salt*
*¼ teaspoon black onion seeds*
  *(optional)*
*about 100 ml warm water*

*This is fresh leavened bread in a thin tear-drop shape—it is made thin to save fuel, and should be eaten very fresh. Excellent with spiced Indian vegetable dishes or Tandoori chicken. Eat it as soon as it is cooked. The black onion seeds (kalonji) are optional but give the bread its characteristic flavour. Buy them from an Indian speciality shop.*

YEAST STARTER:
Mix the yeast with the 5 tablespoons of warm water. Set aside.

THE MIX:
Mix the flour, salt and black onion seeds, then add the yeast mixture and enough warm water to make a pliable dough. Knead thoroughly.

FIRST RISING:
Leave to rise in the bowl, covered with a damp cloth or a sheet of plastic film. When it has doubled in size after about an hour, knead it lightly and divide into 6 pieces. Roll these into balls.

PRE-HEAT OVEN
to 450°F (230°C) Gas 8.

SECOND RISING:
Roll the balls of dough into ovals ¼ in (5 mm) thick and place them on 2 greased baking sheets. Leave, covered, to rise and prove for about 20 minutes while the oven heats up.

BAKING TIME:
Bake for 5 minutes, then turn the bread and bake a further 4 to 5 minutes until just cooked through.

# Calabrian Pizza

*Pizza really means a pie and in this robust version a light, crisp dough holds a moist tuna and tomato filling. It can be made with all white flour, but this is a wholemeal version.*

THE FILLING:
Prepare the filling first. Put the tomatoes in a wide pan with the oil, basil and garlic. Add the chilli pepper and bring to the boil. Simmer until the mixture is thick and the juices have almost evaporated, stirring from time to time to prevent sticking. Then stir in the tuna, olives and anchovies, and cook for 5 minutes. Season. Allow to cool.

THE STARTER:
Mix the yeast with 2 to 3 tablespoons of the warm water.

THE MIX:
Put the flour in a large bowl, make a well in the centre and sprinkle the salt round the edge. When the yeast froths, pour it into the well, add the remaining water and mix to a dough. Knead for 5 minutes.

THE RISING:
Set on a board, cover with a damp cloth or a sheet of oiled polythene and leave to rise until doubled in size, about 40 minutes.

PRE-HEAT OVEN
to 425°F (220°C) Gas 7.

THE SHAPING:
Divide the dough into two and roll out each piece on a well floured board into a large oblong about 14 x 8 in (35.5 x 20 cm). Place one in a well-greased roasting tin and spread the filling over it, leaving a margin of ¾ in (2 cm) round the edge. Lift the other oblong on a rolling pin and place it very carefully over the top.
Press the edges together well and roll them, pinching all the way round to make a tight seal. Brush the top with melted butter.

BAKING TIME:
Bake for 30 to 35 minutes, until golden and crisp.

In colour—page 88

*Makes 1 large pizza*

THE FLOUR:
½ lb strong unbleached white
  flour
½ lb wholemeal flour

THE STARTER:
½ oz fresh yeast
10 fl.oz water, hot to the hand

AND . . .
1 teaspoon salt

THE FILLING:
2 lb tinned Italian tomatoes,
  drained
1 generous tablespoon olive oil
1 tablespoon chopped fresh basil
  or 1 teaspoon dried basil
2 cloves garlic, peeled, crushed
  and chopped
½ red chilli pepper, deseeded and
  flaked or chopped
4 oz tinned tuna, drained and
  mashed
12 black olives, halved and stoned
2 to 3 tablespoons chopped tinned
  anchovy fillets

METRIC EQUIVALENTS:
250 g strong unbleached white flour
250 g wholemeal flour
15 g fresh yeast
300 ml water, hot to the hand
1 teaspoon salt
The filling:
1 kg tinned Italian tomatoes,
  drained
1 generous tablespoon olive oil
1 tablespoon chopped fresh basil
  or 1 teaspoon dried basil
2 cloves garlic, crushed and
  chopped
½ red chilli pepper, chopped
125 g tinned tuna, drained and mashed
12 black olives, halved and stoned
2 to 3 tablespoons chopped tinned
  anchovy fillets

In colour—page 88

*Makes 1 loaf*

THE FLOUR:
*8 oz strong white flour*
*4 oz wholemeal flour*

THE STARTER:
*1 oz fresh yeast*

AND . . .
*6 to 7 fl.oz warm water*
*5 tablespoons olive oil*
*1 teaspoon fine salt*
*10 or 12 cut-up fresh sage*
  *leaves, or 2 teaspoons dried*
  *whole sage leaves*
*small handful of coarse salt*

METRIC EQUIVALENTS:
*25 g strong white flour*
*125 g wholemeal flour*
*30 g fresh yeast*
*150 to 200 ml warm water*
*5 tablespoons olive oil*
*1 teaspoon fine salt*
*10 or 12 cut-up sage leaves*
  *or 2 teaspoons dried whole sage*
  *leaves*
*small handful of coarse salt*

# Focaccia Con La Salvia

*This is adapted from Marcella Hazan's recipe for a lovely Italian flat loaf which is sold hot and so full of olive oil that you can almost squeeze it out of the bread with your hands (Marcella Hazan,* More Classic Italian Cooking, *Knopf, 1978). If you can find a large quarry tile or terracotta gratin dish which can be turned upside-down to expose an unglazed surface, this gives the best kind of heat on which to cook the* focaccia. *It is often served as a snack, but is best eaten soon after it is made. It is traditionally made with all white flour, but you can use the following combination of white and wholemeal flours.*

YEAST STARTER:
Dissolve the yeast in 4 fl.oz (100 ml) of the measured warm water.

FIRST RISING:
Put half the flour into a bowl and add the yeast liquid. Knead thoroughly, put it back in the bowl and leave to rise in a warm place for up to 3 hours, covered with a damp cloth or a sheet of plastic film.

THE MIX:
When it has doubled in size, knead the dough with the remaining flour plus 3 tablespoons of olive oil and the remaining water, the fine salt and the sage.

SECOND RISING:
Knead it very thoroughly for at least 8 minutes, then return it to the bowl and leave to rise as before, until it has doubled in size.

PRE-HEAT OVEN
to 400°F (200°C) Gas 6, and pre-heat the dish or tile for at least 30 minutes before you put in the bread.

THE SHAPING:
Knock the dough down, shape it into a round and roll it into a disc about ½ in (15 mm) thick. Roughen the surface of the dough by dimpling it with your fingertips and sprinkle the remaining olive oil over the top. Sprinkle with a very small quantity of coarse salt. Place the loaf on a floured sheet of cardboard and leave to prove a few minutes in a warm place, then slide on to the heated tile or terracotta dish in the oven. If you're not using a tile, place the dough on a greased baking sheet ready for baking.

BAKING TIME:
Bake for about 25 minutes until it is a rich gold in colour. Cool on a rack until it is just warm, and serve at once.

# Doris Grant

Doris Grant is the inventor of the Grant loaf, which has been an inspiration to housewives for a quarter of a century.

White bread fluffs up in the oven easily enough; but wholemeal contains bran and does not. Commercial bakers succeed in getting volume into wholemeal loaves by mixing the dough for up to an hour—with mechanical mixers and additives. How can the housewife compete?

Doris Grant's answer was to produce a loaf which didn't pretend to be a balloon. The Grant loaf is true to itself: it rises sufficiently to give some volume, but the inside is not airy and expanded like a bakery loaf, but moist, and chewy and retaining the flavour of the wholewheat berry.

The Grant loaf is simplicity itself. She mixes a dough using wholemeal flour (nothing added, nothing taken away); she doesn't knead it at all, or even set her dough to rise a second time. When the dough rises at the end of 40 to 45 minutes, it goes straight into the oven. The result is a denser textured loaf than the baker's "blown-up" version, but, as Mrs. Grant says, a bread of character and flavour. What's more the Grant loaf is an ideal recipe for using soft British wheat.

Some people can't believe you can produce a good bread without kneading. "Try and experiment yourself," she says. "Make two identical loaves, as I have done, kneading one and leaving the other, baking them together. The one you haven't kneaded has goodness and flavour. The other one—no-one bothers to have a second slice.

"I only discovered the method by accident. I had been put on to wholemeal bread by a doctor—to help solve a 15-year problem of indigestion, which it did. As I couldn't buy good wholemeal bread, I had to make my own. One day I was making it, and simply forgot to knead it. In spite of this, the bread was delicious. I began to think then that it was because of not kneading it. I was later told by an old and experienced baker that kneading breaks down the air spaces caused by the yeast, so letting some of the pleasant flavours and goodness of the grain escape. It doesn't matter two hoots if you knead white flour because it has already lost most of its goodness in the milling process."

The Grant loaf wouldn't win any prizes at a convention of modern bakers. The mention of the Grant loaf brings a smile to the faces of the staff at

Chorleywood, Headquarters of the Flour Milling and Baking Research Association, where it's their aim to produce a loaf of good volume, with silky, fine crumbs, evenly aerated, with a thin, crisp, even crust.

Mrs. Grant, however, scorns the efforts of the food technologists to produce a "perfect" loaf. For her, the wholemeal is perfection enough, and the millers are simply playing with the "cosmetics of bread". Worse than that, they are tampering with what's good and removing substances important to our diet, such as all the B complex vitamins. She is not satisfied that the millers later put back some of the nutrients in an "inorganic" form.

"The milling of white bread removes the greater part of 8 vitamins and of 12 minerals. This results in a *distortion* of the natural balance of the nutrients in wholewheat and the totally inadequate restoration to white bread of four statutory additives

(B1, niacin, iron and chalk) may only compound this distortion," she says.

"The subtle inter-relationships between nutrients—which are only now being partly understood—are particularly vulnerable when the nutrients are in an 'inorganic' form."

"Vitamin B1 is part of the Vitamin B complex and one of the body's best safeguards against ill health," she says. "It stimulates the hydrochloric acid in the stomach, which promotes digestion and acts as a natural antibiotic. The whole Vitamin B complex has miraculous qualities, in fact, fairy-tale like powers. It has such a brightening effect on the mind that it has been called the happiness vitamin. It looks after nerves and muscles, particularly of the heart, stomach and colon; it helps the metabolism of carbohydrates (that means the digestion of starches) and the more starches we eat, the more B vitamins we require. Lack of the Vitamin B complex leads to tiredness, nervous exhaustion, intestinal trouble, poor appetite."

Doris Grant goes into the case for Vitamin B very thoroughly in two famous books: *Your Daily Bread*, still quoted although it was published as long ago as 1946, and *Your Daily Food*, published by Faber and Faber in 1973.

She still stands by her arguments, and points out that in spite of all man's technological advances, and especially those of the last hundred years, he is worse off in terms of getting sufficient Vitamin B1 than he was 600—10,000 years ago, when unrefined grain was a staple diet of our ancestors.

"A hundred years ago," she says, "one ounce of genuine unspoiled wholemeal bread contained 30 units of Vitamin B1. Today, one ounce of white bread contains not 30, but only five units of Vitamin B1.

"The body needs about 700 units or more of Vitamin B1 a day to maintain good health. Our wholemeal bread-eating ancestors had 1,200 a day. The average intake today is only about 200. No wonder so many of us are full of aches and pains."

Vitamin B1 resides in the wheat germ and the bran, the parts which millers remove when they make white flour—and sell for animal feed. Farmers know their value! The Grant loaf has all the wheat germ in it, and the bran too. Mrs. Grant also subscribes to the bran movement, and the benefits which bran confers on wholemeal bread eaters.

And yet, if anyone should mistake the strength of her beliefs for fanatacism, she doesn't advocate excessive bread-eating at all. "Don't eat too much," is her advice. "I limit bread and other starch foods to one meal a day. It may seem revolutionary to those who are used to eating bread at every meal, but a small amount of real bread is sufficiently filling and satisfying. It is the refined bread which doesn't satisfy."

Doris Grant would even go as far as to claim her bread is better than those slimming loaves, sometimes advertised on television, whose slices sail up, up and away like a balloon. But a slice of her bread is so filling and satisfying, you don't feel the urge or need to eat too much of it. "And it's nice enough to eat alone, without butter or jam."

Doris Grant is a slim-figured, articulate Scotswoman of 76, who could be taken for her 51-year-old daughter's older sister. She has spent nearly 46 years promoting wholefood and campaigning against refined, commercial foods. She had been ill in her late twenties and became convinced that her diet was not providing the nutrients which should be protecting her.

At home in Poole, Dorset, her husband does the baking these days. Mr. Grant is in semi-retirement, but still is a Director of the Grant family whisky firm of which he was Chairman. He bakes a batch every two weeks, and freezes what they don't immediately want. He cooks the Grant loaf, of course, and Scottish baps using 81% wholewheat flour. If Mrs. Grant happens to be passing the kitchen when he's baking she usually slips some extra bran into the dough.

Their two daughters are grown up and married now; but their elder daughter—an agricultural missionary—has spread the Grant loaf recipe throughout East Africa. And Mrs. Grant's grandson, aged 15, and grand-daughter, aged 13, keep alive the baking tradition, cooking for their parents whenever they can. Their mother, Mrs. Grant's younger daughter, is a Harley Street specialist.

# The Grant Loaf

*Here is the original of the famous loaf which home cooks make all around the world. There isn't an easier loaf you can make. You could substitute 1½ oz (40 g) of medium cut oatmeal for 1½ oz (40 g) of the wholemeal flour for a different texture and flavour.*

YEAST STARTER:
Cream the fresh yeast in a small bowl with the honey or black molasses. Add ¼ pt (150 ml) of the water at 95° to 100°F (35° to 38°C). The temperature is important; it is best to check with a cooking thermometer. Leave for 10 minutes to froth up. If using dried yeast, mix with 3 tablespoons of the water and then add 3 teaspoons honey or black molasses.

THE MIX:
Put the flour into a large bowl and add the salt. In very cold weather warm the flour slightly, just enough to take off the chill. Pour the yeast mixture into the flour and add the rest of the water. Mix well—by hand is best—working from the sides of the bowl to the middle till the dough feels elastic and leaves the sides of the bowl clean. Divide the dough, which should be slippery but not wet between three 2 pt (1¼ litre) bread tins, warmed and greased.

THE RISING:
Cover tins with a cloth and put in a warm place for about 20 minutes, or until the dough is within ½ in (15 mm) from the top of the tins.

PRE-HEAT OVEN
to 400°F (200°C) Gas 6.

BAKING TIME:
Bake for 35 to 40 minutes.

*Makes 3 loaves*

THE FLOUR:
*3 lb stoneground wholemeal flour*

THE STARTER:
*1 oz fresh yeast or 3 level teaspoons dried yeast*
*2 rounded teaspoons honey or black molasses*

AND . . .
*2 pt lukewarm water*
*2 scant teaspoons salt*

METRIC EQUIVALENTS:
*1½ kg stoneground wholemeal flour*
*30 g fresh yeast or 3 level teaspoons dried yeast*
*2 rounded teaspoons honey or black molasses*
*1¼ litres lukewarm water*
*2 scant teaspoons salt*

# The Bran-Plus Loaf

*Makes 2 small loaves*

THE FLOUR:
*2 lb stoneground wholemeal
  flour*

THE STARTER:
*scant 1 oz fresh yeast or 2 level
  teaspoons dried yeast
2 rounded teaspoons honey or
  black molasses*

AND . . .
*1½ teaspoons sea salt
just under 1½ pt lukewarm
  water
3 oz bran*

METRIC EQUIVALENTS:
*1 kg stoneground wholemeal flour
scant 30 g fresh yeast or 2 level
  teaspoons dried yeast
2 rounded teaspoons honey or black
  molasses
1½ teaspoons sea salt
just under 900 ml lukewarm water
90 g bran*

*For those who would like more bran in their diet, here is a
wholemeal recipe with bran. It's a filling and solid bread: a slice at
breakfast-time is good.*

YEAST STARTER:
Cream the fresh yeast in a small bowl with the honey or black
molasses. Add 2 to 3 tablespoons of the warm water. Leave for 10
minutes to froth up.

THE MIX:
Put the flour into a large bowl and add the salt. Add the bran and
mix well. Pour the yeast mixture into the flour and bran and add
the rest of the water. Mix well—by hand is best—working from the
sides of the bowl to the middle until the dough feels elastic and
leaves the sides of the bowl clean. Divide the dough into two
warmed and greased 1 lb (500 g) loaf tins.

THE RISING:
Cover the tins with a cloth and leave in a warm place for about 20
minutes, or until the dough is within ½ in (15 mm) from the top of
the tins.

PRE-HEAT OVEN
to 400°F (200°C) Gas 6.

BAKING TIME:
Bake for 35 to 40 minutes.

# Raisin Loaf

*Makes 2 small loaves*

THE FLOUR:
*1 lb stoneground wholemeal
  flour*

THE STARTER:
*scant ½ oz fresh yeast or 1 level
  teaspoon dried yeast
1 rounded teaspoon honey or
  black treacle*

*A strong-flavoured, tasty loaf for tea-time.*

AND . . .
*8 fl.oz lukewarm water
1 scant teaspoon salt
1 teaspoon mixed spice
4 oz melted butter
3 tablespoons honey
8 oz raisins
1 oz chopped nuts*

METRIC EQUIVALENTS:
*500 g stoneground wholemeal flour
scant 15 g fresh yeast or 1 level
  teaspoon dried yeast
1 rounded teaspoon honey or black
  treacle
250 ml lukewarm water
1 scant teaspoon salt
1 teaspoon mixed spice
125 g melted butter
3 tablespoons honey
250 g raisins
30 g chopped nuts*

YEAST STARTER:
Cream the yeast with 3 tablespoons of the warm water in a cup or
small basin. Add the honey or treacle and leave for 10 minutes.

**THE MIX:**

Mix the salt and spice with the flour in a warmed bowl. Make a well in the centre and pour the yeasty mixture in. Add the melted butter, the honey, and enough of the remaining warm water to make a workable dough. Mix well by hand, adding the raisins and chopped nuts and working from the sides of the bowl to the middle, until the dough feels elastic and leaves the sides of the bowl clean.

**THE RISING:**

Turn out and divide into 2 equal portions. Shape and put into two greased 1 lb (500 g) loaf tins. Cover with greased polythene and leave to rise for 20 to 30 minutes.

**PRE-HEAT OVEN**

to 400°F (200°C) Gas 6.

**BAKING TIME:**

Bake for 40 to 45 minutes.

# Date Loaf

*A moist and fruity tea loaf, which is quick and easy to make, and delicious with butter.*

**PRE-HEAT OVEN**

to 425°F (220°C) Gas 7.

**THE MIX:**

Rub the butter into the flour. Mix together the bicarbonate of soda and cream of tartar and add to the flour. Add the finely chopped dates. Beat the egg yolks with a little of the milk and water, and add to the flour with the honey. Gradually add the remainder of the liquid to make a soft dough. Place in a greased 1 lb (500 g) loaf tin.

**BAKING TIME:**

Bake for about 40 minutes.

*In colour—page 129*

*Makes 1 small loaf*

**THE FLOUR:**
*½ lb wholemeal flour*

**THE RAISING AGENT:**
*½ teaspoon bicarbonate of soda*
*¼ teaspoon cream of tartar*

**AND . . .**
*1 oz butter*
*14 dates, stoned and finely chopped*
*2 egg yolks*
*about ¼ pt milk and water, mixed*
*1 tablespoon honey*

**METRIC EQUIVALENTS:**
*250 g wholemeal flour*
*½ teaspoon bicarbonate of soda*
*¼ teaspoon cream of tartar*
*30 g butter*
*14 dates, stoned and finely chopped*
*2 egg yolks*
*about 150 ml milk and water, mixed*
*1 tablespoon honey*

# Scones

*Makes 6 to 8*

*A simple recipe for scones to serve buttered at tea-time.*

THE FLOUR:
*6 oz wholemeal flour*

THE RAISING AGENT:
*½ teaspoon bicarbonate of soda*
*¼ teaspoon cream of tartar*

AND . . .
*¼ teaspoon salt*
*1 oz butter*
*2 teaspoons honey*
*water or milk to mix, preferably sour milk*

METRIC EQUIVALENTS:
*175 g wholemeal flour*
*½ teaspoon bicarbonate of soda*
*¼ teaspoon cream of tartar*
*¼ teaspoon salt*
*30 g butter*
*2 teaspoons honey*
*water or milk to mix*

THE MIX:
Mix the flour with the bicarbonate of soda, the cream of tartar, and the salt. Rub in the butter and add the honey. Add the milk or water gradually, mixing to a soft dough using a knife. Turn on to a floured board. Roll or press out to a thickness of about 1 in (2.5 cm). Cut into rounds. Brush the tops lightly with a little milk.

PRE-HEAT OVEN
to 425° (220°C) Gas 7.

BAKING TIME:
Bake on a greased baking sheet for about 15 minutes.

# Wholemeal Scones

*Makes 8*

*Unleavened wholemeal scones are ideal when you're in a hurry, but they should also be eaten quickly, as they do not last.*

THE FLOUR:
*1 lb stoneground wholemeal flour*

AND . . .
*6 fl.oz boiling water*

METRIC EQUIVALENTS:
*500 g stoneground wholemeal flour*
*150 ml boiling water*

THE MIX:
Mix the flour with the boiling water until all the water is taken up in the flour to give an almost dry dough. Flatten it into a round cake about 6 in (15 cm) across and cut across four times to give 8 triangular scones.

PRE-HEAT OVEN
to 400°F (200°C) Gas 6.

BAKING TIME:
Bake for 35 minutes. After 15 minutes REDUCE HEAT to 375°F (190°C) Gas 5.

# Sultana Scones

*Sweet scones for tea-time, made with wholemeal flour.*

*Makes 8*

THE FLOUR:
*8 oz wholemeal flour*

THE RAISING AGENT:
*½ teaspoon bicarbonate of soda*
*¼ teaspoon cream of tartar*

AND . . .
*2 egg yolks*
*1 tablespoon water*
*2 oz butter*
*2 oz sultanas*
*1 tablespoon honey*
*about 5 tablespoons milk*

METRIC EQUIVALENTS:
*250 g wholemeal flour*
*½ teaspoon bicarbonate of soda*
*¼ teaspoon cream of tartar*
*2 egg yolks*
*1 tablespoon water*
*60 g butter*
*60 g sultanas*
*1 tablespoon honey*
*about 5 tablespoons milk*

THE MIX:
Beat the egg yolks with the water. Mix the bicarbonate of soda and cream of tartar together well and add to the flour. Rub in the butter. Add the sultanas. Mix in the beaten egg yolks, the honey and sufficient milk to make a stiff dough, using a knife for the mixing. Divide the dough into 2 equal parts, turn out on to a floured board and, using the palm of the hand, flatten into 2 rounds, about ½ in (15 mm) thick. Cut across the top with a floured knife to make 4 scones.

PRE-HEAT OVEN
to 400°F (200°C) Gas 6.

BAKING TIME:
Place scones on a lightly greased baking sheet and bake for 15 minutes.

In colour—page 272

# Ruth's Raisin Scones

*One of the simplest of wholemeal scones to make, with plump, juicy raisins added and no raising agent. Eat the same day.*

*Makes 8*

THE FLOUR:
*8 oz wholemeal flour*

AND . . .
*pinch of salt*
*1½ oz butter*
*milk, preferably sour*
*2 oz raisins*

METRIC EQUIVALENTS:
*250 g wholemeal flour*
*pinch of salt*
*40 g butter*
*milk, preferably sour*
*60 g raisins*

THE MIX:
Put the flour into a large bowl, add the salt and rub in the butter until the mixture is the consistency of breadcrumbs. Add enough milk to make a soft dough. Add the raisins and work well in.
Turn the dough out on to a floured board and flatten into a round cake about 6 in (15 cm) across. Use a floured knife to cut into 8 triangular scones.

PRE-HEAT OVEN
to 375°F (190°C) Gas 5.

BAKING TIME:
Bake for 20 to 25 minutes.

# Scotch Baps

*A distinctive recipe, adapted from the traditional one but using no butter. The texture is fine and smooth and the flavour excellent.*

*Makes 6*

THE FLOUR:
*8 oz 81% wholewheat flour*

THE STARTER:
*¼ pt mixed milk and water*
*½ oz fresh yeast or*
*    1 level teaspoon dried yeast*
*1 teaspoon honey*

AND . . .
*1 level teaspoon salt*
*a little milk for glazing*

METRIC EQUIVALENTS:
*250 g 81% wholewheat flour*
*150 ml mixed milk and water*
*15 g fresh yeast or 1 level teaspoon*
*    dried yeast*
*1 teaspoon honey*
*1 level teaspoon salt*
*a little milk for glazing*

YEAST STARTER:
Warm the milk and water and blend together with the yeast and honey in a small basin. Set aside in a warm place for about 10 minutes or until it becomes frothy. If using dried yeast dissolve the honey in the hand-hot mixed milk and water, and sprinkle on the yeast, stirring into the liquid.

THE MIX:
Sift the flour and salt into a large bowl. Stir the yeast liquid into the flour. Mix by hand in the basin to a rough dough. Turn out on to a floured board and knead until smooth. Put the dough back in the basin and place the basin inside a large polythene bag.

FIRST RISING:
Leave the covered bowl in a warm place until the dough has risen to twice the size, about 1 hour.
Turn the risen dough out and press with the knuckles to knock out the air. Divide the dough into 6 portions and roll each into a ball. Use a rolling pin to flatten each ball into a bap.

SECOND RISING:
Place on a greased baking sheet, brush with milk and dust with flour. Leave, covered, in a warm place until risen and puffy, for up to 40 minutes.

PRE-HEAT OVEN
to 400°F (200°C) Gas 6.

TO BAKE:
Dust the baps well with flour and press a floured thumb into the
centre of each.

BAKING TIME:
Bake for 15 to 20 minutes. Serve warm from the oven, or allow them
to cool and reheat in a hot oven for about 5 minutes before serving.

## Oven Wholemeal Flatties

*Oven flatties are best eaten fresh, as soon as they are cold. They
don't keep. Split them in half, remove the dough-like centre and
butter both halves. They are my favourites—especially good with
egg and cress filling.*

YEAST STARTER:
Cream the yeast in 2 to 3 tablespoons of the warm water, add the
honey or molasses, and leave for 10 minutes to froth up.

THE MIX:
Put the flour and salt in a warmed bowl. Make a well in the centre
and pour in the yeast mixture. Add the rest of the water. Mix
well—by hand is best—for a minute or so, working from the sides
of the bowl to the middle until the dough feels elastic and leaves
the sides of the bowl clean.
Place heaped tablespoons of the dough on a greased baking sheet,
leaving ample room between them. With floured hands press the
spoonfuls into flat rounds—as flat as you can make them.

THE RISING:
Allow to rise in a warm place for about 20 minutes, until the
flatties are nicely puffed.

PRE-HEAT OVEN
to 400°F (200°C) Gas 6.

BAKING TIME:
Bake for about 20 minutes, or until a pale golden-brown on top and
crisp underneath.

*In colour—page 88*

*Makes 12 to 16*

THE FLOUR:
*1 lb stoneground wholemeal
flour*

THE STARTER:
*scant ½ oz fresh yeast or 1
level teaspoon dried yeast*
*1 rounded teaspoon honey
or black molasses*

AND . . .
*13 fl.oz lukewarm water*
*1 scant teaspoon salt*

METRIC EQUIVALENTS:
*500 g stoneground wholemeal flour*
*scant 15 g fresh yeast or 1 level
teaspoon dried yeast*
*1 rounded teaspoon honey or black
molasses*
*370 ml lukewarm water*
*1 scant teaspoon salt*

# George and Cecilia Scurfield

George and Cecilia Scurfield have baked all the bread they are ever going to want to bake. But they still eat plenty of it, nipping across the road from their bookshop in Fakenham, North Norfolk, to Moore's, one of three very good independent bakers in and around the town.

A long time ago, they recall with wry amusement, they were bakers themselves. They were living in the tiny Cambridgeshire village of Shepreth. George had left the army after the war and was trying to make his way as a novelist, playing the part of village postman in the morning, giving him the rest of the day free to write. Two novels were published by Michael Joseph, but the returns weren't coming in fast enough to feed a family of seven (he has two stepchildren beside his own). "I could see my children starving," he said.

The solution offered itself. Since friends praised their bread, why shouldn't they sell it to them?

They had been baking their own bread because shop bread had become so indifferent. It was unappetising, says George, it fell to pieces when you tried to cut it. It didn't keep. Wholemeal bread was almost unobtainable. Brown loaves were like "very distant cousins, several times removed".

Luckily, they lived near a mill, at Fulbourn. They started buying freshly stoneground wholemeal flour in bulk. To make it commercial, they argued, they simply had to step up production. In their kitchen they cooked on an Aga. They would start a batch of four large loaves, putting them in the top oven for 20 minutes, then transferring them to the cooler lower oven for another 20 minutes, putting four more loaves, or six smaller loaves, into the top oven. So they went on till the day's orders were done.

George has a great feeling for self-sufficiency. But Cecilia has no illusions about what they were doing. "It was not romantic. It was not romantic at all."

But here the Scurfields were keeping real bread alive. Soon they were baking three days a week, doing their delivery rounds the day after each bakeday. Mrs. Scurfield would start making the dough in the afternoon, and they'd be baking until after midnight. Their reputation spread by word of mouth. After three months they had over 100 customers.

A health inspector had made a visit, and made some pertinent suggestions relevant to a town bakery but rather alarming in a village kitchen; so the Scurfields had to have the floors up, but in sheer desperation baked on in the midst of building operations, quite expecting that any minute the inspector would arrive, and properly shocked, close them down.

The experience was exhausting and hardly profitable. At the end of a year's efforts, George Scurfield was in Cambridge delivering his bread when he ran into the Bursar of Trinity College. "Ah, Scurfield," he said, "I hear you bake good bread, and I was wondering if . . ."

This must be the moment every small businessman dreams about. The moment to expand; to move to larger premises and take on staff. The Scurfields smile at the memory: "We decided to close down instead."

And close they did. But they wrote a book together, and it has become a bible of the home baker. In 1981 they celebrated 25 years in print; *Home Baked* by George and Cecilia Scurfield. Faber Paperbacks £1.00. The book was happily more profitable than the bakery. And instead of opening another bakery, they opened a kitchenware shop in Cambridge. "I always think Habitat sprang from that," said George thoughtfully.

Their book is enormously simple. "Baking is so easy," says Cecilia. George says he has a fear of books himself: "I'm always afraid I'm not going to understand them." He has good reason; some of the technical books on bread-making are like awkward algebraic exercises; and some of the traditional books put you off with warnings about what can go wrong: like the draughts which might wreck rising dough as surely as they would put the wind up a soufflé.

Cecilia Scurfield: "We used to bake with the windows open. The man who delivered the meat used to be a baker. He was terribly scornful about the open windows. But it's silly. Dough will even rise in the fridge."

George: "A good many people are frightened of baking their own bread, put off by the idea of kneading, mystified by the way yeast works, don't think they have the right sort of oven, or imagine they will have to go round draught-proofing their kitchen.

"The great thing about baking with yeast is the

difficulty of failure. If you should find that the dough doesn't rise, wait just a little longer. It surely will rise if you haven't forgotten the yeast altogether, and even if you have left it out you can always add it with a little more liquid and flour and set the dough to rise again once more.

"Again there's no need to worry if you get some of the ingredients weighed out incorrectly. Flour varies in absorbency, eggs vary in size, fat in oiliness, and so on. You can always add more flour if the dough is too slack, or more liquid if it is too dry.

"Really, the only thing that can go wrong when baking is—leaving the loaves in the oven and forgetting all about them until they've become nothing more than charred remains."

The Scurfields do eat white bread from time to time, but they feel that it's not quite the real thing.

"Most people, especially children, prefer white bread. And if in other ways they eat normal, healthy foods with a fair amount of green vegetables, meat and milk, they should get a plentiful supply of all the vitamins, proteins and minerals they require. All the same, white bread cannot truly qualify as the staff of life . . . .

"The taste, not to mention the texture and the keeping qualities, of home-made bread made from stoneground wholemeal wheat flour is so much pleasanter, so much nuttier, that it really seems unnecessary to go into all the nutritional reasons for preferring it."

# Oatmeal Bread

*A bread with a crispy, nutty flavour that is very good generously spread with butter and honey at tea-time, and also goes well with cheese or pâté.*

PREPARATION:
Put the oatmeal in a large bowl and pour over the milk. Leave to soak for at least 2 hours.

YEAST STARTER:
Cream the yeast with 1 to 2 tablespoons warm water and put aside for about 5 minutes.

THE MIX:
Add the yeast mixture to the flour and oatmeal with the melted butter and the salt to make a smooth, even dough. Knead thoroughly.

FIRST RISING:
Cover the bowl with a damp cloth and leave the dough to rise in a warm place for about 1½ hours, or until it has doubled in size. Shape into 2 small loaves.

SECOND RISING:
Allow the loaves to stand for about 45 minutes.

PRE-HEAT OVEN
to 425°F (220°C) Gas 7.

BAKING TIME:
Bake for 50 minutes to 1 hour. After 30 minutes REDUCE HEAT to 375°F (190°C) Gas 5 and turn the loaves round.

*Makes 2 small loaves*

THE FLOUR:
*about ½ lb wholemeal flour*
*½ lb medium oatmeal*

THE STARTER:
*½ oz fresh yeast or ¼ oz dried yeast*
*1 or 2 tablespoons warm water*

AND . . .
*¾ pt fresh milk*
*2 oz butter, melted but not hot*
*4 teaspoons salt*

METRIC EQUIVALENTS:
*about 250 g wholemeal flour*
*250 g medium oatmeal*
*15 g fresh yeast or 8 g dried yeast*
*1 to 2 tablespoons warm water*
*400 ml fresh milk*
*60 g butter, melted but not hot*
*4 teaspoons salt*

# Milk Steam Cake

*Makes 1 cake*

THE FLOUR:
*½ lb strong white flour*

THE STARTER:
*1 oz fresh yeast or*
  *½ oz dried yeast*
*⅛ pt warm milk*

AND . . .
*2 oz butter*
*2 egg yolks*
*2 teaspoons honey*
*pinch of salt*

TO POUR OVER
AND SPRINKLE:
*¼ pt milk*
*2 tablespoons honey*
*1 heaped teaspoon cinnamon*

METRIC EQUIVALENTS:
*250 g strong white flour*
*30 g fresh yeast or 15 g dried yeast*
*5 tablespoons warm milk*
*60 g butter*
*2 egg yolks*
*2 teaspoons honey*
*pinch of salt*
*To pour over and sprinkle:*
*150 ml milk*
*2 tablespoons honey*
*1 heaped teaspoon cinnamon*

*In England, we might call this French recipe a pudding rather than a cake. It is served hot, painted with honey and sprinkled with cinnamon.*

YEAST STARTER:
Mix the yeast in the warm milk and allow to stand for about 5 minutes.

THE MIX:
Melt the butter and cool until lukewarm. Pour into a bowl and add the egg yolks, honey, salt, and yeast mixture. Stir and mix well. Add the flour and knead until the dough is smooth and creamy. Then roll into a long sausage, cut into ½-in (15 mm) thick slices and put into a well-greased baking tin.

THE RISING:
Cover the baking tin and leave to rise for 45 minutes or until doubled in size.

PRE-HEAT OVEN
to 375°F (190°C) Gas 5.

BAKING TIME:
Bake for about 15 to 20 minutes until the cake is a light golden-brown.
Just before cake is ready heat the ¼ pt (150 ml) milk and stir in 1 tablespoon of the honey. Remove the cake from the oven and pour over the sweetened milk, which will soak in immediately and the cake will rise. Warm the remaining tablespoon of honey, paint the loaf with this and sprinkle with powdered cinnamon. Serve at once.

# Vienna Bread

*A big, generous, smooth, sweetish milk loaf: a good platform for delicious home-made conserves, and very nice toasted.*

YEAST STARTER:
Cream the yeast with 1 to 2 tablespoons of warm water and leave for about 5 minutes.

THE MIX:
Pour the flour into a large bowl. Make a well in the centre and sprinkle the salt around the edge. Pour the yeast mixture into the well. Add the butter, melted but not too hot. Pour in the milk very gradually, as you may need a little more or less. Mix all ingredients lightly and thoroughly. Knead for about 15 to 20 minutes. When the dough is ready it should be a smooth, springy consistency.

FIRST RISING:
Cover the bowl with a damp cloth, and a lid to stop the cloth from drying out or use cling film, and put in a warm place to rise for 2 hours or until it has doubled in size. Knock back, then cut the dough into four and shape into 4 longish loaves. Place them on lightly floured baking sheets.

SECOND RISING:
Leave covered in a warm place for 45 minutes to 1 hour. When ready for the oven the loaves should be soft and slightly puffy to the touch.

PRE-HEAT OVEN
to 425°F (220°C) Gas 7.

BAKING TIME:
Bake for 50 minutes to 1 hour. After 30 minutes REDUCE HEAT to 375°F (190°C) Gas 5 and turn the loaves round, painting the top of each loaf with a little creamy top of the milk.

*Makes 4 loaves*

THE FLOUR:
*2½ lb strong white flour*

THE STARTER:
*1 oz fresh yeast or ½ oz dried yeast*
*1 or 2 tablespoons warm water*

AND . . .
*½ oz salt*
*4 oz butter*
*1 pt warm milk*
*a little top of the milk*

METRIC EQUIVALENTS:
*1 kg strong white flour*
*30 g fresh yeast or 15 g dried yeast*
*1 to 2 tablespoons warm water*
*15 g salt*
*125 g butter*
*600 ml warm milk*
*a little top of the milk*

# Sour Rye Bread

*Makes 4 small loaves*

THE FLOUR:
*1½ lb rye flour*
*1 lb white flour*

THE STARTERS:
*Sourdough paste(see method)*
*½ oz fresh yeast or ¼ oz dried yeast*

AND . . .
*½ oz salt*
*4 oz butter*
*1 pint warm milk and water mixed, as required*

METRIC EQUIVALENTS:
*750 g rye flour*
*500 g white flour*
*Sourdough paste (see method)*
*15 g fresh yeast or 8 g dried yeast*
*15 g salt*
*125 g butter*
*600 ml warm milk and water mixed, as required*

*Not a bread to make on the spur of the moment, because the sour flavour must be allowed to develop over several days. This is the bread enjoyed in Eastern Europe today, but this style of bread was also common in Britain in the Middle Ages. Strictly speaking the yeast is unnecessary.*

SOURDOUGH PASTE STARTER:
A few days before making your bread mix two or three tablespoons of rye flour to a paste with a little warm milk. Leave this in a covered bowl in a warm place until it smells pleasantly sour.

YEAST STARTER:
When you are ready to bake cream the yeast in a little of the warm milk and water.

THE MIX:
Mix the flours in a large bowl. Sprinkle in the salt and stir well together. Melt the butter and allow to cool. Make a well in the flour and pour in the sourdough paste and the butter. Add the yeast mixture. Gradually add the rest of the warm milk and water; the exact quantity will depend upon the absorbency of the flour and this varies. Mix the ingredients lightly and thoroughly with the fingers. Knead for 15 to 20 minutes when the dough should be a smooth, springy consistency.

FIRST RISING:
Cover the bowl with a damp cloth and add a lid to prevent the cloth from drying out. Put in a warm place to rise and leave for about 2 hours or until it has doubled in size. Cut into four and shape into loaves. If you use bread tins, grease them well and half fill with the dough, pressing it well down.

SECOND RISING:
Leave covered in a warm place for 45 minutes to 1 hour. It is better to under than over prove; the latter may give a poor texture.

PRE-HEAT OVEN
to 400°F (200°C) Gas 6.

BAKING TIME:
Bake for 50 to 60 minutes. After 30 minutes REDUCE HEAT to 375°F (190°C) Gas 5, and turn the loaves round. Remove and cool on a wire tray.

# Spice Buns

*These little buns with their deliciously spicy flavour are also known as "wigs". The name, according to the* Encyclopaedia of Gastronomy *is derived from the fact that "A wigg was a wedge and these 'wigs' are wedge-shaped cakes."*

YEAST STARTER:
Mix the yeast with 1 to 2 tablespoons warm water and leave for about 5 minutes.

THE MIX:
Melt the butter and allow to cool. Sift the flour into a large bowl. Add the mixed spice, caraway seeds and salt, and mix well. Make a well in the centre and pour in the yeast, milk, honey and melted butter. Knead thoroughly to a smooth, soft dough. Roll out the dough on a floured board and cut into 24 wedge-shaped buns.

THE RISING:
Place the buns on a floured baking sheet and allow to stand for 30 minutes.

PRE-HEAT OVEN
to 425°F (220°C) Gas 7.

BAKING TIME:
Bake for 20 minutes. Turn them round at half time.

*Makes 24*

THE FLOUR:
*12 oz white flour*
*4 oz wholemeal flour*

THE STARTER:
*½ oz fresh yeast or ¼ oz dried yeast*
*1 to 2 tablespoons warm water*

AND . . .
*2 oz butter*
*1 teaspoon mixed spice*
*¼ oz caraway seeds*
*pinch of salt*
*½ pt milk*
*1 tablespoon honey*

METRIC EQUIVALENTS:
*350 g white flour*
*125 g wholemeal flour*
*15 g fresh yeast or 8 g dried yeast*
*1 to 2 tablespoons warm water*
*60 g butter*
*1 teaspoon mixed spice*
*8 g caraway seeds*
*pinch of salt*
*300 ml milk*
*1 tablespoon honey*

# Gugelhupf

In colour—page 104

*Makes 1 loaf*

THE FLOUR:
*8 oz white flour*

THE STARTER:
*1 oz fresh yeast or ½ oz dried yeast*
*⅛ pt warm milk*

AND...
*2 oz butter, melted but cool*
*2 eggs*
*1 tablespoon honey*
*the zest and juice of 1 orange*
*2 oz seedless raisins (soaked in a little water or rum)*
*1 tablespoon fine breadcrumbs*

METRIC EQUIVALENTS:
*250 g white flour*
*30 g fresh yeast or 15 g dried yeast*
*5 tablespoons warm milk*
*60 g butter, melted but cool*
*2 eggs*
*1 tablespoon honey*
*the zest and juice of 1 orange*
*60 g seedless raisins (soaked in a little water or rum)*
*1 tablespoon fine breadcrumbs*

*Austria is as famous for its rich assortment of delicious cakes and pastries as for its Viennese waltzes. Any yeast cake baked in the traditional centre tube mould qualifies as a Gugelhupf, but you can also use any ordinary ring mould. This cake has a delicate orange flavour, and the plump raisins can be soaked in rum. The cake is traditionally dusted with icing sugar.*

YEAST STARTER:
Cream the yeast with the warm milk. Mix in one or two tablespoons of flour and allow to stand for half an hour in a warm place to rise.

THE MIX:
Add the butter, the eggs, the honey, the orange juice and zest and the raisins to the yeast mix, beating well or whisking after each addition. Finally beat in the rest of the flour very gradually, slapping it in with the fingers. This should be a very slack dough that can almost be poured. Grease the mould carefully and dust it with the breadcrumbs.

THE RISING:
Half fill the mould with dough. Leave to rise for about 1 hour, or until the dough has risen to the top of the mould.

PRE-HEAT OVEN
to 375°F (190°C) Gas 5.

BAKING TIME:
Bake for 30 to 40 minutes. Cool on a wire rack.

# Kolatschen

In colour—page 104

*Makes about 8*

*A delicious croissant dough into which you put fillings to taste—like doughnuts. Rich, but delicate, and when you make it yourself, better than anything you can buy. The recipe may sound complicated for first-timers but it repays the effort. You must use ordinary plain white flour as strong flour will not work. Traditionally Kolatschen are dusted with icing sugar.*

THE FLOUR:
*¾ lb plain white flour*

THE STARTER:
*1 oz fresh yeast or ½ oz dried yeast*
*¼ pt lukewarm milk*
*1 tablespoon honey*
*pinch of salt*

AND...
*2 oz butter, melted but cool*
*2 eggs, well beaten*
*½ lb of butter for spreading*
Fillings: *fruit, poppy seeds, chopped nuts, jam, soured cream or cheese, as liked*

METRIC EQUIVALENTS:
*350 g plain white flour*
*30 g fresh yeast or 15 g dried yeast*
*150 ml lukewarm milk*
*1 tablespoon honey*
*pinch of salt*
*60 g butter, melted but cool*
*2 eggs, well beaten*
*250 g butter for spreading*
Fillings: *see left*

### YEAST STARTER:
Dissolve the yeast in the milk. And the honey and salt and stir. Add enough flour to mix to a thin paste. Leave to rise in a warm place for about 30 minutes.

### THE MIX:
Beat the 2 oz (60 g) melted butter with the eggs in a large bowl. Beat in the yeast mixture. Gradually add the rest of the flour, slapping it in with the fingers. The dough must be soft, smooth and elastic.

### FIRST RISING:
Leave covered in a warm place for 1½ hours or until double in size.

### THE SHAPING AND CHILLING:
Wash the ½ lb (250 g) butter by squeezing it between the fingers in a bowl of cold water until it is soft and easy to spread. Divide in half and leave in a bowl of cold water until you are ready to use it. Knock the dough together and roll it out on a floured board into a strip about ¼ in (5 mm) thick and about three times as long as in width. Shake half of the butter dry and spread it over the centre third of the dough strip. Pull one end over, patting it down at the edges and spread the rest of the butter over that. Pull the remaining end over and pat down the edges. Roll the dough out the other way into a strip the same size. Fold in the ends to make a square. Chill for half an hour in the refrigerator. Roll out the dough again and again fold in. Repeat this twice more at intervals of 30 minutes, placing the dough in the refrigerator each time.

### SECOND RISING:
Allow the dough to rise for 30 minutes or so in a warm place. Roll out on a floured board to ¼ in (5 mm) thickness. Cut into small 3 in (8 cm) squares or circles. Press down with thumb in centre of each to make a hollow. Fill this with fruit, poppy seeds, nuts, jam, soured cream or cheese, according to taste. Fold the dough over the filling, moistening the edges to seal them.

### PRE-HEAT OVEN
to 400°F (200°C) Gas 6.

### BAKING TIME:
Bake for about 30 minutes.

# Mrs. Beeton's Yeast Cake

*Makes 1 cake*

THE FLOUR:
*1 lb white flour*
   *or 12 oz white flour and 4 oz*
   *wholemeal flour*

THE STARTER:
*1 oz fresh yeast or ½ oz dried*
   *yeast*
*1 to 2 tablespoons warm water*

AND ...
*2 oz butter*
*2 eggs*
*4 fl.oz milk*
*2 tablespoons honey*
*6 oz currants*
*2 oz chopped candied peel*

METRIC EQUIVALENTS:
*500 g white flour or 350 g white*
   *flour and 125 g wholemeal flour*
*30 g fresh yeast or 15 g dried*
   *yeast*
*1 to 2 tablespoons warm water*
*60 g butter*
*2 eggs*
*100 ml milk*
*2 tablespoons honey*
*175 g currants*
*60 g chopped candied peel*

*A cut-and-come-again cake that has been a family favourite since it was first made in the last century. Eat quickly or keep in a tin.*

YEAST STARTER:
Cream the yeast with 1 to 2 tablespoons warm water and leave for about 5 minutes.

THE MIX:
Melt the butter and allow to cool. Pour into a bowl. Break in the eggs, pour in the milk and whisk to a froth. Sift the flour into a large bowl. Make a well in the centre and pour in the yeast mixture. Add the honey, the milk, butter and egg mixture, and knead until the dough is smooth and soft and comes away from the sides of the bowl.

FIRST RISING:
Cover the bowl with a damp cloth and leave to rise in a warm place until double in size, at least 1½ hours.

SECOND RISING:
Add fruit and peel, and knead well to make sure they are evenly distributed. Line a 7 in (180 mm) cake tin with grease-proof paper and put in the dough. Leave to prove for 30 minutes.

PRE-HEAT OVEN
to 425°F (220°C) Gas 7.

BAKING TIME:
Bake for 1 hour 30 minutes. After 30 minutes REDUCE HEAT to 375°F (190°C) Gas 5.

# Maria Johnson

Britain is unique in the liberties its bakers take with their loaves. Some of the ingredients they use like Butylated Hydroxytoluene (an antioxidant) sound more appropriate to the laboratory rather than the bakery. In many European countries bread additives are not permitted and bread is made only of flour, water, salt and yeast. In France, for example, bread is legally defined as the product which results from the baking of dough, made from wheat flour, yeast, water and salt. Their bread is apparently none the worse for it.

Maria Johnson is Bulgarian. When she married an Englishman and came to live in Britain in 1965 she was dismayed by the standards of most British shop bread. She couldn't get used to its shining whiteness. Bread in Bulgaria has a warm creamy-white colour because their flour isn't bleached white. "It's a heavier loaf than the British loaf," she says. "But it has more flavour." So she started baking her own.

Maria Johnson, born Maria Kaneva, is a graphic designer and worked with British publishers. She gave this up five years ago to write about food.

Alan Davidson was preparing the second, enlarged edition of his marvellous reference book, *Mediterranean Seafood,* and he asked Maria to contribute some Bulgarian recipes. Her research led her further into the cookery of the Balkan countries than she intended, and soon she decided that a great cuisine deserved to be better known and understood. She must now be the leading authority on Balkan food and regularly contributes to magazines and cookery books (notably Time-Life Publications and *The Sunday Times Guide to the World's Best Food*).

Maria's fondest memories of bread are of the Bulgarian loaf her mother used to buy each day. Maria still buys similar loaves each summer when she returns to Bulgaria.

"It was during the war, when this loaf became hard to come by and bread was rationed like everything else, that I began to bake my own bread. Yeast was no problem. But flour was difficult to find. Maize was added to the usual flour. And to make the maize flour they ground down even the cobs." This combination produced a very yellow loaf. Maria's first attempts were not very successful.

"I began to experiment—and I still am. I remember, shortly after the war, when I was living in Sofia

and studying at the National Academy of Fine Arts, my parents came to visit me. As a special treat, they brought me a really white loaf of bread. This was such a luxury! They gave it to my landlady, who was so delighted, she said: 'Oh, what lovely bread. Do you eat it with bread?'

"Bread mystifies people. Here in England, when I place my simple basic loaf on the table, people are often surprised. They ask how I manage it. They think making bread is something mysterious and prone to failure."

When she's baking her own bread at home Maria makes a large batch at a time. "I use about 3 kilos (over 6 lb) flour. I bake several loaves, then I cut each loaf into three or four pieces and I freeze them. Every day, I unfreeze enough for my husband and myself. It comes out as fresh as the day I made it."

Maria bakes a very basic loaf, which she leaves to rise several times:

"The more times you let a loaf rise, the better the crumb, and it stays fresh longer. It has a good taste—but it's not just a question of taste. That can be achieved by artificial means, by adding chemicals or spraying them into the air to cause the taste-buds to tingle. Oh yes, they do that in some shops. But if you achieve a good tasty loaf in the home by using the slow-rising method, then your taste-buds approve and you have the moral satisfaction of knowing that what you are eating is not harmful."

Her favourite loaf is the *kozounak*, the traditional Bulgarian Easter loaf. In Bulgaria people stay up all night to make it. Here Maria's husband helps her with the kneading:

"He has better muscles for it! The texture of this loaf is delicious—it's in thin long flakes or strands. To get this you knead with melted butter, instead of flour. It's a rich, sweet loaf, almost a cake, like the Russian *kulich*. It can be made in many different fancy shapes—my mother had eight different containers for it. You eat it at breakfast with milk and coffee and at five o'clock for tea. And you eat it over the three days of Easter."

For Maria, whether she's making a basic everyday loaf or a complicated *kozounak*, it's a way of relaxing and getting back to what is natural:

"Everything is so artificial today. When I do something that people have been doing for thousands of years, it gives me some sense of stability. You see, European farming started in the Balkans in the lands on both sides of the Danube. The people there have been growing wheat and baking bread in domed clay ovens since about 6000 BC. Now everything is different. Young people are so busy; they see food as fuel. But soon, thanks to technological advances, people will have too much time and too much leisure. Then cooking will come back. The human species cannot exist without being creative."

NOTE ON DRIED YEAST
*Recently, when reconstituting dried yeast, I found that a sweetening agent wasn't really necessary to activate it. A small amount of flour from the recipe quantity can be mixed instead with the dissolved yeast to form a thin batter. With a little warmth, within 20 to 30 minutes, the yeast starts releasing gases that will raise the dough.*
*Without this preliminary batter the dried yeast takes longer to ferment the dough.*

## Quick Almost-White Bread

*Makes 1 large loaf*

THE FLOUR:
¾ *lb strong white unbleached*
   *flour*
¼ *lb wholemeal flour*

THE STARTER:
¾ *oz fresh yeast*

AND . . .
*just under ½ pt tepid water*
¼ *oz Cheshire (rock) salt**
*a little melted butter or oil for*
   *brushing*

SALT-WATER GLAZE (optional):
*1 teaspoon salt, dissolved in 3*
   *tablespoons warm water*

*This quickly mixed straight dough with only one proving used to be made by country people in the Balkans, when a visitor dropped in unexpectedly and a fresh loaf was needed for the evening meal. (Nowadays they just go to the local baker's.)*
*To speed up the rising time, the dough is given twice the usual amount of yeast for white bread, which, in turn, enriches the loaf with extra protein, vitamins, minerals and trace elements. One point to watch, though: when dealing with high-yeast doughs, you should let the dough rise at a relatively lower temperature, thus avoiding the risk of over fermentation and a resulting sour taste and flavour. Properly fermented and well baked, this bread is light with a pale brown crumb, and an even, honeycombed texture. The crust is neither thick nor hard. It slices well without much crumbling, has a good volume and a lovely yeasty aroma. It stays fresh for two days. The traditional salt-water glaze gives the crust an attractive slightly frosted appearance, but may be omitted if you prefer.*

YEAST STARTER:
Dissolve the yeast in a few tablespoons of the tepid water; dissolve the salt in the remaining water.

### THE MIX:

Lightly grease a large mixing bowl and pour in the flours. Stir them together to mix evenly. Set aside 1 to 2 tablespoons of flour for kneading. Make a well in the centre of the flour and pour in the salt solution and stir it briskly; then add the yeast liquid, stirring as you pour, until most of the flour has been wetted. Gather the mixture with your hands into a ball that leaves the sides of the bowl clean. Knead the dough vigorously with the reserved flour for not less than 10 minutes, until the dough stops sticking to the working surface and is smooth, malleable and elastic. Let it rest for 10 to 15 minutes, then knead it again for a minute or two.

Place the dough in a well buttered or oiled 3½ pt (2 litre) loaf tin or deep round cake tin, pressing it down firmly into the corners. For a light, well aerated loaf, the tin should be no more than a third full. Brush the top with melted butter or oil.

### FIRST RISING:

Cover the tin loosely (the yeast needs air to multiply), with a transparent sheet of polythene and leave it to prove in a cool to slightly warm room (about 70° to 72°F, 21° to 22°C) for about 1½ hours, or until the dough has trebled in size and has reached the top of the tin.

### PRE-HEAT OVEN

to 450°F (230°C) Gas 8.

### BAKING TIME:

Bake in the centre of the oven for about 45 to 50 minutes. After about 25 minutes when the crust starts to colour, brush the surface with the salt-water glaze and REDUCE HEAT to 400°F (200°C) Gas 6. After another 15 minutes, remove the loaf from the tin, brush the sides and bottom of the loaf with the salt-water and place upside-down on the same rack for about 10 minutes, or until golden brown all over. Cool the loaf quickly on a rack before slicing and serving.

### METRIC EQUIVALENTS:

*350 g strong white unbleached flour*
*125 g wholemeal flour*
*20 g fresh yeast*
*just under 300 ml tepid water*
*8 g Cheshire (rock) salt\**
*a little melted butter or oil for*
  *brushing*
Salt-water glaze (optional):
*1 teaspoon salt dissolved in 3*
  *tablespoons warm water*

### NOTE:

*\*When dealing with different types of salt, I prefer not to give the amounts in teaspoons. If someone should substitute the required 3 level teaspoons of Cheshire salt (¼ oz/8 g) with 3 level teaspoons of common cooking salt (½ oz/15 g), it would raise the salt content of the bread from 1.5% to 3%, which is extremely salty and could damage the gluten structure; this will also delay the rising time.*
*Salt, like yeast, has to be weighed.*

In colour—page 105

# Cheese Bread (Toutmanik)

*Serves 4 to 6*

THE DOUGH:
*14 oz Quick Almost-White
    Bread dough (see previous
    recipe)*

AND...
*7 oz sirene or feta cheese,
    crumbled with a fork*
*4 oz butter, melted and cooled to
    lukewarm*
*2 eggs, lightly beaten*

METRIC EQUIVALENTS:
*400 g Quick Almost-White Bread
    dough (see previous recipe)*
*200 g sirene or feta cheese,
    crumbled with a fork*
*125 g butter, melted and cooled to
    lukewarm*
*2 eggs, lightly beaten*

*Toutmanik is one of the oldest Bulgarian dishes and, like the pizza
of southern Italy, is a by-product of bread-making. It is usually
baked during the winter months when something more substantial
and filling is needed. In the villages, lard is often substituted for
butter. Cut into wedges or slices, this bread is ideal for a picnic,
instead of the perennial sandwiches or pies. It is also excellent for a
cheese and wine party or a "Peasants Supper".*
*Sirene cheese is the equivalent of the Greek feta cheese. Both can be
purchased from most Greek food stores; or you could substitute
White Cheshire or White Stilton.*

FIRST RISING:

Prepare half the quantity of the Quick Almost-White Bread recipe
which will give you the required amount of 14 oz (400 g) dough. Put
it to rise in a buttered bowl covered with a warm damp towel, for
about 1 hour. Knock it back and knead it into a long sausage;
divide it into 8 pieces.

On a floured board roll each piece into a circle about the size of a
dinner plate. Brush 6 of the rounds liberally with butter on one

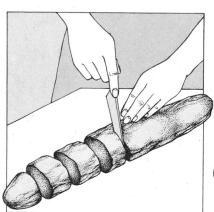  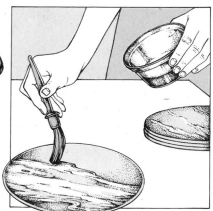

side, then stack them in threes, buttered side up.
Top each pile with an unbuttered round. Leave them to rest for
about 10 minutes. Roll out each pile into a round the size of your
baking dish, about 9 to 10 in (250 mm) in diameter.
Reserve a tablespoon of the beaten egg for glazing; mix the
remainder with the cheese. Cover the baking dish with about half of
the remaining butter. Put one of the dough rounds in the dish.
Sprinkle it lightly with butter. Spoon over the cheese and egg
mixture. Top with the other round. Press down firmly, then prick
the surface with a fork. Pour the rest of the butter on top.

SECOND RISING:
Leave to prove in a reasonably warm place for about 1 hour. The
dough should more than double in volume.

PRE-HEAT OVEN
to 350°F (180°C) Gas 4.

BAKING TIME:
Bake for 45 minutes on a top shelf. After 30 minutes, brush the top
with the reserved beaten egg. Glazing at this stage keeps the crust
from over-browning and losing its lustre.

NOTE:
*Toutmanik cannot be prepared with
ordinary bread dough; to rise
sufficiently, it needs a lot of yeast
as used in the Quick Almost-White
Bread Dough.*

In colour—page 105

*Makes 1 large loaf*

THE FLOUR:
*2½ lb stoneground wholemeal
flour*

THE STARTER:
*1½ oz fresh yeast*

AND . . .
*just over 1 pt tepid water
½ oz* Maldon *sea salt or*
Cheshire *(rock) salt
a little melted butter or oil for
brushing*

GLAZE:
*1 egg yolk mixed with
2 teaspoons water*

METRIC EQUIVALENTS:
*1 kg stoneground wholemeal flour
40 g fresh yeast
about 600 ml tepid water
15 g* Maldon *sea salt or*
Cheshire *rock salt
a little melted butter or oil for
brushing*
Glaze:
*1 egg yolk mixed with 2 teaspoons
water*

OPPOSITE:
Top: *Apricot Bread (Adrian
Bailey) p.211.* Below: *Rice
Bread (Elizabeth David) p.53.*
OVERLEAF LEFT:
Top left: *Focaccia Con La
Salvia p.64 and* right *Calabrian
Pizza p.63 (both from Caroline
Conran).* Below left: *Doris
Grant's Oven Wholemeal
Flatties p.73, split open and
filled with egg and cress.*
OVERLEAF RIGHT:
Top left: *Chalice Bakery's
Fruit Filled Loaf p.174-75.*
Top right: *Tomato Bread
(Mabel Sadler, W.I.) p.142.*
Below centre: *Jane Grigson's
Cretan Olive and Onion Bread
p.57.*

# Wholemeal Panbread

*To improve the appearance of this panbread, egg-wash the top;
this gives it a nice shiny crust. Well wrapped, it keeps moist for
two days.*

YEAST STARTER:
Cream the yeast with a little of the tepid water.

THE MIX:
Put the flour into a lightly oiled mixing bowl; set aside 3 to 4
tablespoons for kneading. Make a well in the centre. Dissolve the
salt in the remaining water. *(This way you achieve a saltier flavour
with a smaller quantity of salt, than when mixing it directly with
the flour.)* Pour the salt-water into the well and stir a few times
to partially moisten the flour.
Add the yeast liquid and mix to form a soft dough. Knead it on a
floured surface with some of the reserved flour for about 5 minutes,
making a soft, slightly sticky dough.

FIRST RISING:
Brush the bowl again with oil and return the dough to it. Cover the
bowl with a warm damp cloth and leave the dough to rise in a
reasonably warm place (about 70°F, 21°C) for about 1½ hours or
until it has more than doubled in size.

SECOND RISING:
Turn out and knead again with a little more flour for about 2
minutes. Leave to rise for about 45 minutes. It is ready when an
indentation made by your finger on the top surface remains without
springing back. Grease a large roasting tin approximately 14 in x
11 in x 2 in (350 mm x 280 mm x 50 mm) and warm it gently.
Knock back the risen dough and knead it with the remaining flour
for a minute or two. Shape to fit into your tin, which should be
just over one-third full. Smooth the top surface with the palm of
your hand dipped in a little melted butter or oil.

THIRD RISING:
Cover loosely and leave in a slightly warmer place (around 75°F,
24°C) for about 30 minutes, until it has almost trebled its size.

PRE-HEAT OVEN
to 400°F (200°C) Gas 6.

BAKING TIME:
Brush the surface of the dough with the egg glaze. Bake on a shelf
above the centre for about 45 minutes. Then turn out of the tin and
bake for a further 5 minutes placed upside-down on the top shelf of
the oven.
Slice when completely cool.

# Rye Bread

In colour—page 216

*Rye bread is often made with a piece of sourdough, left from a previous bread-baking. However, you can make a perfectly acceptable rye bread with a lovely, light-sour smell using yeast.
In the central and north Balkan countries, rye bread is traditionally served with black or red caviar or smoked fish.*

*Makes 4 small loaves*

**YEAST STARTER:**
Dissolve the yeast in 4 tablespoons of the water.

**THE MIX:**
Mix the two flours. Add the salt, dissolved in a few tablespoons of the water. Pour the yeast over the flour. Add enough of the remaining water to make a medium-stiff dough. Turn out on to a floured surface, and knead with a little extra flour for about 10 minutes until rather stiff and no longer sticky. Place in an ungreased bowl.

**FIRST RISING:**
Cover loosely with a wet cloth and a piece of polythene on top and leave in a warm place for about 1 hour. If you have time, knock it down and leave for another ¾ hour or so to rise again.

**THE GLAZE:**
Meanwhile, cream the flour with a little of the water. Dilute this with the remaining water. Bring to the boil over high heat, and boil for 2 to 3 minutes, stirring all the time. Leave to cool.

**THE SHAPING:**
Turn the dough out on to an unfloured surface, and knead for 15 minutes, incorporating the caraway seeds. Divide into 4 equal pieces. Knead and shape into the traditional cigar-shape for rye bread, a slightly pointed oval loaf, a little higher than it is wide.

**SECOND RISING:**
Sprinkle a little semolina on 2 baking sheets. Place the loaves on the sheets, spaced well apart. Cover and set to prove for about 40 minutes until almost double in size. With both hands, gently press each loaf at the sides to push it upwards and make it higher, then glaze it thickly with the flour paste.

**PRE-HEAT OVEN**
to 400°F (200°C) Gas 6.

**BAKING TIME:**
Bake for 1 hour. After 30 minutes remove from oven and glaze again. Return to the oven, setting them this time directly on the oven shelves and REDUCE HEAT to 350°F (180°C) Gas 4. Glaze them again about 15 minutes before baking is complete. Cool on a rack, then wrap in cling-film. Rye bread should should be left to mature for 24 hours before slicing it quite thinly.

**THE FLOURS:**
*1 lb light rye flour*
*1 lb 85% wholewheat flour*

**THE STARTER:**
*½ oz dried yeast*

**AND . . .**
*about 18 fl.oz hand-hot water*
*½ oz rock salt or sea-salt crystals*
*a little extra rye flour for kneading*
*2 to 3 teaspoons caraway seeds*
*a little semolina, for dusting*

**TRADITIONAL GLAZE:**
*½ oz white flour*
*8 fl.oz water*

**METRIC EQUIVALENTS:**
*500 g light rye flour*
*500 g 85% wholewheat flour*
*15 g dried yeast*
*about 500 ml hand-hot water*
*15 g rock salt or sea-salt crystals*
*a little extra rye flour for kneading*
*2 to 3 teaspoons caraway seeds*
*a little semolina for dusting*
*Traditional glaze:*
*15 g white flour*
*250 ml water*

OPPOSITE:
*Oat Bread (Mabel Sadler, W.I.) p.143.*

In colour—page 105

# Sun and Planet

*This bread is pretty to look at and delightful to eat. It's shaped to represent a total eclipse of the sun. It's honey-sweet and has a spicy-buttery flavour. I devised this recipe years ago for the birthday of a ten-year-old nephew who, at that time, spoke of little else but rockets and space travel.*

*Makes 16 rolls and a large bun —enough for 8 to 10 people*

THE FLOUR:
*7 oz strong white unbleached flour*
*5 oz 85% wholewheat flour*

THE STARTER:
*2 teaspoons dried yeast*
*2 fl.oz hand-hot water*

AND . . .
*3½ oz clear honey*
*1 egg*
*3 egg yolks*
*½ level teaspoon ground rock salt*
*½ teaspoon mixed spice (or ½ teaspoon ground ginger and a large pinch of ground cloves)*
*½ teaspoon ground cinnamon*
*¼ teaspoon freshly grated nutmeg*
*⅛ teaspoon freshly ground white pepper*
*1 oz unsalted butter, melted with 1 tablespoon oil*

YEAST STARTER:
Dissolve 2 level teaspoons of the honey in the warm water and sprinkle on the yeast. Leave in a warm place until frothy, about 15 minutes.

THE FILLING:
Stir together all the filling ingredients into a stiff paste. Cover until needed.

THE MIX:
Whisk the whole egg and 2 of the egg yolks with the salt, spices and the remaining honey. Mix the flours in a bowl, reserving 2 rounded tablespoons for kneading. Stir in the egg mixture. Add the yeast liquid and mix to form a dough. Turn out on to a floured surface and knead with most of the remaining flour for about 10 minutes until the dough is quite smooth and stiff—but not hard.

THE SHAPING:
Divide the dough into 3 equal pieces and knead into balls. Spread a little of the butter mixture around a large fluted flan dish 10½ in (270 mm) diameter. Roll 2 of the balls into very thin rounds, slightly larger than your flan dish and brush with the butter mixture. Slice each round with 4 diagonal cuts into 8 triangles (a). To make the "rays": place a triangle on a lightly floured surface with its tip furthest away from you, (b). Put a teaspoon of the filling near the

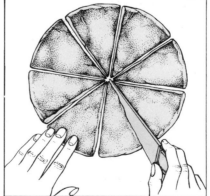

tip. Roll up the triangle from the tip towards you (c), enclosing the filling, and making the base of the roll from the right-hand-side of the triangle. The roll should resemble the shape of a thick pencil about 4 in (10 cm) long (d).

Arrange the 16 rolls peripherally in the dish like the rays of the sun (e). The bases should be touching, and the tips pointing outwards. Leave the flap edge of each roll on top.

Slice the third ball horizontally into 3 or 4 rounds. Spread the remaining filling between the rounds and reform into a smooth ball (the earth). Place in the centre of the dish just touching the base of the rolls.

## THE RISING:

Brush the dough ball and rolls all over with the remaining butter mixture. Cover loosely with an oiled piece of polythene and leave to rise in a warm place for 2½ to 3 hours or until the dough is double in size. Glaze with the remaining egg yolk diluted with 1 teaspoon of water.

## PRE-HEAT OVEN
to 350°F (180°C) Gas 4.

## BAKING TIME:

Bake in the centre of the oven for 20 to 25 minutes or until the top is a deep golden-brown.

To glaze, brush the top quite thickly with the honey immediately it is removed from the oven. Leave to cool in the dish or serve while still warm, with butter, thick cream or on its own. Eat by next day or freeze, but without the glaze.

To use from the freezer: place frozen, wrapped in foil, in the oven at 400°C (200°C) Gas 6 for about 15 minutes or until heated through; then glaze.

## THE FILLING:

3 oz sultanas, chopped

1½ oz walnuts, crushed

1 egg white, beaten until stiff

2 tablespoons clear honey, for glazing

## METRIC EQUIVALENTS:

200 g strong white unbleached flour

150 g 85% wholewheat flour

2 teaspoons dried yeast

50 ml hand-hot water

100 g clear honey

1 egg

3 egg yolks

½ level teaspoon ground rock salt

½ teaspoon mixed spice (or ½ teaspoon ground ginger and a large pinch of ground cloves)

½ teaspoon ground cinnamon

¼ teaspoon freshly grated nutmeg

⅛ teaspoon freshly ground white pepper

30 g unsalted butter melted with 1 tablespoon oil

The filling:

90 g sultanas, chopped

40 g walnuts, crushed

1 egg white, beaten until stiff

2 tablespoons clear honey, for glazing

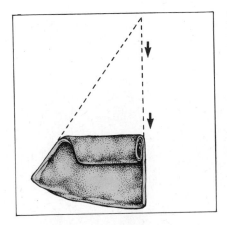
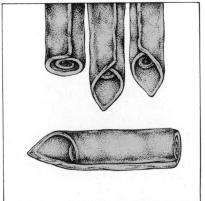

In colour—page 105

# Pogacha (Bulgaria), Pogača (Yugoslavia)

*Makes 1 loaf*

*This soft flat bread is the oldest Slavonic ritual bread. Until Christian times, it was prepared without a leaven and offered to a deity or deities instead of a blood sacrifice. Later, to improve its appearance, small amounts of barm or sourdough were added. In remote mountainous villages, it is still baked directly under the ashes on the hearthstone of an open fireplace. Another paganistic feature is that* pogacha *is never sliced with a knife, nor is it taken to church services to be blessed by the priest. Although, in the larger towns and cities this type of soft flat bread, now raised with yeast and modestly enriched, has lost its initial meaning, it still retains its festive overtones. There are countless variations on the* pogacha *theme—in both Yugoslavia and Bulgaria. This is how I make it:*

THE FLOUR:
*12 oz strong white flour, preferably unbleached*

THE STARTER:
*½ oz fresh yeast*

AND . . .
*4 fl.oz tepid milk*
*1 egg*
*1 level teaspoon cooking salt, or 2 level teaspoons sea salt crystals or rock salt*
*3 tablespoons lukewarm melted butter or oil*
*a little butter or oil for brushing*

METRIC EQUIVALENTS:
*350 g strong white flour*
*15 g fresh yeast*
*100 ml tepid milk*
*1 egg*
*1 level teaspoon cooking salt or 2 level teaspoons sea salt crystals or rock salt*
*3 tablespoons lukewarm melted butter or oil*
*a little butter or oil for brushing*

YEAST STARTER:
Cream the yeast to a thin batter with a little of the milk.

THE MIX:
Tip the flour into a large bowl. Make a hollow in the centre and drop in the whole egg and the salt. Pour in the fat and the yeast mixture. Stir with a round-bladed table knife, adding the rest of the milk gradually to form a fairly stiff dough. Knead it vigorously for about 5 to 10 minutes, then shape it into a ball.

FIRST RISING:
Wash and dry the bowl. Brush it well with oil and roll the dough in it to prevent crusting. Cover the bowl loosely and leave in a not too warm place to rise, for about 2 hours.

SECOND RISING:
When doubled in size, knock it back and knead lightly with a dusting of flour, shaping it into a flattened ball about "two fingers" thick. Place the dough on a greased baking sheet, or in a buttered square baking tin, about 8 in (200 mm) wide. Brush the top with butter or oil. If you like, prick the surface here and there with a fork. Leave to prove for 20 to 30 minutes, to double its bulk.

PRE-HEAT OVEN
to 375°F (190°C) Gas 5.

BAKING TIME:
Bake on a high shelf for approximately 25 to 30 minutes. Remove from the oven and then wrap in a clean cloth and leave to soften, about 15 minutes. Serve warm, broken up in chunks.

Traditionally *pogacha* is brought to the table wrapped in a stiffly-starched white linen napkin, accompanied with a small bowlful of salt, which is placed over the centre of the loaf. (This is a symbolic procedure, marrying 2 basic foods, the bread and the salt.)

# Brown Turban Loaf

In colour—page 105

*Another unusual wholemeal loaf from my kitchen. The mashed potato makes a loaf that retains its moisture for at least three days and is soft and elastic like a sponge. If you wish, you can omit the walnuts, but their taste compliments the wheaty flavour of the wholemeal. The recipe makes one 11 in (28 cm) loaf; its spiral shape and honey glaze make it rather special and perfect for tea.*

*Makes 1 loaf*

THE FLOUR:
*13 oz wholemeal flour*

THE STARTER:
*½ oz dried yeast*
*4 tablespoons hand-hot water*

YEAST STARTER:
Dissolve 1 tablespoon of the honey in the hand-hot water. Add the yeast and leave to stand in a warm place for about 15 minutes.

AND . . .
*2 tablespoons clear honey*
*6 oz (2 medium-sized) floury potatoes*
*¾ level teaspoon cooking salt*
*2 standard eggs, beaten lightly*
*about 4 tablespoons milk*
*2 oz walnuts, chopped into large pieces*
*2 oz butter, melted and cooled to lukewarm or 4 tablespoons oil*
*oil for brushing*
*honey for glazing*

THE MIX:
Boil the potatoes and mash while still hot. Allow to cool. Sprinkle the salt over the cooled mashed potato and beat in the eggs and the second tablespoon of honey.
Whisk the yeast mixture and stir it in. Reserve 3 tablespoons of the flour then add the remaining flour to the potato mixture gradually,' alternating it with the milk, to form a dough. Knead it with most of the reserved flour for about 2 minutes until soft and sticky.

METRIC EQUIVALENTS:
*375 g wholemeal flour*
*15 g dried yeast*
*4 tablespoons hand-hot water*
*2 tablespoons clear honey*
*175 g (2 medium-sized) floury potatoes*
*¾ level teaspoon cooking salt*
*2 standard eggs, beaten lightly*
*about 4 tablespoons milk*
*60 g walnuts, chopped into large pieces*
*60 g butter, melted and cooled to lukewarm or 4 tablespoons oil*
*oil for brushing*
*honey for glazing*

FIRST RISING:
Put the dough into an oiled bowl, brush it with a little oil, cover, and put to rise in a warm place for 3 hours, or until it has almost trebled in size.

THE SHAPING:
Using the rest of the reserved flour, knead the risen dough into a ball, then flatten it into a large round and sprinkle it with the walnuts. Roll it up tightly to form a long sausage-like shape and leave to relax for a few minutes. Put your hands on to the dough and gently roll it out back and forth to elongate it to about 27 in (70 cm). Thoroughly butter or oil a large baking dish about 11 in (280 mm) in diameter. Place one end of the "rope" of dough in the centre of the dish and coil the "rope" into a spiral that fills the entire dish. Pour the remaining butter or oil over the top.

SECOND RISING:
Put the shaped dough to prove in a warm place for about 1½ hours, until just doubled in bulk. (The loaf will continue to rise for a while in the oven.)

PRE-HEAT OVEN
to 350°F (180°C) Gas 4.

BAKING TIME:
Bake in the upper part of the oven for about 50 minutes, until the crust is well browned. Remove from the oven and leave to cool on a rack in its container. To make the loaf shiny, brush the top with a little warmed honey while the bread is cooling.

*In colour—page 105*

# Dee Dee Cake (or wholemeal Kozounak)

*Makes 2 cakes*

THE FLOUR:
1½ lb wholemeal flour

THE STARTER:
2 oz fresh yeast, or 1 oz dried
   yeast
4 fl.oz lukewarm water

AND . . .
7 oz thick opaque honey
1 standard egg
¼ level teaspoon cooking salt
grated rind of 2 large lemons
just under 7 fl.oz tepid milk
4 fl.oz sunflower oil, or
   3½ oz butter, melted and
   cooled to tepid
a little oil for brushing

METRIC EQUIVALENTS:
750 g wholemeal flour
60 g fresh yeast or 30 g dried yeast
100 ml lukewarm water
200 g thick opaque honey
1 standard egg
¼ level teaspoon cooking salt
grated rind of 2 large lemons
just under 200 ml tepid milk
100 ml sunflower oil or 100 g butter,
   melted and cooled to tepid
a little oil for brushing

*The difference between luxury breads in the various European countries lies mainly in the flavouring. For example, in Eastern Europe, i.e. European Russia and the Balkans, rich fermented cakes are traditionally flavoured with lemon rind and possibly small amounts of local spirits, while in the West imported spices like nutmeg, ginger, cinnamon or black pepper are usually added. The Bulgarian kozounak is more closely related to the Russian kulich, the Greek tsourekia, the Yugoslav kuglov and the old-fashioned Viennese gugelhupf than to the English Easter simnel yeast-cake, the Welsh bara brith or the Scotch Christmas bun.*

*The vesicular thread-like structure, characteristic of the Balkan cake-breads, is achieved by kneading the dough not with flour, but with softened butter or oil. The crumb of the baked product pulls apart into attractive longish tufts.*

*This recipe is a variation of the recipe that belonged to my great-grandmother, Stephanie. It was made in huge quantities, using only white flour and a very small amount of yeast. The bulk dough was left to rise overnight. On the next day it was given two more rising periods and a final proof in the tins. This method explains the exceptional keeping qualities of the bread (up to a week). Nowadays, I use wholemeal flour and more yeast and give the dough three risings at the most, as the four small loaves I bake at Easter time are all consumed within a day or two of baking. This wholemeal and honey version, named after my daughter, Diana, was devised especially for children. Use two 3½ pt (2 litre) round, plain or fluted tins with central tubes (sometimes known as gugelhupf or pudding moulds). The advantages of using a mould with a central tube, instead of a deep round cake tin, is that the tube permits the heat to cook the centre of the cake just as well as the outside.*

YEAST STARTER:
Dissolve 1 level teaspoon of the honey in the water. Stir in the yeast and, when dissolved, add ½ oz (15 g) of the flour and mix to a smooth batter. Cover the bowl and leave in a warm place for about 20 minutes, until the yeast-sponge foams.

THE MIX:
Put the remaining flour into a bowl, reserving 2 rounded tablespoons for kneading and shaping. Make a well in the centre. Beat the egg lightly, add the honey, salt, lemon rind and the milk and stir together until blended. Pour the mixture into the well and stir a few times to partially mix with the flour. Add the yeast-sponge and stir everything together, then form into a soft, sticky dough that leaves the bowl completely clean. Turn the dough out on to a floured surface. Knead it with most of the reserved flour for about 10 minutes until moderately stiff and still slightly sticky.

FIRST RISING:
Place the dough into an oiled bowl, turning it over in the bowl to coat the other side with oil, to prevent skinning. Cover loosely with a sheet of plastic and leave to rise in a warm place for about 2 hours, until it has trebled in size.

SECOND RISING:
Turn the dough out on to your work-surface and knead it in the usual manner but without any flour, gradually incorporating small amounts of sunflower oil or lukewarm butter, until the required quantity is used up. The dough will appear somewhat greasy, but this is exactly as it should be. Return the dough to the bowl, cover with polythene and leave to rise in a warm place for about 2 hours, or until it has again trebled its volume.

THIRD RISING:
Oil the two moulds well, not forgetting to grease the central tubes. Sprinkle the work-surface with the remainder of the reserved flour, turn the dough out and divide it in two; knead each piece into a sausage-like shape, long enough to form a complete ring around the central tube of the mould. Press down on the dough with your knuckles to spread it round. It should fill the mould to one-third of its depth. Cover the moulds and set them in a slightly warmer place for the final pre-baking proof. It will take about 1 hour for the dough to reach the mould's rim.

PRE-HEAT OVEN
to 350°F (180°C) Gas 4.

BAKING TIME:
Bake in the centre of the oven for 35 minutes. They are ready when the top is well browned. Leave to cool in the mould for a few minutes, then turn them out on to a wire rack and leave to cool before cutting into wedges. Serve for tea with butter, clotted cream and honey, or on their own. The loaves should be eaten the day they are baked, or stored in the freezer.

# Renny Harrop and The Good Housekeeping Institute

Renny Harrop, now editor of Ebury Press and with direct access to the *Good Housekeeping* kitchens, didn't start baking until she had a flat and oven of her own, and a Belgian girlfriend came to stay: "This girl's mother baked bread every morning for breakfast, which they ate with cheese. While she was with me, she baked it every day." When she left, Renny asked for the recipe. Now, John, who she lives with, bakes it. "But not every day, once a week."

The fact that John does the baking reinforces the theory held by Margaret Coombes, co-director of the Good Housekeeping Institute, that more home-baked bread today is made by men than ever before. Margaret is responsible for the origination and testing of recipes appearing in the *Good Housekeeping* magazine.

She believes that easy-to-bake bread mixes have introduced more home cooks to the idea of having a go themselves. And more recently demand has been supported by the appearance of strong flour in general grocery outlets.

But Margaret does not under-estimate plant-baked sandwich bread which, she says, is fine for toasting. And she applauds wholeheartedly the wider choice, especially the trends towards more brown loaves.

The *Good Housekeeping* magazine is unique in having all the skills and experience of the cooks and home economists of the Good Housekeeping Institute, and has done much to encourage and build up confidence in the hesitant home cook. Three years ago the company moved to new buildings in Broadwick Street, bringing the book company— Ebury Press—and the main magazines —*Good Housekeeping, Harpers & Queen, Cosmopolitan, Company, She, Connoisseur, Antique Collector* and so on—under one roof. In this modern building with lively red doors interlinking open-plan offices filled with furniture designed especially for them, there are five test kitchens. Every recipe that appears in a magazine or a book is tested twice.

Recipes are created and tested, amended and re-tested and critically appraised by a team of home economists and editors and, where necessary, consultant dieticians.

Ebury Press has use of one of the test kitchens. Here they develop and test their own original recipes. Two years ago Renny Harrop was brought in as editor with special responsibility for cookery. Ebury press wanted "to broaden their image into foreign foods and keep up with modern taste trends".

Renny's interest in food didn't come about until she left university. At home she was brought up on white sliced bread, which she loved because "I didn't know there was anything else." Her mother was a good cook, but she knew only seven dishes, which she rotated each week.

After university, Renny went to work for Justin de Blank (the Queen's Baker). "Justin has imagination", she says. "If he likes you and you're reasonably intelligent, he believes you can turn your hand to almost anything. I answered an ad that he pinned on the university notice board. I couldn't type or do shorthand or cook so I ended up dealing with the people who made the food for his shops."

She became very involved with the tasting and testing. "I had the opportunity to try food that I wouldn't otherwise have come across. I loved working in his shops, they are so alive. Justin involves himself in every aspect of the business from personally selecting the quality foods for sale or use in the kitchens to occasionally visiting his bakery in the early hours of the morning and helping to turn out the following day's bread."

Renny left the shop and went to France where she taught English to a French actor, Renaud Verlay. There, she also attended a Cordon Bleu course, but this had little practical application. Most of the students were American heiresses who were only interested in learning how to instruct a chef when they married. Renny's desire for practical experience was more than fulfilled when she returned to England. Justin had opened a restaurant and the cook had walked out. In the resulting crisis, Renny was asked to help out with the cooking. "This was where I had my real training, in a real kitchen, on a big scale."

From there Renny joined Marshall Cavendish as an editor on *Supercook:* "It combined my desire to write and cook. We wrote and tested the recipes ourselves." She became cookery editor of Marshall Cavendish books, before leaving to be editor at Ebury Press: "Here we're interested in health and diet. I work closely with the senior home economist, Susanna Tee, who organises the kitchens. Our special diet books are vetted by dieticians and doctors."

In keeping with recent health trends, they've brought out a book by one of their regular columnists, Gail Duff, *The Good Housekeeping Book of Wholefood Cookery*. Naturally it has some wholemeal bread recipes, and Renny explains, "I said we should include wholefood bread, as long as we had wholemeal croissants. So we did. They're light and fluffy and quite delicious."

Last year Ebury Press also brought out the *Good Housekeeping's Book of Bread Making* for which Susanna Tee feels they must have tested practically every bread recipe possible. But there was one they hadn't quite mastered: "We couldn't work out a really good recipe for French bread," says Renny. "The flour we get in England is different." They're

working on one now using a mixture of cornflour and plain flour, instead of strong bread-making flour: "We think we've got it right this time."

The Good Housekeeping Institute undertakes research in the kitchens—they're now experimenting with bread in microwave ovens. They also keep a close watch on commercial trends: "The bread available today is far nicer than ten years ago," says Renny. "Then you had to go to Crank's to buy a decent loaf. Now good bread is available fresh even in supermarkets, particularly Marks & Spencer and Sainsbury's."

On the other hand, if you want to make it at home, you can't go far wrong with the twice tested Good Housekeeping and Ebury Press recipes adapted below, although here we have substituted honey for sugar.

# Belgian Loaf

*This is a delicious wholemeal bread that only requires a single rising and very little kneading.*

*Makes 1 loaf*

THE MIX:
Lightly grease a 1 lb (500 g) loaf tin with a little butter. Sift the white flour and the salt into a bowl and stir in the wholemeal flour. Make a well in the centre and pour in the water. Crumble the yeast on to the water and trickle the honey over the top. Cut the rest of the butter into small pieces and arrange them round the edge of the mixture. Leave the bowl in a warm place for 5 to 10 minutes, until the yeast has become frothy. Now gradually draw the flour into the liquid with your fingers. Keep mixing in this way until no loose flour remains and the dough leaves the sides of the bowls cleanly. Turn out the dough on to a floured surface and knead for 10 minutes. Make it into a loaf shape and place in the prepared tin.

THE FLOUR:
*4 oz strong white flour*
*12 oz wholemeal flour*

THE STARTER:
*1 oz fresh yeast*
*10 fl.oz lukewarm water*
*1 teaspoon honey*

AND . . .
*1 oz butter*
*2 teaspoons salt*

THE RISING:
Cover the tin with a clean, damp cloth and leave in a warm place for 20 minutes or until the dough has risen to the top of the tin.

PRE-HEAT OVEN
to 400°F (200°C) Gas 6.

METRIC EQUIVALENTS:
*125 g strong white flour*
*350 g wholemeal flour*
*30 g fresh yeast*
*300 ml lukewarm water*
*1 teaspoon honey*
*30 g butter*
*2 teaspoons salt*

BAKING TIME:
Bake for 25 minutes. After 5 minutes REDUCE HEAT to 375°F (190°C) Gas 5. If the loaf does not sound hollow when tapped after this time, REDUCE HEAT again to 350°F (180°C) Gas 4 and put the loaf back for another 5 to 10 minutes.

# Flowerpot Loaves

In colour—page 272

*Makes 2 loaves*

THE FLOUR:
*1 lb 81% or 85% wholewheat flour*

THE STARTER:
*½ oz fresh yeast*
*10 fl.oz lukewarm water*

AND . . .
*2 level teaspoons freshly ground sea salt*
*2 teaspoons honey*
*½ oz butter*
*milk or water to glaze*
*cracked wheat for sprinkling*

METRIC EQUIVALENTS:
*500 g 81% or 85% wholewheat flour*
*15 g fresh yeast*
*300 ml lukewarm water*
*2 level teaspoons freshly ground sea salt*
*2 teaspoons honey*
*15 g butter*
*milk or water to glaze*
*cracked wheat for sprinkling*

*Use new clay flowerpots for this recipe, adapted from* The Good Housekeeping Book of Wholefood Cookery *by Gail Duff. To prevent the pots cracking and the loaves sticking, grease the pots well the first time you use them having previously baked them empty in a hot oven for 30 minutes. This recipe will fill two pots 4 to 5 in (10 to 13 cm) in diameter.*

YEAST STARTER:
Mix the fresh yeast with the water and leave in a warm place for about 10 minutes.

THE MIX:
Mix the flour and salt and rub in the butter. Add the yeast liquid and honey to the flour mixture, and mix to a soft dough that leaves the sides of the bowl cleanly. Knead thoroughly on a floured surface for 10 minutes and divide between the 2 greased flowerpots.

THE RISING:
Cover with a clean cloth and leave to rise until the dough has doubled in size.

PRE-HEAT OVEN
to 450°F (230°C) Gas 8.

BAKING TIME:
Brush the tops of the loaves with milk or water and sprinkle over the cracked wheat. Bake for 30 to 40 minutes until well risen and firm.

# Farmhouse Plait

In colour—page 112

*Makes 1 loaf*

THE FLOUR:
*1½ lb 81% or 85% wholewheat flour*

THE STARTER:
*1 oz fresh yeast*

AND . . .
*¾ pt lukewarm water*
*1 level teaspoon freshly ground sea salt*
*1 oz butter*
*beaten egg to glaze*
*poppy seeds*

*This recipe, adapted from* The Good Housekeeping Book of Wholefood Cookery *by Gail Duff is a wholemeal variation of the traditional plaited loaf.*

YEAST STARTER:
Mix the yeast with ½ pt (300 ml) of the water. Leave in a warm place for 10 minutes.

THE MIX:
Mix the flour and salt together and rub in the butter. Add the yeast mixture and the remaining water to them and mix to a soft dough. Turn out on to a floured surface and knead for 5 minutes.

FIRST RISING:
Cover with a clean cloth and leave in a warm place for 45 minutes or so, until it has doubled in size.

**SECOND RISING:**

Turn the risen dough on to a floured surface and knead again for 10 minutes. Roll into an oblong and cut into 3 lengthwise strips, then pinch them together at the top and plait them. Dampen the ends and seal them together well. Place on a greased baking sheet, cover with a clean cloth, and leave in a warm place for 30 minutes or so, until the dough has doubled in size.

**PRE-HEAT OVEN**

to 425°F (220°C) Gas 7.

**BAKING TIME:**

Brush the loaf with beaten egg and sprinkle some poppy seeds on it. Bake for 40 to 45 minutes. REDUCE HEAT to 375°F (190°C) Gas 5 if the loaf is getting too brown.

**METRIC EQUIVALENTS:**
*750 g 81% or 85% wholewheat flour*
*30 g fresh yeast*
*400 ml lukewarm water*
*1 level teaspoon freshly ground sea*
  *salt*
*30 g butter*
*beaten egg to glaze*
*poppy seeds*

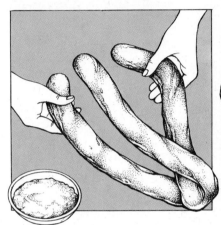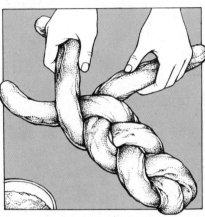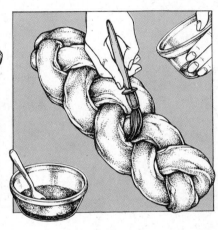

In colour—page 112

# Golden Carrot and Walnut Loaf

*This nourishing loaf has an attractive golden colour and a pleasant crunchy texture.*

*Makes 1 small loaf*

THE FLOUR:
*1 lb wholemeal flour*

THE STARTER:
*½ oz fresh yeast*
*10 fl.oz lukewarm water*

AND . . .
*1 level teaspoon salt*
*½ oz butter*
*4 oz grated carrot*
*3 oz grated Red Leicester cheese*
*1 oz roughly chopped walnuts*
*beaten egg*

METRIC EQUIVALENTS:
*500 g wholemeal flour*
*15 g fresh yeast*
*300 ml lukewarm water*
*1 level teaspoon salt*
*15 g butter*
*125 g grated carrot*
*90 g grated Red Leicester cheese*
*30 g roughly chopped walnuts*
*beaten egg*

YEAST STARTER:
Mix the yeast with the water.

THE MIX:
Mix the flour and salt in a bowl and rub in the butter. Add the yeast mixture, and mix to a soft dough. Knead on a floured surface for about 5 minutes. Add the grated carrot, 2 oz (60 g) of the cheese, and the walnuts, and knead into the dough.

FIRST RISING:
Cover the dough with lightly oiled polythene and leave to rise in a warm place until double in size.

SECOND RISING:
Turn out on to a floured surface and knead for 2 to 3 minutes. Place in a greased 1 lb (500 g) loaf tin, cover with lightly oiled polythene and leave in a warm place until the dough reaches the top of the tin.

PRE-HEAT OVEN
to 400°F (200°C) Gas 6.

BAKING TIME:
Brush with beaten egg and sprinkle with the remaining cheese. Bake for 25 to 30 minutes. Remove from the tin, place on a baking sheet, and bake for 10 minutes more.

# Oatmeal Bread

*This traditional English bread, known as clapbread in Lancashire, is usually eaten with cheese. It also toasts very well, and keeps fresh for some days if stored in an air-tight container.*

*Makes 2 small loaves*

THE FLOUR:
*12 oz strong white flour*
*8 oz medium oatmeal or 8 oz rolled oats*

THE STARTER:
*½ oz fresh yeast*
*5 tablespoons lukewarm water*

AND . . .
*10 fl.oz milk*
*1 level tablespoon salt*
*2 tablespoons oil*

PREPARATION:
Soak the oatmeal or rolled oats in the milk for 30 minutes.

YEAST STARTER:
Crumble the yeast into the water and stir until dissolved.

THE MIX:
Mix the soaked oatmeal with the flour, salt and oil. Add the yeast mixture and beat to a soft but firm dough. Turn on to a floured surface and knead well until firm and elastic.

**FIRST RISING:**
Put the dough in a bowl covered with lightly oiled polythene, and leave to rise in a warm place until double in size, about 1 hour.

**SECOND RISING:**
Turn the dough on to a floured surface, knead lightly and divide into two. Flatten each portion and roll it up like a Swiss roll. Grease two 1 lb (500 g) loaf tins, place the dough in them, cover with lightly oiled polythene and leave to rise until the dough has reached the tops of the tins, about 30 minutes.

**PRE-HEAT OVEN**
to 450°F (230°C) Gas 8.

**BAKING TIME:**
Brush the tops with milk and sprinkle with oatmeal. Bake for 1 hour. After 30 minutes REDUCE HEAT to 300°F (150°C) Gas 2.

METRIC EQUIVALENTS:
*350 g strong white flour*
*250 g medium oatmeal or 250 g rolled oats*
*15 g fresh yeast*
*5 tablespoons lukewarm water*
*300 ml milk*
*1 level tablespoon salt*
*2 tablespoons oil*

# Rosemary Baps

*These savoury rolls are pleasantly aromatic and especially good with cream cheese.*

**YEAST STARTER:**
Mix the yeast, milk and 4 oz (125 g) of the flour to form a batter. Cover and leave in a warm place for 20 minutes until frothy.

**THE MIX:**
Sift together the remaining flour and the salt, and rub in the butter. Stir in the rosemary and the cheese. Beat the yeast mixture into the flour and mix to a soft dough. Turn on to a floured surface and knead for 5 to 10 minutes.

**FIRST RISING:**
Cover with lightly oiled polythene and leave to rise in a warm place until double in size.

**SECOND RISING:**
Turn out on to a floured surface and knead for 10 minutes. Divide into 8 equal pieces and shape into rolls. Put them on a greased baking sheet, cover with lightly oiled polythene and leave to rise in a warm place until double in size.

**PRE-HEAT OVEN**
to 425°F (220°C) Gas 7.

**BAKING TIME:**
Bake for 15 to 20 minutes. After removing from oven, sprinkle with flour.

*In colour—page 112*

*Makes 8*

THE FLOUR:
*1 lb strong white flour*

THE STARTER:
*1 oz fresh yeast*
*10 fl.oz milk*

AND . . .
*2 level teaspoons salt*
*2 oz butter*
*1 level teaspoon dried rosemary*
*2 oz grated Cheddar cheese*

METRIC EQUIVALENTS:
*500 g strong white flour*
*30 g fresh yeast*
*300 ml milk*
*2 level teaspoons salt*
*60 g butter*
*1 level teaspoon dried rosemary*
*60 g grated Cheddar cheese*

# Coconut Clusters

In colour—page 120

Makes 8

THE FLOUR:
4 oz strong white flour
4 oz wholemeal flour

THE STARTER:
½ oz fresh yeast
5 fl.oz lukewarm milk

AND . . .
¼ level teaspoon salt
3 oz desiccated coconut
2 teaspoons honey
finely grated rind of 1 lemon
milk or beaten egg for glazing
toasted long thread or shredded
    coconut for topping
    (optional)

METRIC EQUIVALENTS:
125 g strong white flour
125 g wholemeal flour
15 g fresh yeast
150 ml lukewarm milk
¼ level teaspoon salt
90 g desiccated coconut
2 teaspoons honey
finely grated rind of 1 lemon
milk or beaten egg for glazing
toasted long thread or shredded
    coconut for topping (optional)

This attractive crown-shaped loaf makes an ideal tea bread. Serve with butter.

YEAST STARTER:
Mix the yeast with the milk.

THE MIX:
Sift the flours and salt into a bowl, then add the desiccated coconut. Pour in the yeast mixture, and add the honey and lemon rind. Knead to a soft dough in the bowl, then turn out on to a floured surface and knead for a further 5 minutes until the dough is smooth. Cover with lightly oiled polythene.

FIRST RISING:
Leave in a warm place for about 50 minutes until double in bulk.

SECOND RISING:
Knead the dough on a lightly floured surface for 2 to 3 minutes. Divide into 8 equal pieces, knead them into smooth balls, and place in a greased spring-release or loose-bottomed 8 in (200 mm) cake tin in a circle with one in the centre. Cover with lightly oiled polythene and leave in a warm place for about 45 minutes, until double in bulk.

PRE-HEAT OVEN:
to 400°F (200°C) Gas 6.

BAKING TIME:
Brush with milk or beaten egg and bake for about 25 minutes, until golden brown and firm to the touch. Sprinkle with toasted long thread or shredded coconut after removing from the oven.

# Savoury Walnut Bread

Makes 1 loaf

THE FLOUR:
1 lb strong white flour

THE STARTER:
½ oz fresh yeast
5 fl.oz lukewarm water

This makes a good picnic loaf, which is delicious with sharp Cheddar cheese. It uses a 10 in (255 mm) shallow cake tin.

AND . . .
1½ level teaspoons salt
1 level teaspoon paprika
¼ level teaspoon bicarbonate of
    soda
2 oz chopped walnuts
10 fl.oz soured cream

METRIC EQUIVALENTS:
500 g strong white flour
15 g fresh yeast
150 ml lukewarm water
1½ level teaspoons salt
1 level teaspoon paprika
¼ level teaspoon bicarbonate of
    soda
60 g chopped walnuts
300 ml soured cream

YEAST STARTER:
Mix the yeast with the water.

THE MIX:
Sift the flour, salt, paprika and bicarbonate of soda into a large
bowl, and stir in the walnuts. Add the yeast mixture and the soured
cream and mix to a soft dough. Turn on to a lightly floured surface
and knead for 5 minutes, until the dough is smooth.

FIRST RISING:
Cover with lightly oiled polythene and leave in a warm place for
about an hour, until double in size.

SECOND RISING:
Turn on to a floured surface and knead for 2 to 3 minutes. Place in a
greased 10 in (255 mm) shallow cake tin and cover with lightly oiled
polythene. Leave in a warm place to rise for 30 minutes.

PRE-HEAT OVEN
to 425°F (220°C) Gas 7.

BAKING TIME:
Bake for 35 to 40 minutes.

## Cheese Pull-Aparts

*This bread is at its best served hot and buttered.*

*Makes 8*

YEAST STARTER:
Mix the yeast with the milk.

THE FLOUR:
*8 oz strong white flour*

THE MIX:
Mix together the flour, salt, mustard and cheese. Sauté the celery or
onion in the butter until soft and add to the dry ingredients. Add
the yeast mixture and mix to a firm dough; knead for 10 minutes.
Cover with lightly oiled polythene.

THE STARTER:
*½ oz fresh yeast*
*5 fl.oz lukewarm milk*

AND . . .
*½ level teaspoon salt*
*1 level teaspoon dry mustard*
*2 oz grated Cheddar cheese*
*2 oz finely chopped celery or
  onion*
*1 oz butter*
*beaten egg for glazing*

FIRST RISING:
Leave in a warm place until double in size.

SECOND RISING:
Turn out and knead for 5 minutes, then divide into 8 sausage-
shaped pieces. Make a ¼ in (5 mm) cut down the length of each
piece with a sharp knife. Place the sausages of dough, side by side
but not quite touching one another, in a greased tin 7 x 9¾ in
(180 x 250 mm). Cover with lightly oiled polythene and leave to rise
in a warm place for about 45 minutes.

METRIC EQUIVALENTS:
*250 g strong white flour*
*15 g fresh yeast*
*150 ml milk*
*½ level teaspoon salt*
*1 level teaspoon dry mustard*
*60 g grated Cheddar cheese*
*60 g finely chopped celery or onion*
*30 g butter*
*beaten egg for glazing*

PRE-HEAT OVEN
to 375°F (190°C) Gas 5.

BAKING TIME:
Brush with beaten egg and bake for about 25 minutes.

# Cotswold Loaf

*Makes 1 large loaf*

THE FLOUR:
*1 lb wholemeal flour*

THE STARTER:
*½ oz fresh yeast*
*10 fl.oz lukewarm water*

AND...
*1 level teaspoon salt*
*1 oz butter*
*beaten egg for glazing*

THE FILLING:
*8 oz tomatoes, skinned and sliced*
*2 sticks celery, finely sliced*
*1 level teaspoon dried mixed*
*    herbs*
*salt*
*freshly ground pepper*
*4 oz grated Cotswold (Double*
*    Gloucester with chives) cheese*

METRIC EQUIVALENTS:
*500 g wholemeal flour*
*15 g fresh yeast*
*300 ml lukewarm water*
*1 level teaspoon salt*
*30 g butter*
*beaten egg for glazing*
*The filling:*
*250 g tomatoes, skinned and sliced*
*2 sticks celery, finely sliced*
*1 level teaspoon dried*
*    mixed herbs*
*salt*
*freshly ground pepper*
*125 g grated Cotswold (Double*
*    Gloucester with chives) cheese*

*A colourful, layered wholemeal loaf which makes a welcome change from sandwiches for a picnic.*

YEAST STARTER:
Mix the yeast with the water.

THE FILLING:
Mix together the tomatoes, finely sliced celery and dried herbs. Season with salt and pepper. Add three-quarters of the grated cheese, keep the rest on one side.

THE MIX:
Mix together the flour and salt, and rub in the butter. Add the yeast liquid and mix it to a soft dough; add more water if necessary. Turn on to a floured surface and knead thoroughly for 10 minutes or so. Divide into 3 equal pieces and roll out to oblongs 5 x 9 in (13 x 23 cm). Put one of these in the base of a greased 2 lb (1 kg) loaf tin. Cover with half of the filling. Put the second piece of dough on top and spread with rest of filling. Cover with the third oblong of dough.

THE RISING:
Cover with lightly oiled polythene and leave in a warm place until the dough reaches the top of the tin.

PRE-HEAT OVEN
to 400°F (200°C) Gas 6.

BAKING TIME:
Brush the loaf with beaten egg and sprinkle over the remaining cheese. Bake for 25 to 30 minutes until golden brown. Remove from the tin, place on a baking sheet, and put back in the oven for 5 minutes.

OPPOSITE:
Top: *Kolatschen p.80-81 and* below: *Gugelhupf p.80, seen here traditionally dusted with icing sugar (both from George and Cecilia Scurfield).*

# Biscottes

In colour—page 217

*These crisp breads are good with pâté or cheese, as a change from bread or toast. Prepare a day in advance. They need to be baked twice.*

*Makes 24 to 28*

**YEAST STARTER:**
Mix the yeast with a little of the milk. Sift the flour into a large bowl, make a well in the centre and pour in the yeast mixture and half the remaining milk. Sprinkle lightly with flour and leave in a warm place for 20 minutes.

**THE MIX:**
Cream the butter and honey, and beat in the eggs. Stir this into the yeast mixture with the remaining milk. Knead on a floured surface for 5 minutes, until smooth.

**FIRST RISING:**
Cover with lightly oiled polythene and leave to rise in a warm place for about an hour, until the dough is three times its original bulk.

**PRE-HEAT OVEN**
to 400°F (200°C) Gas 6.

**SECOND RISING:**
Knead for 2 to 3 minutes on a floured surface. Shape into long, flat rolls and place on a greased baking sheet. Cover with lightly oiled polythene and leave to rise for 10 minutes.

**FIRST BAKING TIME:**
Brush with beaten egg and bake for 20 to 25 minutes. Cool on a wire rack and leave overnight.

**SECOND BAKING TIME:**
Next day, cut into thin slices and bake in a pre-heated oven, 300°F (150°C) Gas 2 for about 30 minutes until crisp and brown. Cool on a wire rack. When cool, store in an air-tight container.

**THE FLOUR:**
*2 lb strong white flour*

**THE STARTER:**
*1½ oz fresh yeast*

**AND . . .**
*scant ¾ pt lukewarm milk*
*6 oz butter, softened*
*2 tablespoons honey*
*2 beaten eggs*
*beaten egg for glazing*

**METRIC EQUIVALENTS:**
*1 kg strong white flour*
*40 g fresh yeast*
*scant 400 ml lukewarm milk*
*175 g butter*
*2 tablespoons honey*
*2 beaten eggs*
*beaten egg for glazing*

**OPPOSITE:**
Top: *Dee Dee Cake or Wholemeal Kozounak (Maria Johnson) p.94-95.* Centre: *Bath Buns (Brian Binns) p.130.* Bottom left: *Sun and Planet (Maria Johnson) p.90-91.*
**PREVIOUS SPREAD LEFT:**
Top left: *Toutmanik (Cheese Bread) p.86-87.* Below centre: *Wholemeal Panbread p.88, both from Maria Johnson.* Top right: *Brian Binns' Herb Bread, topped with fennel seeds p.131.*
**PREVIOUS SPREAD RIGHT:**
Top: *Poppy Seed Roll (Nina Froud) p.112.* Centre: *Brown Turban Loaf p.93* and bottom: *Pogacha p.92 (both from Maria Johnson). Serve Pogacha with fresh yoghurt as shown here.*

# Wholemeal Croissants

*Makes about 16*

THE FLOUR:
*1 lb 4 oz wholemeal flour*

THE STARTER:
*1 oz fresh yeast or ½ oz dried
 yeast*

AND...
*¾ pt warm milk and water,
 mixed*
*½ level teaspoon freshly ground
 sea salt*
*11 oz butter*
*1 egg, beaten*

*Surprisingly light and buttery, these wholemeal croissants,
adapted from* The Good Housekeeping Book of Wholefood Cookery
*by Gail Duff, combine goodness with continental verve.*

YEAST STARTER:
Blend the yeast with about ¼ pt (150 ml) milk and water and leave
for about 15 minutes.

THE MIX:
Mix the flour and salt together and stir in the yeast mixture. Melt
1½ oz (40 g) butter and add to the flour with enough of the
remaining milk and water to make a fairly soft dough. Knead
lightly

FIRST RISING:
Cover and leave in a warm place to rise for about 30 minutes until
double in size.

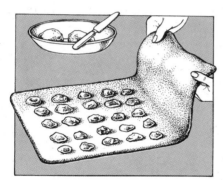

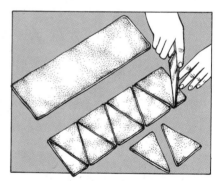

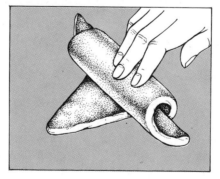

**THE SHAPING AND RESTING:**
Knead lightly then roll into an oblong measuring 7 x 21 in (18 x 53.5 cm) keeping the edges straight. Soften the remaining butter with a knife and divide into 3 portions. Dot one portion of butter in small pieces over the top two thirds of the dough. Fold the bottom third of the dough up and the top third down, sealing the edges well with a rolling pin. Turn the dough, so that the folded edges are at the side. Cover and place in the fridge for 20 minutes.
Roll out again into an oblong, dot as before with butter, fold, seal and turn again. Cover and place in the fridge for 20 minutes. This prevents the butter from becoming too soft with overhandling. Repeat with the final portion of butter and place in the fridge, as before, for 20 minutes.
Finally, roll out the dough quite thinly and cut into triangles with sides longer than bases, measuring 9 x 9 x 6 in (23 x 23 x 15 cm). Roll up each triangle from the base and curl the ends round to form a crescent.

**SECOND RISING:**
Place on a greased baking tray, cover and leave to rise for 15 to 20 minutes, until double in size.

**PRE-HEAT OVEN**
to 450°F (230°C) Gas 8.

**BAKING TIME:**
Brush with beaten egg and bake for 10 to 15 minutes until risen.

*METRIC EQUIVALENTS:*
*600 g wholemeal flour*
*30 g fresh yeast or 15 g dried yeast*
*400 ml warm milk and water, mixed*
*½ level teaspoon freshly ground sea salt*
*325 g butter*
*1 egg, beaten*

# Nina Froud

In the Far East they do not bake bread. The staple food is rice; wheat is used primarily to make noodles. But in the mountainous north of China, they make steamed yeasty dumplings with sweet or savoury fillings that are, in effect, a kind of bread.

Nina Froud sampled these dumplings at a very early age, when she travelled on pilgrimages through China with her godmother, a Buddhist from Shanghai. Vegetarian dishes were the diet in the monasteries where they stayed. To appease the desire for meat, *tofu*—soya bean paste—was dressed in the shape of an animal, and brought to the table as a whole goose or a perfect fish.

In the kitchens of Nina's childhood home in Hong Kong the cook prepared less elaborate but still very intricate dishes. Nina's part-Georgian, part-English mother did not cook: "She had a love of eating," says Nina, "which she passed on to me."

This love of eating has been with Nina throughout her life. It enables her to indulge in her chief pleasures—people, languages and travel. She is co-director of a London literary agency, speaks nine languages—at the moment she's studying Hebrew, Chinese and Turkish—has travelled throughout Europe, the Americas and the Far East, and has translated works from several languages including Chekhov's *Uncle Vanya* from the Russian and *Larousse Gastronomique* from the French. She is also author and co-author of thirty-eight cookery books.

Her mother taught her to appreciate only the best in food, but could not teach Nina to cook. At home, she was not even allowed into the kitchens. But sometimes, when illness kept her away from school, she would sneak into these forbidden rooms: "I watched the cook stuff prawns with almonds. I was mesmerized by him."

Her own cooking skills developed much later — out of necessity. When she was eighteen she married her first husband, a sailor. He was part-Italian, part-English, born in India, and he brought his young bride to England. They stayed at various British naval bases: "They were not exciting, gastronomically speaking." Finally, they landed in Northumberland, at Blyth —"There was nothing blithe about that"— and Nina who had always been serviced by cooks and housekeepers now had her first try at running a home and doing her own shopping: "There was only one shop in Seaton Sluice along the coast—a Co-op. I went there with my shopping list and waited in the queue to be served. Bread was the first item on my list. When it was my turn I asked, 'Can I have a loaf of bread, please?' The Northumberland lady behind me said, 'you don't buy bread here. You make it.'

This lady went on to give Nina her first shopping and cooking lesson: "She told me what to buy—flour and fresh yeast. Then she followed me home, and then and there in my own kitchen she showed me how to make bread. And sure enough among the items in the kitchen of our rented house, there was a bread tin."

Nina loved making bread: "The smell had me converted immediately. Home-made bread smells good and keeps well. It has good eating qualities and good keeping qualities."

She began to experiment with bread-making and cooking in general. She cooked everything, and loved the whole experience. Her skills were greatly increased when her father-in-law by her second marriage, George Froud, joined the household. George, an engineer, and the only true Englishman in the family, had been brought up in Russia and had married a Russian. At seventy, he suffered a stroke and in order not to be a burden to his son and daughter-in-law he took over the running of their kitchen: "We had never eaten so well. An engineer, artistic by temperament, is an ideal combination in a cook. He was especially good at baking. He understood all about heat penetration."

To get grandfather George to accept some money from them, Nina, who had by now written and published one cookery book in collaboration with a Spanish friend, embarked on a second book with grandfather. Naturally, it was about Russian food: *The Homebook of Russian Cookery*. Among the many recipes, there were several on bread:

"Russians are great bakers. In the small towns and villages there isn't a baker for miles around. The stove is going all day; grandmother even sleeps on it. So they have to bake."

They bake light yeasty *blinis* to fill with caviar or smoked salmon: "Grandfather's version uses kippers and is quite delicious." And they bake a heavy sour black bread that is like the soil itself. They sniff the bread and breathe it in, then they down it with a small glass of sharp vodka—the perfect combination of earthy flavours.

Nina learnt a lot from grandfather George. Above all she learned how much she didn't know about cooking. Her love of good food is still with her and is now equalled by her culinary skills and love of cooking. And whenever she can she bakes her own bread. "I'm very grateful to that Northum-berland miner's wife. When I have guests I like to do my own baking. There are so many different shapes and sizes and flavours. Bread is inter-national, and the thing about foreign breads is that they live well together. *They* don't quarrel. In Israel you can eat Arab pitta bread in the street and Jewish cholla in the home."

# Blini

In colour—page 200

*Light, yeast pancakes—a time-honoured way of serving caviar. Also delicious with thin slices of smoked salmon—or with kippers and chopped hard-boiled egg. They make a good starter to a meal.*

*Serves 4 to 6*

THE FLOUR:
*7 oz buckwheat flour*

YEAST STARTER:
Take a large mixing bowl and cream the yeast with the warm water and 4 fl.oz (100 ml) of the warm milk. Mix in half the flour.

THE STARTER:
*scant 1 oz fresh yeast*
*7 fl.oz lukewarm water*

FIRST RISING:
Stir well, cover and leave in a warm place for 2 to 3 hours.

AND . . .
*7 fl.oz lukewarm milk*
*2 eggs, separated*
*¼ teaspoon salt*
*1 teaspoon honey*
*½ oz melted butter*

THE MIX:
Beat the egg yolks with the salt and honey and beat in the rest of the milk. Add the melted butter and mix again. Add this to the yeast mixture, stir thoroughly and stir in the rest of the flour. Beat the egg whites until stiff and fold them into the batter.

THE FILLING:
*caviar or*
  *4 oz smoked salmon or*
  *2 plump kippers, boned*
    *and 2 hard-boiled eggs*
*with 7 fl.oz soured cream*
  *2 oz melted butter*
  *chopped spring onions*
    *(for red caviar)*

SECOND RISING:
Cover and leave undisturbed for 45 to 50 minutes. The final batter should be like thick cream.

COOKING TIME:
It is important to make all the *blini* of equal size, not more than 4 in (10 cm) across. Lightly grease a heavy-based frying-pan, put it over a hot flame and drop in some batter. Shake the pan to spread the batter to about 3 or 4 in (8 to 10 cm). Cook for about 1 minute until the underside browns, turn and cook the other side.
Stack the cooked *blini* and cover with a cloth to keep warm.

METRIC EQUIVALENTS:
*200 g buckwheat flour*
*scant 30 g fresh yeast*
*200 ml lukewarm water*
*200 ml lukewarm milk*
*2 eggs, separated*
*¼ teaspoon salt*
*1 teaspoon honey*
*15 g melted butter*
The filling:
*caviar or 125 g smoked salmon*
  *or 2 plump kippers, boned, and*
    *2 hard-boiled eggs*
*with 200 ml soured cream*
  *60 g melted butter*
  *chopped spring onions*
    *(for red caviar)*

TO SERVE:
Serve the *blini* and put the caviar or smoked salmon, melted butter and soured cream in separate dishes. Let each person help himself. If using red caviar, add a bowl of chopped spring onions for sprinkling on the caviar. If using kippers, add the chopped hard-boiled eggs to the butter.

In colour—page 113

*Makes 3 large cakes*

THE FLOUR:
*2 lb 2 oz white flour*

THE STARTER:
*1 oz fresh yeast*
*4 tablespoons lukewarm water*

AND . . .
*7 fl.oz lukewarm milk*
*6 tablespoons honey*
*3 to 4 drops vanilla essence*
*pinch of salt*
*3 to 4 filaments saffron*
*2 tablespoons vodka (optional)*
  *or water*
*2 oz seedless raisins*
*8 oz unsalted butter*
*4 eggs*
*4 oz sultanas*
*2 oz candied peel, chopped*
*2 oz blanched almonds, chopped*

THE GLAZE:
*1 egg yolk, diluted with*
  *2 teaspoons water*
*1 tablespoon fine breadcrumbs*

# *Kulich*

*This tall, cylindrical cake is the traditional Russian Easter cake. Russians use a special kulich tin, but you can use a tall fruit juice tin, a salad oil tin or a big coffee container. In Russia a thin smooth wooden spill is usually inserted into the unbaked* kulich *reaching right down to its base. The cake is done when the spill is removed without any dough sticking to it. It is usual to bake one* kulich *for each member of the family with small ones for the children. There must always be enough* kulich *to offer the endless stream of visitors who drop in over Easter.*

YEAST STARTER:
Cream the yeast with the lukewarm water and set aside.

FIRST RISING:
Put the warm milk in a large mixing bowl with 1 tablespoon of the honey, the vanilla essence, the salt and one-third of the flour. Stir in the creamed yeast and mix well. Cover and leave in a warm place to rise until double in size, about 1 hour.

PREPARATION:
Put the saffron filaments (these are far better than powdered saffron) in a small glass and cover with the vodka or water. Leave to soak until the vodka or water has become a deep orange colour. In a separate small bowl cover the raisins in water and leave to soak.

THE MIX:
Gently heat the butter with the remaining honey and beat in the eggs. Cool and stir this into the yeast mixture.
Drain the raisins and add them to the mixture. Strain the saffron infusion into the mixture and discard the saffron filaments. Stir in the sultanas, chopped peel and chopped almonds and the remaining flour. Mix well.
Turn out onto a floured board and knead well for 15 to 20 minutes adding more flour or warm water, if necessary, to make an elastic dough that is silky smooth.

SECOND RISING:
Place in a clean bowl, cover and leave in a warm place to double in size. This may take about 1 hour or more, as the dough may be slow rising and fairly stiff.

THE SHAPING:
Grease the base and sides of three cylindrical baking tins 1¾ pt (1 litre) size well, and sprinkle with flour. Line the bottoms with a circle of buttered greaseproof paper or tin foil. Shape the dough into a ball for larger tins and into cylindrical rolls for the smaller tins. Do not fill the containers more than half full of dough.

### THIRD RISING:

Cover with a cloth and leave in a warm place to prove until the dough rises almost to the top of the tins, about 45 minutes to 1 hour.

### PRE-HEAT OVEN

to 400°F (200°C) Gas 6.

### THE GLAZE:

Brush the tops with the diluted egg yolk and sprinkle with breadcrumbs.

### BAKING TIME:

Bake on the bottom shelf of the oven for 50 to 55 minutes. After 15 minutes REDUCE HEAT to 350°F (180°C) Gas 4. Remove the *kulich* from its tin, cover with a cloth and leave on a cake rack to cool.

*Kulich* is traditionally iced and then decorated with hundreds and thousands. To serve, first cut off the decorated top, then cut the cake into round slices about ¾ in (2 cm) thick. If the slices are large, halve and quarter them. Replace the top as a lid.

METRIC EQUIVALENTS:
*1 kg white flour*
*30 g fresh yeast*
*4 tablespoons lukewarm water*
*200 ml lukewarm milk*
*6 tablespoons honey*
*3 to 4 drops vanilla essence*
*pinch of salt*
*3 to 4 filaments saffron*
*2 tablespoons vodka (optional) or water*
*60 g seedless raisins*
*250 g unsalted butter*
*4 eggs*
*125 g sultanas*
*60 g candied peel, chopped*
*60 g blanched almonds, chopped*
The glaze:
*1 egg yolk diluted with 2 teaspoons water*
*1 tablespoon fine breadcrumbs*

In colour—page 105

*Makes 1 cake*

THE FLOUR:
*15 oz white flour*

THE STARTER:
*1 oz fresh yeast*
*warm water*
*6 fl.oz milk*
*4 oz butter*
*2 tablespoons honey*

AND...
*pinch of salt*
*2 large eggs or 3 small eggs*

THE FILLING:
*10 oz poppy seeds*
*6 fl.oz milk*
*4 tablespoons honey*
*2 to 3 drops vanilla essence*
*2 tablespoons chopped candied
  peel*
*1 teaspoon ground cinnamon*
*½ oz melted butter*

METRIC EQUIVALENTS:
*425 g white flour*
*30 g fresh yeast*
*warm water*
*150 to 200 ml milk*
*125 g butter*
*2 tablespoons honey*
*pinch of salt*
*2 large or 3 small eggs*
*The filling:*
*300 g poppy seeds*
*150 to 200 ml milk*
*4 tablespoons honey*
*2 to 3 drops vanilla essence*
*2 tablespoons chopped candied peel*
*1 teaspoon ground cinnamon*
*15 g melted butter*

OPPOSITE:
Top: *Rosemary Baps p.101.*
Right: *Golden Carrot and Walnut
Loaf p.100.* Left: *Farmhouse
Plait p.98-99. All from The
Good Housekeeping Institute.*

# Poppy Seed Roll

*This traditional Polish cake is served with morning coffee or afternoon tea. It is sometimes also served as a dessert. To vary the cake, you can add chopped nuts and/or dried fruit to the filling.*

YEAST STARTER:
Cream the yeast with a little warm water. Warm the milk, butter and honey gently in a small saucepan until the butter melts and the milk is lukewarm. Do not let it get too hot. Pour this over the yeast and mix well.

THE MIX:
Sift the flour and salt into a large warmed mixing bowl. Make a well in the centre and pour in the yeast and milk mixture. Work in the flour and knead to make a smooth dough.

FIRST RISING:
Cover the bowl with a lightly floured cloth and put it in a warm place for 1½ to 2 hours until the dough doubles in size.

THE FILLING:
Rinse the poppy seeds with hot water and drain them well (this is best done through muslin). Grind the seeds finely. Heat the milk in a small saucepan, add the honey and bring gently to the boil. Add the ground poppy seeds and vanilla essence and cook, stirring frequently, until the mixture thickens. Stir in the candied peel, cinnamon and melted butter. Remove from the heat and leave to cool.

THE SHAPING:
Knock down the dough and work in the eggs, beating well. Turn out and knead on a floured board. Then roll out the dough into a rectangle until it is just over ¼ in (5 mm) thick. Moisten the edges and spread the filling thickly over the rectangle almost to the edges. Roll it up.

SECOND RISING:
Place on a lightly greased baking tray, cover with a cloth and leave to rise in warm place for a further 1½ to 2 hours.

PRE-HEAT OVEN
to 375°F (190°C) Gas 5.

BAKING TIME:
Brush the top of the poppy seed roll with the melted butter and bake for 35 to 45 minutes.

# Bagels

*Bagels originated in Eastern Europe. The Russians made up songs about them and sold them at fairs like quoits on a string. Because they are circular in shape, having "no beginning and no end", bagels are said to be magical; they are supposed to bring luck. In the Jewish tradition this round shape also symbolizes the cycle of life without end. Bagels are boiled first and then baked.*

YEAST STARTER:
Cream the yeast in half the lukewarm water and leave for 5 minutes.

THE MIX:
Add the oil, 1 tablespoon of the honey and the rest of the warm water to the yeast mixture. Beat the egg and add this. Sift the flour and salt into a bowl. Add the yeast mixture and make into a firm smooth dough. Knead for 3 to 4 minutes.

FIRST RISING:
Cover with a cloth and leave in a warm place to rise for 1 hour. Turn out on to a floured board, knead well until the dough acquires elasticity.

THE SHAPING:
Divide the dough into 12 equal pieces and shape each into a roll about 5 in (13 cm) long and ¾ in (2 cm) thick. Make these into rings, pinching the ends together and smoothing them out as evenly as possible.

SECOND RISING:
Leave covered on a floured board for 10 to 15 minutes.

PRE-HEAT OVEN
to 400°F (200°C) Gas 6.

COOKING TIME:
Add the remaining 2 tablespoons honey to the boiling water in a very large wide saucepan and bring to a rolling boil. Drop the bagels in one by one. When they are all in the saucepan (or as many as will fit in) and the water has been brought back to the boil, reduce the heat and allow the bagels to simmer gently for 10 to 15 minutes, until they become light enough to float up to the surface.
Remove the bagels with a slotted spoon and drain well on kitchen paper. Place them on a greased baking sheet. Brush each bagel with the diluted egg yolk to glaze. Sprinkle with poppy or caraway seeds.

BAKING TIME:
Bake for 25 to 30 minutes until smooth, crisp and golden brown.

*Makes 12*

THE FLOUR:
*12 oz white flour*

THE STARTER:
*1 oz fresh yeast*

AND . . .
*5 fl.oz lukewarm water*
*1½ teaspoons salt*
*3 tablespoons honey*
*4 tablespoons oil*
*1 egg*
*7 pt boiling water*
*1 tablespoon cold water*
*poppy seeds or caraway seeds*

THE GLAZE:
*1 egg yolk diluted with*
*  2 teaspoons cold water*

METRIC EQUIVALENTS:
*350 g white flour*
*30 g fresh yeast*
*150 ml lukewarm water*
*1½ teaspoons salt*
*3 tablespoons honey*
*4 tablespoons oil*
*1 egg*
*4 litres boiling water*
*1 tablespoon cold water*
*poppy seeds or caraway seeds*
The glaze:
*1 egg yolk diluted with 2 teaspoons*
*  cold water*

OPPOSITE:
*Kulich (Nina Froud) p.110-111; shown here made into small and big cakes for all the family, and traditionally iced.*

# Coulibiac

*Serves 4 to 6*

*Coulibiac is a tall Russian pie with one or more fillings in layers. It can be made with puff pastry or, as here, with a quick brioche dough. It can be served hot or cold. For best results use generous helpings of fish filling: salmon, tuna or halibut.*

THE FLOUR:
*6 oz strong white flour*
*7 oz wholemeal flour*

THE STARTER:
*½ oz fresh yeast*
*1 teaspoon honey*
*5 fl.oz lukewarm water*
*2 eggs*

AND . . .
*pinch of salt*
*4 oz butter*

THE SAUCE:
*1 oz mushrooms*
*2 oz butter*
*3 to 4 sprigs of parsley*
*10 peppercorns*
*2 oz white flour*
*7 fl.oz fish stock*
*3½ fl.oz cream*

THE FILLING:
*1 lb cooked salmon, tuna or*
*    halibut (skinned and boned)*
*1 finely chopped onion*
*4 oz butter*
*2 oz mushrooms*
*4 oz rice or buckwheat, cooked*
*3 to 4 sliced hard-boiled eggs*
*2 to 3 tablespoons chopped*
*    parsley, chervil and tarragon*
*salt and pepper*

THE GLAZE:
*1 egg yolk mixed with 1*
*    teaspoon water*

YEAST STARTER:
Dissolve the yeast and honey in the warm water and mix with about one-third of the flour.

THE MIX:
Put the remaining flour in a large mixing bowl, make a well in the centre and add the eggs, salt and yeast mixture. Mix well. Melt the butter and add this to the flour. Beat the dough. Turn out and knead until smooth and soft.

THE RISING:
Cover and leave to stand in a warm place for about 1 to 1½ hours.

THE SAUCE:
Fry the whole mushrooms in the butter for about 5 minutes. Add the parsley and peppercorns and cook for 3 to 4 minutes over a low heat. Blend in the flour and cook the roux for a few minutes, without allowing it to colour. Stir in the stock and bring to the boil, stirring with a wooden spoon until the first bubble appears. Reduce the heat and simmer gently for 45 to 50 minutes, skimming from time to time. Strain the sauce through damp muslin and continue to stir until quite cold. When ready to use, reheat gently, blend in the cream and check seasoning.

THE FILLING:

Flake the cooked fish or cut it into very thin pieces. Lightly fry the onion in about ½ oz (15 g) butter. Slice and lightly fry the mushrooms in butter.

PRE-HEAT OVEN
to 425°F (220°C) Gas 7.

THE SHAPING:

Roll the dough into a thin rectangle and cut in half. Place one sheet on a lightly greased baking tray and moisten the edges. Spread a layer of cooked rice or buckwheat evenly across the dough, leaving the edges untouched. Spoon over some of the reheated sauce. Follow with a layer of egg slices, more sauce, then a layer of fish. Season with salt and pepper. Sprinkle with herbs, onion and mushrooms and spoon over some more sauce. Finish with the remaining rice or buckwheat. Season and sprinkle liberally with the remaining butter, melted down. Cover with the second sheet of dough and press down to seal the edges.

BAKING TIME:

Brush the top with the diluted egg yolk, prick all over with a fork and bake for 30 to 35 minutes.

METRIC EQUIVALENTS:
*175 g strong white flour*
*200 g wholemeal flour*
*15 g fresh yeast*
*1 teaspoon honey*
*150 ml lukewarm water*
*2 eggs*
*pinch of salt*
*125 g butter*
The sauce:
*30 g mushrooms*
*60 g butter*
*3 to 4 sprigs of parsley*
*10 peppercorns*
*60 g white flour*
*200 ml fish stock*
*90 ml cream*
The filling:
*500 g cooked salmon, tuna or*
   *halibut (skinned and boned)*
*1 finely chopped onion*
*125 g butter*
*60 g mushrooms*
*125 g cooked rice or buckwheat*
*3 or 4 sliced hard-boiled eggs*
*2 to 3 tablespoons chopped parsley,*
   *tarragon and chervil*
*salt and pepper*
The glaze:
*1 egg yolk mixed with 1 teaspoon*
   *water*

# Chinese Dumplings

*These steamed dumplings are quick and easy to make and can have a variety of savoury—in this case pork—or sweet fillings.*

*Makes 16*

THE FLOUR:
*8 oz white flour*

THE RAISING AGENT:
*2 teaspoons baking powder*

AND ...
*1 teaspoon honey*
*1 tablespoon sesame or peanut oil*
*4 fl.oz warm water*

THE FILLING:
*4 oz lean pork, finely chopped*
*1 tablespoon peanut oil*
*1 tablespoon onion, finely chopped*
*2 oz mushrooms, finely chopped*
*pinch of salt*
*½ teaspoon soya sauce*
*1 teaspoon cornflour*
*1 teaspoon oyster sauce*
*2 tablespoons cold water*

METRIC EQUIVALENTS:
*250 g white flour*
*2 teaspoons baking powder*
*1 teaspoon honey*
*1 tablespoon sesame or peanut oil*
*100 ml warm water*
The filling:
*125 g lean pork, finely chopped*
*1 tablespoon peanut oil*
*1 tablespoon onion, finely chopped*
*60 g mushrooms, finely chopped*
*pinch of salt*
*½ teaspoon soya sauce*
*1 teaspoon cornflour*
*1 teaspoon oyster sauce*
*2 tablespoons cold water*

THE FILLING:
First prepare the filling by frying the pork quickly for about one minute in the heated peanut oil. This seals in the juices. Add the onion and mushrooms, stir well and cook for one minute. Season with salt and soya sauce. Mix the cornflour with the oyster sauce and cold water. Blend into the ingredients in the frying-pan and cook for one more minute. Remove from the heat.

THE MIX:
Mix the flour with the baking powder, add the honey, oil and enough warm water to make a stiff dough. Knead on a floured board until springy. Divide the dough into 16 pieces, shape each into a ball, then roll out into 2½ to 3 in (6.5 to 8 cm) circles.
Put a teaspoon of filling on each circle. Moisten the edges and pinch together. Arrange the parcels on a piece of moist cloth in a steamer or place each in the steamer on a piece of greaseproof paper cut to size.

COOKING TIME:
Steam over a high heat for 12 to 15 minutes. Serve with vinegar or soya sauce.

# Yeast Raised Pie

*In this Georgian recipe, tender beef is encased in yeast-risen pastry. It's a good way of making the best meat go further and is ideal for a picnic or buffet lunch.*

YEAST STARTER:
Dissolve the yeast and honey in the warm water and mix with one-third of the mixed flour.

THE MIX:
Put the remaining mixed flours in a bowl, make a well in the middle and add the eggs, salt and yeast mixture. Mix well and add the melted butter. Beat the dough until smooth.

THE RISING:
Cover and leave in a warm place for about 1 to 1½ hours.

THE FILLING:
Cut the steak into strips about 1 in (2.5 cm) long and ½ in (1.5 cm) thick, and fry it in half the butter. When brown on all sides, add the spring onions, mushrooms, parsley and chives. Mix and cook for about five minutes. Season with salt and pepper, and moisten with stock.

PRE-HEAT OVEN
to 400°F (200°C) Gas 6.

THE SHAPING:
Using two-thirds of the dough, roll out the bottom sheet which should be thicker and longer than the top covering. Place this on a flat, lightly greased baking tray and spread the filling over it, avoiding the edges. Dot with tiny pieces of butter. Moisten the edges. Roll out the rest of the dough and carefully cover the filling with it, drawing up the edges of the lower sheet to cover the edges of the upper sheet and pinch to seal well together. Make a hole in the centre for steam to escape. Brush the top with melted butter and sprinkle with breadcrumbs.

BAKING TIME:
Bake for 1 hour. Remove from the oven, pour 2 to 3 tablespoons melted butter into the hole in the centre and serve hot or cold.

*Makes 1 pie*

THE FLOUR:
*7 oz white flour*
*6 oz wholemeal flour*

THE STARTER:
*½ oz fresh yeast*
*½ teaspoon honey*
*5 fl.oz warm water*

AND . . .
*2 eggs*
*pinch of salt*
*4 oz butter, melted*

THE FILLING:
*1½ lb beef, preferably rump or
   fillet steak*
*4 oz butter*
*1 bunch spring onions, chopped*
*½ lb mushrooms, sliced*
*2 tablespoons chopped parsley*
*1 tablespoon chopped chives*
*salt and pepper*
*2 to 3 tablespoons stock*
*2 to 3 tablespoons fine
   breadcrumbs*

METRIC EQUIVALENTS:
*200 g white flour*
*175 g wholemeal flour*
*15 g fresh yeast*
*½ teaspoon honey*
*150 ml warm water*
*2 eggs*
*pinch of salt*
*125 g butter, melted*
The filling:
*750 g beef*
*125 g butter*
*1 bunch spring onions, chopped*
*250 g sliced mushrooms*
*2 tablespoons chopped parsley*
*1 tablespoon chopped chives*
*salt and pepper*
*2 to 3 tablespoons stock*
*2 to 3 tablespoons fine breadcrumbs*

# Miriam Polunin

Miriam Polunin is a working woman—managing editor of *Here's Health* magazine—and makes her wholemeal bread the quick way. By adding Vitamin C to the dough mixture she cuts out the need for a second rising.

Government regulations on what you can and what you can't put in bread puzzle health food people. For example, they give their blessing to potassium bromate as an additive to white bread. But they do not permit Vitamin C in wholemeal bread.

Potassium bromate is a chemical which is added to new white flour to mature it. It is also used in baking as an oxidising agent. It is used in minutely small quantities, 10 to 60 parts per million. But health food people say it should not be used at all; if there was an error in dosage, it could have awful consequences. Potassium bromate is a poison which causes nausea, vomiting, severe abdominal pain, diarrhoea. The ensuing apathy leads to irritation. Loss of consciousness or convulsions may follow. In South Africa in the sixties 816 people were poisoned when they ate bread prepared from dough which contained an excessive amount, 1.1 per cent of the weight. In New Zealand 55 people were poisoned after eating sugar which had been contaminated with the bromate.

By a curious twist of logic, Vitamin C (ascorbic acid), which is freely used in the baking industry as an antioxidant, is not permitted by law in bread sold as wholemeal.

It seems that civil servants, pressed to remove unwanted additives from white bread, didn't budge, but in a gesture to the wholefood lobby, removed the inoffensive Vitamin C from wholemeal bread. A government committee actually recommended seven years ago that it should be put back, but it hasn't been. (Food Standards Committee's Second report on Bread and Flour 1974.) The recommendation was reinforced in 1980 in another government committee inquiry known as the COMA report (dealing with the medical aspects of food policy).

Vitamin C, is of course, one of the vitamins vital to our health, but its beneficial properties are lost in the fermentation and baking process; however, it does help produce a smooth-textured, well-risen loaf, although some purists find the results too cakey, and prefer a rougher, heavier wholemeal loaf.

If, like Miriam Polunin, you eat wholemeal bread for health reasons, there is no difference in health value at all between bread with Vitamin C or bread without it.

"I only have time to bake once a week," she explains, "so I use all the short cuts I can. I add a crumbled Vitamin C tablet to my yeast starter. I used dried yeast because it is more convenient to store. With this method, I only need one rise. I get a good texture, and it is not crumbly or wet in the middle.

"I make the same dough every week. I took the recipe off a packet of Allinson's flour. From this basic recipe I make wholemeal bread, pitta bread and some pizzas. For special occasions I bake fancy breads with fruity flavours—no sugar, that's against *Here's Health* thinking.

"I bake the breads and at once freeze everything we're not eating. You take it out of the freezer about two hours before you want to use it."

*Here's Health* is the largest circulation health magazine in Great Britain. It has doubled in circulation since Miriam took charge—and they have a healthy 76,000 readers.

It began 25 years ago, homing in on a minority group of people, whose anxiety about their health amounted almost to panic. Today it is closely associated with the wholefood movement and is the most consistent source of information on natural foods. The balance is sometimes slightly thrown by advertisers, fewer these days, proclaiming the merits of elixirs like Royal Jelly, pollen, extract of ginseng root and essence of green lipped mussels.

Miriam Polunin smiles, but chooses not to comment. Her own contributions to the magazine are usually about wholefoods. She ran the first consumer test on organic and stoneground flours, comparing them for workability and baking properties. Their cookery pages frequently include recipes showing how wholemeal flour can be used instead of white flour, with results which are not only healthier but tastier too.

Miriam does not come from a wholefood background unless you count her birthplace, Macclesfield, home of Hovis. "We ate it. It's not wholemeal, but its a lot better for you than white bread."

She went to the London School of Economics, where she read English and Economics. Her first job was with Rolls-Royce, on the finance side. She wasn't surprised when the firm went bankrupt. "They never listened to the accountants."

When a boyfriend left for Japan, she threw up her job to join him. It was in the Far East she discovered a different, healthier style of eating. Among Zen Buddhists she ate brown rice for the first time and enjoyed it. They ate little or no meat, but delicious vegetable dishes. Travelling in Malaysia and Indonesia, she noted that meat-eating Europeans were bloated, sluggish and unhealthy; and the locals, eating a more vegetarian diet, were quick-witted, lithe and bursting with energy.

She had never made bread until she got to Australia. During her travels she helped some wives in a ranch kitchen in the outback and by the time she got to Perth, felt ready to do it by herself. "I made my first wholemeal loaf. It was laughable. Square, solid and heavy as a brick."

She had no intention of becoming a food freak. But back in England, now married, and living in Godalming, she saw an advertisement for a tea-boy with *Health Food Trader*, sister magazine to *Here's Health*, published in nearby West Byfleet. She got the job and over the years has become one of the company's most potent converts.

Having originally started in a career which some thought a little bit cranky, she often finds herself today in the swim of approved medical thinking, which she finds very pleasant. Like the current views on bran and dietary fibre: "But I hope people aren't going to think that a good dose of bran is the easy answer," she says. "It's not just a question of ladling crude fibrous bran into the bowels. The more bran you eat the more phytic acid you consume; this acid can bind useful mineral substances, like calcium. This doesn't happen when you eat bran as part of the whole grain."

Here are some of the wholemeal recipes she has developed at home.

# Everyday Bread

*Makes 2 small loaves and either 8 rolls or 2 pitta breads or 1 pizza base*

THE FLOUR:
*1½ lb wholemeal flour*

THE STARTER:
*½ oz dried yeast or 1 oz fresh yeast*
*1 teaspoon honey*
*1 Vitamin C tablet (25 mg)*

AND...
*¾ pt lukewarm water*
*2 teaspoons salt*
*2 teaspoons oil*
*1 oz sesame seed (optional)*

METRIC EQUIVALENTS:
*750 g wholemeal flour*
*15 g dried yeast or 30 g fresh yeast*
*1 teaspoon honey*
*1 Vitamin C tablet (25 mg)*
*400 ml lukewarm water*
*2 teaspoons salt*
*2 teaspoons oil*
*30 g sesame seeds (optional)*

OPPOSITE:
Top: *Wholemeal Farl (Brian Binns) p.135.* Below: *Miriam Polunin's Hairy Bread p.121.*
OVERLEAF LEFT:
Top left: *Tea Brack (Theodora FitzGibbon) p.221.* Top right: *Coconut Clusters (Good Housekeeping Institute) p.102.* Centre: *Soda Bread (Theodora FitzGibbon) p.219.* Centre left and front: *Pikelets and Crumpets (Alan Long) p.238.*
OVERLEAF RIGHT:
Top: *Apricot and Hazelnut Loaf (Olive Odell, W.I.) p.140.* Centre right: *Yorkshire Tea Cakes (Brian Binns) p.128.* Bottom left: *Apple Muffins (Olive Odell, W.I.) p.138.*

*The quickest conventional wholemeal bread you can make that isn't a Grant loaf—it takes as little as 95 minutes, including baking.*

YEAST STARTER:
Put the yeast, honey and Vitamin C tablet in a cup and fill not more than two-thirds full with lukewarm water. Whisk with a fork and leave in a warm place for 10 minutes until it has a "head" like a pint of stout.

THE MIX:
Meanwhile mix the flour, salt and oil in a large bowl. If you are using sesame seeds, toast them over a low heat in an ungreased frying-pan for a minute or two, then add to the flour. Warm and grease two 1 lb (500 g) bread tins. Pour the yeast mixture and enough of the remaining water on to the flour mixture to make a dough. Mix and turn on to a floured surface. Knead for about 6 to 8 minutes or until smooth and springy. Take 2 pieces from the dough, each weighing about 1 lb (500 g). Knead each separately for half a minute, then shape into rectangles as wide as the tins. Fold into three, and drop into the tins with the seam at the bottom.

THE RISING:
Place the tins in a polythene bag and leave in a warm place for about 35 to 40 minutes.

PRE-HEAT OVEN
to 475°F (240°C) Gas 9.

VARIATIONS:
Shape the remaining dough into (a) rolls—it will make 8 small 1 oz (30 g) ones—or (b) pitta bread, making 2 thinly rolled ovals—brush lightly with oil, fold over and roll into ¼ in (5 mm) thick ovals again, or (c) pizza base, in which case leave the dough to soften for about 15 minutes before rolling it out as thinly as you can. Place on a baking sheet, cover generously with tomato purée and tomatoes, chopped mushrooms or anchovies, grated cheese and lots of oregano or basil. All these alternatives need about 15 minutes to rise, so should be ready for baking with the loaves.

BAKING TIME:
Bake the loaves for 30 to 35 minutes; if browning too quickly REDUCE HEAT to 425°F (220°C) Gas 7. Bake pitta or rolls for 10 to 15 minutes, pizza for 15 to 20. Cool the loaves on a wire tray. For pitta, wrap immediately in a tea-towel, unwrapping after a few minutes to cut along one edge and open it into a 'pocket' to stuff with salad and cheese or meat.

# Hairy Bread

*A rough bread for those who have progressed beyond wanting to produce wholemeal bread that looks just like the brown loaves the baker makes. It was christened by a friend.*

YEAST STARTER:
Place the yeast, molasses and Vitamin C tablet in a bowl or jug and fill not more than two-thirds full with lukewarm water. Leave in a warm place for 10 minutes, until frothy.

THE MIX:
Meanwhile mix the flour and the other dry ingredients in a bowl. Rub in the fat. Pour on the yeast mixture, add the egg and rest of the water, mix and turn out on to a floured surface. Knead for 10 minutes or until fairly smooth. Warm and grease a large bread tin or a baking sheet. Roll the dough in flakes of bran or wheat germ if used, then shape it into a neat oblong mound to fit the tin or sit on the sheet.

THE RISING:
Cover with polythene and leave to rise for about 50 minutes.

PRE-HEAT OVEN
to 475°F (240°C) Gas 9.

BAKING TIME:
Bake for 45 to 50 minutes. After 20 minutes, REDUCE HEAT to 400°F (200°C) Gas 6 and continue baking until the loaf parts slightly from the sides of the tin or is well browned on the baking sheet.

*In colour—page 120*

*Makes 1 loaf*

THE FLOUR:
*1 lb coarse wholemeal flour*

THE STARTER:
*¼ oz dried yeast or ½ oz fresh yeast*
*1 teaspoon molasses*
*1 Vitamin C tablet (25 mg)*

AND . . .
*¾ pt lukewarm water*
*1 oz rolled oats or bran*
*1 oz wheat germ*
*1 oz cooked brown rice or other whole grain*
*1 oz toasted sesame seeds*
*1 teaspoon sea salt*
*1 oz butter or oil*
*1 egg*
*bran or wheat germ for rolling (optional)*

METRIC EQUIVALENTS:
*500 g coarse wholemeal flour*
*8 g dried yeast or 15 g fresh yeast*
*1 teaspoon molasses*
*1 Vitamin C tablet (25 mg)*
*400m lukewarm water*
*30 g rolled oats or bran*
*30 g wheat germ*
*30 g cooked brown rice or other whole grain*
*30 g toasted sesame seeds*
*1 teaspoon sea salt*
*30 g butter or oil*
*1 egg*
*bran or wheat germ for rolling (optional)*

OPPOSITE:
Top left: *Yvonne Townsend's Dough Cake p.156-57.* Top right: *Cornish Splits, baked as a crown loaf with four splits and one on top (Mabel Sadler) p.144.* Bottom left: *Lardy Cake (Betty Grant) p.152-53. All from The Women's Institute.*

In colour—page 32

# Wholemeal Bagels

*Makes about 15*

*This is the lightest wholemeal bread and the easiest way to make rolls using wholemeal flour. Bagels are boiled before baking.*

THE FLOUR:
*1 lb wholemeal flour*

THE STARTER:
*¼ oz dried yeast or ½ oz fresh yeast*
*1 Vitamin C tablet (25 mg)*
*1 teaspoon honey*

AND . . .
*½ pt lukewarm milk*
*1 teaspoon salt*
*2 oz softened butter*
*1 egg yolk*

METRIC EQUIVALENTS:
*500 g wholemeal flour*
*8 g dried yeast or 15 g fresh yeast*
*1 Vitamin C tablet (25 mg)*
*1 teaspoon honey*
*300 ml lukewarm milk*
*1 teaspoon salt*
*60 g softened butter*
*1 egg yolk*

YEAST STARTER:
Put the yeast, Vitamin C tablet and honey in a cup with some of the milk, and leave in a warm place for 10 minutes.

THE MIX:
Put the flour and salt in a large bowl and rub in the butter. When the yeast mixture is frothy add it to the flour with the egg yolk and enough of the warm milk to make a dough. Mix and turn out on to a floured surface. Knead for about 8 minutes, until the dough is smooth and springy.

FIRST RISING:
Return to the bowl, cover and leave in a warm place for 30 minutes.

SECOND RISING:
Re-knead the dough for about half a minute. Roll into ¾ in (2 cm) diameter sausage strips, then cut off 6 in (15 cm) lengths and pinch the ends together to make rings. Place on a greased baking sheet and leave for about 15 minutes.

PRE-HEAT OVEN
to 475°F (240°C) Gas 9.

COOKING AND BAKING TIME:
Fill a wide saucepan or deep frying-pan with water, and bring to the boil. Then let the water simmer gently. Drop the rings one at a time into the simmering water. They will float. Cook for 2 minutes on each side and remove them with a fish slice. Do not let the water boil, and don't try to poach too many rings at once or they will stick to each other. Transfer to a baking sheet. Place in the pre-heated oven and bake until golden and crisp, about 20 minutes, reducing the temperature if they brown too quickly.

VARIATIONS:
Traditional toppings for bagels include caraway seeds, poppy or sesame seeds and herbs. Sprinkle the toppings on just before baking.

# Granary Croissants

*A good variation of the usual croissant made with white flour, this recipe uses Granary flour. The croissants freeze well for 3 months and come up crisp in the oven when you want to eat them.*

YEAST STARTER:
Place the yeast, honey, Vitamin C tablet and half the water in a small bowl, whisk with a fork and leave in a warm place for 10 minutes or until frothy.

THE MIX:
Beat one of the eggs. Put the flour and salt in a warm mixing bowl. Add the egg, the yeast mixture, and enough of the remaining water to make a softish but workable dough. Knead thoroughly for 8 to 10 minutes.

FIRST SHAPING:
Roll into an oblong, about 6 x 21 in (15 x 53.5 cm). Divide the butter into three pieces. Cut one piece into small cubes and dot evenly over two-thirds of the dough. Fold the unbuttered end over, then the other end on top. Turn the dough sideways anti-clockwise, and repeat this process twice, using the remaining butter.
Put the folded dough on a floured sheet and cover with polythene. Place in the refrigerator for 30 minutes.

SECOND SHAPING:
Roll and fold the dough as before (but without butter) a further three times. Chill for another 30 minutes.
On a floured surface, roll the dough out into a large circle, about 17 in (43 cm) across. Don't stretch the dough—it must be moving without sticking to the surface beneath. Don't worry if the edge of the circle is not perfectly even!
Let the dough sit for 10 minutes. Cut the circle into 12 even wedges. Let them rest for a few minutes. Warm and slightly grease one or two baking sheets. Beat up the second egg in a cup with 2 teaspoons of water and a pinch of sea salt, and brush the wedges. Roll up each wedge *loosely* towards the point, finishing with the point underneath.

THE RISING:
Place on the baking sheets and brush with the egg mix again. Cover with polythene and leave to rise for about 40 minutes.

PRE-HEAT OVEN
to 475°F (240°C) Gas 9.

BAKING TIME:
Bake for 15 to 20 minutes. After 10 minutes REDUCE HEAT to 425°F (220°C) Gas 7. Cool on a rack.

*Makes 12 large croissants*

THE FLOUR:
*1 lb* Granary *flour*

THE STARTER:
*1 tablespoon dried yeast*
*1 teaspoon honey*
*1 Vitamin C tablet (25 mg)*

AND...
*8 fl.oz lukewarm water*
*2 eggs*
*1 good teaspoon sea salt*
*8 oz butter, chilled*

METRIC EQUIVALENTS:
*500 g Granary flour*
*1 tablespoon dried yeast*
*1 teaspoon honey*
*1 Vitamin C tablet (25 mg)*
*250 ml lukewarm water*
*2 eggs*
*1 good teaspoon sea salt*
*250 g butter, chilled*

# Fruit Cake With Yeast

*Makes 1 large cake*

THE FLOUR:
*5 oz wholemeal flour*

THE STARTER:
*2 teaspoons dried yeast*
*1 teaspoon honey*
*about 6 fl.oz lukewarm water*

AND...
*3 oz chopped dried apricots*
*    (a chopped, scrubbed lemon*
*    or orange could be*
*    substituted)*
*3 oz raisins*
*3 oz sultanas*
*2 tablespoons honey*
*2 generous teaspoons mixed*
*    spice*
*1 heaped teaspoon cinnamon*
*3 oz chopped nuts or peanuts*
*½ oz softened butter*
*3 oz chopped apple*
*sesame seeds to decorate*
*    (optional)*

METRIC EQUIVALENTS:
*150 g wholemeal flour*
*2 teaspoons dried yeast*
*1 teaspoon honey*
*about 150 to 200 ml lukewarm water*
*90 g chopped dried apricots (or a*
*    chopped, scrubbed lemon or*
*    orange)*
*90 g raisins*
*90 g sultanas*
*2 tablespoons honey*
*2 generous teaspoons mixed spice*
*1 heaped teaspoon cinnamon*
*90 g chopped nuts or peanuts*
*15 g softened butter*
*90 g chopped apple*
*sesame seeds to decorate (optional)*

*A large amount of fruit and spice is used in this yeast-risen cake. The attraction of raising cakes with yeast is both nutritional and practical. It's a way of making very enjoyable cakes with only a little fat and sweetener in them. Normal cakes depend a lot on fat and sweeteners for texture as well as for flavour. It also gives an even rise—no cracked peaks in the middle of flat cakes.*

PREPARATION:
Clean the dried fruits by covering them with water and bringing to the boil. Drain well and discard the water.

YEAST STARTER:
Mix the yeast, the teaspoon of honey, and the water in a small bowl. Whisk with a fork and leave in a warm place for 10 minutes until frothy.

THE MIX:
Put the flour into a large mixing bowl. Add the honey, mixed spice, cinnamon, dried fruits (and lemon or orange if using), chopped nuts, butter, and chopped apple. Now add the yeast mixture and stir quite vigorously for about 2 minutes. Add a little more liquid if necessary to make a dropping consistency. Transfer to a large well greased bread or cake tin. Cover with polythene and leave in a warm place until slightly risen and puffy, about 1 hour.

TO DECORATE:
Sprinkle with sesame seeds before putting in the oven if liked. For an alternative decoration, lay a row of orange or apple slices and nuts along the top and glaze with honey after baking.

PRE-HEAT OVEN
to 475°F (240°C) Gas 9.

BAKING TIME:
Bake for 40 minutes until firm on top. After 10 minutes REDUCE HEAT to 425°F (220°C) Gas 7. Cool on a cake rack.

# Brian Binns

Brian Binns, who trained as a professional baker and was a Chief Executive with Allied Bakeries, is also a gifted and inventive home cook. In 1977 he won The Sunday Times Meat Cookery competition, and has since published two cookery books.

At home in Lancashire he and his wife Vanessa often entertain and they usually bake their own bread. "When we want something good", says Brian, "we make it at home ourselves, but sometimes we buy from small bakeries. We're very selective."

He has serious reservations about plant bread: "It needs more fermentation and should be baked longer." He also finds many small bakeries wanting: "It isn't easy to change the big industries; wrapped and sliced is needed by the country as a whole. But the small baker could make more of the present trend. Some small bakers produce excellent bread but others, particularly the "hot bread" merchants, take short cuts using additives and short processes, ending up with bread that may be fresher but is not as well made or as cheap as that supplied by plant bakeries." Brian knows what a small baker can achieve. He also knows what the small baker is up against.

He has worked in several bakeries and has experienced the long unsociable hours and physical discomforts of the job, as well as the pleasures of learning and using a skill. At 15, Brian was apprenticed to Bill Hurrel's bakery in Middleton, near Manchester. Work started at six each morning and went on until the evening:

"There were old pine tables and a pine dresser. Leslie Williams, the baker, taught me how to mould and shape the loaves. I learnt the whole process of fermentation, leaving the dough for 3 hours or a whole day. We made brown bread, Hovis and a bread that isn't often available now called Turog. And we made real oven-bottom muffins."

He was fascinated by the skill and speed with which you had to use the peel—a flat-based pole for manoeuvering the muffins, and taking goods from the oven. "You set the muffins in the oven with it, then you had to whip it away quickly leaving the muffins on the oven floor. You had to position them correctly so that halfway through baking you could turn them over. And then, whisk, and out they came. Delicious."

Brian learnt the skills and also the fun of baking.

Ex-policeman, Bill Hurrel, gave a lot of freedom to the bakers. Sometimes he would "come on the table" with them and mould tea cakes and bread and he sang in a deep baritone voice as he rolled the dough.

At the next bakery where Brian worked, Fittons of Heywood, he learnt to use the slip, a long narrow peel, like a long shelf, demanding greater dexterity and accuracy than the peel. "We would spend three or four hours a day just making and baking oven-bottom muffins. We had coke-fired stone-bottom ovens. The muffins had a big crust, they were slightly tough and charred, with a great flavour."

Here they baked "good old traditional" breads: Coburgs and bloomers and cottage loaves; and they prepared overnight sponges—ferments that were left for twelve or even twenty-four hours.

Brian was fascinated by the fermentation process. His knowledge increased as he experimented with cooking methods in the test kitchens of Southern Oil Company and Sayer's Confectioners Limited. But it was Peter Bakalarski, an ex-Battle of Britain pilot, who ran a small bakery near Blackburn, who taught him most: "Peter gave me my first experience in the use of barms. He had about twenty tubs fermenting away in his bakery. They were different colours, made with different flours. He put my skills to shame."

He made Kaiser rolls—small white rolls with pleats and pointed corners: "I watched him fold and shape the pleats, doing work that is now done by machines. It was a wonderful experience."

Brian perfected his craft by watching others at work, and practising. He entered—and on several occasions won—competitions. He met all the great bakers of his time—Ronnie Adams, who made Princess Margaret's wedding cake, Harold Waterfield, Frank Webster, who had his own method of fermentation, Joe Horspool, and Bill Spencer.

"These men all had businesses that made good bread. They entered and won competitions. They know the subject inside out and they were respected by their trade for their knowledge of baking. Then, it was bread, not wrapped and sliced."

Today, Brian who used to bring home bread straight from the oven at Allied Bakeries, teaches his five-year-old daughter to bake.

He is a perfectionist. To him the average home-made loaf is not good enough. "You need space. No draughts. The water temperature must be right. You can't be haphazard about making bread—not if you want good results. Don't take short cuts—there aren't any, unless you're an expert."

He admits that in days gone by people made bread under all sorts of conditions, some even worse than bad: "Their bread was probably passable, but why make it if you can buy better?"

If plant-baked bread is lacking and home-made bread is at best only passable, what is the answer for the average family?

"The small baker couldn't take over from the plant baker, but the good small baker is doing well. There are queues outside his bakery. The public is discerning but the small baker isn't exploiting the opportunity he has. The labour cost is high in confectionery, not so with bread. He has to realise this potential and exploit it."

While we wait for this to happen, here are some of Brian's own favourite loaves.

# Rye Bread

*Makes 1 tin loaf and 1 baton loaf*

THE FLOUR:
*14 oz strong white flour*
*14 oz rye flour or meal*

THE STARTER:
*¾ oz fresh yeast*
*1 teaspoon honey*
*1 teaspoon black treacle*
*about 16 fl.oz warm water*

AND...
*½ oz caraway seeds*
*3 level teaspoons salt*

METRIC EQUIVALENTS:
*400 g strong white flour*
*400 g rye flour or meal*
*20 g fresh yeast*
*1 teaspoon honey*
*1 teaspoon black treacle*
*about 450 ml warm water*
*15 g caraway seeds*
*3 level teaspoons salt*

*This recipe makes two good nutritional loaves with a fairly close texture, using equal quantities of rye and white flour and a sprinkling of caraway seeds.*

YEAST STARTER:
Mix the honey, treacle and water together in a bowl and whisk in the yeast until thoroughly blended.

THE MIX:
Mix the white flour, rye flour, caraway seeds, and salt together in a large bowl. Make a well in the centre and pour in the yeast mixture. Gradually draw in the flour, mixing vigorously to make a soft, sticky dough.

FIRST RISING:
Put the dough in a warm, greased bowl, cover with greased polythene and leave to rise in a warm place for 1 hour.

SECOND RISING:
Turn out the dough onto a work-surface, knock out the air and knead to a smooth ball. Return to the bowl, cover again and put to rise for another 30 minutes.

THE SHAPING:
Cut off about one-third of the dough and mould this to fit a warmed and greased 1 lb (500 g) bread tin. Knead and mould the remaining two-thirds into a fat baton, like a heavy rolling pin and place on a greased and warm baking sheet.

THIRD RISING:
Cover both the tin and baking sheet with greased polythene and put to rise for 25 minutes.

FOURTH RISING:
Using a razor blade or very sharp knife make a ½ in (1.5 cm) deep
cut from end to end of the tin loaf. Make diagonal cuts in the baton
loaf about ¼ in (5 mm) deep and ¾ in (2 cm) apart. Sprinkle each
loaf with a little rye flour, cover and put back to rise for 15 minutes.

PRE-HEAT OVEN
to 425°F (220°C) Gas 7.

BAKING TIME:
Bake for 30 to 35 minutes.

## *Sally Lunn Loaf*

*This sweetened bread is said to have been first made in the late
eighteenth century by the pastry-cook Sally Lunn of Bath. She
sold her cakes mainly to the wealthy, who came to take the waters.
Serve the bread as soon as it's cool enough to cut with a knife.*

YEAST STARTER:
Warm a basin and mix the yeast, honey and 2 oz (60 g) of the flour
in it, gradually stirring in the water to make a smooth, thin paste.
Cover with greased polythene and put in a warm place to rise for
20 minutes.

THE MIX:
Sieve the rest of the flour into a large mixing bowl. Make a well in
the centre and put in the honey, beaten egg and lemon rind. Pour in
the yeast mixture, mix vigorously and knead to make a smooth
dough. Knead in the softened butter, shape the dough into a ball,
and put in a warm, lightly buttered bowl.

FIRST RISING:
Cover with greased polythene and put in a warm place to rise for
30 minutes.

SECOND RISING:
Divide the risen dough into three, shape each piece into a ball and
put into warm, lightly buttered 5 in (13 cm) cake tins. Cover with
greased polythene and leave to rise in a warm place for 35 to 40
minutes. After 20 minutes brush the top with beaten egg.

PRE-HEAT OVEN
to 450°F (230°C) Gas 8.

BAKING TIME:
Bake for 15 minutes.

*Makes 3 loaves*

THE FLOUR:
*12 oz strong white flour*

THE STARTER:
*¾ oz fresh yeast*
*1 level teaspoon honey*
*¼ pt warm water*

AND . . .
*1 tablespoon honey*
*1 egg, beaten*
*finely grated rind of 1 lemon*
*2 oz softened butter*
*a little beaten egg to glaze*

METRIC EQUIVALENTS:
*350 g strong white flour*
*20 g fresh yeast*
*1 level teaspoon honey*
*150 ml warm water*
*1 tablespoon honey*
*1 egg, beaten*
*finely grated rind of 1 lemon*
*60 g softened butter*
*a little beaten egg to glaze*

# Yorkshire Tea Cakes

In colour—page 120

*Makes 10 to 12*

THE FLOUR:
10 oz strong white flour
6 oz wholemeal flour

THE STARTER:
1 oz fresh yeast
1 tablespoon honey
½ pt warm milk

AND . . .
2 oz currants
2 oz sultanas
1 level teaspoon salt
1½ oz butter

METRIC EQUIVALENTS:
300 g strong white flour
175 g wholemeal flour
30 g fresh yeast
1 tablespoon honey
300 ml warm milk
60 g currants
60 g sultanas
1 level teaspoon salt
40 g butter

*Fruit tea cakes were originally prepared at Lent. Serve them split open and buttered or toasted and buttered. Traditionally these tea cakes were made with all white flour. This recipe uses a mixture of wholemeal and white flour.*

YEAST STARTER:
Dissolve the honey in the milk and use 3 tablespoons of the liquid to mix the yeast to a smooth paste. Stir in the rest of the milk.

THE MIX:
Wash the currants and sultanas in warm water, pat dry with kitchen paper and leave in a warm place. Sieve the flour and salt into a large bowl, rub in the butter and make a well in the middle. Pour in the yeast liquid. Mix well in, then knead until dough is smooth and elastic in texture. Work in the warm slightly moist fruit. Shape the dough into a ball and put in a warm, greased bowl.

FIRST RISING:
Cover the bowl with greased polythene and set in a warm place to rise for 45 minutes.

SECOND RISING:
Turn the dough out on to a lightly floured board and knead for a few minutes to a smooth, even texture. Reshape dough into a ball, cover again and put to rise for 15 minutes.
Divide the dough into 10 to 12 pieces, each weighing about 3 oz (90 g). Shape each piece into a smooth ball, and set to one side under a sheet of greased polythene. Leave for about 5 minutes while you warm two lightly buttered baking sheets.
Roll out the dough balls with a rolling pin into 3½ in (9 cm) discs. Place on the baking sheets about 1 in (2.5 cm) apart.

THIRD RISING:
Cover with greased polythene and set to rise in a warm place for 35 to 45 minutes.

PRE-HEAT OVEN
to 435°F (225°C) Gas 7½.

BAKING TIME:
Bake for about 10 minutes, or until golden-brown.

OPPOSITE:
Top left: *Wholemeal Sourdough Bread, baked in a French stick style from Margaret Oldman p.147.* Top right: *Cheese and Herb Plait from Shirley Nash p.148.* Below: *Walnut and Onion Loaf (Dinah Morrison) p.180.*

# *Pikelets and Crumpets*

*Pikelets are thin versions of crumpets, baked on a griddle without the need for a ring to hold their shape. Crumpets are descendants of "crompid cake"—a griddle-baked cake, first recorded in the seventeenth century, which was so thin that it curled up. Make rings for crumpets out of small cans with the top and bottom removed, such as a baked bean can. Eat pikelets hot from the pan or leave to cool then toast and butter. Serve crumpets toasted and buttered.*

*Makes 8 to 10*

THE FLOUR:
*8 oz strong white flour*

THE STARTER:
*½ oz fresh yeast*

AND . . .
*1 level teaspoon salt*
*¼ pt warm milk*
*¼ pt warm water*
*¼ teaspoon bicarbonate of soda*
*4 tablespoons cold water*
*1 lightly beaten egg white*

METRIC EQUIVALENTS:
*250 g strong white flour*
*15 g fresh yeast*
*1 level teaspoon salt*
*150 ml warm milk*
*150 ml warm water*
*¼ teaspoon bicarbonate of soda*
*4 tablespoons cold water*
*1 lightly beaten egg white*

THE MIX:
Sieve the flour and salt together in a large mixing bowl and mix in the yeast. Mix together the warm milk and warm water and pour into the bowl.

THE RISING:
Beat vigorously for 5 minutes to make a smooth batter, then cover and put in a warm place for about 30 minutes or until the risen mixture starts to drop.
Dissolve the bicarbonate of soda in the cold water and beat it into the batter. Carefully fold in the beaten egg white to produce a batter the consistency of thick pouring cream.

COOKING TIME:
Heat a lightly greased griddle, hot plate or heavy based frying-pan until a drop of the batter sizzles immediately on contact.
Put a full tablespoon of the batter on to the hot surface and cook until the top of the pikelet is no longer wet.
Turn over with a palette knife, and cook until the other side is lightly browned. Continue until all the batter is used.

TO MAKE CRUMPETS:
Prepare the batter with 1 oz (30 g) more flour and cook on one side only. Cook with the batter in a greased 3 in (8 cm) ring in the pan or on the cooking surface.

OPPOSITE:
Top: *Peggy Williams' Doughnuts, split open and filled with jam and cream p.154.* Centre: *Doris Grant's Date Loaf p.69.* Below: *Dinah Morrison's Buckwheat and Buttermilk Waffles p.180-81.*

In colour—page 105

# Bath Buns

*Makes 16*

*Bath buns are probably the easiest buns to make, using the sponge or ferment method. Originally they were made without fruit, but with added spices. They were decorated with sugar-coated caraway seeds. An early seventeenth century recipe for Bath Cake uses the same ingredients.*

THE FLOUR:
*12 oz strong white flour*

THE STARTER:
*¾ oz fresh yeast*
*1 large egg, beaten*
*¼ pt warm water*
*1 rounded teaspoon honey*

AND . . .
*1 tablespoon honey*
*3 oz softened butter*
*4 oz sultanas*
*1 oz chopped candied lemon peel*
*finely grated rind of 1 lemon*
*a little beaten egg to glaze*

METRIC EQUIVALENTS:
*350 g strong white flour*
*20 g fresh yeast*
*1 large egg, beaten*
*150 ml warm water*
*1 rounded teaspoon honey*
*1 tablespoon honey*
*90 g softened butter*
*125 g sultanas*
*30 g chopped candied lemon peel*
*finely grated rind of 1 lemon*
*a little beaten egg to glaze*

YEAST STARTER:
Stir the beaten egg and warm water together to make up 7½ fl.oz (225 ml) of liquid comfortably warm to the touch. Dissolve the teaspoon of honey in it. Use 3 tablespoons of this liquid to mix the yeast to a smooth paste in a large bowl. Stir in the remaining liquid and whisk in 2 oz (60 g) of the flour to make a smooth batter. Cover the bowl with polythene and put in a warm place to rise for 30 minutes.

THE MIX:
Sieve the rest of the flour into a large bowl and make a well in the centre. Add the tablespoon of honey to the yeast mixture and pour this into the well. Gradually draw in the flour and work the ingredients together to form a stiff dough. Knead in the softened butter a little at a time until the dough has a silky look. Shape it into a ball, place in a greased bowl that has been slightly warmed.

FIRST RISING:
Cover with a greased sheet of polythene and stand in a warm place for 1 hour, or until the dough has nearly trebled in size.
Turn the dough onto a work-surface and put the sultanas, candied peel and lemon rind on top. Knead them in until they are evenly distributed and the dough has a smooth texture. Cover it with polythene and leave for 5 minutes.

SECOND RISING:
Divide the dough into 16 pieces, by pulling and tearing, not by cutting. Put the rough pieces, well spaced out, on a lightly buttered warmed baking sheet. Cover with polythene and put to rise in a warm place for 15 to 20 minutes.

THIRD RISING:
Brush the buns over lightly with beaten egg, and put to rise, uncovered, for 20 minutes.

PRE-HEAT OVEN
to 450°F (230°C) Gas 8.

BAKING TIME:
Bake for about 10 minutes or until golden-brown.

# Herb Bread

In colour—page 105

*The herbs in this light, open-textured loaf can be varied to suit individual taste, for example you may wish to use marjoram and thyme instead of the tarragon. Serve with cheese or pâté or any cold meat.*

*Makes 2 small loaves*

YEAST STARTER:
Mix the beaten egg with the warm milk and use 3 tablespoons of this to mix the fresh yeast into a thin paste. Put aside for about 5 to 10 minutes to allow the yeast to work.

THE FLOUR:
*6 oz wholemeal flour*
*6 oz strong white flour*

THE STARTER:
*¾ oz fresh yeast*
*1 large egg, beaten*
*about 6 fl.oz warm milk*

THE MIX:
Stir the rest of the mixed egg and milk into the yeast mixture. Add the oil, honey and herbs.
Mix the salt with the flours and sieve three-quarters of it into the liquid ingredients. Beat well, with a wooden spoon for 4 to 5 minutes until you have a soft, creamy dough. Stir in the remaining flour and divide the mixture between two well-greased 1 lb (500 g) loaf tins, preferably long and narrow.

AND . . .
*1 tablespoon sunflower oil*
*2 level teaspoons honey*
*1 level teaspoon tarragon or*
*  other herbs*
*1½ level teaspoons salt*
*fennel seeds for sprinkling*

THE RISING:
Cover the tins with greased polythene and put in a warm place for 30 to 35 minutes for the dough to rise.

METRIC EQUIVALENTS:
*175 g wholemeal flour*
*175 g strong white flour*
*20 g fresh yeast*
*1 large egg, beaten*
*150 to 200 ml warm milk*
*1 tablespoon sunflower oil*
*2 level teaspoons honey*
*1 level teaspoon tarragon or other*
*  herbs*
*1½ level teaspoons salt*
*fennel seeds for sprinkling*

PRE-HEAT OVEN
to 350°F (180°C) Gas 4.

BAKING TIME:
Sprinkle the tops of the loaves with fennel seeds and bake for 25 to 30 minutes.

# *Butter Buns*

*Makes 20*

*These rich, sweet buns have a lemon curd filling.*

THE FLOUR:
*1 lb 2 oz strong white flour*

THE STARTER:
*1 oz fresh yeast*
*1 large egg, beaten*
*about 6 fl.oz warm water*
*1 teaspoon honey*

AND . . .
*¼ teaspoon salt*
*2 tablespoons honey*
*2 oz softened butter*
*2 oz melted butter*
*lemon curd for filling*
*a little beaten egg to glaze*

METRIC EQUIVALENTS:
*560 g strong white flour*
*30 g fresh yeast*
*1 large egg, beaten*
*150 to 200 ml warm water*
*1 teaspoon honey*
*¼ teaspoon salt*
*2 tablespoons honey*
*60 g softened butter*
*60 g melted butter*
*lemon curd for filling*
*a little beaten egg to glaze*

YEAST STARTER:
Mix the beaten egg with enough warm water to give ½ pt (300 ml) of liquid. Mix the yeast and 1 teaspoon of honey to a smooth paste in 3 tablespoons of the liquid. Add the remaining liquid and whisk in 4 oz (125 g) of the flour. Cover and put in a warm place for 30 minutes.

THE MIX:
Sieve the remaining flour and salt into a large bowl and make a well in the centre. Pour on the yeast mixture and add the 2 tablespoons of honey. Mix vigorously until you have a soft, sticky dough.

FIRST RISING:
Knead in the softened butter well, then mould the dough into a ball and put in a warm, greased bowl. Cover with greased polythene and put in a warm place to rise for 45 minutes.
Turn out the risen dough onto a work-surface, knock out any bubbles and divide it into 20 equal parts. Mould these into balls, cover them with the polythene and leave to rest for 5 minutes.
Roll out each ball into a disc ⅛ in (3 mm) thick, brush with melted butter, almost to the edge and place ½ teaspoon of lemon curd in the centre. Fold the disc in half, brush again with melted butter and fold again to make a quarter-circle.

SECOND RISING:
Space out on greased baking sheets. Brush over with beaten egg. Put in a warm place, uncovered, for 25 to 30 minutes.

PRE-HEAT OVEN
to 425°F (220°C) Gas 7.

BAKING TIME:
Bake for about 10 minutes.

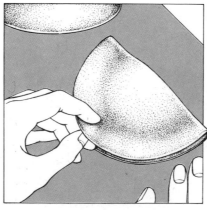
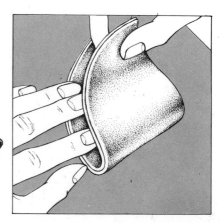

# Christmas Loaf

*This Christmas loaf was originally baked during the days of the Depression between the two wars, as a substitute for Christmas cake. It is now more often served on a special occasion. If possible, prepare it two weeks in advance and pour some ale over the cooked loaf to give a rich and improved texture.*

YEAST STARTER:
Mix the beaten egg and warm milk together in a large bowl to give ¼ pt (150 ml) of liquid. Whisk the yeast, 2 teaspoons of honey and 2 oz (60 g) of the flour into the liquid until thoroughly blended. Cover with polythene and put in a warm place for 30 minutes.

THE MIX:
Cream the butter in a large bowl and gradually add the 3 tablespoons of honey and the black treacle. Beat in the egg, then sieve in the flour, salt, baking powder, nutmeg and mixed spice. Mix together roughly then pour in the yeast mixture and mix well until the ingredients are well blended and smooth. Work currants, sultanas and peel into the mixture until evenly distributed. Divide the dough in half and shape each portion to fit into a 1 lb (500 g) loaf tin, warmed and well greased.

THE RISING:
Cover the tins with greased polythene and put to rise in a warm place for 45 minutes.

PRE-HEAT OVEN
to 400°F (200°C) Gas 6.

BAKING TIME:
Bake for 35 to 40 minutes.
A larger cake can be made by using one 2 lb (1 kg) tin and baking the cake for 1 hour.

*Makes 2 small loaves*

THE FLOUR:
*10 oz strong white flour*

THE STARTER:
*½ oz fresh yeast*
*1 large egg, beaten*
*about 5 tablespoons warm milk*
*2 teaspoons honey*

AND . . .
*4 oz butter*
*3 tablespoons honey*
*1 tablespoon black treacle*
*1 large egg, beaten*
*1 level teaspoon salt*
*2 level teaspoons baking powder*
*1 level teaspoon grated nutmeg*
*2 level teaspoons ground mixed spice*
*8 oz currants*
*4 oz sultanas*
*1 oz mixed, chopped dried peel*

METRIC EQUIVALENTS:
*300 g strong white flour*
*15 g fresh yeast*
*1 large egg, beaten*
*about 5 tablespoons warm milk*
*2 teaspoons honey*
*125 g butter*
*3 tablespoons honey*
*1 tablespoon black treacle*
*1 large egg, beaten*
*1 level teaspoon salt*
*2 level teaspoons baking powder*
*1 level teaspoon grated nutmeg*
*2 level teaspoons ground mixed spice*
*250 g currants*
*125 g sultanas*
*30 g mixed, chopped dried peel*

*In colour—page 217*

# Farthing Buns

*In Victorian times, a farthing could buy one of these sweet buttery buns.*

*Makes about 40*

THE FLOUR:
*1 lb 2 oz strong white flour*

THE STARTER:
*1 large egg, beaten*
*about 7½ fl. oz warm water*
*1 oz fresh yeast*
*1 teaspoon honey*

AND . . .
*¼ teaspoon salt*
*3 tablespoons honey*
*2 oz butter, softened but not oily*
*4 oz mixed dried fruit*
*1 oz melted butter for brushing*
*1 teaspoon clear honey*

METRIC EQUIVALENTS:
*560 g strong white flour*
*1 large egg, beaten*
*about 225 ml warm water*
*30 g fresh yeast*
*1 teaspoon honey*
*¼ teaspoon salt*
*3 tablespoons honey*
*60 g butter, softened but not oily*
*125 g mixed dried fruit*
*30 g melted butter to brush over*
*1 teaspoon clear honey*

YEAST STARTER:
Combine the beaten egg with enough warm water to make ½ pt (300 ml). Mix the yeast to a smooth paste in 3 tablespoons of the liquid. Add the rest of the liquid and whisk in 4 oz (125 g) of the flour and 1 teaspoon of honey to make a smooth batter. Cover and put in a warm place for 30 minutes.

THE MIX:
Sieve the remaining flour and salt into a large bowl. Make a well in the centre, pour in the yeast mixture and add the 3 tablespoons of honey. Gradually draw in the flour and mix vigorously to a soft, sticky dough.
Knead in the softened butter thoroughly until the dough is smooth and silky in texture. Mould into a ball, place in a lightly greased bowl, that has been warmed.

FIRST RISING:
Cover with greased polythene and put in a warm place to rise for 45 minutes.
Turn out the risen dough on to a work-surface, knock out any air bubbles and knead in the dried fruit. Cover the dough with the greased polythene and leave on the work-surface to rest for 5 minutes.
Roll out the dough to a rectangle about ¼ in (5 mm) thick and brush some of the melted butter over the surface, starting at one of the shorter ends of the rectangle and continuing over two-thirds of the sheet of dough. Fold the unbuttered third over the centre third

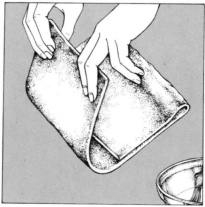

of the dough and the remaining third over these two. Cover the dough again and leave it to rest on the work-surface for 10 minutes. Roll out the dough again into a rectangle not more than ¼ in (5 mm) thick. Add the teaspoon of honey to the rest of the melted butter and brush this over all the surface. Cut the dough into pieces about 3 in (8 cm) and 1 in (2.5 cm) wide.

SECOND RISING:
Arrange the pieces about ½ in (1.5 cm) apart on a greased baking sheet. Cover with greased polythene and put in a warm place to rise for 35 minutes.

PRE-HEAT OVEN
to 425°F (220°C) Gas 7.

BAKING TIME:
Bake for about 10 minutes or until golden-brown.

# Wholemeal Farl

In colour—page 120

*A farl is a "cake" made of flour or oatmeal. This version incorporates both; the result is delicious.*

*Makes 8*

YEAST STARTER:
Cream the yeast with the honey in the lukewarm water. Add the Vitamin C. Set aside for about 10 minutes.

THE FLOUR:
*1 lb 12 oz wholemeal flour*
*4 oz medium oatmeal*

THE MIX:
Mix the wholemeal flour, oatmeal, salt and baking powder in a large bowl and rub in the butter. Add the yeast mixture and mix vigorously to a nice dough—not too soft.

THE STARTER:
*2 oz fresh yeast*
*2 teaspoons honey*
*2 Vitamin C tablets (50 mg)*

THE SHAPING:
Divide the dough into two equal portions. Shape each into a round ball and place on baking sheets dusted with oatmeal. Press the balls into discs about 1¼ in (3 cm) thick. Cut each disc into 4 segments and separate the segments by about ¼ in (5 mm). Sprinkle with oatmeal.

AND...
*about 1 pt lukewarm water*
*1 level tablespoon baking
    powder*
*½ oz salt*
*2 oz butter*

THE RISING:
Cover with a moist cloth or polythene and leave to prove at room temperature for about 1¼ hours.

METRIC EQUIVALENTS:
*850 g wholemeal flour*
*125 g medium oatmeal*
*60 g fresh yeast*
*2 teaspoons honey*
*2 Vitamin C tablets (50 mg)*
*about 600 ml lukewarm water*
*1 level tablespoon baking powder*
*15 g salt*
*60 g butter*

PRE-HEAT OVEN
to 400°F (200°C) Gas 6.

BAKING TIME:
Bake for about 35 minutes until golden-brown.

# Olive Odell and The Women's Institute

As long as The Women's Institute exists, its enthusiasm will keep alive many home crafts, like baking.

One of the most inspiring figures of The Women's Institute is Olive Odell, cookery writer, lecturer, food consultant and former National Vice-chairman of the W.I. Not only is she a superb cook who specialises in preserves (her recent invention is a masterful peach, orange and walnut jam), she is also constantly in touch with the best cooks in all the counties. She has selected some of her own favourite breads, and put together a collection of breads from some of the good home bakers she has come across in her travels across the country.

Olive Odell lives in Worcestershire in a seventeenth-century farmhouse on the land her husband Alan has farmed for more than 40 years. The pantry off the surprisingly modern and spotless kitchen is lined with jars of Olive's home-made preserves.

She's been baking since she was sixteen, which was shortly after her mother let her loose in the kitchen. Her mother was a great encouragement. She didn't watch over her daughter's first attempts —and they were disastrous.

"I believed that if one teaspoon of anything was good, then two must be better. I was using brewer's yeast. It's very runny. The bread overflowed everywhere. It smelt like a brewhouse—and was quite inedible. Only I enjoyed it. But it did teach me the principle of always following a recipe. It also made me more determined."

Her determination led her to master a wholemeal and white mixed loaf and a plain white loaf. During her years as a medical student her time was limited, though she did extend her range to cheese bread, herb bread, tea rings and Chelsea buns. These weren't always successful—either to her husband's taste—"he's quite conservative"—or to her father's. When she proudly produced her first herb bread, her father remarked: "Jolly good job we've got three hungry dogs."

Olive was not deterred: "Whatever you make, not everything will be appreciated. Especially not by your own family. If I don't succeed, I want to know why."

As a mother of three young children, Olive joined The Women's Institute with the intention of learning more about home crafts. Here, her love of

cooking was encouraged, and soon she was studying to take her W.I. advanced cookery exams. She is now a qualified judge of cookery, specialising in preserves. And these preserves she often serves on her own home-made bread.

One of Olive's favourite loaves is the soda bread her mother used to make: "Father was a brewer, so mother usually made her bread with brewer's yeast. It was called barm—the old name for yeast, and looked like the white froth on top of stout. But when we were in Ireland, which was for about six months of the year, mother made the local bread, without yeast. She cooked it in a *bastable*—a shallow iron cooking pot with three legs." This is how they've made bread in Ireland for thousands of years—the average family had no oven.

"We stood the pot on the red ashes of a fire and heaped ashes on top. Then we ate the bread, hot and buttered, right there on the grass. It was fun. And from mother's point of view it had the whole family involved."

Olive turned cooking from a hobby into a profession. She is the author of two cookery books and was consultant for several others, including the Reader's Digest *Farmhouse Cookery* and *Food from your Garden.* She's also an informal teacher, giving occasional cooking—including bread-making—classes in her own kitchen. Here are her tips to anyone starting out for the first time:

1. Get used to handling the dough. A lot of people think it's a delicate and complicated process. In fact, you should knock it about roughly.
2. Don't be put off by first disasters.
3. Master the basics first. Try plain wholemeal bread; it's the simplest to make.

## Bastable or Soda Bread

*This bread was first made in lidded iron pots, and baked over a fire-place, sometimes with smouldering turfs of peat laid on the lid to give even heat. The* bastable *had three legs and could stand on the hearthstone. Not a loaf for keeping: eat it within 48 hours. Best eaten warm, with butter, honey or herb cream cheese. This recipe uses all wholemeal flour, but it can also be made with a mixture of wholemeal and white flour, e.g. two-thirds wholemeal, one-third white.*

PRE-HEAT OVEN
to 350°F (180°C) Gas 4.

THE MIX:
Mix the flour, cream of tartar, bicarbonate of soda and the salt thoroughly, then rub in the butter. Add the honey and mix to a soft dough with the milk. Some flours take up more liquid than others, so it is difficult to be absolutely exact. Pat into a flattish round loaf and place on a greased baking sheet. Using the back of a knife, mark into quarters.

BAKING TIME:
Bake for about 45 minutes.

*Makes 1 small loaf*

THE FLOUR:
*1 lb wholemeal flour*

THE RAISING AGENTS:
*½ teaspoon cream of tartar*
*¾ teaspoon bicarbonate of soda*

AND . . .
*pinch of salt*
*½ oz butter*
*1 teaspoon honey*
*½ pt (approx) milk, buttermilk, or sour milk*

METRIC EQUIVALENTS:
*500 g wholemeal flour*
*½ teaspoon cream of tartar*
*¾ teaspoon bicarbonate of soda*
*pinch of salt*
*15 g butter*
*1 teaspoon honey*
*300 ml (approx) milk, buttermilk, or sour milk*

# Apple Muffins

In colour—page 120

*Makes 12*

THE FLOUR:
*4 oz white flour*
*4 oz wholemeal flour*

THE RAISING AGENT:
*1 teaspoon baking powder*

AND...
*3 oz butter*
*3 cooking apples*
*1 egg, beaten*
*1 tablespoon honey*
*milk, if needed*

METRIC EQUIVALENTS:
*125 g white flour*
*125 g wholemeal flour*
*1 teaspoon baking powder*
*90 g butter*
*3 cooking apples*
*1 egg, beaten*
*1 tablespoon honey*
*milk, if needed*

*Apples give these soft muffins a sweet and sour flavour. Eat them hot and split open with a hunk of mature Cheddar cheese. They also toast well when cold. These muffins can be made with all white flour if your prefer.*

THE MIX:
Mix the flours and baking powder together. Rub in the butter. Peel, core and grate the apples and mix with the beaten egg and honey. Add to the dry ingredients and mix well together. Add a little milk if the mixture is too dry, but the mixture should not be too wet, as the apples release their juice during cooking. Roll the dough out to ½ in (1.5 cm) thick. Cut into small rounds and place on a greased baking sheet.

PRE-HEAT OVEN
to 350°F (180°C) Gas 4.

BAKING TIME:
Bake for 25 to 30 minutes.

# Christmas Bread

*Makes 2 small loaves*

THE FLOUR:
*1 lb strong white flour*

THE STARTER:
*½ oz fresh yeast or ¼ oz dried yeast*

AND...
*5 fl.oz lukewarm milk*
*1 tablespoon honey*
*½ teaspoon salt*
*2 oz butter at room temperature*
*1 egg, beaten*
*a little melted butter*
*4 oz raisins or sultanas*
*2 oz chopped glacé cherries*
*2 oz chopped glacé fruits
   or candied peel*

*A bread bursting with good Christmas ingredients, full of promise, but not too rich.*

YEAST STARTER:
Mix the yeast with 2 tablespoons of the warm milk and leave for about 5 minutes.

THE MIX:
Sift the flour into a large bowl. Put the honey, salt, butter and beaten egg in with the remaining warm milk, and mix well. Add the yeast mixture to the egg and butter liquid. Mix well, and pour all at once into the flour. Mix and knead until the dough leaves the sides of the bowl and has a shiny appearance.

FIRST RISING:
Brush the dough with melted butter, cover and leave until double in size, about 1 hour.

SECOND RISING:
Knock back and knead in the dried and glacé fruits. Divide the mixture between two greased 1 lb (500 g) loaf tins. Leave, covered, in a warm place, until double in size, about 30 to 40 minutes.

PRE-HEAT OVEN
to 400°F (200°C) Gas 6.

BAKING TIME:
Bake for 45 to 50 minutes. After 20 minutes REDUCE HEAT to 375°F (190°C) Gas 5. If you like, you can brush the loaves with a little melted honey for the last 5 minutes.

METRIC EQUIVALENTS:
*500 g strong white flour*
*15 g fresh yeast or 8 g dried yeast*
*150 ml lukewarm milk*
*1 tablespoon honey*
*½ teaspoon salt*
*60 g butter at room temperature*
*1 egg, beaten*
*a little melted butter*
*125 g raisins or sultanas*
*60 g chopped glacé cherries*
*60 g chopped glacé fruits*
*or candied peel*

## Quick Malt Bread

*A fruity sticky textured bread to serve in slices with butter and soft cheese. 1 oz (30 g) of the dried fruit in this recipe can be replaced with chopped walnuts or hazelnuts or a mixture of both, if you prefer.*

*Makes 1 small loaf*

THE FLOUR:
*8 oz white flour*

PRE-HEAT OVEN
to 325°F (170°C) Gas 3.

THE MIX:
Sift the flour, baking powder and salt into a basin, and add the dried fruit. Put the milk, honey, malt extract and black treacle into a saucepan, and stir over a low heat until lukewarm. Pour into the flour and dried fruit mixture, mix well, and beat to a soft dough (a wooden spoon is best). Grease and line a 1 lb (500 g) bread tin, and press the dough into the tin.

THE RAISING AGENT:
*1 heaped teaspoon baking powder*

AND . . .
*1 teaspoon salt*
*4 oz raisins or sultanas*
*2 oz chopped dates*
*½ pt milk*
*2 teaspoons honey*
*2 tablespoons malt extract*
*1 tablespoon black treacle*

BAKING TIME:
Bake for 1 hour.

METRIC EQUIVALENTS:
*250 g white flour*
*1 heaped teaspoon baking powder*
*1 teaspoon salt*
*125 g raisins or sultanas*
*60 g chopped dates*
*300 ml milk*
*2 teaspoons honey*
*2 tablespoons malt extract*
*1 tablespoon black treacle*

# Apricot and Hazelnut Loaf

In colour—page 120

*This is a good textured tea loaf with the crunchiness of nuts and the tart rich flavour of apricots.*

*Makes 2 small loaves*

THE FLOUR:
*8 oz wholemeal flour*
*8 oz white flour*

THE STARTER:
*½ oz fresh yeast or ¼ oz dried yeast*
*1 teaspoon honey*
*scant ½ pt lukewarm milk*

AND . . .
*1 teaspoon salt*
*4 oz dried apricots, chopped*
*2 oz hazelnuts, chopped*
*2 oz butter at room temperature*
*2 teaspoons honey*
*1 egg, beaten*

METRIC EQUIVALENTS:
*250 g wholemeal flour*
*250 g white flour*
*15 g fresh yeast or 8 g dried yeast*
*1 teaspoon honey*
*scant 300 ml lukewarm milk*
*1 teaspoon salt*
*125 g dried apricots, chopped*
*60 g hazelnuts, chopped*
*60 g butter at room temperature*
*2 teaspoons honey*
*1 egg, beaten*

YEAST STARTER:
Add the yeast and honey to the warm milk and leave for 5 minutes to froth.

THE MIX:
Put the flours, salt, dried fruit and nuts in a bowl and mix well. Add the softened butter, honey and beaten egg to the yeast liquid, then pour into the dry ingredients. Mix well, and knead to a stiffish dough.

FIRST RISING:
Leave, covered, in a warm place until double in size, about 1 hour.

SECOND RISING:
Knock back and knead again. Divide the mixture between two greased 1 lb (500 g) loaf tins. Leave, covered, in a warm place, until double in size, about 30 to 40 minutes.

PRE-HEAT OVEN
to 425°F (220°C) Gas 7.

BAKING TIME:
Bake for 35 to 40 minutes. After 25 minutes REDUCE HEAT to 400°F (200°C) Gas 6.
If you like, you can glaze with egg white mixed with a little honey before placing the dough in the oven.

# Irish Barm Brack

*Makes 2 small loaves*

*Barm is another name for yeast—it is the frothing yeast which bubbles to the top of ale when it is fermenting and, until the turn of the century when commercial yeast preparations became available, bakers usually had to use ale barm. The name lives on in this traditional sweet tea loaf, but today ordinary yeast is used.*

THE FLOUR:
*1 lb strong white flour*

THE STARTER:
*¾ oz fresh yeast or ½ oz dried yeast*
*1 teaspoon honey*

AND . . .
*scant ½ pt lukewarm milk*
*1 level teaspoon salt*
*½ teaspoon grated nutmeg*
*2 oz butter*

*1 tablespoon honey*
*1 egg, beaten*
*4 oz raisins or sultanas*
*4 oz currants*
*2 oz mixed peel*

YEAST STARTER:
Put the yeast and the teaspoon of honey in half the warm milk and leave for 5 minutes to froth up.

THE MIX:
Sieve the flour, salt and spice together in a bowl. Rub in the butter. Add the tablespoon of honey, the beaten egg and the rest of the warm milk to the yeast mixture. Pour into the flour, then knead until the dough leaves the sides of the bowl. Add the dried fruit and peel and knead lightly to distribute them evenly.

FIRST RISING:
Leave the dough covered, in a warm place until double in size, about 1 hour.

SECOND RISING:
Knock back, knead again and divide the dough between two greased cake tins or 1 lb (500 g) loaf tins. Allow to rise again until double in size, about 40 minutes.

PRE-HEAT OVEN
to 400°F (200°C) Gas 6.

BAKING TIME:
Bake for 55 to 60 minutes. After 30 minutes REDUCE HEAT to 350°F (180°C) Gas 4.

METRIC EQUIVALENTS:
*500 g strong white flour*
*20 g fresh yeast or 15 g dried yeast*
*1 teaspoon honey*
*scant 300 ml lukewarm milk*
*1 level teaspoon salt*
*½ teaspoon grated nutmeg*
*60 g butter*
*1 tablespoon honey*
*1 egg, beaten*
*125 g raisins or sultanas*
*125 g currants*
*60 g mixed peel*

# *Potato Scones*

*This recipe is a variation on the traditional scone, using mashed potatoes and rolled oats.*

THE MIX:
Mash the potatoes while they are still warm. Put the flour into a bowl with the rolled oats, salt and baking powder. Rub in the butter. Mix the mashed potatoes in well.
Roll out the mixture lightly to about ¾ in (2 cm) thick and cut it into 6 to 8 rounds about 2 in (5 cm) across.

PRE-HEAT OVEN
to 350°F (180°C) Gas 4.

BAKING TIME:
Place the scones on a greased baking sheet and bake for about 20 minutes or until golden-brown.
Cold boiled potatoes can be sieved and used, but the dough will then need 1 tablespoon of milk added to bind it.

See colour—page 272

*Makes 6 to 8*

THE FLOUR:
*2 oz white flour*
*1 oz rolled oats*

THE RAISING AGENT:
*3 level teaspoons baking powder*

AND . . .
*3 oz potatoes, freshly boiled*
*¼ teaspoon salt*
*1 oz butter*

METRIC EQUIVALENTS:
*60 g white flour*
*30 g rolled oats*
*3 level teaspoons baking powder*
*90 g potatoes, freshly boiled*
*¼ teaspoon salt*
*30 g butter*

## W.I. Home Bakers
# MABEL SADLER

*Seventy-eight-year-old Mabel Sadler has been a member of The Women's Institute for thirty years. As the eldest daughter of a family of twelve, she always had to work hard and never had a cookery lesson until she joined the W.I. She's now a competition winner and cookery demonstrator throughout Cornwall. In 1973 she demonstrated cookery at the Ideal Home Exhibition. Mabel says: "I always bake everything we eat and am no good to shopkeepers except to buy the ingredients". Here are four of her recipes: Tomato Bread, Oat Bread, Cornish Splits and Quick Brown Bread.*

In colour—page 88

# Tomato Bread

*Makes 1 large or 2 small loaves*

*Mabel usually makes this bread with all white flour. The variation below uses a mixture of wholemeal and white flour.*

THE FLOUR:
1 lb strong white flour
4 oz wholemeal flour

THE STARTER:
½ oz fresh yeast
1 teaspoon honey

AND...
½ pt warm water
1 small (2¼ oz) tin tomato purée
1 tablespoon olive oil
1 teaspoon salt

METRIC EQUIVALENTS
500 g strong white flour
125 g wholemeal flour
15 g fresh yeast
1 teaspoon honey
300 ml warm water
1 small (64 g) tin tomato purée
1 tablespoon olive oil
1 teaspoon salt

YEAST STARTER:
Mix the yeast and honey in ¼ pt of the warm water and leave for about 5 minutes to froth.

THE MIX:
Add the tomato purée and the oil to the remaining ¼ pt of warm water and warm up in a saucepan.
Mix the flours and salt in a large mixing bowl. Make a well in the centre and add the yeast mixture. Gradually add the tomato liquid and mix together to form a workable dough. Go easy on the liquid. Knead for 5 minutes or so until the dough has an even, springy texture.

THE RISING:
Cover and leave to rise for about 1 hour, or until double in size.

PRE-HEAT OVEN
to 410°F (210°C) Gas 6½.

BAKING TIME:
Bake for 30 minutes. After 10 minutes REDUCE HEAT to 400°F (200°C) Gas 6.

# Oat Bread

In colour—page 89

*This delicious oat bread can be made with white flour instead of 81% or 85% wholewheat flour if your prefer.*

*Makes 2 small loaves*

THE FLOUR:
*1½ lb 81% or 85% wholewheat*
*    flour*
*12 oz rolled oats*

YEAST STARTER:
Mix the yeast, ½ teaspoon of honey and warm water together in a small bowl and leave for 5 minutes to froth.

THE MIX:
Warm the milk to scalding point and stir in 2 oz (60 g) of the butter. Put the flour into a large bowl and add the salt and rolled oats. Pour in the yeast mixture and stir well. Add the tablespoon of honey, the vegetable oil and enough of the milk mixture to make a dough. Knead until smooth.

THE STARTER:
*¾ oz fresh yeast or ½ oz dried*
*    yeast*
*½ teaspoon honey*
*3 tablespoons warm water*

AND . . .
*about 1 pt milk*
*3 oz butter*
*1 teaspoon salt*
*1 tablespoon honey*
*2 teaspoons vegetable oil*

FIRST RISING:
Cover the bowl and put the dough to rise in a warm place for 1 hour, or until double in size.

SECOND RISING:
Grease two 1 lb (500 g) loaf tins. Knead the dough again for 5 to 10 minutes, then divide into two and shape into loaves. Place the loaves in the tins. Melt the rest of the butter slightly and brush over the loaves. Leave to rise again in a warm place for about 30 minutes.

METRIC EQUIVALENTS:
*750 g 81% or 85% wholewheat flour*
*350 g rolled oats*
*20 g fresh yeast or 15 g dried yeast*
*½ teaspoon honey*
*3 tablespoons warm water*
*600 ml milk*
*90 g butter*
*1 teaspoon salt*
*1 tablespoon honey*
*2 teaspoons vegetable oil*

PRE-HEAT OVEN
to 410°F (210°C) Gas 6½.

BAKING TIME:
Bake for 30 to 35 minutes in the centre of the oven. After 15 minutes REDUCE HEAT to 375°F (190°C) Gas 5. Sprinkle lightly with dry rolled oats while still hot.

In colour—page 121

# Cornish Splits

*Traditionally, these splits are made with white flour and served split open, with clotted cream and strawberry jam, but you can use a mixture of half wholemeal flour and half white flour if you prefer. You can make an attractive crown loaf by baking 4 splits in a 5 in (13 cm) round baking tin and placing one on top.*

*Makes about 15*

THE FLOUR:
*1 lb strong white flour*

THE STARTER:
*1 oz fresh yeast or ½ dried yeast*
*1 teaspoon honey*
*½ pt warm milk*

AND . . .
*1 teaspoon salt*
*2 oz butter*

METRIC EQUIVALENTS:
*500 g strong white flour*
*30 g fresh yeast or 15 g dried yeast*
*1 teaspoon honey*
*300 ml warm milk*
*1 teaspoon salt*
*60 g butter*

YEAST STARTER:
Mix the yeast and honey in the warm milk. Leave for 5 minutes.

THE MIX:
Sift the flour and salt into a large bowl and rub in the butter until the mixture is the consistency of breadcrumbs. Gradually pour the yeast liquid into the flour stirring thoroughly, and knead well.

FIRST RISING:
Cover and leave to rise in a warm place for about 1 hour or until the dough has doubled in size.
Knead well again. Shape into about 15 rolls or buns and place on a lightly floured baking sheet.

SECOND RISING:
Cover and leave to rise again in a warm place until doubled in size.

PRE-HEAT OVEN
to 400°F (200°C) Gas 6.

BAKING TIME:
Bake for 15 to 20 minutes.

# Quick Brown Bread

*This delicious brown bread is ideal for everyday use. It is quick to make and has a lighter texture than bread made with all wholemeal flour.*

*Makes 6 small loaves*

THE FLOUR:
*3¼ lb wholemeal flour*
*4 oz strong white flour*

THE STARTER:
*1 oz fresh yeast*

AND . . .
*4 rounded teaspoons salt*
*2 oz butter*
*scant 2 pt warm water*

THE MIX:
Mix the flours in a large bowl with the salt. Rub in the butter, and make a well in the centre. Add almost all the water, keeping back about ¼ pt (150 ml). Crumble in the yeast and stir it around. Draw some of the dry flour over it and leave to sponge for about 10 minutes.
Mix all together thoroughly, adding remaining water if necessary. Knead well until you have a smooth, springy dough which comes away from the sides of the bowl.

THE RISING:
Divide into 6 equal portions, shape into loaves and put into 6 well-greased 1 lb (500 g) loaf tins. Cover and put in a warm place for about 1 hour until the dough reaches to the top of the tins.

PRE-HEAT OVEN
to 400°F (200°C) Gas 6.

BAKING TIME:
Bake for 25 to 30 minutes, or until each loaf sounds hollow when tapped on the bottom.

METRIC EQUIVALENTS:
*1½ kg wholemeal flour*
*125 g strong white flour*
*30 g fresh yeast*
*4 rounded teaspoons salt*
*60 g butter*
*scant 1¼ litres warm water*

# MOLLY ANDREWS
## *Lincolnshire Plum Bread*

*This bread is one of Molly Andrews' specialities. A farmer's wife for 34 years and a member of the W.I. for 18, she's now County Vice-chairman of Lincolnshire North Federation, Chairman of the Home Economics sub-committee, and a cookery judge. Her recipe is unusual because it uses baking powder and yeast and requires no kneading or rising, but it does need two hours' cooking. She says: "This bread is better for keeping a few days in an air-tight tin. Serve buttered with a good mature Cheddar cheese."*

YEAST STARTER:
Stir the yeast into ¼ pt (150 ml) of the warm milk.

THE MIX:
Sift the flour and baking powder into a large bowl and rub in the butter. Add the dried fruit. Add the eggs and the honey to the rest of the warm milk, and mix with the yeasty milk.
Make a well in the centre of the flour, pour in the liquid, and mix. This is a stiff mix.
Put into three 2 lb (1 kg) loaf tins.

PRE-HEAT OVEN
to 300°F (150°C) Gas 2.

BAKING TIME:
Bake for about 2 hours.

*Makes 3 large loaves*

THE FLOUR:
*2 lb white flour*

THE STARTER:
*1 oz fresh yeast or ½ oz dried yeast*
*4 teaspoons baking powder*

AND . . .
*about ¾ pt lukewarm milk*
*½ lb butter*
*2 lb mixed dried fruit*
*2 eggs, beaten*
*scant ¼ pt clear honey, warmed*

METRIC EQUIVALENTS:
*1 kg white flour*
*30 g fresh yeast or 15 g dried yeast*
*4 teaspoons baking powder*
*about 400 ml lukewarm milk*
*250 g butter*
*1 kg mixed dried fruit*
*2 eggs, beaten*
*scant 150 ml clear honey, warmed*

# MARGARET OLDMAN
## *Wholemeal Pizza*

*Makes one 12 in (30 cm) pizza*

THE FLOUR:
*8 oz wholemeal flour*

THE STARTER:
*½ oz fresh yeast*
*1 teaspoon honey*

AND...
*¼ pt warm milk and water*
*½ teaspoon salt*

THE TOPPING:
*1 medium-sized onion*
*1 tablespoon olive or vegetable oil*
*8 oz tomatoes, fresh or tinned*
Your choice from:
  *black olives, flaked tuna fish, sardines, anchovies, sliced green peppers, sliced mushrooms, salami slices, shredded ham*
*4 to 6 oz cheese, such as Edam*
*basil, oregano, marjoram*

METRIC EQUIVALENTS:
*250 g wholemeal flour*
*15 g fresh yeast*
*1 teaspoon honey*
*150 ml warm milk and water*
*½ teaspoon salt*
The topping:
*1 medium-sized onion*
*1 tablespoon olive or vegetable oil*
*250 g tomatoes, fresh or tinned*
*other ingredients of your choice, as above*
*125 to 175 g cheese, such as Edam*
*basil, oregano, marjoram*

*Margaret Oldman became interested in wholefood when she was living in California. She firmly believes in the use of raw fruit and vegetables and whole-grain cereal foods, high in fibre. As well as practising her own beliefs, she gives talks on wholefood nutrition and cookery to a variety of groups and runs wholefood courses for the Workers' Educational Association (W.E.A.).*
*At home in Cheshire, the bread-making is now in the hands of her husband and five-year-old daughter. Here's her wholemeal version of a pizza. She says: "For a well-balanced meal serve it hot with a mixed green salad."*

YEAST STARTER:
Cream the yeast with the honey and a little of the warm liquid. Leave until frothy, about 10 minutes.

THE MIX:
Mix the flour and salt and add the yeast mixture and the rest of the liquid. Mix well and knead into a smooth dough. Roll out or press to fit a pizza pan 12 in (300 mm) in diameter or a raised-edge baking sheet. Cover and leave in a warm place while you prepare the topping.

PRE-HEAT OVEN
to 475° to 500°F (240° to 260°C) Gas 9.

THE TOPPING:
Chop the onion and sauté in the oil. Add the tomatoes and cook until soft. Spread over the pizza base and add the other topping ingredients of your choice. Grate the cheese. Sprinkle with the herbs, then with the grated cheese.

BAKING TIME:
Bake in the very hot oven for 10 to 15 minutes. Alternatively the pizza can be frozen and baked later.

# Wholemeal Sourdough Bread

In colour—page 128

*Margaret uses Sam Mayall's organically grown stoneground wholemeal flour from Harmer Hill, near Shrewsbury. She says, "the result is the most delicious, light-textured wholemeal bread I've ever tasted." This recipe requires no kneading. Prepare the sourdough starter at least one day in advance.*

*Makes 2 stick loaves, French-style*

**SOURDOUGH STARTER:**
*½ oz fresh yeast*
*½ teaspoon honey*
*3 tablespoons lukewarm water*
*1 tablespoon milk*
*½ teaspoon vegetable oil*
*1 teaspoon sea salt*
*2 oz wholemeal flour*

DAY ONE
SOURDOUGH STARTER:
Blend the yeast with the honey and 1 tablespoon warm water.
Put the milk, vegetable oil and remaining 2 tablespoons water in a small saucepan. Bring to the boil, then cool to lukewarm.
Add the yeast mixture to the cooled milk liquid. Add the salt and stir in the flour. Cover and leave in a warm place for 12 to 24 hours.

**THE FLOUR:**
*1½ lb wholemeal flour*

DAY TWO
YEAST STARTER:
Blend the yeast with ½ tablespoon of the honey and 4 tablespoons of the warm water. Set aside until frothy, about 10 minutes.

**YEAST STARTER:**
*1½ oz fresh yeast*

**AND . .**
*1½ tablespoons honey*
*9 fl.oz warm water*
*1½ tablespoons vegetable oil*
*4 fl.oz milk*
*2 teaspoons sea salt*

THE MIX:
Put the vegetable oil, milk and remaining water in a small saucepan, bring to the boil, and stir in the remaining honey, then cool to lukewarm. Place the flour in a large mixing bowl with the salt. Pour in the yeast liquid and the milk mixture. Add the sourdough starter and stir until well blended into a soft dough.

**METRIC EQUIVALENTS:**
Sourdough starter:
*15 g fresh yeast*
*½ teaspoon honey*
*3 tablespoons lukewarm water*
*1 tablespoon milk*
*½ teaspoon vegetable oil*
*1 teaspoon sea salt*
*60 g wholemeal flour*
Rest of ingredients:
*750 g wholemeal flour*
*40 g fresh yeast*
*1½ tablespoons honey*
*275 ml warm water*
*1½ tablespoons vegetable oil*
*100 ml milk*
*2 teaspoons sea salt*

FIRST RISING:
Place in a greased bowl, cover and let rise in a warm place until double in size, about 1 hour.

THE SHAPING:
Turn on to a lightly floured surface. Divide into 2 equal pieces and roll each into a rectangle about 15 x 10 in (38 x 25.5 cm). Roll up, with the wide side towards you, pinching the edges to seal them as you roll. Roll gently back and forth using both hands so that the ends taper slightly.

SECOND RISING:
Place on an oiled baking sheet. Make diagonal cuts about 2 in (5 cm) apart. Leave to prove, uncovered, for about 1 hour.

PRE-HEAT OVEN
to 475°F (240°C) Gas 9. When the loaves have risen slightly more than double in size, REDUCE OVEN to 425°F (220°C) Gas 7.

BAKING TIME:
Place the bread in the centre of the oven and bake for 35 to 40 minutes. After 15 minutes REDUCE HEAT to 350°F (180°C) Gas 4. Cool on a wire rack.

# SHIRLEY NASH
## Cheese and Herb Plait

In colour—page 128

*Makes 1 large or 2 small plaits*

THE FLOUR:
*10 oz wholemeal flour*
*6 oz strong white flour*

THE STARTER:
*½ oz fresh yeast*
*1 level teaspoon honey*
*¼ pt warm milk*

AND . . .
*2 level teaspoons salt*
*¼ pt lukewarm water*
*½ oz butter*
*1 teaspoon mixed dried herbs*
*3 oz grated cheese*
*paprika pepper*

METRIC EQUIVALENTS:
*300 g wholemeal flour*
*175 g strong white flour*
*15 g fresh yeast*
*1 level teaspoon honey*
*150 ml warm milk*
*2 level teaspoons salt*
*150 ml lukewarm water*
*15 g butter*
*1 teaspoon mixed dried herbs*
*90 g grated cheese*
*paprika pepper*

*Shirley Nash moved from London to Bedfordshire in the early 1960s. A keen W.I. member, she grows most of her own vegetables and enjoys cooking for an appreciative family. This plaited loaf is excellent for cheese and wine parties but equally suitable for serving with soup.*

YEAST STARTER:
Dissolve the honey and yeast in the warm milk.

THE MIX:
Mix the flours together. Dissolve the salt in the water. Rub the butter into the flour. Add the salt water and yeast liquid to the flour, mix well, then knead to a smooth dough, about 10 minutes.

FIRST RISING:
Leave the dough in a covered bowl in a warm place to rise until doubled in bulk, about 1 to 1½ hours.

SECOND RISING:
Knock back the dough then work in the herbs and cheese, saving ½ oz (15 g) cheese for the top. Leave to rise for about 30 minutes.

PRE-HEAT OVEN
to 400°F (200°C) Gas 6.

THIRD RISING:
Re-knead and make into 1 large or 2 smaller plaits. Cover and leave to rise until doubled in size, about 30 minutes.

BAKING TIME:
Brush gently with some milk, sprinkle with the remaining cheese and paprika pepper. Bake for about 35 minutes.

## Baps

*Makes 12*

*Lovely, floury soft brown rolls that are especially good for filling with beefburgers or sausages.*

THE FLOUR:
*½ lb wholemeal flour*
*½ lb strong white flour*

THE STARTER:
*1 oz fresh yeast*
*¼ pt warm milk*

AND . . .
*1 level teaspoon salt*
*¼ pt warm water*
*3 oz butter*

YEAST STARTER:
Dissolve the yeast in the milk.

THE MIX:
Dissolve the salt in the water. Mix the flours together and rub in the butter. Add the salt and yeast liquids to the flour, mix well, and then knead until a smooth dough is obtained, about 10 minutes.

FIRST RISING:
Leave the dough to rise in a covered bowl in a warm place until doubled in bulk, about 1 hour.

SECOND RISING:
Knock back, knead lightly and divide the dough into 12 pieces. Knead and shape these into oval or round pieces, ½ in (1.5 cm) thick. Place on a greased and floured baking sheet, flatten each one slightly and dredge with flour. Cover and leave to rise until doubled in size, about 30 minutes.

PRE-HEAT OVEN
to 425°F (220°C) Gas 7.

BAKING TIME:
Bake for 10 to 15 minutes. Place on a wire tray, cover with a clean, dry tea towel, and leave to cool.

METRIC EQUIVALENTS:
*250 g wholemeal flour*
*250 g strong white flour*
*30 g fresh yeast*
*150 ml warm milk*
*1 level teaspoon salt*
*150 ml warm water*
*90 g butter*

# Apple Bread

*A very light, moist tea-bread made with apples.*

*Makes 2 small loaves*

YEAST STARTER:
Dissolve the honey and yeast in a *very* little warm water.

THE MIX:
Mix the flours, add the yeast mixture and apple pulp. Mix well and knead until a smooth dough is obtained.

FIRST RISING:
Leave the dough in a covered bowl in a warm place to rise until doubled in bulk, about 2 to 2½ hours.

SECOND RISING:
Knead lightly, and shape to fit into two 1 lb (500 g) loaf tins. Cover and leave to rise until the dough has doubled in size and reaches the top of the tins, about 30 minutes.

PRE-HEAT OVEN
to 375°F (190°C) Gas 5.

BAKING TIME:
Brush the loaves with a little milk and bake for about 30 minutes, until the bases sound hollow when tapped.

THE FLOUR:
*1 lb wholemeal flour*
*1 lb strong white flour*

THE STARTER:
*1 oz fresh yeast*
*1 teaspoon honey*

AND . . .
*1 lb warm apple pulp*

METRIC EQUIVALENTS:
*500 g wholemeal flour*
*500 g strong white flour*
*30 g fresh yeast*
*1 teaspoon honey*
*500 g warm apple pulp*

# DOREEN ADAMSON
## *Cheese Plaits*

*Makes 1 plait*

THE FLOUR:
*½ lb strong white flour*
*½ lb wholemeal flour*

THE STARTER:
*½ oz fresh yeast*
*½ pt warm water*

AND . . .
*1 teaspoon salt*
*½ teaspoon dry mustard*
*large pinch of pepper*
*½ oz butter*
*4 oz grated Cheddar cheese*

METRIC EQUIVALENTS:
*250 g strong white flour*
*250 g wholemeal flour*
*15 g fresh yeast*
*300 ml warm water*
*1 teaspoon salt*
*½ teaspoon dry mustard*
*large pinch of pepper*
*15 g butter*
*125 g grated Cheddar cheese*

*Doreen Adamson makes these delicious cheese plaits early each Friday morning, so that they are still warm when they go on sale at the local W.I. market in Derbyshire. She's been a member for 20 years and is now a Controller of the local market. These markets were started in the 1920s and '30s to enable country people to augment their income by selling surplus produce. You do not need to be a W.I. member to produce for the market, and many husbands take part.*

YEAST STARTER:
Dissolve the yeast in the warm water.

THE MIX:
Mix the flours in a large bowl and add the salt, mustard and pepper. Rub in the butter. Stir in the cheese, keeping back a tablespoon for sprinkling on top of the loaf. Add the yeast liquid, stirring well to make a dough. Turn out on to a floured board and knead well.

FIRST RISING:
Cover and leave for about 1 hour or until double in size.
Knock back the risen dough and cut into 3 equal portions. Roll each piece into a long strip. Join the pieces together at the top and plait; then pinch ends together.

SECOND RISING:
Place on a greased baking sheet and sprinkle with the rest of the cheese. Leave to rise for about 30 minutes.

PRE-HEAT OVEN
to 400°F (200°C) Gas 6.

BAKING TIME:
Bake for about 40 minutes or until the loaf sounds hollow when tapped on the bottom.

# BETTY GRANT
## *Wholemeal Bread*

*Contrasting recipes from Betty Grant: wholesome Wholemeal Bread, Savoury French Loaf and rich Lardy Cake. Betty has enjoyed cooking from a very early age and much of her life has been connected with it. She took courses in Housewifery and Advanced Cookery, followed by Institutional Catering; has cooked in a private school, managed a hotel and helped run a restaurant. She's been with the W.I. for 22 years. Until recently she was President and now she is Secretary of her local group in Lincolnshire.*

YEAST STARTER:
Cream the yeast and honey with ¾ pt (400 ml) of the lukewarm water, and leave for about 10 minutes to froth.

THE MIX:
Mix the flour and salt in a large bowl and rub in the butter. Add the yeast mixture, the black treacle liquid and enough of the remaining warm water to make a pliable dough. Mix thoroughly and knead until the dough is soft and smooth.

FIRST RISING:
Cover and leave in a warm place to rise for about 1½ hours. Knock back and weigh out as required for rolls or loaves.

SECOND RISING:
Place in greased bread tins or on a greased baking tray. Leave to rise: 45 minutes for the loaves, 30 minutes for the rolls.

PRE-HEAT OVEN
to 450°F (230°C) Gas 8.

BAKING TIME:
Bake loaves for about 40 to 50 minutes, or until the bread sounds hollow when tapped on the bottom. Bake rolls for 15 to 20 minutes.

*Makes about 3 loaves*

THE FLOUR:
*3 lb wholemeal flour*

THE STARTER:
*1 oz fresh yeast or 4 teaspoons*
    *dried yeast*
*1 teaspoon honey*

AND . . .
*1½ pt lukewarm water*
*4 teaspoons salt*
*1 oz butter*
*1 tablespoon black treacle,*
    *dissolved in ½ pt warm water*

METRIC EQUIVALENTS:
*1½ kg wholemeal flour*
*30 g fresh yeast or 4 teaspoons*
    *dried yeast*
*1 teaspoon honey*
*900 ml lukewarm water*
*4 teaspoons salt*
*30 g butter*
*1 tablespoon black treacle,*
    *dissolved in 300 ml warm water*

# Savoury French Loaf

*Makes 1 small loaf*

THE DOUGH:
½ *basic wholemeal bread
    dough, risen once* (see previous
    recipe)

AND...
*2 oz grated cheese
4 oz chopped fried bacon
mixed herbs for sprinkling
beaten egg for glazing*

METRIC EQUIVALENTS:
½ *basic wholemeal bread dough,
    risen once* (see previous recipe)
*60 g grated cheese
125 g chopped fried bacon
mixed herbs for sprinkling
beaten egg for glazing*

*For variety, you can use the wholemeal bread dough in the
previous recipe to make one standard wholemeal loaf and transform
the other half of the dough into this savoury bread.*

THE SHAPING:
Roll the dough into a rectangle 12 x 8 in (30 x 20 cm). Sprinkle the
cheese, bacon and mixed herbs over the dough and roll it up into a
flat roll. Slash across the top at 1 in (2.5 cm) intervals. Place on a
greased baking sheet.

SECOND RISING:
Cover with greased polythene and leave to rise for about 30 minutes.

PRE-HEAT OVEN
to 450°F (230°C) Gas 8.

BAKING TIME:
Brush with beaten egg and sprinkle lightly with mixed herbs. Bake
in the centre of the oven for 20 to 25 minutes.

In colour—page 121

# Lardy Cake

*Makes 1 cake*

THE FLOUR:
*8 oz wholemeal flour*

THE STARTER:
½ *oz fresh yeast or 1 teaspoon
    dried yeast*
½ *teaspoon honey*
½ *pt lukewarm water*

AND...
½ *teaspoon salt*
½ *oz lard*

THE FILLING:
*4 oz lard
4 oz sultanas
1 teaspoon mixed spice
4 oz clear honey, warmed*

*Betty Grant makes Lardy Cake in the traditional way with strong
white flour and castor sugar. This variation uses wholemeal flour
and honey.*

YEAST STARTER:
Mix the yeast and honey with the warm water and leave for about
10 minutes to froth.

THE MIX:
Mix the flour and salt in a large bowl and rub in the ½ oz (30 g)
lard. Make a well in the centre and stir in the yeast liquid. Knead
the dough thoroughly until the mixture is smooth.

FIRST RISING:
Cover and leave in a warm place to rise for about 45 minutes to
1 hour or until double in size.

THE FILLING:
Turn out on to a work-surface and roll out to an oblong
approximately 12 in x 9 in (30 cm x 23 cm) and about ½ in (1.5 cm)
thick. Dot a third of the lard over two-thirds of the dough. Sprinkle
with sultanas and mixed spice, and trickle honey over them. Fold
the bottom uncovered pastry up over the filling and the top of the
pastry down over this. Give a quarter turn and repeat this process
twice more with the remaining two-thirds. Fold once more, ending
with an oblong about 3 in (8 cm) deep.

## SECOND RISING:

Put on a greased, deep-sided baking dish and slash across the top in a criss-cross fashion. Cover and leave to rise in a warm place for 1 hour, or until soft and risen.

## PRE-HEAT OVEN

to 425°F (220°C) Gas 7.

## BAKING TIME:

Bake for about 40 minutes. Just before removing from the oven, spoon over some of the syrup which has run out in the cooking, or dribble a tablespoon of honey over it. Cool on a wire rack. Serve warm, cut in thick slices.

## METRIC EQUIVALENTS:

250 g wholemeal flour
15 g fresh yeast or 1 teaspoon dried yeast
½ teaspoon honey
300 ml lukewarm water
½ teaspoon salt
15 g lard
The filling:
125 g lard
125 g sultanas
1 teaspoon mixed spice
125 g clear honey, warmed

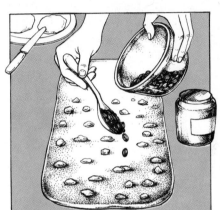
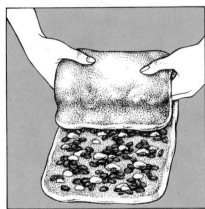
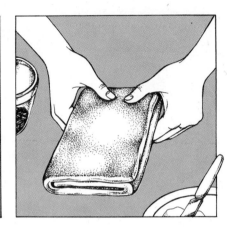

# PEGGY WILLIAMS
## *Doughnuts*

In colour—page 129

*Makes about 16*

THE FLOUR:
*½ lb strong white flour*
*½ lb wholemeal flour*

THE STARTER:
*1 oz fresh yeast*
*8 fl.oz warm milk*
*1 teaspoon honey*
*1 Vitamin C tablet (25 mg)*

AND . . .
*1 level teaspoon salt*
*2 oz butter*
*1 egg, beaten*
*oil for frying*
*powdered cinnamon (optional)*
*strawberry jam or redcurrant*
  *jelly*
*whipped cream*

METRIC EQUIVALENTS:
*250 g strong white flour*
*250 g wholemeal flour*
*30 g fresh yeast*
*250 ml warm milk*
*1 teaspoon honey*
*1 Vitamin C tablet (25 mg)*
*1 level teaspoon salt*
*60 g butter*
*1 egg, beaten*
*oil for frying*
*powdered cinnamon (optional)*
*strawberry jam or redcurrant jelly*
*whipped cream*

*Peggy Williams is a retired farmer's wife still very actively involved in country pursuits. She judges for summer shows and W.I. events, and is famous for her doughnuts. She usually makes them with all white flour and rolls them in castor sugar while they are still hot. This variation of her recipe uses half white and half wholemeal flour. They freeze well, lasting up to 3 months.*

YEAST STARTER:
Crumble the yeast into the milk in a jug and add the honey and Vitamin C tablet. Whisk with a fork until the tablet has dissolved.

THE MIX:
Mix the flours and salt in a bowl and rub in the butter until the mixture resembles fine breadcrumbs. Add the egg and the yeast liquid and mix to a soft dough. Turn on to a floured board. Knead and stretch the dough for about 10 minutes until it is elastic and no longer sticky.

FIRST RISING:
Replace the dough in the bowl, cover with greased polythene and leave for 10 minutes. Meanwhile grease a baking sheet.

SECOND RISING:
Cut the dough in half and replace one piece in the covered basin. Cut the first portion of dough into 8 pieces and shape each piece into a 4 in (10 cm) roll. Do the same with the other half, or make it into round balls. Place on the greased baking tray, cover loosely with greased polythene, and allow to rise until double in size, about 30 minutes.

THE FRYING:
Fill a deep-fat fryer one-third full with oil and heat to 350°F (180°C). Place crumpled kitchen paper on a plate and powdered cinnamon if liked on another. Carefully lift the doughnuts from the tin and fry 3 at a time for about 4 minutes, turning once. Drain on the kitchen paper and then roll in the cinnamon. Put on a wire rack to cool. Make a cut in each, then spread with jam and pipe or spread on cream.

# JUDY ROJÉ
## Lemon Chelsea Buns

*Judy Rojé, a Londoner by birth, now lives in Cheshire where she and her family run a six-acre smallholding. They grow most of their own fruit and vegetables and keep hens, calves and sheep. Judy is an ex-President of Bunbury W.I., and took up home-baking a few years ago after attending a W.I. day course on yeast cookery. She now bakes all the bread for the family, including these delicious lemon Chelsea buns and the following Granary bread. The buns should be eaten within 48 hours.*

**YEAST STARTER:**
Dissolve the yeast in the lemon juice and enough warm water to make 6 fl.oz. Leave in a warm place for about 10 minutes to start fermentation.

**THE MIX:**
Add the liquid to the white flour and salt and mix well. Cream 2 oz (60 g) of the butter with the honey and beat into the flour mixture.

**FIRST RISING:**
Cover and leave to double in size.

**SECOND RISING:**
Beat the egg into the mixture, and knead with the 2 to 3 oz (60 to 90 g) wholemeal flour (more if necessary). The dough must be dry enough to knead and subsequently roll out. Cover and leave to rise for about 30 minutes.

**THE FILLING:**
To make the filling, mix the grated lemon rind with the candied peel and honey.

**THIRD RISING:**
Roll out the dough to about 16 x 18 in (40.5 x 45.5 cm) and about ¼ in (5 mm) thick. Dot with the rest of the butter. Spread the filling mixture on the dough. Roll up tightly and cut ¾ in (2 cm) thick slices with a very sharp or saw-edge knife. Set fairly close together on a greased baking tray. Cover and leave to rise again for about 30 minutes.

**PRE-HEAT OVEN**
to 425°F (220°C) Gas 7.

**BAKING TIME:**
Bake for 15 to 20 minutes (the closer together the buns are, the longer it takes to cook them). Glaze while hot with the honey glaze. If you like, return them to the oven for 2 to 3 minutes so the tops are not soggy. Cool on the baking tray covered with a clean cloth.

*Makes 16*

THE FLOUR:
*6 oz strong white flour*
*2 to 3 oz wholemeal flour*

THE STARTER:
*1 oz fresh yeast*
*juice of 1 lemon*
*about 5 fl.oz warm water*

AND . . .
*¼ teaspoon salt*
*4 oz butter*
*1 tablespoon honey*
*1 egg*

THE FILLING:
*grated rind of 2 lemons*
*3 tablespoons candied peel*
*1 tablespoon clear honey,*
*  warmed*

THE GLAZE:
*1 dessertspoon honey dissolved*
*  in 1 to 2 tablespoons hot water*

METRIC EQUIVALENTS:
*175 g strong white flour*
*60 g to 90 g wholemeal flour*
*30 g fresh yeast*
*juice of 1 lemon*
*about 150 ml warm water*
*¼ teaspoon salt*
*125 g butter*
*1 tablespoon honey*
*1 egg*
*grated rind of 2 lemons*
*3 tablespoons candied peel*
*1 tablespoon clear honey, warmed*
*1 dessertspoon honey dissolved in 1*
*  to 2 tablespoons hot water*

# Granary Bread

*Makes 4 loaves*

THE FLOUR:
*1½ lb Granary flour*
*1½ lb wholemeal flour*

THE STARTER:
*1 to 1½ oz fresh yeast*
*1 teaspoon honey*

AND . . .
*just under 1½ pt warm water*
*2 level tablespoons salt*
*1 oz butter*

METRIC EQUIVALENTS:
*750 g Granary flour*
*750 g wholemeal flour*
*30 to 40 g fresh yeast*
*1 teaspoon honey*
*just under 900 ml warm water*
*2 level tablespoons salt*
*30 g butter*

*Granary flour gives an interesting flavour and texture. By mixing it with wholemeal, Judy produces a loaf that is less sweet than all Granary, and less dense than all wholemeal.*

YEAST STARTER:
Cream the yeast with the honey and a little of the warm water.

THE MIX:
Mix the two flours with the salt and rub in the butter. Make a well in the centre, pour in the yeast mixture and sufficient warm water to make a workable dough. Knead well.

FIRST RISING:
Cover and put in a warm place until double in size, about 1 hour.

SECOND RISING:
Knock back, shape into 4 loaves and place on greased baking trays. Cover and allow to rise, about 30 minutes.

PRE-HEAT OVEN
to 425°F (220°C) Gas 7.

BAKING TIME:
Bake for about 30 to 40 minutes.

# YVONNE TOWNSEND
# Dough Cake

*In colour—page 121*

*Makes 1 large cake*

THE FLOUR:
*1 lb strong white flour*

THE STARTER:
*½ oz fresh yeast or ¼ oz dried yeast*
*1 teaspoon honey*

AND . . .
*2 tablespoons honey, warmed*
*scant ½ pt lukewarm milk*
*1½ teaspoons salt*
*4 oz lard or softened butter*
*4 oz mixed currants and sultanas*

*Yvonne Townsend grew up in a bakery in Oxfordshire, which her brother now runs. It has a brick oven and still produces the superb crusty bread Yvonne used to deliver with her father on his horse-drawn van. In those days some people gave them home-grown vegetables in exchange for bread and cakes.*
*Yvonne has kept up the family tradition, started by her grandfather in 1892, and runs a bakery and confectionery shop in Witney. Her breads and cakes are made to the recipes handed down through the family. Of the following recipe she says: "Customers can buy a couple of pounds of dough, from which they like to make their own Dough Cake or Lardies, as I do myself." For those not fortunate enough to be able to buy Yvonne's ready-made dough, here's the complete recipe. It is traditionally made with lard.*

YEAST STARTER:
Mix the yeast and teaspoon of honey with ¼ pt (150 ml) of the warm milk. Stir and leave for about 10 minutes until frothy.

## THE MIX:

Sift the flour and salt into a large bowl. Make a well in the centre and pour in the yeast liquid, the warmed honey and the remaining warm milk. Mix thoroughly.

Knead well. Break up the dough with your fingers, then work in the lard or softened butter little by little until completely integrated. Work the currants and sultanas into the mixture evenly. Place the dough in a greased 2 lb (1 kg) loaf tin.

## THE RISING:

Cover with a cloth and put in a warm place to rise for about 45 minutes.

## PRE-HEAT OVEN

to 375°F (190°C) Gas 5.

## BAKING TIME:

Bake for 40 to 45 minutes.

METRIC EQUIVALENTS:
*500 g strong white flour*
*15 g fresh yeast or 8 g dried yeast*
*1 teaspoon honey*
*2 tablespoons honey, warmed*
*1½ teaspoons salt*
*125 g lard or softened butter*
*125 g mixed currants and sultanas*

# BEVERLEY EVANS
## *Bara Brith*

*Mrs. Beverley Evans has been a member of the W.I. since she was 14 years old. She's now Chairman of Crafts and Home Economics of Anglesey County Federation. Her Anglesey version of this well known Welsh bread uses yeast.*

## THE MIX:

Melt the butter in the warm milk. Put all the dry ingredients in a warm bowl with the crumbled yeast. Stir the warm liquid into the egg and add the honey. Pour into the dry ingredients and mix well.

## FIRST RISING:

Allow to rise until it has doubled in bulk.

## SECOND RISING:

Turn on to a floured board. Knead and shape into a loaf and put into a greased 2 lb (1 kg) tin. Allow to rise again for 10 minutes.

## PRE-HEAT OVEN

to 350°F (180°C) Gas 4.

## BAKING TIME:

Bake for 30 minutes.

*Makes 1 large loaf*

THE FLOUR:
*1 lb white flour*

THE STARTER:
*½ oz fresh yeast, crumbled*

AND . . .
*3 oz butter*
*½ pt warm milk*
*6 oz dried fruit*
*pinch of salt*
*little grated nutmeg*
*1 egg, beaten*
*2 tablespoons clear honey*

METRIC EQUIVALENTS:
*500 g white flour*
*15 g fresh yeast, crumbled*
*90 g butter*
*300 ml warm milk*
*175 g dried fruit*
*pinch of salt*
*little grated nutmeg*
*1 egg, beaten*
*2 tablespoons clear honey*

# Elisabeth Lambert Ortiz

Many British people who bake tend to stick to the one or two basic loaves they know well—perhaps a white loaf and a wholemeal one, maybe one that's half and half. For variety they change the shape. But in some countries bread forms a major feature of the diet as a whole. It may be eaten alone, without even the addition of butter, or served as something special for breakfast or morning coffee. Or it may be presented as a pudding at the end of a meal. This is often so in the West Indies, where Elisabeth Lambert Ortiz lived. (Lambert is her maiden name, Ortiz the name she gained from her Mexican husband, Cesar).

Elisabeth was born and grew up in England, lived for some years in the West Indies, and became a journalist in Australia. It was while working in New York, scripting documentaries for the United Nations, that she met and married her husband, chief of radio broadcasting at the UN. They have lived in Mexico, Latin America and the Far East, which provided Elisabeth with the material for her food books. She's now written five and has been consultant for many more, including the Time-Life series. She's also a regular contributor to *Gourmet* magazine. (It was through her *Gourmet* articles that James Beard, High Priest of American cook-books, urged her to write books.)

She first started making bread in the West Indies. "I remember my first lesson well. We had the most glamorous beautiful teacher. It was time to start sex education—they called it biology in those days. The teacher didn't think it was a very nice subject. First she taught us about the spine, then she taught us about the composition of the blood. Then she said, 'Oh, let's make bread'. So, I have whole areas of total ignorance, but I do know all about bread. And that makes me very happy.

"Most of the flour in the Caribbean countries is imported from the States. They add their own ingredients like banana and coconut to give bulk as well as flavour. And they make many quick breads, using baking powder, because it used to be very difficult to come across yeast, even in packets. Many people didn't have ovens, but they still made bread."

After her first bread-making lesson, Elisabeth never looked back. Now she makes bread without even thinking about it: "The thing is that it's so co-operative. You can think things through as you make it and still have a good loaf of bread. You can't do that with pastry. You have to behave yourself with pastry. With bread you can do what you like. And there's that wonderful moment after the first rising, when you go plonk and down it all goes. It's very satisfying. And it's good exercise. Dough likes to be mistreated."

Elisabeth, who has worked in the test kitchens at Time-Life in New York, remembers seeing the slightest, slimmest of young girls beating the dough with a force you wouldn't have imagined her capable of: "Bread's like that. It gives you a sense of authority. It must be good for people. You can have a really good work-out—as good as jogging. And then, there's that extraordinary smell. It's marvellous. Far out of proportion to the ingredients. Good pastry doesn't have that smell."

Some manufacturers have now brought out a spray that is said to artificially recreate the smell of freshly baked bread. This is apparently being used in some supermarkets to tempt buyers up to the bread counter. "Well," laughs Elisabeth "at least it shows they recognise that fresh bread does have a good smell. Plant bread may not have much flavour, but at least they're making it smell good."

Elisabeth's hunger for the smell and flavour of fresh bread led her to unprecedented extremes when she and her husband were posted to Bangkok for four years. There was no such thing as fresh bread out there. Flour was imported from the United States, and yeast, even dried yeast, was difficult to track down. When Elisabeth found the ingredients, she had to use her Thai oven: "I baked the bread in this oven made from a kerosene tin. We placed the tin oven on top of our charcoal stove and put charcoal on top of it to reproduce the effect of an oven. Our Thai servant Tongdee thought I was crazy, out there in the tropical heat stoking up the coals. I put a thermometer in the tin and Tongdee used a palm leaf fan to fan up the coals. If they got too hot, he'd take some off with tongs. And if the temperature dropped too low, I'd shout and he'd start fanning away again. We did this for 40 minutes."

*Was the loaf a success?*

"Well, it wasn't the loaf I'd intended, but it was very passable. An Italian-Vienna type loaf, with good texture."

"Yes, very good texture," adds Cesar, who remembers with delight all the many loaves Elisabeth has cooked. "And she makes very good *tortillas*."

"Yes, but for *tortillas* you must have the right flour. You can't use ordinary maize flour. It has to be *masa harina*. There's a very important difference.

To make *masa harina* the dried corn is boiled in water with slaked lime to loosen and soften the skins. Then, it is drained and boiled lightly and ground into a paste. This is a cooked flour. It's the only cooked flour there is."

Elisabeth loves making *tortillas* and also *arepas* —the Venezuelan and Colombian cousin of the *tortilla*: "*Arepas* are more bready. They're crusty on the outside and doughy inside. You pull out the dough and throw it away. Then you fill it with butter and cream cheese. You bite into it and it all runs down your face. Delicious." (There is a recipe for *arepas* on p.166).

Elisabeth has a good memory for the many breads she's tasted. She remembers the "divine" lardy cake, greasy and heavy with fruit, she bought from a small bakery near Wallingford. And she will never forget the semolina bread made by an Italian baker in New York: "It was so wonderful. I'm determined to work out how he made it. I'll know immediately if I get it right. In fact, I'll give you the recipe. That'll give me an excuse to spend the week-end experimenting."

*Does she have any tips for the beginner?*

"Don't fuss. If the dough doesn't rise, wait another hour. Perhaps the yeast is old or the room is too cold. Just leave it—it'll work in the end. Bread is very accommodating."

Here are some of her recipes for breads, mostly from the Caribbean, Mexico and Latin America.

# Boija (Coconut Corn Bread)

*An unusual Caribbean loaf that uses yeast. A good, solid bread, very well flavoured with a nice crunchy texture from the cornmeal.*

*Makes 2 loaves*

THE FLOUR:
*¾ lb white flour*
*½ lb cornmeal*

THE STARTER:
*1 oz fresh yeast or ½ oz dried yeast*
*about ½ pt lukewarm milk*

AND . . .
*¼ lb finely grated coconut*
*2 large ripe bananas, mashed*
*¼ lb unsalted butter, melted and cooled*
*2 tablespoons honey*
*½ teaspoon ground allspice*
*1 teaspoon salt*

METRIC EQUIVALENTS:
*350 g white flour*
*250 g cornmeal*
*30 g fresh yeast or 15 g dried yeast*
*about 300 ml lukewarm milk*
*125 g finely grated coconut*
*2 large ripe bananas, mashed*
*125 g unsalted butter, melted and cooled*
*2 tablespoons honey*
*½ teaspoon ground allspice*
*1 teaspoon salt*

*In colour — page 200*

YEAST STARTER:
Cream the yeast in half the lukewarm milk. Mix the flour and cornmeal together. Pour the yeast liquid into a mixing bowl and add half the flour mixture to make a sponge.

FIRST RISING:
Cover with a cloth and leave in a warm place to rise for about 1½ hours, until double in size.

THE MIX:
Add the rest of the flour mixture and all the remaining ingredients to the yeast and flour mixture and enough water to make a stiff batter. Beat thoroughly with a wooden spoon.

SECOND RISING:
Pour the mixture into 2 greased 9 x 5 x 3 in (230 x 130 x 80 mm) loaf tins. Cover loosely with a cloth and leave in a warm place to rise for about 30 minutes.

PRE-HEAT OVEN
to 350°F (180°C) Gas 4.

BAKING TIME:
Bake for 45 minutes to 1 hour, or until the bread begins to shrink from the sides of the tin and the top is lightly browned. Cool in the tin for a few minutes before turning out on to a wire rack.

# Floats

*These fried crispy breads are a lovely accompaniment to fish. They can also be eaten as a bread or to accompany drinks. Always serve them warm.*

*Makes about 18*

THE FLOUR:
*7 oz wholemeal flour*
*7 oz white flour*

THE STARTER:
*½ oz fresh yeast or ¼ oz dried yeast*
*3 tablespoons lukewarm water*

AND . . .
*1 teaspoon salt*
*4 oz butter, chilled and diced*
*1 teaspoon honey*
*about 7 fl.oz lukewarm water*
*¾ pt vegetable oil*

METRIC EQUIVALENTS:
*200 g wholemeal flour*
*200 g white flour*
*15 g fresh yeast or 8 g dried yeast*
*3 tablespoons lukewarm water*
*1 teaspoon salt*
*125 g butter, chilled and diced*
*1 teaspoon honey*
*about 200 ml lukewarm water*
*400 ml vegetable oil*

YEAST STARTER:
Mix the yeast with the lukewarm water and leave for a few minutes in a warm place.

THE MIX:
Mix the flours and salt together. Rub the butter into the flour until the mixture looks like breadcrumbs. Make a well in the centre and pour in the yeast liquid. Then add the honey and enough of the lukewarm water to make a fairly soft dough. Mix thoroughly, then knead for about 5 minutes on a lightly floured board until the dough is smooth and elastic.

FIRST RISING:
Return the dough to the bowl and leave in a warm place to rest for about 1 hour, until it has doubled in size.

SECOND RISING:
Mould the dough into small balls, about 1½ in (4 cm) in diameter. Arrange on a baking sheet and leave in a warm place until they have doubled in size, 45 minutes to 1 hour.

COOKING TIME:
Roll the floats out paper thin. Heat the oil in a large frying-pan and fry the floats for 2 to 3 minutes each side, until golden-brown. Drain them on paper towels.

## Banana Bread

*This bread is ideal at tea-time or for breakfast. The bananas add bulk and flavour, and the pecan nuts give texture. You can top slices of bread with ice-cream and fruit, and serve it as a dessert.*

THE MIX:
Cream the butter until fluffy, gradually adding the honey. Beat the egg in thoroughly. In a separate bowl, sieve together the flour, baking powder, salt and nutmeg. Add the vanilla to the mashed bananas. Gradually stir the dry ingredients and bananas alternately into the butter mixture. Beat well after each addition so that the ingredients are thoroughly blended. Dust the raisins with a teaspoon of flour and add them and the pecans to the mixture, mixing well. Pour into a greased 9 x 5 in (230 x 130 mm) bread tin.

PRE-HEAT OVEN
to 350°F (180°C) Gas 4.

BAKING TIME:
Bake for about 1 hour.

In colour—page 201

*Makes 1 loaf*

THE FLOUR:
*8 oz white flour*

THE RAISING AGENT:
*3 teaspoons baking powder*

AND . . .
*4 oz unsalted butter*
*2 tablespoons honey*
*1 egg*
*½ teaspoon salt*
*½ teaspoon nutmeg*
*1 to 2 drops vanilla essence*
*3 large ripe bananas, mashed*
*3 oz seedless raisins*
*3 tablespoons pecan nuts,*
  *coarsely chopped*

METRIC EQUIVALENTS:
*250 g white flour*
*3 teaspoons baking powder*
*125 g unsalted butter*
*2 tablespoons honey*
*1 egg*
*½ teaspoon salt*

*½ teaspoon nutmeg*
*1 to 2 drops vanilla essence*
*3 large ripe bananas, mashed*
*90 g seedless raisins*
*3 tablespoons pecan nuts, coarsely*
  *chopped*

# Pumpkin Buns

*Makes 12*

*Delightful sweet buns from Trinidad to eat instead of cake.*

THE FLOUR:
*½ lb white flour*

THE STARTER:
*1 oz fresh yeast or ½ oz dried
   yeast*
*2 tablespoons lukewarm water*
*1 tablespoon honey*

AND . . .
*½ teaspoon salt*
*1 teaspoon ground allspice*
*1 teaspoon ground ginger*
*3 oz seedless raisins*
*½ lb pumpkin, cooked, drained
   and mashed*
*1 oz unsalted butter*
*2 eggs, well beaten*
*grated rind of 1 lime or lemon*

METRIC EQUIVALENTS:
*250 g white flour*
*30 g fresh yeast or 15 g dried yeast*
*2 tablespoons lukewarm water*
*1 tablespoon honey*
*½ teaspoon salt*
*1 teaspoon ground allspice*
*1 teaspoon ground ginger*
*90 g seedless raisins*
*250 g pumpkin, cooked, drained
   and mashed*
*30 g unsalted butter*
*2 eggs, well beaten*
*grated rind of 1 lime or lemon*

YEAST STARTER:
Cream the yeast with the water and honey and leave in a warm place for about 10 minutes.

THE MIX:
Mix together the flour, salt, allspice and ginger. Add the raisins. While the pumpkin is still warm, add the butter to it and blend well together.
Make a well in the flour mixture, and add the yeast liquid, pumpkin mixture, eggs and grated rind. Draw in the flour and mix thoroughly. Knead into a smooth dough.

FIRST RISING:
Cover the dough and leave to rest in a warm place for about 30 minutes.

SECOND RISING:
Mould the dough into 12 buns, and arrange on a greased baking sheet. Leave to rise in a warm place for about 20 to 30 minutes.

PRE-HEAT OVEN
to 400°F (200°C) Gas 6.

BAKING TIME:
Bake for about 15 minutes and serve warm.

In colour—page 200

# Roti

*Makes about 4 large roti*

*Roti are of Indian origin; the term simply means bread, but like everything else in Trinidad, roti—basically parathas—have their own flavour and character. A large roti makes a good lunch, folded up like an envelope with some curry inside. A small roti is usually served as an accompaniment to a curry.*

THE FLOUR:
*½ lb wholemeal flour*

THE STARTER:
*½ oz fresh yeast*
*2 to 3 tablespoons warm water*

AND . . .
*1 teaspoon salt*
*1½ oz butter*
*2 oz clarified butter, melted*
*extra flour and water, as needed*

METRIC EQUIVALENTS:
*250 g wholemeal flour*
*15 g fresh yeast*
*2 to 3 tablespoons warm water*
*1 teaspoon salt*
*40 g butter*
*60 g clarified butter, melted*
*extra flour and water, as needed*

YEAST STARTER:
Cream the yeast in 2 to 3 tablespoons warm water.

THE MIX:
Mix the flour and salt in a bowl. Rub in the 1½ oz (40 g) butter with
your fingertips until the mixture resembles breadcrumbs. Make a
well in the centre and pour in the yeast liquid. Mix thoroughly with
a wooden spoon, then knead to make a fairly stiff dough. Add more
water, one tablespoon at a time, until the dough becomes softer and
more elastic but is not sticky. Knead well.

FIRST RISING:
Cover the dough and leave for 30 minutes.

SECOND RISING:
Knead again for 3 to 4 minutes, then divide into 4 balls. Roll out on
a floured board into 12 in or 8 in (30 cm or 20 cm) rounds as desired.
Brush lightly all over with clarified butter and sprinkle with flour.
Fold them in half twice so that they form a four-layered quarter-
circle. Cover and leave for 30 minutes.
Roughly shape the roti into circles with the hands and roll out on a
floured board into 12 in or 8 in (30 cm or 20 cm) rounds.

COOKING TIME:
Heat a cast-iron frying-pan or griddle until a little flour sprinkled
on it will instantly brown or water dropped on it splutters. Place
one of the roti in the pan and cook for about 1 minute. Turn and
spread with a thin layer of melted clarified butter. Cook for another
2 minutes and spread again with the butter. Cook for a minute
longer and turn. Cook for a minute on this side, and remove from
the pan to a board.
Hit all over with a wooden mallet until it is flaky. Wrap the roti in a
towel and keep warm until the other roti are cooked. Serve at once.

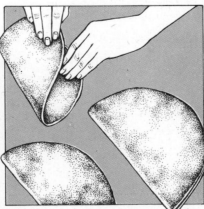
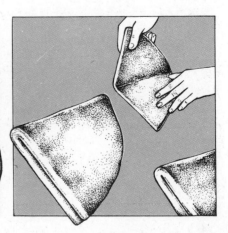

# Coconut Bread

In colour—page 200

*Makes 2 loaves*

THE FLOUR:
*¾ lb white flour*

THE RAISING AGENT:
*3 teaspoons baking powder*

AND...
*1 teaspoon salt*
*½ lb fresh coconut, finely grated*
*1 egg, well beaten*
*3 fl.oz evaporated milk*
*¼ lb honey*
*2 to 3 drops vanilla essence*
*4 oz unsalted butter, melted and
    cooled*

*Coconut is a traditional flavouring in the Caribbean. Make coconut
bread for breakfast or afternoon tea. Or wait until the evening and
serve it as a dessert with stewed fruit.*

THE MIX:
Sieve the flour, baking powder and salt into a large mixing bowl.
Add the coconut. Make a well in the centre and add the beaten egg,
milk, honey, vanilla and butter, mixing well. Divide the mixture
between 2 greased 9 x 5 in (230 x 130 mm) loaf tins and fill each
about half full.

PRE-HEAT OVEN
to 350°F (180°C) Gas 4.

BAKING TIME:
Bake for 50 to 55 minutes. Allow loaves to cool in the tins before
turning out on to a wire rack.

METRIC EQUIVALENTS:
*350 g white flour*
*3 teaspoons baking powder*
*1 teaspoon salt*
*250 g fresh coconut, finely grated*
*1 egg, well beaten*

*80 ml evaporated milk*
*125 g honey*
*2 to 3 drops vanilla essence*
*125 g unsalted butter, melted and
    cooled*

# Dal Puri (Bread stuffed with split peas) In colour—page 200

*This Trinidadian stuffed bread is usually served as a snack with drinks or as an accompaniment to a main dish. You need light fingers to roll the* puris, *so that the peas do not burst through.*

PREPARATION:
Soak the peas overnight and drain unless they are the quick cooking variety. Put the peas into a saucepan with enough water to cover. Stir in the massala. Bring to the boil and simmer, covered, until tender, about 1 hour. Add the cumin, onion and garlic, and salt and pepper to taste. Stir the mixture, which should be fairly dry, and set aside.

THE MIX:
Mix the flours with the baking powder and salt. Make a well in the centre and pour in the vegetable oil which has been mixed with the water. Mix together well with a wooden spoon to make a stiff dough. Add more water if the dough is too stiff, but it should not be soft. Knead thoroughly.

STANDING TIME:
Cover with a cloth and allow to stand for 1 hour.
Knead the dough again and divide into 4 equal size balls. Leave the balls to rest for 10 minutes.
Roll out lightly into circles. Put a quarter of the split pea mixture in the centre of each circle of dough. Moisten the edges with water and gather up the dough to cover the split peas, sealing it firmly.
Roll out the *puris* very gently until they are ¼ in (5 mm) thick. Be very careful or the stuffing will come through the dough. Using a pastry brush, paint the *puris* with clarified butter or oil.

COOKING TIME:
Cook them on a hot greased griddle, turning frequently and brushing with more butter or oil. Cook for about 10 minutes, until lightly browned and puffy. Serve any leftover filling with the *puris*.

*Makes 4*

THE FLOUR:
*¼ lb wholemeal flour*
*¼ lb white flour*

THE RAISING AGENT:
*1 teaspoon baking powder*

AND . . .
*4 oz split peas*
*1 tablespoon massala (curry powder)*
*1 teaspoon ground cumin*
*1 small onion, finely chopped*
*1 clove garlic, crushed*
*salt and freshly ground pepper*
*½ teaspoon salt*
*1 tablespoon vegetable oil*
*about 4 fl.oz water*
*clarified butter or oil for frying*

METRIC EQUIVALENTS:
*125 g wholemeal flour*
*125 g white flour*
*1 teaspoon baking powder*
*125 g split peas*
*1 tablespoon massala (curry powder)*
*1 teaspoon ground cumin*
*1 small onion, finely chopped*
*1 clove garlic, crushed*
*salt and freshly ground pepper*
*½ teaspoon salt*
*1 tablespoon vegetable oil*
*about 100 ml water*
*clarified butter or oil for frying*

# Traditional Tortillas

*Makes about 12*

THE FLOUR:
7 oz masa harina*

AND...
*1 teaspoon salt*
*8 fl.oz warm water*

METRIC EQUIVALENTS:
*200 g* masa harina*
*1 teaspoon salt*
*250 ml warm water*

*\*Masa harina is available from Harrods Food Store and some speciality shops.*

*These flat breads were made in early Mexico before the Spaniards introduced wheat. They form part of almost every meal in Mexico and several Central American countries. They are served fresh and warm, and are kept wrapped in a tea towel to keep their freshness. Cold tortillas can be warmed up over direct heat, but they should be turned continually. If they become dry, pat each one with damp hands.*

THE MIX:
Sift the *masa harina\** and salt into a bowl. Make a well in the centre and pour in the water. Gradually draw in the *masa harina\** and mix well to form a soft dough. Divide the dough into egg-sized balls. Flatten them on a *tortilla* press between 2 sheets of grease-proof paper to form thin pancakes about 4 in (10 cm) in diameter. If the *tortillas* stick, the dough is too moist. Add a little more *masa harina\** to the dough and begin again.

COOKING TIME:
Place a heavy frying-pan or griddle over a medium heat and cook the *tortillas,* one at a time, for about 1 minute on each side. The edges will begin to lift and the *tortillas* will be slightly browned.

# Arepas

*Makes 8 to 10*

THE FLOUR:
7 oz masa harina*

AND...
*1 teaspoon salt*
*about 9 fl.oz warm water*

METRIC EQUIVALENTS:
*200g* masa harina*
*1 teaspoon salt*
*about 275 ml warm water*

*\*Masa harina is available from Harrods Food Store and some speciality shops.*

*Arepas look like pure white round bread rolls or scones, yet they are made from maize flour processed in the same way as Mexican tortillas. These breads from Venezuela and Colombia are doughy inside, and deliciously crisp on the outside. To vary the flavour, add 4 oz (125 g) grated Gruyère cheese.*

THE MIX:
Mix the flour with the salt in a bowl. Stir in the water to make a stiffish dough. Add a little more if necessary. Let the dough stand for 5 minutes, then form into slightly flattened balls about 3 in (8 cm) across and about ½ in (1.5 cm) thick.

PRE-HEAT OVEN
to 350°F (180°C) Gas 4.

COOKING TIME:
Cook on a heavy, lightly greased griddle over a moderate heat for 5 minutes each side.

BAKING TIME:
Bake in the oven for 20 to 30 minutes, turning 2 or 3 times during the cooking. They are done when they sound hollow when tapped.

# Wheat Tortillas

*With the arrival of wheat in Mexico in the sixteenth century, a new kind of tortilla was made.*

THE MIX:
Sift the flour, baking powder and salt into a mixing bowl. Rub in the butter. Make a well in the centre and pour in enough water to make a stiff dough. Divide the dough into balls the size of small eggs. Roll them out on a lightly floured board, making them as thin as possible.

COOKING TIME:
Cook for about 2 minutes on each side in a heavy frying-pan or griddle over a medium heat.

Makes about 12

THE FLOUR:
*7 oz unbleached white flour*

THE RAISING AGENT:
*1 teaspoon baking powder*

AND . . .
*1 teaspoon salt*
*1 oz butter*
*about ¼ pt cold water*

METRIC EQUIVALENTS:
*200 g unbleached white flour*
*1 teaspoon baking powder*
*1 teaspoon salt*
*30 g butter*
*about 150 ml cold water*

# Sweet Corn Bread

*This spicy soft bread with a crunchy bite is more of a cake than a bread. The amount of baking powder may look surprising, but it is necessary as the cornmeal is very dense in texture.*

THE MIX:
Sift together all the dry ingredients, including the spices.
Cream the butter until light and fluffy and add the cornmeal mixture.
Gradually add the milk, coconut milk, honey, eggs and grated rind, and mix well with a wooden spoon. Stir in the grated coconut and the dried fruit and peel which have been tossed in a little flour.
Pour the mixture into 2 greased 9 x 5 in (230 x 130 mm) loaf tins.

PRE-HEAT OVEN
to 350°F (180°C) Gas 4.

BAKING TIME:
Bake for about 35 minutes in the centre of the oven.

METRIC EQUIVALENTS:
*350 g yellow cornmeal*
*125 g white flour*
*2 tablespoons baking powder*
*½ teaspoon each ground cinnamon,*
  *nutmeg and cloves*
*1 teaspoon salt*
*175 g butter*

*6 tablespoons milk*
*6 tablespoons coconut milk\**
*2 tablespoons honey*
*4 eggs, well beaten*
*grated rind of 1 lime or lemon*
*250 g fresh coconut, finely grated*
*250 g mixed dried fruit and peel*

In colour—page 201

Makes 2 loaves

THE FLOUR:
*¾ lb yellow cornmeal*
*¼ lb white flour*

THE RAISING AGENT:
*2 tablespoons baking powder*

AND . . .
*½ teaspoon each ground*
  *cinnamon, nutmeg and cloves*
*1 teaspoon salt*
*6 oz butter*
*6 tablespoons milk*
*6 tablespoons coconut milk\**
*2 tablespoons honey*
*4 eggs, well beaten*
*grated rind of 1 lime or lemon*
*½ lb fresh coconut, finely grated*
*½ lb mixed dried fruit and peel*

*\*Coconut Milk is available from some health food shops, or you can make it by steeping grated or desiccated coconut in boiling water for 1 hour.*

## Sopa Paraguaya (Paraguayan Corn Bread)

In colour—page 200

*Serves 6 to 8*

THE FLOUR:
*7 oz cornmeal*

AND...
*4 oz butter*
*2 medium onions, finely chopped*
*8 oz cottage cheese*
*8 oz grated Gruyère or Cheddar cheese*
*10½ oz can creamed sweet corn*
*1 teaspoon sea salt*
*⅓ pt milk*
*6 eggs, separated*

METRIC EQUIVALENTS:
*200 g cornmeal*
*125 g butter*
*2 medium onions, finely chopped*
*250 g cottage cheese*
*250 g Gruyère or Cheddar cheese*
*325 g can creamed sweet corn*
*1 teaspoon sea salt*
*200 ml milk*
*6 eggs, separated*

*This well-flavoured corn bread is traditionally served with beef soup and grilled steaks, but it is excellent with any meat or poultry dish or by itself. A pinch of dried aniseed may be added with the dry ingredients, if liked. To vary the texture, cut 2 oz (60 g) of the Gruyère into tiny cubes and stir this into the mixture at the last moment.*

THE MIX:
Heat half the butter in a frying-pan and sauté the onions until softened. Put to one side.
Cream the remaining butter and add to the cottage cheese, blending thoroughly. Add the Gruyère or Cheddar cheese and the onions. In another bowl mix the cornmeal, sweet corn, salt and milk thoroughly. Blend the cornmeal mixture with the cheese mixture. Beat the egg whites until they form soft peaks. Beat the yolks separately. Combine the two and stir them into the cornmeal and cheese mixture. Grease and flour a 10 x 13 in (255 x 330 mm) baking tin. Pour in the mixture.

PRE-HEAT OVEN
to 400°F (200°C) Gas 6.

BAKING TIME:
Bake for 45 minutes or until a skewer inserted into the loaf comes out clean.

## Bolillos (Mexican Bread Rolls)

*Makes 18*

THE FLOUR:
*½ lb wholemeal flour*
*½ lb strong white flour*

THE STARTER:
*½ oz fresh yeast or ¼ oz dried yeast*
*3 tablespoons lukewarm water*

AND...
*about 10 fl.oz lukewarm water*
*1½ teaspoons salt*

*These petit pains of Mexico, traditionally made with all white flour, were acquired during the short, unhappy reign of Maximilian that was imposed on the Mexicans by Napoleon III. Mexico preferred to remain independent but was not reluctant to accept French bread. Today, bolillos are sold fresh twice a day and are as good as any bread you will find in France.*

YEAST STARTER:
Put the yeast into a large bowl and soften it with 3 tablespoons lukewarm water.

THE MIX:
When the yeast has liquefied completely, stir in the rest of the lukewarm water and the salt, and mix. Gradually mix in the flours to make a dough that comes away from the sides of the bowl with a little stickiness. Knead the dough on a lightly floured board for 10 minutes, or until it is smooth and elastic and has lost its stickiness.

**FIRST RISING:**
Put the dough into a greased bowl, cover it with a clean cloth, and leave to rise for about 2 hours in a warm place until it has doubled in size

**SECOND RISING:**
Punch the dough down, cover it, and let it rise a second time for about 1 hour, until again doubled in bulk. Turn it out on to a lightly floured board and knead for about 5 minutes. Divide the dough in half. Roll each piece out into a strip about 18 in (45.5 cm) long and 6 in (15 cm) wide. Then roll each piece up like a Swiss roll. Cut each roll into 9 slices, making 18 in all. Pinch the ends of each slice and arrange on a greased baking sheet. (See diagram)

**THIRD RISING:**
Cover and let the rolls rise for about 1 hour until they have doubled in size.

**PRE-HEAT OVEN**
to 400°F (200°C) Gas 6.

**BAKING TIME:**
Brush the rolls lightly with water and bake for about 30 minutes, or until they are golden-brown.

**METRIC EQUIVALENTS:**
*250 g wholemeal flour*
*250 g strong white flour*
*15 g fresh yeast or 8 g dried yeast*
*3 tablespoons lukewarm water*
*about 300 ml lukewarm water*
*1½ teaspoons salt*

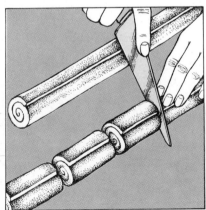
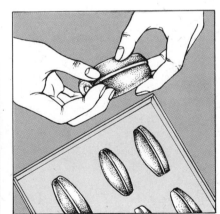

# Fouace (Walnut Hearth Cake)

In colour—page 256

*Makes 1 loaf*

THE FLOUR:
*8 oz white flour*

THE STARTER:
*scant ½ oz fresh yeast*
*4 tablespoons lukewarm milk*
*2 teaspoons honey*

AND...
*½ teaspoon salt*
*2 oz butter, cut into small pieces*
*1 egg, lightly beaten*
*4 oz chopped walnuts*
*1 egg yolk*
*1 teaspoon water*

METRIC EQUIVALENTS:
*250 g white flour*
*scant 15 g dried yeast*
*4 tablespoons lukewarm milk*
*2 teaspoons honey*
*½ teaspoon salt*
*60 g butter, cut into small pieces*
*1 egg, lightly beaten*
*125 g chopped walnuts*
*1 egg yolk*
*1 teaspoon water*

*This bread from the Périgord in France is delicious on its own or with a soft cheese such as Brie or Camembert; a pungent goat's cheese offsets the sweet walnuts perfectly. Serve the bread warm or at room temperature, buttered, or toasted and buttered for breakfast, or with coffee.*

YEAST STARTER:
In a small bowl mix together the yeast, milk and honey and let it stand in a warm place until the yeast is bubbly.

THE MIX:
Sift the flour and salt into a large bowl. Mix in the butter until the mixture resembles breadcrumbs. Make a well in the centre and add the egg and the yeast mixture. Mix to a soft but not sticky dough. If necessary add a little water. Turn the dough out on to a lightly floured board and knead until it is smooth and satiny, about 10 minutes. Knead the walnuts into the dough.

THE RISING:
Form the dough into a ball and place it on a buttered baking sheet. With a sharp knife slash the bread in 4 equidistant places. Cover with a cloth and leave in a warm, draught-free place until it has doubled in bulk, 2 to 3 hours.

PRE-HEAT OVEN
to 350°F (180°C) Gas 4.

BAKING TIME:
Beat the egg yolk with 1 teaspoon of water and brush the dough lightly with this egg wash. Bake for about 30 minutes or until it is browned and the bottom sounds hollow when tapped. Transfer to a rack to cool.

# Semolina Bread

*An Italian bread with a difference—the crunchy taste of semolina.*

*Makes 1 loaf*

YEAST STARTER:
Put the yeast into a small bowl with the lukewarm water and teaspoon of honey. Mix and let stand in a warm place until bubbly.

THE FLOUR:
*5 oz white flour*
*8 oz semolina*

THE MIX:
In a large bowl sift together the semolina, flour and salt. Rub the butter into the flour mixture with the fingertips until it resembles coarse breadcrumbs. Make a well in the centre, add the egg, the yeast mixture and the tablespoon of honey. Mix to a soft dough. Turn out on to a floured surface and knead for 5 to 10 minutes.

THE STARTER:
*1 oz fresh yeast or ½ oz dried*
  *yeast*
*3 fl.oz lukewarm water*
*1 teaspoon honey*

AND . . .
*1 teaspoon salt*
*2 oz butter, cut into small pieces*
*1 egg, lightly beaten*
*1 tablespoon honey*
*1 egg yolk*
*1 teaspoon water*

THE RISING:
Form the dough into a ball and place on a greased baking sheet. Make 4 equidistant slashes in the dough and cover it with a cloth. Put in a warm, draught-free place to rise until double in bulk, 2 to 3 hours.

PRE-HEAT OVEN
to 350°F (180°C) Gas 4.

METRIC EQUIVALENTS:
*150 g white flour*
*250 g semolina*
*30 g fresh yeast or 15 g dried yeast*
*6 tablespoons lukewarm water*
*1 teaspoon honey*
*1 teaspoon salt*
*60 g butter, cut into small pieces*
*1 egg, lightly beaten*
*1 tablespoon honey*
*1 egg yolk*
*1 teaspoon water*

BAKING TIME:
Beat the egg yolk with the teaspoon of water, and brush over the dough. Bake for about 30 minutes.

# Chalice

John Reynard opened the Chalice wholemeal bakery in Bury St. Edmunds in Suffolk at the age of 33. Five years ago he was disillusioned with his job, market researching detergents for Unilever in France. "I started to look for something else. I left my job. I didn't know what I was looking for. But I knew what I was coming from."

He travelled to America. "I was on holiday in California and I went to the Tassajara Centre which is just north of San Francisco. It is a Zen centre, all about meditation, and food." It was a profound experience.

It was only afterwards that he discovered that the place was famous for *The Tassajara Bread Book*—which was to prove an inspiration later. The book is by a former cook at the Zen Centre, Edward Espe Brown. This is how he describes making bread:

*"Bread makes itself, by your kindness, with your help, with imagination running through you, with dough under hand, you are bread-making itself, which is why bread-making is so fulfilling and rewarding.*

*"A recipe doesn't belong to anyone. Given to me, I give it to you. Only a guide, only a skeletal framework. You must fill in the flesh according to your nature and desire. Your life, your love will bring these words into full creation. This cannot be taught. You already know. So please cook, love, feel, create."*

These ideals were alien to those Reynard had accepted in his career in marketing. And Tassajara bread was a world apart from the packets of white sliced his mother sold in a grocer's shop in South Yorkshire. But he was converted. He loved their sense of caring.

"It's very Zen to be in touch with what you're doing even if it's only preparing vegetables, and especially when making bread. You really know when someone cares: the Life Force comes through. It's very different from the junk food that's turned out ad lib. I mean the positive side, what you put into it; it's about compassion and respect reflected in everything you do."

He decided to open a vegetarian restaurant. He bought an old bakery in Bury St. Edmunds, Suffolk, planning to convert it. The deep brick oven, a hundred years old, had never cooled. The brothers who were selling it assumed he would go

on baking. And he did; first of all with a fortnight's tuition from the brothers, and then with the help of a German baker. "He showed us how to use a local flour, *Hofel's*. We learnt that English wheat is too soft for a wholemeal that rises. *Hofel's* is 60 per cent imported organic flour to 40 per cent English. We discovered you can add natural gluten—up to about 5 per cent."

John Reynard found a baker, Robb Halliday, whose background was art college. Robb had to learn by trial and error: a few days' apprenticeship here and there to improve his skills, such as working with the Bamboo Grove, Powis Mews, W11, one of the biggest producers of wholemeal bread in London.

The bakery was hard work: they would bake 200 loaves in one batch, and sell about 500 a day, But the mark-up on a loaf is small and Reynard needed a restaurant to make it commercially viable. "I hope I'm business-like. You can't be airy-fairy in the wholefood business. You must be strong. There's nothing wrong with business. It's only the way some people do it."

The following breads were inspired by Tassajara with some variations:

# Cinnamon Rolls

*These rolls are really breads with fillings, but their shape is based on Swedish tea rings.*

**YEAST STARTER:**
Mix the yeast with the teaspoon of honey and a little of the warm water.

**THE MIX:**
Dissolve the dried milk in the remaining warm water or just use the warm water. Mix with the flour, salt, vegetable oil or melted butter, and the egg. Add the yeast mixture. Mix to a firm but pliable dough. Knead lightly.

**FIRST RISING:**
Cover the dough and leave to rise for 2 hours.

**SECOND RISING:**
Knock back, then roll out on a floured surface into a rectangle about ¼ in (5 mm) thick. Brush with honey and sprinkle with raisins or sultanas and cinnamon. Roll up like a Swiss roll, with the seam downwards, touching the tin. Cut into sections or cut part way and bend into a circle, forming a lovely crown and put on a greased baking tin to rise for 30 minutes in a warm place.

**PRE-HEAT OVEN**
to 375°F (190°C) Gas 5.

**BAKING TIME:**
Brush with the beaten egg mixture and bake for 20 minutes. Cool on a wire rack.

**VARIATIONS:**
Instead of cinnamon, use home-made fruit purées; home-made conserves; or mixtures of dates, dried fruits and nuts.

*Makes about 20*

THE FLOUR:
*1 lb wholemeal flour*

THE STARTER:
*1 oz fresh yeast or ½ oz dried yeast*
*1 teaspoon honey*

AND . . .
*8 fl.oz warm water*
*2 oz dried milk (optional)*
*1 teaspoon salt*
*2 tablespoons vegetable oil or melted butter*
*1 egg, beaten*
*2 tablespoons honey*
*4 oz raisins or sultanas*
*cinnamon for sprinkling*
*1 egg beaten with 2 teaspoons water*

METRIC EQUIVALENTS:
*500 g wholemeal flour*
*30 g fresh yeast or 15 g dried yeast*
*1 teaspoon honey*
*250 ml warm water*
*60 g dried milk (optional)*
*1 teaspoon salt*
*2 tablespoons vegetable oil or melted butter*
*1 egg, beaten*
*2 tablespoons honey*
*125 g raisins or sultanas*
*cinnamon for sprinkling*
*1 egg beaten with 2 teaspoons water*

# Fruit or Vegetable Filled Loaves

In colour—page 88

*Makes 2 loaves*

THE FLOUR:
*1½ lb wholemeal flour*

THE STARTER:
*½ oz fresh yeast or ¼ oz dried
    yeast
4 tablespoons warm water
1 teaspoon honey*

AND . . .
*1½ teaspoons salt
2 tablespoons vegetable oil
12 fl.oz warm water
1 egg
fillings, of your choice, see below
1 egg, beaten
poppy seeds*

*The wholemeal dough is rolled out thin and flat like a pizza, a filling is laid on top and then the sides are cut into flaps and folded over. It's a loaf which is a pie, and can have a variety of fillings.*

YEAST STARTER:
Dissolve the yeast in the warm water with the honey, and wait until it bubbles.

THE MIX:
Sieve the flour once to remove the coarser bran. Mix the flour, salt, oil, yeast mixture, and 12 fl.oz (350 ml) of warm water. Mix to an elastic dough.

FIRST RISING:
Leave the dough in a covered bowl to rise, about 2 hours.

FILLING:
Roll the dough into a flat rectangle ½ in (1.5 cm) thick. Mark lengthwise into 3 equal widths. Place ample filling along the centre strip. Make 6 to 8 cuts from centre to outside edge on the outer strips, so that folds can be lifted to make covering flaps. Fold over, one from each side so that they overlap, criss-crossing.

*FILLINGS
FRUIT:
*1 lb (500 g) sliced, cooked apples
    sweetened with honey,
    sprinkled with dried fruit,
    ground nutmeg, cinnamon,
    and cloves*

OR
*4 bananas mashed with honey*

OR
*1 lb (500 g) sliced, cooking pears
    mixed with 2 sliced bananas,
    honey and spices*

OR
*½ lb (250 g) dates, nuts, sultanas,
    raisins mixed with spices*

OR
*Any fruit purée with mixed
    dried fruit and nuts*

VEGETABLE:
*1 lb (500 g) leeks, blanched 5
    minutes, drained, sliced thinly,
    and seasoned*

OR
*1 lb (500 g) carrots, sliced thinly
    and parboiled for 10 minutes,
    drained and seasoned*

OR
*1 lb (500 g) mixed diced
    vegetables: blanched 5 minutes
    in boiling water, drained and
    seasoned*

SAVOURY:
*1 to 2 eggs beaten with
    8 oz (250 g) grated cheese
    1 teaspoon powdered mustard
    ½ oz (15 g) melted butter*

OR
*Left-over cooked brown rice
    flavoured with tamari sauce*

**SECOND RISING:**
Place on a greased baking tray and cover to prove for 30 minutes.

**PRE-HEAT OVEN**
to 350°F (180°C) Gas 4.

**BAKING TIME:**
Brush with the beaten egg and sprinkle with poppy seeds. Bake for 1 hour.

**METRIC EQUIVALENTS:**
*750 g wholemeal flour*
*15 g fresh yeast or 8 g dried yeast*
*4 tablespoons warm water*
*1 teaspoon honey*
*1½ teaspoons salt*
*2 tablespoons vegetable oil*
*350 ml warm water*
*1 egg*
*fillings of your choice, see above*
*1 egg, beaten*
*poppy seeds*

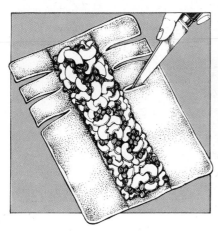
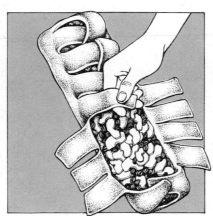
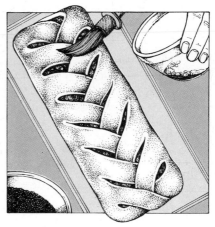

# Dinah Morrison

Dinah Morrison is a food stylist. She baked the bread for this book and cooks for leading British photographers like Tessa Traeger and Christine Hanscomb. You will see her beautifully baked loaves in magnificent cookery books and illustrated food articles in the best magazines. They do not merely satisfy the demands of taste; they also have to live up to the camera's exacting scrutiny. This, she says, is not difficult with bread: "Bread is very photogenic. It isn't too delicate. You can exaggerate the shapes. And it has such nice surfaces. You can cover them with flour or different glazes, or sprinkle them with seeds."

It's the shape of bread that really intrigues Dinah: "I love playing with the dough. It's like plasticine or clay. I suppose I'm a frustrated potter really. I like the feel of it."

Bread brings back memories: "When we were children in the war, we lived near Welwyn in Hertfordshire. Our bread was delivered once a week from Harrods. It was OK at the beginning of the week, but by the end it was rather stale, but terribly wholesome. At boarding school we were given sliced white bread, which wasn't very nice. But we spread our own jam on it and we had bread-eating competitions. Far better than school dinners."

When Dinah first started making her own bread, she made hot cross buns. "I felt that Easter wasn't right without them. Mother always made them, so when I became a mother, I felt I should make them too."

Dinah didn't begin to take cooking seriously until she went to America in her early thirties. There she worked as assistant to Joe Hyde, a chef who had trained in France with the Troisgros brothers. "Helping him behind the scenes and watching him give cookery classes made me want to be more professional about my own cooking."

Three years in Germany with three small children gave her ample time to extend her range of dishes. She entertained a lot at home. Sometimes she brought the German rye bread from the local shop, but for variety she made her own.

She also bought a powerful electric mixer, a

Braun. And she soon stopped following recipes: "Once I'd learned the basics—flour, yeast, liquid, salt—I began to make up my own variations. It's always a different loaf. Even if you use the same ingredients, it comes out differently. The joy of home-made bread is that it's never boring. It's also therapeutic. When I'm in a bad temper, I like kneading the dough and giving it a good bashing."

Dinah has taught her three children to bake. Eighteen-year-old Miranda, the only girl, is the most enthusiastic. But she doesn't like using dried yeast, the instructions on the packet are too vague. What did Miranda start off with? "Oh, hot cross buns, like mum, of course."

Dinah's useful hints for the beginner: "Don't be afraid. Apart from the odd failure with packet yeast which may have been exposed to the air, you can't really go wrong. Yeast will work anywhere. It just takes longer if it's too cold. And you don't need to watch it. You can go out and leave it in the refrigerator or a cool larder, then bake it in the evening. But don't try to make too much bread at once. It's jolly hard work."

# Hot Cross Buns

*A family favourite at any time of year, though tradition has it that they should be eaten at Easter. A splendid spicy fragrance fills the kitchen when they are cooking.*

YEAST STARTER:
Warm half the milk, mix with the yeast and leave for about 5 minutes.

THE MIX:
Mix the flours, salt and spice in a large warmed bowl. Heat the rest of the milk to boiling point and stir in the honey, butter, and saffron, if used. Allow to cool. Add to the flour with the drained currants and yeast mixture. Knead well, adding a little more milk or flour, if necessary, to make a smooth, even dough.

FIRST RISING:
Cover with greased cling film and a tea-cloth, and allow to rise for 50 to 60 minutes or until double in size.

SECOND RISING:
Punch down the dough, turn out on to a work-surface and cut into 12 equal sized pieces. Turn the cut edges under on each of these to make nice round buns. Place on a lightly greased baking sheet and leave to rise in a warm place for 30 to 40 minutes.

THIRD RISING:
Cut a cross in the top of each bun using a very sharp knife. Leave to rise again for 10 minutes.

PRE-HEAT OVEN
to 400°F (200°C) Gas 6.

BAKING TIME:
Bake for 20 to 25 minutes. (A pan of hot water on the bottom shelf of the oven will help to keep the buns soft.) When cooked, remove from the oven and glaze by brushing over with the warmed honey while still hot to give a nice glossy finish.

*Makes 12*

THE FLOUR:
*10 oz unbleached strong white flour*
*6 oz wholemeal flour*

THE STARTER:
*¾ oz fresh yeast*

AND . . .
*½ pt milk*
*1 teaspoon salt*
*1 rounded teaspoon mixed spice*
*2 tablespoons honey*
*2 oz butter*
*saffron (optional)*
*2 oz currants, soaked in hot water until soft*
*For glazing;*
*3 tablespoons warmed honey*

METRIC EQUIVALENTS:
*300 g unbleached strong white flour*
*175 g wholemeal flour*
*20 g fresh yeast*
*300 ml milk*
*1 teaspoon salt*
*1 rounded teaspoon mixed spice*
*2 tablespoons honey*
*60 g butter*
*saffron (optional)*
*60 g currants, soaked in hot water until soft*
*For glazing:*
*3 tablespoons warmed honey*

# Double Plaited Loaf

*A decorative loaf, delicious as it is, and excellent toasted.*

*Makes 1 large loaf*

THE FLOUR:
*1 lb unbleached strong white
    flour*
*½ lb wholemeal flour*

THE STARTER:
*¾ oz fresh yeast*

AND . . .
*8 fl.oz warm milk*
*1½ teaspoons salt*
*1 egg, beaten*
*5 fl.oz water*
*For the top:*
*1 egg yolk*
*pinch of salt*
*1 teaspoon water*
*poppy seeds to decorate*

YEAST STARTER:
Dissolve the yeast in 3 tablespoons of the warm milk and leave to stand for about 5 minutes to froth.

THE MIX:
Mix the flours and salt in a large, warmed bowl. Make a well in the centre of the flour and pour in the yeast mixture, the rest of the milk, the beaten egg, and enough warm water to make a manageable dough. Knead well.

FIRST RISING:
Cover the bowl with oiled cling film and a tea-cloth. Allow to rise in a warm place for about an hour.
Punch down the dough and divide into 4 equal pieces. Cover one piece with cling film. Roll the other three into long, thin strips and plait them together, sealing the ends with a little water. Place on a greased baking sheet.
Take the remaining piece of dough, and divide it into 3 pieces. Roll these into long thin strips and plait as before.

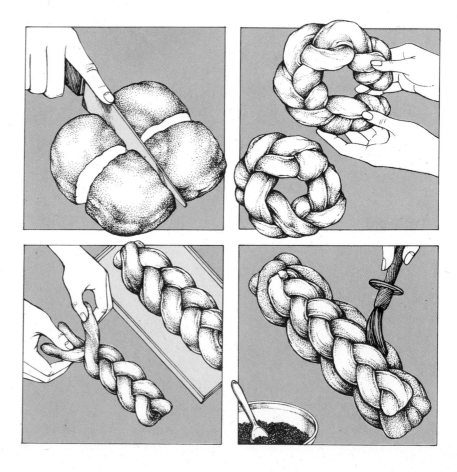

For the top: Beat the egg yolk with a pinch of salt and a teaspoon of water. Brush the larger plait with some of this and place the small plait firmly on top. Brush this over, too, with the egg mix.

SECOND RISING:
Cover with oiled cling film and leave in a warm place to rise for about 40 minutes. When nicely risen, paint the whole top of the loaf again with the egg mix and sprinkle over with poppy seeds.

PRE-HEAT OVEN
to 400°F (200°C) Gas 6.

BAKING TIME:
Bake for 45 minutes. After 40 minutes turn the loaf over, and cook for a further 5 minutes, or until the bread sounds hollow when tapped on the bottom.

METRIC EQUIVALENTS:
*500 g unbleached strong white flour*
*250 g wholemeal flour*
*20 g fresh yeast*
*250 ml warm milk*
*1½ teaspoons salt*
*1 egg, beaten*
*150 ml water*
For the top:
*1 egg yolk*
*pinch of salt*
*1 teaspoon water*
*poppy seeds to decorate*

# Wholemeal Pitta Bread

*An unusual wholemeal version of this Middle Eastern and Mediterranean bread. Serve it alone or split open and filled with salad and kebabs or cheese and onion.*

YEAST STARTER:
Cream the yeast with 2 tablespoons of the warm water and leave for about 5 minutes to froth.

THE MIX:
Sift the white flour into a large warmed bowl and mix in the wholemeal flour. Dissolve the salt in the rest of the warm water. Make a well in the centre of the flour and gradually pour in the yeast liquid, olive oil and enough of the warm water to make a soft dough. Knead well.

FIRST RISING:
Cover with a piece of greased cling film and a tea towel. Leave to rise in a warm place for about 1 hour, or until double in size. Turn the dough out on to a work-surface and punch down. Cut into 8 pieces of equal size. Fold the edges of each piece under and roll them into flat oval shapes.

SECOND RISING:
Put the oval breads on to 2 greased baking sheets. Leave them to rise for 15 minutes, covered as above.

PRE-HEAT OVEN
to 425°F (220°C) Gas 7.

BAKING TIME:
Bake for 20 minutes.

*Makes 8*

THE FLOUR:
*12 oz wholemeal flour*
*4 oz unbleached strong white flour*

THE STARTER:
*½ oz fresh yeast*

AND . . .
*about 10 fl.oz warm water*
*2 teaspoons* Maldon *sea salt*
*2 to 3 tablespoons olive oil*

METRIC EQUIVALENTS:
*350 g wholemeal flour*
*125 g unbleached strong white flour*
*15 g fresh yeast*
*about 300 ml warm water*
*2 teaspoons* Maldon *sea salt*
*2 to 3 tablespoons olive oil*

In colour—page 128

*Makes 2 small loaves*

THE FLOUR:
*1½ lb* Granary *flour*

THE STARTER:
*¾ oz fresh yeast*

AND...
*about 12 fl.oz warm water*
*4 oz walnuts*
*2 teaspoons* Maldon *sea salt*
*2 to 3 tablespoons oil, walnut if*
    *possible*
*6 oz finely chopped onion*

METRIC EQUIVALENTS:
*750 g* Granary *flour*
*20 g fresh yeast*
*about 350 ml warm water*
*125 g walnuts*
*2 teaspoons* Maldon *sea salt*
*2 to 3 tablespoons oil, walnut if*
    *possible*
*175 g finely chopped onion*

# Walnut and Onion Loaf

*The combination of nuts and onions give this* Granary *bread a delicious savoury flavour, ideal on its own or with cheese.*

YEAST STARTER:
Cream the yeast with 3 tablespoons of the warm water and leave aside for about 5 minutes to dissolve.

THE MIX:
Put aside 8 of the best walnuts for decoration, and chop the others.
Dissolve the *Maldon* sea salt in the rest of the water.
Put the flour into a large mixing bowl. Mix the yeast liquid and salt-water into the flour with the oil. Gradually add a little more water, or flour, if needed to make a fairly wet but manageable dough. Knead well. Blend in the chopped onions and walnuts.

FIRST RISING:
Cover the dough with oiled cling film and a tea-cloth and allow to rise for about 1 hour, or until double in size.
Knock down the dough and divide into pieces of equal size. Fold each piece over, making four quarter-turns, so that it is smooth on top and has a neat join or seam beneath. Put each portion of dough into a well-greased 1 lb (500 g) loaf tin, with the seam underneath.

SECOND RISING:
Cover with oiled cling film and put to rise for a further 40 minutes in a warm place, or until the dough has risen to the tops of the tins. Arrange the walnuts in a row on top of the loaves, moistening them underneath with a little water to help them stay in position.

PRE-HEAT OVEN
to 400°F (200°C) Gas 6.

BAKING TIME:
Bake for 40 to 45 minutes. Cover the loaves with grease-proof paper if the walnuts start to become too brown.

# Buckwheat and Buttermilk Waffles

In colour—page 129

*Makes about 20*

THE FLOUR:
*4 oz buckwheat flour*
*2 oz white flour*

THE RAISING AGENTS:
*1 teaspoon cream of tartar*
*½ teaspoon bicarbonate of soda*

*To make these delicious waffles you will need a special waffle-iron, available from most kitchenware departments. Serve with honey or maple syrup.*

THE MIX:
Sift together the two flours, the cream of tartar and bicarbonate of soda. Make a well in the centre and put in the egg yolks, the buttermilk and the melted butter. Mix together quickly.
Beat the egg whites with a pinch of salt until stiff, then fold them into the batter and add up to 2 fl.oz (60 ml) of milk to make the

batter fluid enough to spread on to the waffle-iron.

**PRE-HEAT IRON**
to moderately hot and pour in enough batter to fill the bottom half of it.

**COOKING TIME:**
Close the iron and cook on both sides, about 2 minutes, until the waffle is golden-brown, crisp on the outside and still slightly soft inside. Keep the waffles warm in a low oven.

AND . . .
*2 eggs, separated*
*9 fl.oz buttermilk*
*2 oz butter, melted*
*pinch of salt*
*2 fl.oz milk*

METRIC EQUIVALENTS:
*125 g buckwheat flour*
*60 g white flour*
*1 teaspoon cream of tartar*
*½ teaspoon bicarbonate of soda*
*2 eggs, separated*
*275 ml buttermilk*
*60 g butter, melted*
*pinch of salt*
*60 ml milk*

# Yorkshire Oat Cakes

*A delicious oatmeal breakfast. Toast and serve with butter and marmalade.*

**YEAST STARTER:**
Crumble the yeast into 3 to 4 tablespoons of the warm water and leave to stand for 10 minutes.

**THE MIX:**
Mix the yeast liquid with the fine oatmeal and the rest of the warm water.

**THE RISING:**
Leave to rise for 30 minutes in a warm place. Stir in 2 oz (60 g) of the medium oatmeal.

**PRE-HEAT**
a heavy griddle or heavy frying-pan until moderately hot. Wipe with a little sunflower oil on a piece of kitchen paper.

**COOKING TIME:**
Sprinkle on a teaspoon of the remaining oatmeal and pour on a ladleful of batter. Spread this out quickly with a spatula as thinly as possible until it is approximately 6 in (15 cm) in diameter. When the top is dry, sprinkle this with a little more of the oatmeal and turn it over to cook on the other side. When this too is dry put the oat cake on a rack to cool, and repeat the process until the batter is finished. If it gets too thick at the bottom, add a little more water. These very unpromising floppy oat cakes should now be toasted and served deliciously hot.

*Makes about 12*

THE FLOUR:
*4 oz fine oatmeal*
*4 oz medium oatmeal*

THE STARTER:
*½ oz fresh yeast*

AND . . .
*½ pt warm water*
*a little sunflower oil*

METRIC EQUIVALENTS:
*125 g fine oatmeal*
*125 g medium oatmeal*
*15 g fresh yeast*
*300 ml warm water*
*a little sunflower oil*

# Grodzinski

Grodzinski's is one of the leading three or four bakeries in London which serve the Jewish community. They provide a taste of Europe with traditional rye breads and black breads, Sabbath cholla brushed with egg yolk and speckled with poppy seeds, and sweet yeasty tea cakes.

The head of this famous family firm is Harry Grodzinski, now in his seventies. It is over a hundred years since his grandmother, Judith, was the first Grodzinski to bake in London, selling her "wedding rolls" from a basket in a street market.

The Grodzinskis had been bakers in Lithuania as long as anyone can remember, and there was a Grodzinski's there until 1939: but Harry Grodzinski's grandparents left in 1888, fleeing from the *pogroms*.

"My grandmother, Judith, née Goide—another name in baking—started by baking wedding rolls: *bulkalech*. You make them with the same dough as cholla, but you take two strips of the dough and twist them into a little bun. You brush it with egg and sprinkle with poppy seeds. You don't add egg to the mixture, because it makes it too cakey. Jewish people don't like it so cakey."

In those far off days Judith Grodzinski didn't have a large, modernised bakery at her disposal. She didn't even have an oven: "She had to hire the oven of master-baker Galevitz. She arrived at his bakery at 6 a.m. every morning and when he finished baking his bread she carried on with her own. Her husband took the rolls to Wentworth market in a big basket, then he sat on a stool and sold them from the basket."

The continuous *pogroms* in Russia and Poland at the turn of the century brought a lot of Jewish people to London. And they all wanted bread: "Around 1900, grandfather Aaron opened his own bakery, first in Bedford Street, then in Fieldgate Street, in the East End. At first he had one double-decker oven, but soon he had three coal-fired double-decker ovens. They did all the work by hand. They made all their own dough until 1916, when they got a dough-making machine. By 1920 they were producing about 20,000 loaves a week, under the direction of master-baker Rosenblatt."

Apart from grandmother Judith, none of the Grodzinskis were true bakers. They all had training at bakery school, but soon found that their strength lay in administration and organisation rather than

baking. However, they had a knack for choosing good bakers: "We've always had good bakers, like Rosenblatt. He was a real craftsman. And we've got a wonderful staff-director relationship. We only ever had one strike, and that was in 1916."

Harry and his two brothers and two sisters were all born in the premises above the bakery in Fieldgate Street. They were bought up with the smell of bread—and with the smell of ovens. This was not the pleasant aroma that today's home bakers enjoy: "It was really bad. The ovens were coal-fired. You couldn't open the windows because of the soot. The neighbours were always complaining, because they couldn't hang their washing out to dry."

Harry was in his twenties before he moved away from the bakery to Hampstead Garden Suburb: "It was like Paradise. You could smell the flowers. The night-scented stock was wonderful." But his career in the bakery began long before that. He was set to work at the age of sixteen, when one of the van drivers was taken ill: "We had two horse-drawn vans. One delivered to the West End and one to the East End of London. We had to start loading at about four in the morning and it could take up to two hours to load the vans. I didn't know the route. The driver said, 'Don't worry, the horse knows all the shops'. But the horse just stopped to drink at the water fountain in front of the Royal Exchange. I had to work it out for myself."

He's been working it out ever since. He joined the firm at the age of twenty and he and his brother Reuben soon took over from their widowed mother. But Harry does not put the success of the business down to his own or his family's endeavours alone: "This firm runs on *muzzel* (luck). Twice we were almost hit in the war. Once a gas cylinder blew up right near our house in the Garden Suburb but we were unhurt. And once the bakery was hit. It was about six in the morning. The bread was baked and waiting to be loaded. All the windows were broken, but instead of blowing in, they blew out. The glass fell into the street. All the loaves were saved."

Grodzinski's loaves met no losses in the war, but he did lose his labels: "It was the custom for Jewish bakers to attach a label to the underside of each loaf, so you could identify your bread. People would go in and ask for a Grodzinski loaf. They do the same thing now with paper wrappers. But in the war they complained that the labels were wasteful. People were throwing away the piece of the bread with the label attached."

Now, Grodzinski's have no such identification problems. They sell the bread from their own shops. The company has expanded and been modernised, and about ten years ago, Harry's sons, David and Jonathan, joined him in the company.

Harry was born with the smell of bread in his nostrils, a smell he can recognise anywhere in the world: "In 1930 I went touring in a Riley through France, Germany and Switzerland. At five in the morning we reached the top of the St. Gotthard's Pass. We stopped to breathe in the fresh air — and I smelt bread. On a cold night, you can smell it from miles away. Twenty minutes later we were eating hot rolls."

Harry still eats hot rolls and bread and pastries. "I hear I'm making rum babas these days," he said to his head baker. "I'll have a dozen of those." But he also likes to keep on the go, and goes for long walks and hikes two or three times a year, and swims whenever he can. Which of his many breads does he prefer? "Black bread in the week and cholla at the week-end. In Hebrew, we have a saying, cholla and butter is a taste of paradise'." And who could deny himself that?

Here are some recipes for Jewish breads and buns, as grandmother Judith Grodzinski might have made them.

# Curd Cheese Buns

*Makes about 12*

THE FLOUR:
*8 oz white flour*

THE STARTER:
*scant ½ oz fresh yeast*
*2 teaspoons honey*

AND . . .
*about ¼ pt warm water*
*¼ teaspoon salt*
*5 oz butter*
*1 egg, beaten*

THE FILLING:
*1 lb curd or cream cheese*
*1 egg*
*2 tablespoons honey*
*2 oz sultanas*

METRIC EQUIVALENTS:
*250 g white flour*
*scant 15 g fresh yeast*
*2 teaspoons honey*
*about 150 ml warm water*
*¼ teaspoon salt*
*150 g butter*
*1 egg, beaten*
For the filling:
*500 g curd or cream cheese*
*1 egg*
*2 tablespoons honey*
*60 g sultanas*

*Small light morsels, something like croissants with slightly sweetened curd cheese centres. Chill the dough overnight in the refrigerator and serve them with coffee for breakfast.*

YEAST STARTER:
Add the honey to the yeast, cream with 1 to 2 tablespoons of the warm water and leave for 5 minutes.

THE MIX:
Mix the flour and salt. Rub in 1 oz (30 g) of the butter. Make a well in the flour and add the egg, the yeast mixture and enough of the water to make a soft dough. Turn out on to a floured board and knead well.
Roll the dough into an oblong about 12 in (30 cm) long. Cut the rest of the butter into small pieces and cover two-thirds of the oblong with one-third of the butter. Fold the unbuttered piece up one-third and bring the other piece over it. Seal the edges. Turn to the left, roll out into an oblong, and repeat the process using another one-third of the butter. Repeat a third time using the last of the butter. Repeat once more without butter.

CHILLING TIME:
Place in the refrigerator and chill well for about 1 hour or more.

THE FILLING:
Beat the filling ingredients together well. Roll out the dough thinly and cut in 2 in (5 cm) squares. Place on a greased baking tray. Spoon some cheese mixture in the centre of each square. Damp the edges and fold each corner up towards the middle.

THE RISING:
Allow to rise in a cool place for about 1 hour until puffed up.

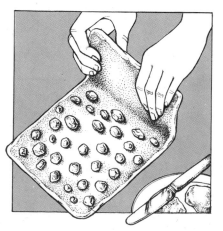

PRE-HEAT OVEN
to 450°F (230°C) Gas 8.

BAKING TIME:
Bake for 15 minutes.

VARIATION:
*To make a fruit bun, you will need sultanas and/or other dried fruit, honey, cinnamon and chopped almonds. Make the dough and chill well as above. Roll the dough into a square. Brush it with melted butter. Coat with honey and sprinkle with dried fruit, cinnamon and nuts, leaving a margin around the edges. Wet the edges and roll the dough into a Swiss roll shape. Cut into ½ in (1.5 cm) slices. Place the slices on a greased baking tin and bake in the pre-heated oven as above.*

## Platzels

*A traditional Jewish crusty roll with a "dimple" in the middle, sprinkled with poppy seeds.*

*Makes 12*

YEAST STARTER:
Cream the yeast with 1 or 2 tablespoons of the water and leave for 5 minutes.

THE FLOUR:
*1 lb white flour*

THE MIX:
Put the flour in a large mixing bowl with the salt. Add the honey, the oil, the yeast mixture, and enough water to make a soft dough. Turn out on to a floured board and knead well.

THE STARTER:
*½ oz fresh yeast*

AND . . .
*about 10 fl.oz lukewarm water
scant teaspoon salt
1 teaspoon honey
1 teaspoon vegetable oil
1 egg
poppy seeds*

FIRST RISING:
Leave to rise, covered, in a warm place for about 1 hour until double in size.

SECOND RISING:
Knock back, knead again. Divide into 12 pieces, about 1 to 2 oz each (30 to 60 g). Roll each piece into a ball and place on a greased baking tray. Flatten each ball with the palm of your hand or a rolling pin. Cover and leave to rise for about 30 minutes in a warm place.

METRIC EQUIVALENTS:
*500 g white flour
15 g fresh yeast
about 300 ml lukewarm water
scant teaspoon salt
1 teaspoon honey
1 teaspoon vegetable oil
1 egg
poppy seeds*

PRE-HEAT OVEN
to 450°F (230°C) Gas 8.

BAKING TIME:
Press a dimple in the middle of each *platzel* with a floured finger. Beat the egg and add 1 tablespoon of the remaining water. Brush each roll with the egg wash and sprinkle with poppy seeds. Bake for about 10 minutes until brown.

# Cholla and Bulkalech (Wedding Rolls)

*Plaited cholla is the traditional Jewish Sabbath bread: the plait makes it easy to break the bread without using a knife. At Purim the cooked bread is covered with a layer of boiled apricot jam and sprinkled with hundreds and thousands. A round cholla is usually made for the Jewish New Year, representing the fullness of the year to come. And this same cholla dough is twisted into the wedding rolls or* bulkalech *that Judith Grodzinski's husband once sold from a basket in the market.*

*Makes about 12*

THE FLOUR:
*1 lb white flour*

THE STARTER:
*½ oz fresh yeast*
*1 teaspoon honey*

AND . . .
*about 8 fl.oz lukewarm water*
*1 teaspoon salt*
*2 tablespoons vegetable oil*

TO GLAZE:
*1 egg, beaten*
*poppy seeds for sprinkling*

METRIC EQUIVALENTS:
*500 g white flour*
*15 g fresh yeast*
*1 teaspoon honey*
*about 250 ml lukewarm water*
*1 teaspoon salt*
*2 tablespoons vegetable oil*
*1 egg, beaten*
*poppy seeds for sprinkling*

YEAST STARTER:
Cream together the yeast, honey and 1 to 2 tablespoons of the warm water. Leave for about 5 minutes to froth.

THE MIX:
Put the flour and salt in a bowl. Make a well in the centre and add the yeast mixture, the oil and enough warm water to make a stiff, pliable dough. Turn out and knead on a floured board.

FIRST RISING:
Leave to rise in a warm place until double in size.

THE SHAPING:
To make a plaited cholla divide the dough into 3 pieces of equal size. Roll each piece out to about 10 to 12 in (25.5 to 30 cm) in length, join the pieces at one end and make a plait, squeezing the pieces together at the other end.
To make a round cholla: roll out the dough in one piece to about 12 in (30 cm) in length. Then coil it.

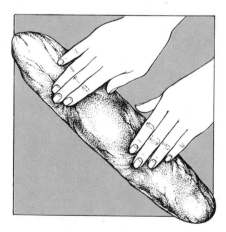

To make wedding rolls: break off small pieces of dough, about 2 oz (60 g) each. Divide each piece in 2 unequal pieces of 1½ oz (45 g) and ½ oz (15 g). Roll each piece into a thin sausage. Place the small strip diagonally on top of the larger one. Twist the two together and form a knot, squeeze lightly and tuck the ends underneath. Repeat with all the rolls.

SECOND RISING:
Place on a greased baking sheet, cover and leave to rise for about 30 minutes.

PRE-HEAT OVEN
to 400°F (200°C) Gas 6.

THE GLAZE:
Add 1 to 2 tablespoons of the water to the beaten egg. Brush the cholla or rolls with the egg wash and sprinkle liberally with poppy seeds.

BAKING TIME:
Bake the round or plaited cholla for about 50 minutes. After 10 minutes REDUCE HEAT to 375°F (190°C) Gas 5. Bake the wedding rolls in a hot oven for about 10 minutes until brown.

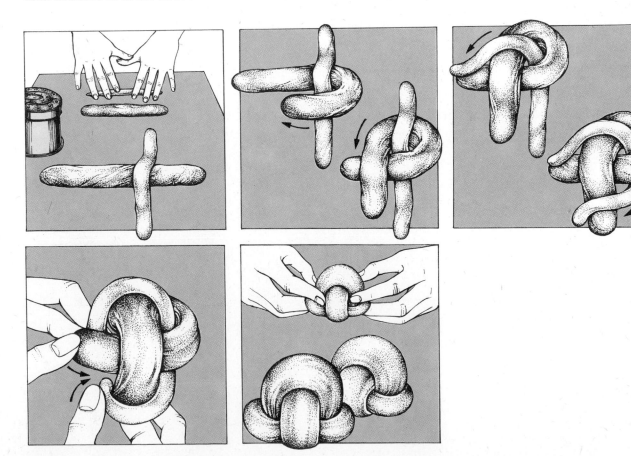

# Danish Ring

*Makes 1 ring*

THE FLOUR:
*4 oz white flour*

THE STARTER:
*¼ oz fresh yeast or 1 teaspoon
  dried yeast*
*1 teaspoon honey*

AND . . .
*about 3 tablespoons warm water*
*pinch of salt*
*3 oz butter*
*1 egg, beaten*

THE FILLING:
*4 oz ground almonds*
*2 tablespoons honey*
*1 teaspoon lemon juice*
*yolk of 1 egg*

METRIC EQUIVALENTS:
*125 g white flour*
*8 g fresh yeast or 1 teaspoon dried
  yeast*
*1 teaspoon honey*
*about 3 tablespoons warm water*
*pinch of salt*
*90 g butter*
*1 egg, beaten*
For the filling:
*125 g ground almonds*
*2 tablespoons honey*
*1 teaspoon lemon juice*
*yolk of 1 egg*

*One of the many variations of this world-famous yeast pastry. This ring is traditionally decorated with icing, glacé cherries, almonds and angelica.*

YEAST STARTER:
Cream the yeast with the honey and 1 tablespoon of the warm water and set aside for 5 minutes in a warm place.

THE MIX:
Mix the flour and salt in a bowl and rub in ½ oz (15 g) of the butter. Make a well in the flour and add the egg, the yeast mixture and enough warm water to make a soft dough.
Turn on to a floured board and knead well. Roll into an oblong. Cut the rest of the butter into small pieces and cover two-thirds of the oblong with one-third of the butter. Fold the unbuttered piece up one-third and bring the other piece over it. Seal the edges. Turn to the left, roll out into an oblong, and repeat with the next one-third of the butter. Repeat again with the final one-third of the butter. Repeat once more (the fourth time) without any butter.

CHILLING TIME:
Place in the refrigerator and chill well for about 1 hour.

THE FILLING:
Mix the ground almonds, honey, lemon juice and egg yolk together. Roll the pastry into a square. Spread with the filling, leaving a margin at the edges. Wet the edges and roll up, like a Swiss roll. Arrange in a circle on a greased baking sheet.

THE RISING:
Leave to rise in a cool place until slightly puffed up—about 1 hour.

PRE-HEAT OVEN
to 450°F (230°C) Gas 8.

BAKING TIME:
Bake for 25 minutes. Remove from oven and leave to cool.

# *Rum Baba*

*Some say these sweet cakes came from Poland via France. Baba means woman and the cakes are said to resemble a woman in a full skirt.*

YEAST STARTER:
Dissolve the yeast in the warm milk and water and set aside for 5 minutes.

THE MIX:
Sift the flour and salt into a warm mixing bowl. Beat the eggs with the vanilla essence and honey. Add the yeast mixture to the flour, then add the egg mixture a little at a time, mixing the sticky dough lightly with your hands.

FIRST RISING:
When you've formed a dough, dot it with small pieces of softened butter, cover with a cloth and leave in a warm place to rise for 45 to 60 minutes, but not longer.

SECOND RISING:
Knock back the dough, knead lightly and shape to fill small well-buttered ring moulds (or one large mould) one-third full. Cover and put in a warm place to rise to the top of the moulds, about 30 minutes.

PRE-HEAT OVEN
to 400°F (200°C) Gas 6 for small babas *or* to 450°F (230°C) Gas 8 for a larger cake.

BAKING TIME:
Bake small babas for about 10 to 15 minutes or until quite golden. Bake a large cake for about 30 minutes. After 10 minutes REDUCE HEAT to 375°F (190°C) Gas 5. Cook until quite golden on top. Cool a little, then turn out.

THE SYRUP:
Add the water to the honey and warm through. Stir in the rum. Prick the babas all over with a fork. Pour the hot syrup over before they cool completely. Keep spooning until most of the syrup is absorbed. Sprinkle with more rum as you serve them.

*In colour—page 201*

*Makes 1 large cake or several small ones*

THE FLOUR:
*8 oz white flour*

THE STARTER:
*½ oz fresh yeast*
*8 tablespoons warm milk and*
*    water, mixed*

AND . . .
*pinch of salt*
*2 eggs, beaten*
*4 to 5 drops vanilla essence*
*1 tablespoon honey*
*2 oz softened butter*

THE SYRUP:
*¼ lb honey*
*4 fl. oz water*
*6 tablespoons rum*

METRIC EQUIVALENTS:
*250 g white flour*
*15 g fresh yeast*
*8 tablespoons warm milk and water,*
*    mixed*
*pinch of salt*
*2 eggs, beaten*
*4 to 5 drops vanilla essence*
*1 tablespoon honey*
*60 g softened butter*
*The syrup:*
*125 g honey*
*100 ml water*
*6 tablespoons rum*

# Bobby Freeman

"... crusty, home-baked bread, with the mealy savour of ripe wheat roundly in your mouth and under your teeth, roasted sweet and crisp and deep brown..."

In *How Green Was My Valley*, Richard Llewellyn brought alive the everyday details of Welsh life, a life that Bobby Freeman—then running an advertising consultancy in Birmingham—felt strongly drawn towards: "My mother was Welsh, we spent most of our family holidays in north Wales, but it was Pembrokeshire, when I discovered it, which exerted a compelling attraction."

That was in 1962. Now, as a result of having run her own restaurant and hotel in Fishguard, worked for the Wales Tourist Board and written widely about Wales, she has researched and written *First Catch Your Peacock*—a very thorough look at Welsh cookery.

"At the restaurant we served good regional dishes from all over the world, including Wales. Customers kept urging me to bring out a book of Welsh recipes." She faced opposition from the Welsh themselves: "They couldn't understand why I wanted to put their dishes on a menu. In rural Wales they didn't see a meal as a social occasion so much as fuel for the hard work needed on the farm. The dishes are simple but very enjoyable."

Bobby did her research in Welsh records offices and libraries. "But very little had been written down. There's an oral tradition in Wales—but I don't speak Welsh. So I needed help."

This she found, and the book finally emerged. It covers all aspects of food and cookery in Wales and, of course, there is a chapter on bread. In fact bread was one of the factors that drew Bobby to Wales: "One of the delights of going to Pembrokeshire after Birmingham was to get proper crusty oven-baked bread from the local bakery. Its isolation, you see, had kept the area traditional, but eventually the multiple bakeries' steam-baked product reached the far west. Now even the locally-baked bread tastes more like 'shop bread' than it used to—with a few notable exceptions. They must have changed the mix because they're still using the lovely old ovens."

Much more is changing in Wales, but until relatively recently the traditional cookery that grew out of the life of the farming people remained almost intact.

The early Celts developed yeast breads; they also invented the bakestone (griddle) for scones and quick-breads. After the Norman invasion when the Welsh were driven into the uplands, barley bread was the prime bread, eaten with all meals, and continued so until the end of the eighteenth century. Rye bread was eaten mainly for its so-called medicinal properties. White bread was little known even among the gentry until the end of the eighteenth century. White bread was a special treat, baked in the pot-oven or *ffwrn fach,* an iron pot placed upon a tripod over the fire with burning coals or peat heaped on top so it was heated above and below. It was popular in areas where peat was the main fuel.

Traditional Welsh breads are mainly rough, even coarse. They're made of wholemeal flour, barley meal, oatmeal or rye. They were traditionally baked either in a wall oven or in a separate oven-house out in the yard.

Today the availability of good bread in Wales is about the same as elsewhere in Britain: "Some independent small bakers have survived. Country people are going back to baking their own, and the 'self-sufficiency' people who have settled in the north and west have created a demand there."

Old mills are being restored to produce stone-ground wholemeal flour, like Felin Geri at Cwm Cou in west Wales and the mill run by Mrs. Horsfield at Pentrefoelas, near Blaenau Ffestiniog.

In urban areas, such as Cardiff and Swansea, the younger middle classes are taking an interest in good, home-baked bread. Here are some traditional Welsh loaves, adapted from Bobby's book, which you can try for yourself.

## Bakestone Bread

*The "bakestone" is the iron plate, or griddle (Welsh—*planc, maen, llechwan, gradell*) on which all kinds of cakes and quick breads were baked. The dough was placed on the heated bakestone standing on a tripod over an indoor or outdoor fire, and then covered with an inverted cast-iron pan on to which glowing embers were heaped. Today you can use your cooker.*

THE MIX:
Mix the flours and salt in a large bowl. Dissolve the bicarbonate of soda in the buttermilk and add to the flour. Mix well to form a soft dough, adding a little water if necessary. Knead lightly until the dough leaves the sides of the bowl and turn on to a floured board. Shape into a round, flat loaf, flattening the top lightly with a rolling pin. Transfer to a greased, moderately hot bakestone or heavy frying-pan.

COOKING TIME:
Cook over a moderate heat until the surface begins to harden, about 20 minutes, then turn and cook for another 20 minutes on the other side.

*Makes 1 loaf*

THE FLOUR:
*½ lb strong white flour*
*½ lb 85% wholewheat flour*

THE RAISING AGENT:
*1 teaspoon bicarbonate of soda*

AND . . .
*½ teaspoon salt*
*½ pt buttermilk*

METRIC EQUIVALENTS:
*250 g strong white flour*
*250 g 85% wholewheat flour*
*1 teaspoon bicarbonate of soda*
*½ teaspoon salt*
*300 ml buttermilk*

## Barley Bread on the Bakestone

*Unleavened barley bread,* bara cancar, *was baked when supplies of ordinary bread were short or when yeast was unobtainable. These barley "biscuits" should be very thin indeed.*

THE MIX:
Put the barley flour or meal in an earthenware dish. Add sufficient cold water to make a dough, using your hands to mix well. Remove a little dough at a time and roll into a ball between the hands. Press with the palm on to a floured surface into a small round, then roll out as thin as possible to resemble a large oat cake (but not too thin or too big or it will be impossible to transfer to the bakestone).

COOKING TIME:
Cook one at a time on a hot, greased bakestone or in a heavy frying-pan, until the surface begins to harden. Turn and cook the other side. It cooks quickly.

*Makes 1* bara cancar

THE FLOUR:
*1 lb barley flour or meal*

AND . . .
*cold water*

METRIC EQUIVALENTS:
*500 g barley flour or meal*
*cold water*

# Steamed Brown Bread

*An interesting method of making bread from Caernarvonshire. Especially useful in hot weather when it would be preferable not to have to use the oven. Use cleaned 1 lb (500 g) food cans, such as empty baked bean cans with one end completely removed.*

*Makes 2 loaves*

THE FLOUR:
*8 oz strong white flour*
*4 oz bran*
*4 oz wholemeal flour*

AND...
*1 teaspoon bicarbonate of soda*
*12 fl.oz thick sour milk or buttermilk*
*½ teaspoon salt*
*1½ tablespoons black treacle*
*3 oz raisins or sultanas*

METRIC EQUIVALENTS:
*250 g strong white flour*
*125 g bran*
*125 g wholemeal flour*
*1 teaspoon bicarbonate of soda*
*350 ml thick sour milk or buttermilk*
*½ teaspoon salt*
*1½ tablespoons black treacle*
*90 g raisins or sultanas*

In colour—page 216

THE MIX:
Mix the white flour and salt in a large bowl. Add the bran, wholemeal flour and bicarbonate of soda and mix well. Heat the sour milk or buttermilk, add the treacle and mix well. Stir into the flour mixture and add the raisins or sultanas. Pour the mixture into greased cans so that they are not more than two-thirds full, cover loosely with foil and place in a large saucepan, half filled with boiling water.

STEAMING TIME:
Steam for 3 hours, maintaining the level of the water throughout.

# Maslin Bread

*An old bread made from a mixture of grains—barley or rye mixed with wheat. This version uses rye and wheat and gives a delicious, close-textured loaf with a slight malty flavour.*

*Makes 1 very large loaf or 2 smaller loaves*

THE FLOUR:
*1 lb 4 oz 85% wholewheat flour*
*4 oz rye flour*

THE STARTER:
*2 teaspoons dried yeast*
*1 teaspoon honey*

AND...
*about ¾ pt warm water*
*2 teaspoons salt*

METRIC EQUIVALENTS:
*600 g 85% wholewheat flour*
*125 g rye flour*
*2 teaspoons dried yeast*
*1 teaspoon honey*
*about 400 ml warm water*
*2 teaspoons salt*

YEAST STARTER:
Dissolve the yeast and honey in about ¼ pt (150 ml) of the warm water and set aside until frothy.

THE MIX:
Mix the flours together in a large, warmed bowl. Make a well in the centre and pour in the frothed yeast. Add the salt to the remaining warm water and add enough of this to make a workable dough. Knead for a few minutes only.

FIRST RISING.
Leave in a warm bowl, covered with oiled polythene, in a warm place until double in size, about 1 hour.

SECOND RISING:
Knock back, knead lightly what is now a very pliable, pleasant dough, and shape into a greased and floured 3 lb (1½ kg) loaf tin, or a 2 lb (1 kg) and 1 lb (500 g) tin. Cover with polythene again and leave to rise a second time, about 40 minutes.

PRE-HEAT OVEN
to 400°F (200°C) Gas 6.

BAKING TIME:
Bake for 35 to 45 minutes. After 15 minutes REDUCE HEAT to 325°F
(170°C) Gas 3.

## Planc Bread

*A traditional recipe from Anglesey, adapted to use honey and butter
instead of sugar and lard.*

YEAST STARTER:
Mix the yeast and honey with the milk and water and leave for
about 5 minutes to froth.

THE MIX:
Mix the flours and salt in a large, warmed bowl, and rub in the
butter. Make a well in the centre of the mixture and pour in the
yeast liquid. Mix and knead until the dough leaves the sides of the
bowl.

FIRST RISING:
Cover with a warm cloth and leave until double in size, about 2
hours. Mould into a large, flat cake, kneading and pressing towards
the sides with the hands. When shaped it should be about 1 in
(2.5 cm) thick.

SECOND RISING:
Leave to rise for 15 minutes.

COOKING TIME:
Transfer to a greased, moderately hot bakestone, "planc", or heavy
frying-pan. Cook over moderate heat for 20 minutes on one side,
then turn and cook for another 20 minutes on the other side.

*Makes 1 large loaf*

THE FLOUR:
*1½ lb wholemeal flour*
*½ lb strong white flour*

THE STARTER:
*1 oz fresh yeast or ½ oz dried*
*  yeast*
*1 teaspoon honey*
*12 fl.oz lukewarm milk and*
*  water*

AND . . .
*1 teaspoon salt*
*1 oz butter*

METRIC EQUIVALENTS:
*750 g wholemeal flour*
*250 g strong white flour*
*30 g fresh yeast or 15 g dried yeast*
*1 teaspoon honey*
*350 ml lukewarm milk and water*
*1 teaspoon salt*
*30 g butter*

*In colour—page 216*

# Wholemeal Bara Brith

*Makes 2 loaves*

*The various versions of this "speckled bread" are legion. This one comes from Montgomeryshire. The flavour is improved by plumping the fruit beforehand in warm tea. It is best to wait 1 or 2 days before eating, keeping the cake sealed in a tin.*

THE FLOUR:
*1 lb wholemeal flour*

THE STARTER:
*½ oz fresh yeast*

AND . . .
*about 8 fl.oz warm milk and
    water, mixed
3 oz sultanas or raisins
3 oz currants
4 oz butter
½ teaspoon salt
½ teaspoon mixed spice
2 oz candied peel*

METRIC EQUIVALENTS:
*500 g wholemeal flour
15 g fresh yeast
about 250 ml warm milk and water,
    mixed
90 g sultanas or raisins
90 g currants
125 g butter
½ teaspoon salt
½ teaspoon mixed spice
60 g candied peel*

YEAST STARTER:
Cream the yeast with a little of the warm milk and water.

THE MIX:
Soak the dried fruit in warm water or tea for 10 minutes. Put half the flour in a large mixing bowl. Rub in the butter. Add the salt and mixed spice, the dried fruit, the peel, the yeast liquid, and some of the warm milk and water. Stir well together.

FIRST RISING:
Cover and leave this sponge for 2 hours.

SECOND RISING:
Knock back and knead in the remaining flour and more of the milk and water, if necessary, to make a workable dough. Do not make it too stiff. Knead well. Cover and leave for 2 hours.

PRE-HEAT OVEN
to 375°F (190°C) Gas 5.

BAKING TIME:
Without kneading, lift the dough into greased baking tins. Bake for 1 to 1½ hours. Cool. Serve cold, cut into thin slices, and butter liberally.

# Oat Cakes

In colour—page 273

*Oats were the only reliable crop in the wet cold upland regions of Wales and were much respected for their body-building properties. They were most frequently made into oat cakes, either with or without fat. Oat cakes were cooked on the bakestone. The traditional instrument for turning them was a wooden slice called a* crafell *and they were dried on a wooden rack, a* diogyn. *Some were cooked on one side only and then dried before the fire. Oat cakes were formed by a deft "palming" method. Balls of dough were first flattened with the palm of the hand, then piled on top of each other with plenty of oatmeal in between. One hand cupped the pile to keep it round and even, while the other worked on the whole pile, flattening with the palm, until miraculously the oat cakes emerged very thin and about 10 in (25 cm) across. This recipe is adapted from Mattie Thomas' collection, and you can use a rolling pin to make them, if you cannot master the "palming" method.*

*Makes about 20*

THE FLOUR:
*1 lb oatmeal*

AND . . .
*about ½ pt skimmed milk*

METRIC EQUIVALENTS:
*500 g oatmeal*
*about 300 ml skimmed milk*

THE MIX:
Put the oatmeal in a large bowl. Add sufficient of the skimmed milk to moisten, and mix with a wooden spoon, until a soft dough is formed. It must be soft.

THE SHAPING:
Remove to a floured board, break off a handful of dough and shape into a ball. Roll out into a circle. The first "loaf" should be fairly thick. Sprinkle with oatmeal and set aside. Make a second "loaf" in the same way—this one and all the others should be wafer thin. Sprinkle over a little oatmeal. Continue making "loaves" until all the dough is used up.

COOKING TIME:
Heat a bakestone or heavy frying-pan to moderately hot. Cook the oat cakes on one side only. Place the unbaked side towards the fire to dry out. Repeat for each loaf. They are dinner plate size and almost transparent in thinness. Alternatively, you can bake them in a very low oven on a baking sheet. They are done when the edges begin to curl.

*An alternative recipe mixes 4 tablespoons medium oatmeal with ½ tablespoon vegetable oil and 3 tablespoons water; the oat cakes are baked in a moderate oven for about 10 minutes. It is best to use these small quantities, and mix and roll out only a few oat cakes at a time.*

# *Barley Bread*

*Makes 3 small loaves*

THE FLOUR:
½ lb barley flour
1 lb wholemeal flour

THE STARTER:
1 oz fresh yeast or ½ oz dried
    yeast
1 teaspoon honey

AND . . .
1 pt lukewarm water
2 teaspoons salt

METRIC EQUIVALENTS:
250 g barley flour
500 g wholemeal flour
30 g fresh yeast or 15 g dried yeast
1 teaspoon honey
600 ml lukewarm water
2 teaspoons salt

*According to Mattie Thomas, who put together a valuable collection of traditional Welsh recipes in 1925, barley bread (bara barlys) was the "prime bread in the old days, eaten with all meals". Baking was done once a week, so that by the end of the week the bread must have become quite hard. The custom of breaking bread into soups and pouring tea or buttermilk over it was probably devised as a means of softening it up to avoid waste. Before baking, barley meal was sprinkled over the loaf, "the surplus being whisked off with a goose wing . . ." Below is an adaptation of the traditional loaf; this close-textured loaf was originally made with brewer's barm and baked in a wall oven heated with a culm fire.*

YEAST STARTER:
Mix the yeast and honey with 5 tablespoons of the warm water, and leave for about 5 minutes to froth.

THE MIX:
Mix the flours together and put in an ovenproof bowl in a low oven for 5 to 10 minutes to warm through. Dissolve the salt in the remaining water. Add the salted water to the yeast mixture, make a well in the centre of the flour and pour in. Mix quickly with one hand until the mixture forms a dough. Knead until the dough leaves the side of the bowl, turn on to a floured board and knead very thoroughly, about 15 minutes.

FIRST RISING:
Place the dough in a greased bowl, cover and leave in a warm place until double in size, about 1 hour. Knock back and knead the risen dough for 5 minutes. Divide the mixture between 3 greased 1 lb (500 g) loaf tins.

SECOND RISING:
Leave, covered, in a warm place, until risen again, about 20 minutes.

PRE-HEAT OVEN
to 400°F (200°C) Gas 6.

BAKING TIME:
Bake for 45 to 50 minutes. Wrap the hot loaves in a thick towel until cool to prevent the crusts from becoming too hard.

# Rye Bread

*Rye bread* (bara rhyg) *was eaten by the Welsh for its medicinal value, although they did not like its dark appearance and strong flavour. Originally it was made with brewer's barm. This makes a very dense loaf. Prepare the dough the night before.*

**YEAST STARTER:**
Mix the yeast with 3 tablespoons of the warm water and set aside for 10 minutes.

**THE MIX:**
Place the rye and barley flours and salt in a large bowl. Add the yeast mixture and enough of the warm water to make a workable dough. Knead and place in a bowl.

**FIRST RISING:**
Cover and leave to rise in a warm place overnight.

**SECOND RISING:**
The following morning knock back and knead the dough again. Leave to rise for 1 hour. Turn on to a floured board and shape into a flat round.

**PRE-HEAT OVEN**
to 425°F (220°C) Gas 7.

**BAKING TIME:**
Bake for about 1 hour. After 15 minutes REDUCE HEAT to 375°F (190°C) Gas 5.

*Makes 1 loaf*

THE FLOUR:
*½ lb rye flour*
*½ lb barley flour*

THE STARTER:
*1 oz fresh yeast or ½ oz*
*dried yeast*

AND . . .
*about ½ pt lukewarm water*
*1 teaspoon salt*

METRIC EQUIVALENTS:
*250 g rye flour*
*250 g barley flour*
*30 g fresh yeast or 15 g dried yeast*
*about 300 ml lukewarm water*
*1 teaspoon salt*

# Ursel Norman

When Ursel Norman married an Englishman and came to live in Britain she immediately started to bake her own bread. "English bread wasn't worth buying," she recalls. "It was hardly worth eating."

She was born in West Germany where she was brought up to enjoy good bread. Her husband, Derek, was delighted with her efforts; a steady daily output of good wholemeal loaves, with a milk and egg twist, decorated with poppy seeds, on Sundays.

Attempting to expand her repertoire it quickly became evident that there were no good books available on the subject. So she set about writing one of her own. She combined her baking with her husband's artistic skills and together they produced *Use Your Loaf* (Collins) which gives a step-by-step account of 24 good wholesome breads to bake at home with appetizing illustrations of the finished results.

As she didn't have any books to draw on, she wrote to all her friends for recipes: Italian friends in Milan gave her pizza, other friends in Chicago gave her a pumpernickel recipe. Relations also helped; Derek's mother—a wonderful English pastry cook, and Ursel's own German mother, provided interesting and well tried family recipes. Ursel cooked and tested, and every time she had a success her husband took it away and drew it. Their children helped by eating the bread. They are teenagers now: a daughter, Julia, and two sons, Marcus and Carl.

The book was an instant success in Britain. It has also made them famous in America where they now live. According to Ursel, bread in America is "plastic stuff" so the book had a ready market.

American life has modified her approach to bread-baking; all her friends are making their own in revolt against poor commercial products. "The shops recognise this, and better bread flours have been made available. I make more sweet tasting breads now."

The bread book started Ursel off as a cookery writer; she and Derek followed it with similar books on salads, pasta, soups, and chicken. In Chicago they became local celebrities with a cookery strip in the local paper, *The Pioneer Press*, which covers the North shore of Lake Michigan.

What advice would she offer to beginners? "Remember, baking is essentially a technique, once mastered you should experiment. Try adding extra ingredients. I started to add too much extra bran and that was a flop, it made it too heavy. But one day I felt hungry for something really heavy and coarse, and I added whole wheat kernels, which I soaked in water overnight. That was very satisfying. Now I quite often do it. I add raisins, sometimes, dried apricots, dried apples, some strange things: I think I'm becoming a little bit Americanised."

## Pizza

*Makes one 10 in (25.5 cm) pizza*

*More delicious than any you can buy in shops; as good as any you can get in restaurants, because you make sure the filling is that much better. Satisfying, pleasantly easy, and rewarding.*

THE FLOUR:
*4 oz wholemeal flour*
*4 oz white flour*

THE STARTER:
*½ oz fresh yeast or ¼ oz dried yeast*
*1 teaspoon honey*

AND . . .
*¼ pt warm water*
*1 teaspoon salt*
*5 tablespoons olive oil*

THE SAUCE:
*1 large chopped onion*
*olive oil*
*1 clove garlic, crushed*
*1 x 15 oz can tomatoes*
*small can tomato purée*
*salt and pepper, oregano, basil and 1 bay leaf*
*½ lb Mozzarella or Cheddar cheese*
*Parmesan for sprinkling*

AND . . .
*your choice of the following:*
*sliced hot salami, flaked tuna, black olives, strips of anchovy, sliced green peppers, mushrooms*

YEAST STARTER:
Put the yeast and 2 tablespoons of the warm water in a cup with the honey. Stir to dissolve and leave for 10 minutes to froth.

THE MIX:
Mix the two flours and salt in bowl. Make a well in the centre and pour in the yeast mixture, the rest of the warm water and the olive oil. Mix together to a soft dough, and then knead for 10 minutes until it is fairly elastic.

FIRST RISING:
Cover with a cloth and leave to rise for 1 hour.

THE SAUCE:
Fry the onion in the olive oil until brown, add the garlic and fry for 1 or 2 minutes. Add the tomatoes, tomato purée, and seasonings, and simmer, partially covered, for about 1 hour. The sauce should be quite thick. Cool a little before use.

THE SHAPING:
Remove the dough, and knock it back to bring it down to its original size. Make the dough into a ball, and then flatten it with your hands. Pick it up and gradually stretch it, turning it round between your fingers, letting its weight pull it longer. Don't let it tear. It may be stiff at first but gradually it will loosen. Continue gently until you have a circle 10 in (25.5 cm) across. Put it on a greased baking sheet or floured pizza tray. Spread on the cooled sauce. Cover with layers of fillings of your choice. Top with a thick layer of grated Mozzarella or Cheddar cheese. Sprinkle with Parmesan and a few drops of olive oil.

SECOND RISING:
Leave the pizza to rise for 30 minutes in a warm place.

PRE-HEAT OVEN
to 425°F (220°C) Gas 7.

BAKING TIME:
Bake for 30 minutes on a low shelf in the oven.

METRIC EQUIVALENTS:
*125 g wholemeal flour*
*125 g white flour*
*15 g fresh yeast or 8 g dried yeast*
*1 teaspoon honey*
*150 ml warm water*
*1 teaspoon salt*
*5 tablespoons olive oil*
For the sauce:
*1 large chopped onion*
*olive oil*
*1 clove garlic, crushed*
*1 x 425 g can tomatoes*
*small can tomato purée*
*salt and pepper, oregano, basil and*
  *1 bay leaf*
*250 g Mozzarella or Cheddar cheese*
*Parmesan for sprinkling*
Your choice of the following:
*sliced hot salami, flaked tuna, black*
  *olives, strips of anchovy, sliced*
  *green peppers, mushrooms*

# Monastery Oat Bread

In colour—page 256

*Makes 2 long oval loaves*

THE FLOUR:
*12 oz white flour*
*1½ lb wholemeal flour*
*1 lb rolled oats*

THE STARTER:
*1 oz fresh yeast or ½ oz dried yeast*
*2 teaspoons honey*
*1½ pt warm milk*

AND . . .
*1 teaspoon salt*
*3 oz melted butter*

METRIC EQUIVALENTS:
*350 g white flour*
*750 g wholemeal flour*
*500 g rolled oats*
*30 g fresh yeast or 15 g dried yeast*
*2 teaspoons honey*
*900 ml warm milk*
*1 teaspoon salt*
*90 g melted butter*

*Rolled oats give a chewy, tasty feel to a loaf, and a nutty crust. Be patient making it, as you leave it to rise four times. But it's no real trouble.*

YEAST STARTER:
Dissolve the yeast with the honey and stir into the warm milk.

FIRST MIX:
Put the white flour and 12 oz (350 g) of the wholemeal flour in a bowl. Stir in the yeast mixture.

FIRST RISING:
Cover with a damp cloth and leave to rise for 1 hour.

SECOND MIX:
Now add the salt, the melted butter, the rolled oats, and the rest of the wholemeal flour, and knead to a soft dough for 10 to 15 minutes.

SECOND RISING:
Cover with a damp cloth and leave to rise for 50 minutes in a warm place.

THIRD RISING:
Knock it back and knead again. Leave to rise for 40 minutes.

FOURTH RISING:
Knock the dough back again. Shape into two long ovals and place in greased baking tins. They should come up to halfway. Cut diagonal lines across the top with a sharp knife. Leave to rise again, covered with a cloth for about 1 hour.

PRE-HEAT OVEN
to 425°F (220°C) Gas 7.

BAKING TIME:
Bake for about 1 hour.

OPPOSITE:
Top left in napkin: *Chappatis (Caroline Conran) p.61.* Top right: *Roti (Elisabeth Lambert Ortiz) p.162-63.* Bottom left: *Naan (Caroline Conran) p.62.* Bottom right: *Dal Puri (Elisabeth Lambert Ortiz) p.165.*
OVERLEAF LEFT:
Top in napkin: *Blini (Nina Froud) p.109; serve with soured cream and red caviar.* Below: *Floats (Elisabeth Lambert Ortiz) p.160-61.*
OVERLEAF RIGHT:
Top: *Coconut Bread p.164.* Below: *Sopa Paraguaya (Paraguayan Corn Bread) p.168 (both from Elisabeth Lambert Ortiz.)*

# Cottage Loaf

In colour—page 216

*One of the most traditional of English loaves, a round loaf with another rounded loaf on top, which tilts like a chef's hat in the heat of the oven. This is a wholemeal version, but it can be made with white flour, or half wholemeal, half white.*

*Makes 2 loaves*

THE FLOUR:
*2½ lb stoneground wholemeal flour*

YEAST STARTER:
Dissolve the yeast in a cup with a little of the warm water and leave for 10 minutes.

THE STARTER:
*1 oz fresh yeast or ½ oz dried yeast*

THE MIX:
Put the flour and salt in a bowl. Add the yeast liquid, the melted butter and enough of the remaining water to make a dough. Knead for 10 to 15 minutes until shiny and elastic.

AND . . .
*about 1 pt warm water*
*2 teaspoons salt*
*2 oz melted butter*
*2 tablespons milk or cream for glaze*

FIRST RISING:
Put the dough in a bowl, covered with a damp cloth, and leave in a warm place for 1 to 1½ hours until double in size.

METRIC EQUIVALENTS:
*1 kg stoneground wholemeal flour*
*30 g fresh yeast or 15 g dried yeast*
*about 600 ml warm water*
*2 teaspoons salt*
*60 g melted butter*
*2 tablespoons milk or cream for glaze*

THE SHAPING:
Cut the dough in half. From each piece cut off one-third. Roll the 2 large pieces into balls and place them on a greased baking tray. Roll the 2 smaller pieces into balls, and place them on top of the 2 large balls. Dip a floured finger or thumb down through the centre to the bottom of each loaf to anchor them.

SECOND RISING:
Cover with a dry cloth and leave for about 30 to 40 minutes to double in size.

PRE-HEAT OVEN
to 425°F (220°C) Gas 7.

BAKING TIME:
Bake for 35 to 40 minutes. After 15 minutes REDUCE HEAT to 375°F (190°C) Gas 5. Remove the loaves briefly 10 minutes before they are done and brush them with milk or cream to give a shiny glaze.

OPPOSITE:
Top: *Banana Bread (Elisabeth Lambert Ortiz) p.161.* Below right: *Rum Baba (Grodzinski) p.189.* Bottom left: *Sweet Corn Bread (Elisabeth Lambert Ortiz) p.167.*

In colour—page 216

# Oatmeal Rye Country Style

*Makes 2 oval loaves*

*Rich, dark and moist, with the light crunchiness of the oatmeal inside. Solid and good.*

THE FLOUR:
*1 lb wholemeal flour*
*1 lb white flour*
*½ lb rye flour*
*½ lb oatmeal (not rolled oats)*

THE STARTER:
*1 oz fresh yeast or ½ oz dried yeast*
*1½ pt warm milk and water (half and half)*
*1 tablespoon honey*

AND . . .
*2 teaspoons salt*
*4 fl. oz sunflower oil (or vegetable oil)*
*milk or cream for glaze*

METRIC EQUIVALENTS:
*500 g wholemeal flour*
*500 g white flour*
*250 g rye flour*
*250 g oatmeal (not rolled oats)*
*30 g fresh yeast or 15 g dried yeast*
*900 ml warm milk and water (half and half)*
*1 tablespoon honey*
*2 teaspoons salt*
*100 ml sunflower oil (or vegetable oil)*
*milk or cream for glaze*

YEAST STARTER:
Dissolve the yeast in the warm milk and water and stir in the honey.

FIRST MIX:
Mix the wholemeal flour and white flour in a bowl and stir in the creamy yeast and milk liquid, beating to a thick batter.

FIRST RISING:
Cover and leave to ferment for 30 minutes.

SECOND MIX:
Mix in the rye flour and oatmeal, the salt and oil, and make a soft dough. Knead for 15 minutes.

SECOND RISING:
Leave in a covered bowl for 1 hour to rise.

THE SHAPING:
Knock back the dough, and shape into two oval loaves. Place on greased baking sheets. With a floured finger punch two rows of holes down the sides of each loaf: this allows moisture to escape as the dough rises and prevents stickiness.

THIRD RISING:
Cover with a cloth and leave to prove until double in size, about 30 to 40 minutes.

PRE-HEAT OVEN
to 425°F (220°C) Gas 7.

BAKING TIME:
Bake for about 1 hour. Brush the loaves with milk or cream 10 minutes before they are done to give a shiny finish.

# Buttermilk Rolls

*Soft rolls from New England, which are crispy outside and soft inside. They always surprise and impress guests, and taste lovely too.*

**YEAST STARTER:**
Dissolve the yeast in a little of the warm buttermilk.

**THE MIX:**
Add the bicarbonate of soda, salt, honey, and the yeast mixture to the remaining buttermilk. Beat well then gradually add half of the flour. Add 1 oz (30 g) of the melted butter, and the rest of the flour. Make a soft dough, and knead for 5 minutes.

**FIRST RISING:**
Leave, covered with a damp cloth, to rise in a warm place for 1 hour.

**THE SHAPING:**
Knock back the dough, cut into 2 pieces and roll them out to ⅛ in (3 mm) thick. Brush both pieces with the rest of the melted butter. Cut the dough into strips 1½ in (4 cm) wide, and stack the strips on top of one another, stacking them 7 or 8 strips high. With a sharp knife, cut them into squares of about 1½ in (4 cm).

**SECOND RISING:**
Grease some bun or mince pie tins, and stand the squares in them, vertically, cut side up. Cover and leave them to rise for 40 minutes.

**PRE-HEAT OVEN**
to 425°F (220°C) Gas 7.

**BAKING TIME:**
Bake for 15 to 20 minutes, until golden.

*Makes 6 to 8*

THE FLOUR:
*1 lb 10 oz white flour*

THE STARTER:
*1 oz fresh yeast or ½ oz dried yeast*
*¼ teaspoon bicarbonate of soda*

AND...
*1 pt warm buttermilk*
*1 teaspoon salt*
*½ tablespoon honey*
*3 oz melted butter*

METRIC EQUIVALENTS:
*800 g white flour*
*30 g fresh yeast or 15 g dried yeast*
*¼ teaspoon bicarbonate of soda*
*600 ml warm buttermilk*
*1 teaspoon salt*
*½ tablespoon honey*
*90 g melted butter*

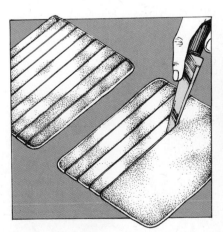

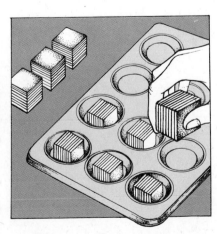

In colour—page 216

# Chicago Pumpernickel—or Black Bread

*A dense German loaf which German immigrants took with them to America's Mid-West in the nineteenth century. Wrap it in foil to keep it moist; it lasts a long time. Slice thinly.*

*Makes 2 small loaves*

THE FLOUR:
*1½ lb rye flour*

THE STARTER:
*1 oz fresh yeast or ½ oz dried*
  *yeast*
*¼ pt warm water*

AND . . .
*2 oz butter*
*½ pt warm milk*
*5 tablespoons molasses or black*
  *treacle*
*1 egg, beaten*
*1 teaspoon salt*
*2 tablespoons caraway seeds*
*2 tablespoons cream for glaze*

METRIC EQUIVALENTS:
*750 g rye flour*
*30 g fresh yeast or 15 g dried yeast*
*150 ml warm water*
*60 g butter*
*300 ml warm milk*
*5 tablespoons molasses or black*
  *treacle*
*1 egg, beaten*
*1 teaspoon salt*
*2 tablespoons caraway seeds*
*2 tablespoons cream for glaze*

YEAST STARTER:
Dissolve the yeast in the warm water.

THE MIX:
Melt the butter in the warm milk. When it cools to lukewarm, dissolve the molasses in it, adding the beaten egg, salt, and the yeast liquid. Add the caraway seeds and ½ lb (250 g) of the rye flour. Beat until smooth.

FIRST RISING:
Leave this wet mixture to rise for 30 minutes.

SECOND RISING:
Mix in another ½ lb (250 g) rye flour. Cover the bowl with a damp cloth and leave for 30 minutes or more to rise further.

THIRD RISING:
Now stir in the rest of the rye flour, and knead well for 10 minutes. If the dough is too sticky, add a little more flour. Make the dough into 2 oval shapes, and put them into 2 greased 1 lb (500 g) baking tins, pressing them down until they come up to the halfway mark. Cover with a dry cloth and leave to prove for 1 hour.

PRE-HEAT OVEN
to 400°F (200°C) Gas 6.

BAKING TIME:
Bake for 40 minutes. After 30 minutes, brush with cream. Remove and cool on a wire tray. Do not eat until cold.

# Basic Wheat Germ Brown Bread

In colour—page 273

*A soft, moist brown bread with a sweet, nutty flavour. Rich in protein, iron and vitamins. If you wish to experiment—add extra nutrition by kneading in a handful or two of raisins, currants or nuts.*

*Makes 1 large or 2 small loaves*

PREPARATION:
Heat the milk, oil, honey and salt to almost boiling. Leave to cool until lukewarm.

THE FLOUR:
*10 oz wholemeal flour*
*10 oz strong white flour*
*8 oz toasted wheat germ*
*8 oz bran (optional)*

YEAST STARTER:
Mix the yeast and warm water and leave to prove for 5 minutes.

THE STARTER:
*1 oz fresh yeast or ½ oz dried yeast*
*4 fl.oz warm water*

THE MIX:
Add the yeast liquid to the warm milk mixture, together with the beaten egg and half the wholemeal and half the strong white flour. Beat with a wooden spoon until smooth.
Mix in the wheat germ (and bran, if used) and enough of the remaining flour to make a medium firm, elastic dough. Knead thoroughly.

AND . . .
*¾ pt milk*
*4 fl.oz vegetable oil*
*2 level tablespoons honey*
*2 teaspoons salt*
*1 egg, beaten*

FIRST RISING:
Place in a clean bowl, cover with a damp cloth and leave to rise until double in size, about 1½ hours.
Knock back by kneading a little. Shape into a long loaf and place on a greased baking sheet (or two if they are small).

METRIC EQUIVALENTS:
*300 g wholemeal flour*
*300 g strong white flour*
*250 g toasted wheat germ*
*250 g bran (optional)*
*30 g fresh yeast or 15 g dried yeast*
*100 ml warm water*
*400 ml milk*
*100 ml vegetable oil*
*2 level tablespoons honey*
*2 teaspoons salt*
*1 egg, beaten*

SECOND RISING:
Cover with a dry cloth and leave to rise until doubled, about 1 hour.

PRE-HEAT OVEN
to 400°F (200°C) Gas 6.

BAKING TIME:
Bake for about 35 to 45 minutes.

# Adrian Bailey

Adrian Bailey is an artist who turned food writer; he developed an early interest in food because his father ran hotels, and the young Adrian made friends with the chefs. As an art student at St. Martin's School in London he became friends with Len Deighton, also an art student. They shared a flat; drawing and cooking; producing a stream; of ambitious dishes which had fellow students hammering on the doors to share.

Deighton went on to create a cookery strip in *The Observer*, before switching to writing best-sellers; Bailey went on to become food correspondent of *Queen* magazine, and then *Harper's Bazaar*, illustrating his articles with his own exciting drawings. He has written seven books on food including *Cooking of the British Isles* (a Time-Life book); *Mrs. Bridges' Upstairs, Downstairs Cookery Book*; *The World Atlas of Cheese*; and *The Book of Ingredients*.

After six months of intensive research in a library which contains 11,000 references to breads, Adrian Bailey determined that bread is about 10,000 years old: some kinds of barley cake were eaten about that time in Santa Barbara on America's West Coast; along the Danube; and in settlements along the Persian Gulf.

The Egyptians are credited with inventing risen bread, (just as they are credited with discovering brewing), but Bailey takes the view that all primitive man has made leavened bread of a sort, because wild yeasts come to dough mixtures without even being summoned. Many a wet, warm grain mixture must have started to ferment, and therefore given a lighter result as our ancestors heated it on their hot hearthstones.

As Bailey points out drily, yeast isn't the only "starter" agent which can make bread rise. "Practically anything can be used to make a starter," he says. "Flour and milk, flour and water; cornmeal, beer and tea leaves; old shoes; hot water and sugar mixed with the pulp of old books about bread, and magazines devoted to food and wine; hops, a slice of onion, a large slice of cheese-cake and a finely shredded copy of an old *Sunday Times* announcing the launch of the Campaign for Real Bread."

You could also make a white dough mix with honey, and leave it in a warm place, and the wild yeasts might descend on it, and you'd have a light bread. "That's how they did it in Ancient Greece,"

says Bailey. He makes the last 100 years of bread-making seem rudely modern.

Bailey did all this research for his history of bread, *Blessings of Bread*, which traces the uncertain agricultural, economic, religious and political ups-and-downs of our staple food. He became particularly intrigued by the early Greek and Roman breads and set out to recreate them: *Artologanos*, which includes freshly ground black pepper, and flat hearth loaves like *Melitutes* and the bread of *Cappodocia*. "I can't tell if I got them right: I tested them quite a few times, and had to throw out some."

The research into bread took him further than he'd planned as he only intended to include a handful of recipes; he actually produced nearly 200. Bailey found himself baking every day, and rushing out to his neighbours in Islington, unloading buns, crumpets, Chelsea buns. "It's a simple process. Housewives have been doing it for 6,000 years, so it can't be that difficult."

Bailey suspects the language of baking makes it sound more mysterious than it is: *kneading* the dough, *proving* it, *knocking* it back, *proving* it again; and then leaving it 45 minutes, and then . . . waiting for it to cool. "You've got to get the flour, the yeast; it all takes time; I can see that someone might say, it's easier to go down the road and buy a loaf from the nearest shop.

"But once you start baking, it's enjoyable, it's therapeutic. It generates an enormous amount of pride. You have bread to take to your neighbours who may, or may not, be impressed; or even envious. If you bake your own bread for a meal and everything else goes wrong, you are still a success."

If you think you might want to begin, let's finish with some advice from Bailey in a lighter vein. "Several trial runs may be needed to produce bread to your satisfaction. Some recipe books neglect to point out certain basic, important facts, such as explaining that some doughs can be very sticky indeed, those which are too warm, or contain eggs and honey. It is a good idea, therefore, to unplug the telephone and disconnect the doorbell when making rich dough breads. Unsuspecting cooks have been known to become inextricably wedded to telephones, electric blenders, door handles, small animals and children, by liaison of adhesive bun dough studded with currants."

## Muesli Loaf

*This is a light, brownish loaf with a slightly sweet and nutty taste. Here and there an occasional raisin or two.*

*Makes 2 small loaves*

YEAST STARTER:
Work the yeast with about ¼ pt (150 ml) of the warm water at "blood heat", or about 98°F (37°C), and the honey. Leave for 10 minutes until frothy.

THE MIX:
Mix the white and wholemeal flours with the salt in a warm bowl. Add the yeast mixture to the flour with the remaining water, mix thoroughly, then knead for 7 to 10 minutes until smooth and springy.

FIRST RISING:
Leave for 2 hours, or until doubled in bulk.

SECOND RISING:
Now work in the muesli, knead for a few minutes, separate the dough in half, and pack into greased 1 lb (500 g) bread tins. Leave until risen above the edge of the tins, about 45 minutes to 1 hour.

PRE-HEAT OVEN
to 450°F (230°C) Gas 8.

BAKING TIME:
Bake for about 30 to 40 minutes. The loaves should sound hollow when tapped underneath. (In fact, a cooked loaf will sound hollow when tapped on top, as well.)

*THE FLOUR:*
*1 lb 5 oz strong white flour*
*3 oz wholemeal flour*
*3 to 4 oz muesli*

*THE STARTER:*
*½ oz fresh yeast, or ¼ oz dried yeast*
*1 teaspoon honey*

*AND . . .*
*¾ pt warm water*
*2 teaspoons salt*

*METRIC EQUIVALENTS:*
*650 g strong white flour*
*90 g wholemeal flour*
*90 to 125 g muesli*
*15 g fresh yeast, or 8 g dried yeast*
*1 teaspoon honey*
*400 ml warm water*
*2 teaspoons salt*

In colour—page 217

*Makes 1 ring*

THE FLOUR:
*1¼ lb strong white flour*

THE STARTER:
*1 oz fresh yeast or ½ oz dried
    yeast*
*4 tablespoons lukewarm water*

AND...
*8 fl.oz milk*
*2 tablespoons honey*
*4 oz butter*
*2 teaspoons salt*
*2 eggs, beaten*

THE FILLING:
*1 oz melted butter*
*6 oz raisins or currants*
*2 oz chopped almonds*
*2 teaspoons cinnamon*

# Swedish Tea Ring

*An attractive style of tea-bread: tear off pieces instead of cutting.
Traditionally this bread is iced when cool.*

YEAST STARTER:
Mix the yeast and 1 teaspoon of the honey with the warm water.
Leave for about 5 minutes to froth.

THE MIX:
Scald the milk and add the butter and the remaining honey. Stir
until most of the butter melts. Sift the flour with the salt into
another bowl and stir in the yeast mixture. Cool the milk to
lukewarm and add it to the flour mixture. Add the eggs. Mix to a
soft dough, adding more flour if necessary. Knead until smooth.

FIRST RISING:
Leave, covered in a greased bowl, in a warm place to double in size,
about 1 hour. Knock back and knead again until smooth. Roll out to
a rectangle 12 x 5 in (30 x 13 cm) and ½ in (1.5 cm) thick.

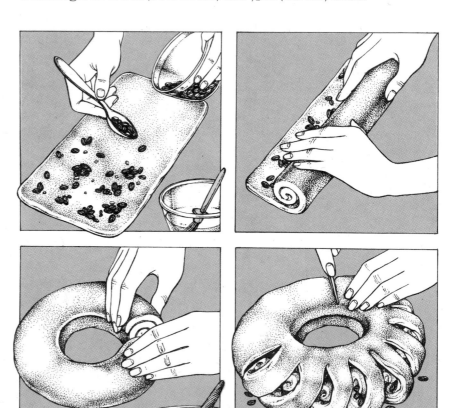

**THE FILLING:**
Brush the dough with the melted butter. Scatter the dried fruit, nuts and cinnamon over the surface. Roll the dough up fairly tightly to form a 12 in (30 cm) length. Brush the ends with water and join them to form a circle.

**SECOND RISING:**
Leave, covered in a warm place, until doubled in size, about 30 to 40 minutes. With a sharp knife or scissors, make deep cuts almost through the ring at intervals of 1 in (2.5 cm), twisting each segment at an angle. Place the ring on a greased baking sheet.

**PRE-HEAT OVEN**
to 375°F (190°C) Gas 5.

**BAKING TIME:**
Bake for 25 minutes.

**METRIC EQUIVALENTS:**
*625 g strong white flour*
*30 g fresh yeast or 15 g dried yeast*
*4 tablespoons lukewarm water*
*250 ml milk*
*2 tablespoons honey*
*125 g butter*
*2 teaspoons salt*
*2 eggs, beaten*
*The filling:*
*30 g melted butter*
*175 g raisins or currants*
*60 g chopped almonds*
*2 teaspoons cinnamon*

# Grissini

*Pencil-thin Italian bread sticks to serve with drinks before a meal.*

**YEAST STARTER:**
Mix the yeast and the 1 teaspoon of honey with the warm water and leave for 5 minutes to froth.

**THE MIX:**
Sift the flour and salt into a large bowl. Scald the milk and add the butter and 2 teaspoons of honey to it, stirring until the butter has melted. When the milk mixture has cooled to lukewarm, add it to the flour with the yeast mixture. Mix and knead until the dough leaves the sides of the bowl and has a slimy appearance.

**FIRST RISING:**
Leave, covered, in a warm place until double in size, about 1 hour. Knock back and knead again until smooth. Divide the dough into pieces and roll them out in lengths the thickness of a pencil and about 9 to 12 in (23 to 30 cm) long.

**SECOND RISING:**
Place the dough sticks on a greased baking sheet and leave, covered, in a warm place to double in size, about 20 to 30 minutes.

**PRE-HEAT OVEN**
to 425°F (220°C) Gas 7.

**BAKING TIME:**
Brush with cold water and bake the *grissini* for 30 minutes. After 10 minutes REDUCE HEAT to 350°F (180°C) Gas 4.

*Makes about 12 long or 24 short sticks*

**THE FLOUR:**
*1 lb strong white flour*

**THE STARTER:**
*1 oz fresh yeast or ½ oz dried yeast*
*1 teaspoon honey*
*4 fl.oz lukewarm water*

**AND . . .**
*2 teaspoons salt*
*4 fl.oz milk*
*1 oz butter*
*2 teaspoons honey*

**METRIC EQUIVALENTS:**
*500 g strong white flour*
*30 g fresh yeast or 15 g dried yeast*
*1 teaspoon honey*
*100 ml lukewarm water*
*2 teaspoons salt*
*100 ml milk*
*30 g butter*
*2 teaspoons honey*

# Date, Pecan and Orange Bread

*Makes 1 large loaf*

*Moist, chewy, nutty and full of natural sweetness: very popular with children.*

THE FLOUR:
*10 oz strong white flour*

THE MIX:
Sift the flour, baking powder and salt into a large bowl. In another bowl, cream the butter and honey. Add the egg, still beating. Gradually beat the flour mixture, a little at a time, into the egg mixture. Use the orange juice to moisten it and continue adding until all the flour and juice are used up and blended. Dust the nuts, dates and orange rind in a little extra flour and stir into the mixture. Pour the batter into a greased 2 lb (1 kg) loaf tin.

THE RAISING AGENT:
*2 teaspoons baking powder*

AND . . .
*1 teaspoon salt*
*2 oz softened butter*
*4 tablespoons honey*
*1 egg, beaten*
*5 fl.oz pure orange juice*
*3 oz chopped pecans or walnuts*
*3 oz chopped, stoned dates*
*1 tablespoon grated orange rind*

PRE-HEAT OVEN
to 350°F (180°C) Gas 4.

BAKING TIME:
Bake for 1 hour or until a clean warm knife blade inserted into the centre comes out clean.

METRIC EQUIVALENTS:
*300 g strong white flour*          *1 egg, beaten*
*2 teaspoons baking powder*        *150 ml pure orange juice*
*1 teaspoon salt*                  *90 g chopped pecans or walnuts*
*60 g softened butter*             *90 g chopped, stoned dates*
*4 tablespoons honey*              *1 tablespoon grated orange rind*

# Rice Bread

*Makes 2 small loaves*

*A good loaf and an ideal way of using up left-over cooked rice.*

THE FLOUR:
*12 oz strong white flour*
*4 oz wholemeal flour*

YEAST STARTER:
Pour the milk into a bowl and add the butter, honey and salt. Stir until they have dissolved. When the milk has cooled to lukewarm, sprinkle over the yeast. Leave for about 5 minutes to froth.

THE STARTER:
*1 oz fresh yeast or ½ oz dried yeast*
*8 fl.oz milk, scalded*
*1½ oz butter*
*1 tablespoon honey*
*1 teaspoon salt*

THE MIX:
Mix the flours into the yeast mixture, and add the cooked rice. Turn out on to a floured board and knead thoroughly, as the dough will be sticky. This dough is not as smooth textured as most bread doughs, because of the rice.

AND . . .
*8 oz cooked rice*

FIRST RISING:
Leave, covered in a greased bowl, until double in size, about 1 hour. Knock back and knead again. Divide between 2 greased 1 lb (500 g) loaf tins.

SECOND RISING:
Leave, covered, in a warm place, until double in size, about 30 to 40 minutes.

PRE-HEAT OVEN
to 375°F (190°C) Gas 5.

BAKING TIME:
Bake for 30 to 35 minutes.

METRIC EQUIVALENTS:
*350 g strong white flour*
*125 g wholemeal flour*
*30 g fresh yeast or 15 g dried yeast*
*250 ml milk, scalded*
*40 g butter*
*1 tablespoon honey*
*1 teaspoon salt*
*250 g cooked rice*

# Apricot Bread

In colour—page 88

*The sweet-sour flavours of the apricot make a tart and colourful loaf.*

*Makes 1 large loaf*

THE MIX:
Cream the butter and honey in a large bowl. Add the beaten eggs gradually, and stir in the orange juice, bran, almonds, and orange rind. Drain and chop the cooked apricots then add them to the egg mixture.
Sift the flour, salt, baking powder and bicarbonate of soda into the egg and orange juice mixture and mix well. Pour into a greased 2 lb (1 kg) loaf tin.

THE FLOUR:
*8 oz strong white flour*

THE RAISING AGENTS:
*4 teaspoons baking powder*
*½ teaspoon bicarbonate of soda*

THE RISING:
Leave, covered, in a warm place, until double in size, about 30 minutes.

AND . . .
*1 oz butter*
*2 tablespoons honey*
*2 eggs, beaten*
*8 fl.oz pure orange juice*
*½ oz bran*
*2½ oz chopped almonds*
*1 teaspoon grated orange rind*
*6 oz cooked apricots*
*½ teaspoon salt*

PRE-HEAT OVEN
to 325°F (170°C) Gas 3.

BAKING TIME:
Bake for ¾ to 1 hour.

METRIC EQUIVALENTS:
*250 g strong white flour*
*4 teaspoons baking powder*
*½ teaspoon bicarbonate of soda*
*30 g butter*
*2 tablespoons honey*
*2 eggs, beaten*

*250 ml pure orange juice*
*15 g bran*
*75 g chopped almonds*
*1 teaspoon grated orange rind*
*175 g cooked apricots*
*½ teaspoon salt*

# Boston Brown Bread

In colour—page 216

*Makes about 4 loaves*

THE FLOUR:
*8 oz wholemeal flour*
*8 oz rye flour*
*8 oz cornmeal*

THE RAISING AGENT:
*2 teaspoons bicarbonate of soda*

AND...
*2 teaspoons salt*
*6 oz raisins*
*6 fl.oz molasses or black treacle*
*about 1 pt buttermilk*

METRIC EQUIVALENTS:
*250 g wholemeal flour*
*250 g rye flour*
*250 g cornmeal*
*2 teaspoons bicarbonate of soda*
*2 teaspoons salt*
*175 g raisins*
*175 g molasses or black treacle*
*450 ml buttermilk*

*This steamed bread originates from the days before ovens were commonplace in most homes. After steaming, the bread was dried out before a fire. It was probably cooked by early American settlers. To make cylindrical moulds, remove the lid from any empty can, such as a can of tomatoes.*

THE MIX:
Mix the flours and cornmeal with the salt and bicarbonate of soda in a large bowl and add the raisins. Stir the molasses or black treacle into the buttermilk and when they are mixed add to the flour mixture. Mix to a batter and pour into greased, cylindrical moulds. Cover tightly with greaseproof paper or foil and place the moulds in a casserole dish. Fill the casserole dish with boiling water to reach three-quarters up the sides of the moulds and cover with a lid.

STEAMING TIME:
Steam for at least 2 hours, adding more water if necessary.

PRE-HEAT OVEN
to 350°F (180°C) Gas 4.

BAKING TIME:
Remove the bread from the moulds and bake in the oven for a few minutes to dry.

# Southern Spoonbread

*Makes 1 loaf*

THE FLOUR:
*5 oz cornmeal*

AND...
*1¼ pt milk*
*1¼ teaspoons salt*
*1 oz softened butter*
*4 eggs, separated*

METRIC EQUIVALENTS:
*150 g cornmeal*
*750 ml milk*
*1¼ teaspoons salt*
*30 g softened butter*
*4 eggs, separated*

*This bread derives from the "Indian Pudding" that was a mainstay in early colonial America. It is sometimes served today as a substitute for potatoes or rice. It looks like a soufflé—brown and crusty on top with a pale yellow moist inside. Serve very hot.*

THE MIX:
Blend the milk, cornmeal and salt over a low heat until the mixture thickens—about 15 minutes. Stir in the butter and allow the mixture to cool. Beat the egg yolks and separately whisk the egg whites until very stiff. Stir the beaten egg yolks into the mixture and fold in the whites. Pour the mixture into a greased soufflé or baking dish.

PRE-HEAT OVEN
to 400°F (200°C) Gas 6.

BAKING TIME:
Bake for about 45 to 50 minutes or until puffed up and brown and firm on top.

# Dutch Honey Bread

*This bread probably dates back to the days when Amsterdam was the centre of the spice trade.*

THE MIX:
Stir the bicarbonate of soda into the honey then stir in the buttermilk. Cream the butter with the 3 tablespoons of honey in a large bowl. Add the eggs and beat until they are well mixed. Sift the flour, salt, cinnamon, ginger and cloves and stir into the egg mixture. Add the buttermilk liquid and mix to a batter. Dust the almonds and raisins with a little flour and fold them into the batter. Pour the batter into a greased 2 lb (1 kg) loaf tin.

THE RISING:
Leave, covered, in a warm place until double in size, about 1 hour.

PRE-HEAT OVEN
to 350°F (180°C) Gas 4.

BAKING TIME:
Bake for 50 minutes or until a warm knife blade inserted in the centre of the loaf comes out clean.

*Makes 1 large loaf*

THE FLOUR:
*8 oz strong white flour*

THE RAISING AGENT:
*1 teaspoon bicarbonate of soda*

AND...
*6 oz clear honey*
*6 fl.oz buttermilk*
*4 oz softened butter*
*3 tablespoons honey*
*3 eggs, beaten*
*¼ teaspoon salt*
*½ teaspoon cinnamon*
*½ teaspoon ground ginger*
*½ teaspoon ground cloves*
*1½ oz blanched almonds*
*1½ oz raisins*

METRIC EQUIVALENTS:
*250 g strong white flour*
*1 teaspoon bicarbonate of soda*
*175 g clear honey*
*150 to 200 ml buttermilk*
*125 g softened butter*
*3 tablespoons honey*
*3 eggs, beaten*
*¼ teaspoon salt*
*½ teaspoon cinnamon*
*½ teaspoon ground ginger*
*½ teaspoon ground cloves*
*40 g blanched almonds*
*40 g raisins*

# Corn Muffins

*An excellent substitute for the usual bread roll. Particularly good with ham.*

*Makes about 18*

THE FLOUR:
*8 oz strong white flour*
*4 oz cornmeal*

THE STARTER:
*½ oz fresh yeast or ¼ oz dried yeast*
*4 tablespoons lukewarm water*

AND...
*8 fl.oz milk*
*1 teaspoon salt*
*1 tablespoon honey*
*2 oz butter*
*2 eggs, beaten*

METRIC EQUIVALENTS:
*250 g strong white flour*
*125 g cornmeal*
*15 g fresh yeast or 8 g dried yeast*
*4 tablespoons lukewarm water*
*250 ml milk*
*1 teaspoon salt*
*1 tablespoon honey*
*60 g butter*
*2 eggs, beaten*

YEAST STARTER:
Mix the yeast with the lukewarm water and leave for about 5 minutes.

THE MIX:
Gently heat the milk with the salt and honey until hot but not boiling. Pour into a large bowl and stir in the cornmeal and butter, cut into small pieces. When the milk mixture has cooled to lukewarm, add the yeast liquid and the beaten eggs. Stir together and mix well. Turn out on to a floured board and knead until smooth.

THE RISING:
Leave, covered, in a warm place until double in size, about 1 hour. Knock back and knead again until smooth. Roll the dough out on a floured surface and divide it into walnut-sized pieces. Place in greased deep patty pans.

PRE-HEAT OVEN
to 425°F (220°C) Gas 7.

BAKING TIME:
Bake for about 20 minutes.

# Cappodocia

*Alleged to have been the finest bread in Ancient Rome, kept only for the tables of the wealthy: the addition of white flour gave it luxury status.*

*Makes 1 loaf*

THE FLOUR:
*6 oz wholemeal flour*
*4 oz strong white flour*

THE STARTER:
*½ oz fresh yeast or ¼ oz dried yeast*
*1 teaspoon honey*

AND...
*8 fl.oz lukewarm milk*
*1 tablespoon olive oil*

YEAST STARTER:
Mix the yeast, honey and 2 tablespoons of the warm milk together and leave for 5 minutes to froth.

THE MIX:
Mix the flours in a large bowl and add the yeast mixture, olive oil and the remaining milk. Knead until springy.

FIRST RISING:
Leave, covered, in a greased bowl, in a warm place until double in size, about 1 hour.
Knock back and knead again until smooth. Shape into a dome and place on a greased baking sheet.

SECOND RISING:
Leave, covered, in a warm place until double in size, about 30 to 40 minutes. Mark with a cross.

PRE-HEAT OVEN
to 400°F (200°C) Gas 6.

BAKING TIME:
Bake for 25 minutes or until well risen and light brown.

METRIC EQUIVALENTS:
*175 g wholemeal flour*
*125 g strong white flour*
*15 g fresh yeast or 8 g dried yeast*
*1 teaspoon honey*
*250 ml lukewarm milk*
*1 tablespoon olive oil*

# Artologanos

*This recipe is based on an ancient Greek bread, which at one time also included wine and not milk. It was highly praised by the writer Herodotus.*

*Makes 1 loaf*

YEAST STARTER:
Mix the yeast and honey with 2 tablespoons of the warm milk and leave for about 5 minutes to froth.

THE FLOUR:
*6 oz wholemeal flour*
*4 oz barley flour*

THE MIX:
Mix the flours with the salt and pepper in a large bowl. Add the oil and the yeast mixture and mix well. Add the remaining milk and mix and knead until smooth and springy.

THE STARTER:
*½ oz fresh yeast or ¼ oz dried yeast*
*1 teaspoon honey*

THE RISING:
Leave, covered, in a warm place until double in size, about 1 hour. Knock back and knead again until smooth. Shape into a flat hearth loaf and place on a greased baking sheet.

AND . . .
*6 fl.oz lukewarm milk*
*½ teaspoon salt*
*1 teaspoon freshly ground black pepper*
*1 tablespoon olive oil*

PRE-HEAT OVEN
to 400°F (200°C) Gas 6.

BAKING TIME:
Bake for 30 minutes until well risen and brown.

METRIC EQUIVALENTS:
*175 g wholemeal flour*
*125 g barley flour*
*15 g fresh yeast or 8 g dried yeast*
*1 teaspoon honey*
*150 to 200 ml lukewarm milk*
*½ teaspoon salt*
*1 teaspoon freshly ground black pepper*
*1 tablespoon olive oil*

# Melitutes

*A recipe based on the bread of early Athens: originally made with the precious honey of Mount Hymettus.*

*Makes 1 loaf*

THE FLOUR:
*6 oz strong white flour*
*3 oz wholemeal flour*

THE STARTER:
*½ oz fresh yeast or ¼ oz dried yeast*

AND . . .
*½ teaspoon salt*
*2 tablespoons honey*
*8 fl.oz lukewarm milk*

METRIC EQUIVALENTS:
*175 g strong white flour*
*90 g wholemeal flour*
*15 g fresh yeast or 8 g dried yeast*
*½ teaspoon salt*
*2 tablespoons honey*
*250 ml lukewarm water*

YEAST STARTER:
Mix the yeast and 1 teaspoon of the honey with 2 tablespoons of the warm milk, and leave for about 5 minutes to froth.

THE MIX:
Mix the flours in a large bowl with the salt and add the rest of the milk and honey. Knead to a springy dough.

FIRST RISING:
Leave, covered, in a warm place until double in size, about 1 hour. Knock back and knead again. Shape the loaf into a dome and place on a greased baking sheet.

SECOND RISING:
Leave to prove a second time for about 30 minutes. Mark with a cross.

PRE-HEAT OVEN
to 400°F (200°C) Gas 6.

BAKING TIME:
Bake for 25 minutes.

OPPOSITE:
Left: *A round Oatmeal Rye Country Style Loaf p.202* and right: *Cottage Loaf p.201 (both by Ursel Norman).* Centre: *Maslin Bread (Bobby Freeman) p.192-93.*
OVERLEAF LEFT:
Top: *Two loaves of Mild Barley Bread (Elizabeth David) p.54 one baked in a sandwich tin and the other hand moulded with a decorative criss-cross top.*
Centre left: *Wholemeal Bara Brith (Bobby Freeman) p.194.*
Centre right: *Parker House Rolls (Adrian Bailey) p.217.*
Below: *Rye Bread) Maria Johnson) p.89.*
OVERLEAF RIGHT:
Top: *Boston Brown Bread (Adrian Bailey) p.212.* Centre: *Chicago Pumpernikel (Ursel Norman) p.204.* Below: *Corn Bread (Alan Long) p.241.*

# Parker House Rolls

*A delicate, soft and slightly sweet roll created at the famous nineteenth-century hotel in Boston, Parker House.*

YEAST STARTER:
Mix the yeast and 1 teaspoon honey with the warm water. Leave for about 5 minutes to froth.

THE MIX:
Mix the milk with the salt, butter and 3 teaspoons of honey and heat until lukewarm. Sift 12 oz (350 g) of the flour into a large bowl and stir in the milk and yeast mixtures. Beat well, cover and leave for 30 minutes. Beat the egg and add it with the remaining flour. Knead well.

FIRST RISING:
Leave, covered, in a warm place to double in size, about 1 hour. Knock back and knead again until smooth. Rest for several minutes, then roll out to ½ in (1.5 cm) thick and cut into 3 in (8 cm) rounds. With a knife, make a crease in each round, slightly off centre. Brush with melted butter. Fold the small section into the larger one and pinch the edges together.

SECOND RISING:
Place the rolls on a greased baking sheet, brush again with melted butter, and leave, covered, in a warm place until double in size. about 30 to 40 minutes.

PRE-HEAT OVEN
to 425°F (220°C) Gas 7.

BAKING TIME:
Bake for 15 minutes.

*In colour—page 216*

*Makes about 36*

THE FLOUR:
*1¾ lb strong white flour*

THE STARTER:
*1 oz fresh yeast or ½ oz dried yeast*
*1 teaspoon honey*
*4 tablespoons lukewarm water*

AND . . :
*about 14 fl.oz milk*
*1 teaspoon salt*
*1 oz butter*
*3 teaspoons honey*
*1 egg*
*about ½ oz melted butter*

METRIC EQUIVALENTS:
*850 g strong white flour*
*30 g fresh yeast or 15 g dried yeast*
*1 teaspoon honey*
*4 tablespoons lukewarm water*
*450 ml milk*
*1 teaspoon salt*
*30 g butter*
*3 teaspoons honey*
*1 egg*
*about 15 g melted butter*

OPPOSITE:
Top left: *Biscottes (Good Housekeeping Institute) p.105.*
Top right: *Farthing Buns (Brian Binns) p.134.* Centre: *Swedish Tea Ring, dusted with icing sugar (Adrian Bailey) p.208-209.*

# Theodora FitzGibbon

Theodora FitzGibbon and George Morrison have probably done more than anyone to reclaim the vanishing traditions of Irish cookery. Theodora is a renowned cookery writer and George is a film maker and picture archivist. His selection of period photographs in her books and her evocative writing recreate the life of the past with its haunting memories.

But it's often a hard and poor tradition and, like the peasant cookery of many lands, has depended on the ingenuity and skills of the cook working with only a few simple basic ingredients, whether it's a potato, oatmeal flour or another cereal. "There's a tradition in Ireland of making your own bread," says Theodora. "High tea was once a great meal of the day, with as many as fifty breads which could be served at the table. During and after the ten-year famine from 1840-50 people lived on bread with the scrapings of bacon and cabbage." But the breads were made from many cereals: combinations of oatmeal and rye, sometimes Indian meal or maize, too. "They developed interesting loaves out of necessity."

As a rule, traditional Irish loaves are made without yeast, because until quite recently many people didn't have the means to bake them properly. "Even 30 years ago some people in the outlying districts didn't have ovens." They baked bread in a three-legged pot over an open turf fire with hot turf sods heaped on top of the lid. "You couldn't bake yeast-risen loaves this way. The heat was too uneven. It was fine for soda bread."

"The soda bread or farls were marked on top with a cross. This wasn't for religious reasons, it was to ensure the even distribution of the raising agent. Griddle cakes and scones were also popular."

Theodora, the daughter of a surgeon in the Indian Army, was educated at several convents abroad, but remembers spending happy school holidays with her Irish relatives in County Clare. It was a more pleasant experience than some aspects of her education, and more instructive, she says.

At finishing school in Paris, she attended classes given by an elderly exiled queen, where she was taught many outmoded rules of etiquette, such as learning to eat fiery mustard dishes and hot peppers, without changing the expression on her face: "I suppose we were expected to marry Ambassadors or something like that. It was

assumed that we would have to eat strange foods and, of course, it would be quite improper to show that they were distasteful to us." She actually trained for the stage, and had enjoyed some success as an actress until she married.

Theodora's first husband was the writer Constantine FitzGibbon. Together they lived in Bermuda, Capri, Rome and the United States, and in these faraway places, she did all the cooking. It wasn't until several years later, in 1952, that she published a book, *Cosmopolitan Cookery in an English Kitchen*—one of the first books to suggest foreign dishes to the post-war British housewife. The shops had few of the right ingredients. Theodora carefully sought out British alternatives.

This book was soon followed by others—25 in all. The most comprehensive is *The Food of the Western World* which took 15 years to research and write. It covers 34 countries and there are entries in 32 languages.

Now she's writing a book she feels will be the most important of all. It's about Irish food, and she thinks it will be the most thorough work ever written on the subject: "It's taken me five years to research. I've talked to elderly people all over and I've found little bits here and there, in the British

Museum and in old eighteenth and nineteenth century diaries and journals."

Dipping into the past makes her very aware of the changes that have taken place in her own lifetime. When *she* was a child, everybody baked their own soda bread. And even the loaves from the bakery were crusty because they were cooked in a brick oven: they had "that lovely yeasty smell that bread doesn't seem to have today. Now people buy that awful yammy stuff. We call it pan bread; it's so soft that if you pick it up too violently your fingers meet in the middle. Children eat it as sandwiches at lunch-time: we don't have school dinners in Ireland."

In her family's house they made soda bread once or twice a week. They cooked half a dozen loaves at a time—enough to feed the farmworkers too. It was baked in a solid fuel range, like an Aga: "It had such an inviting and appetizing smell. When the loaves were done, they were wrapped in tea towels and stood up on their sides. By wrapping them in tea towels, you let the steam out and keep them soft. That way the crust doesn't go too hard. The soda loaf or cake, as it's called in the country, is flat and a too hard crust makes it too chewy."

Today, there's a revival in home-baking in Ireland: "People are asking for bread recipes." In Theodora's own home, if guests arrive unexpectedly, she makes soda bread: "It's so simple and quick. It's ready in about an hour. You don't even need buttermilk. I use yoghurt diluted with a little water."

## Soda Bread

*An Irish speciality, from the days when it was cooked on a griddle over a peat fire, or in a pot with a lid called a bastable oven with glowing turf piled on top to give an all-round heat. Soda bread is still baked all over Ireland.*

THE MIX:
Mix all the dry ingredients together in a bowl and make a well in the centre. Add the egg and enough of the yoghurt mixture or buttermilk to make a thick dough, stirring with a wooden spoon. The mixture should be slack but not too thin and the mixing done lightly and quickly. Add a little more liquid if the dough seems too thick.
Flour your hands and place the dough on a lightly floured board. Flatten it into 2 circles about 1½ in (4 cm) thick. Place on a baking sheet or put into a 2 lb (1 kg) loaf tin, and make a large cross on the top of each loaf using a floured knife. This is to ensure even distribution of heat.

PRE-HEAT OVEN
to 375°F (190°C) Gas 5.

BAKING TIME:
Bake for 40 to 60 minutes. Test the centre with a skewer before removing from the oven. Keep the bread soft by wrapping it in a clean tea towel.

In colour—page 120

*Makes 2 loaves*

THE FLOUR:
*½ lb wholemeal flour*
*½ lb white flour*

THE RAISING AGENTS:
*1¼ teaspoons bicarbonate of soda*
  *(1 teaspoon only if using*
    *buttermilk)*
*3 teaspoons baking powder*

AND . . .
*1 teaspoon salt*
*1 egg*
*about ½ pt natural yoghurt and*
  *¼ pt water, or scant ¾ pt*
  *buttermilk*

METRIC EQUIVALENTS:
*250 g wholemeal flour*
*250 g white flour*
*1¼ teaspoons bicarbonate of soda*
  *(1 teaspoon only if using*
    *buttermilk)*
*3 teaspoons baking powder*
*1 teaspoon salt*
*1 egg*
*about 300 ml natural yoghurt and*
  *150 ml water, or scant 450 ml*
  *buttermilk*

In colour—page 233

# Boxty Bread

*An Irish potato bread, traditionally served hot, split in two with butter, on Hallowe'en. And there's a rhyme to go with it:*
*"Boxty on the griddle, boxty in the pan*
*If you don't eat boxty, you'll never get a man."*
*This version is boxty in the pan. The starch in the potatoes acts as a raising agent.*

*Makes about 4 flat cakes (16 farls)*

THE FLOUR:
*1 lb white flour*

AND . . .
*1 lb raw potatoes*
*1 lb cooked potatoes, mashed*
*salt and pepper to taste*
*4 oz butter, melted*

METRIC EQUIVALENTS:
*500 g white flour*
*500 g raw potatoes*
*500 g cooked potatoes, mashed*
*salt and pepper to taste*
*125 g butter, melted*

THE MIX:
Peel 1 lb (500 g) potatoes and grate them into a clean cloth. Wring them tightly over a basin, catching the liquid. Put the grated potatoes into another basin and cover with the cooked, mashed potatoes.
When the starch has sunk to the bottom of the raw potato liquid, pour off the water and scrape the starch on to the mashed potato mixture. Mix well. Sieve the flour over it and add salt and pepper. Finally add the melted butter. Mix together.
Knead, then roll out on a floured board, and shape into flat round cakes. Make a cross over each with a floured knife, so that when cooked they will divide into quarters or farls.

PRE-HEAT OVEN
to 300°F (150°C) Gas 2.

BAKING TIME:
Cook on a greased baking sheet for about 40 minutes.

# Yeasted Fruit Loaf

*This raisin bread, also known as Fruit Pan, is a special favourite at tea-time in Ireland. It can also be made without the fruit.*

*Makes 2 large loaves*

THE FLOUR:
*1 lb 5 oz wholemeal flour*

THE STARTER:
*2 oz fresh yeast or 1 oz dried yeast*
*4 fl.oz warm potato water or plain water*
*2 tablespoons lukewarm mashed potatoes*

AND . . .
*5 level tablespoons honey*
*4 oz butter*
*2 eggs, beaten*
*5 oz seedless raisins*
*1 teaspoon salt*

YEAST STARTER:
Dissolve the yeast in the water in a large bowl until it becomes creamy. Add the mashed potatoes, 2 tablespoons of the honey and 4 oz (125 g) of the flour. Mix well until smooth. Cover with a cloth, and leave for about 30 minutes in a warm place.

THE MIX:
Stir again. Add another 4 oz (125 g) of the flour to the yeast mixture and beat until smooth. Melt the butter and allow to cool. Add this and the beaten eggs and the remaining honey. Stir in the raisins, the remaining flour and the salt and mix to a soft dough. Knead for about 5 minutes and put in a greased bowl, turning once.

FIRST RISING:
Cover again, as before, and leave for 1 hour in a warm place. Punch it down, using the knuckles and leave for 5 minutes. Divide in half, and shape to fit two 2 lb (1 kg) bread tins.

SECOND RISING:
Put into greased tins, cover and leave in a warm place until it has doubled in bulk—about 35 to 40 minutes.

PRE-HEAT OVEN
to 350°F (180°C) Gas 4.

BAKING TIME:
Bake for 50 to 60 minutes. When properly cooked the loaf will have a hollow sound when tapped at the bottom. Test with a skewer if in doubt.

METRIC EQUIVALENTS:
*650 g wholemeal flour*
*60 g fresh yeast or*
  *30 g dried yeast*
*100 ml warm potato water or plain*
  *water*
*2 tablespoons lukewarm mashed*
  *potatoes*
*5 level tablespoons honey*
*125 g butter*
*2 eggs, beaten*
*150 g seedless raisins*
*1 teaspoon salt*

# Tea Brack

*A simplified (but spirited!) version of the traditional Barm Brack. It is richly fruited with plump sultanas and raisins which can be soaked in a mixture of whisky and tea instead of the more homely tea for special occasions.*

PREPARATION:
Soak the dried fruits and honey overnight in the tea.

THE MIX:
Next day, alternately add the flour and beaten eggs to the dried fruit mixture. Finally add the baking powder. Blend well together and add the mixed spice if liked. Turn into 3 greased 2 lb (1 kg) loaf tins.

PRE-HEAT OVEN
to 300°F (150°C) Gas 2.

BAKING TIME:
Bake for 1½ hours. If you like you can brush the tops with a little melted honey to give a fine glaze.

In colour—page 120

*Makes 3 large loaves*

THE FLOUR:
*1 lb white flour*

THE RAISING AGENT:
*3 level teaspoons baking powder*

AND . . .
*1 lb sultanas*
*1 lb raisins*
*½ lb honey*
*1 pt cold, milkless tea*
*3 eggs, beaten*
*3 teaspoons mixed spice*
  *(optional)*

METRIC EQUIVALENTS:
*500 g white flour*
*3 level teapoons baking powder*
*500 g sultanas*
*500 g raisins*
*250 g honey*
*600 ml cold, milkless tea*
*3 eggs, beaten*
*3 teaspoons mixed spice (optional)*

# Arabella Boxer

Arabella Boxer has written about food with distinction for 15 years; first as the author of one of the most original books ever devised, *First Slice Your Cookbook*, and recently as the *Vogue* cook, and a *Sunday Times* contributor. She has twice won the Glenfiddich Award for the Best Food Writer.

She has for several years worked with the photographer Tessa Traeger, to produce dishes which are as beautiful as they are tasty. She especially loves fresh vegetables, and has written one book exclusively about them: *Arabella Boxer's Garden Cookbook*.

She is a self-taught cook. In recent years she has grown deeply interested in food as a source of good health, and shares with many others a growing concern for the intrinsic goodness of food. She makes her own bread, using for the most part wholemeal or *Granary* flour.

## Wholemeal Onion Bread

*Makes 1 loaf*

THE FLOUR:
*1 lb wholemeal flour*

THE STARTER:
*½ oz fresh yeast*

AND...
*about ½ pt warm water*
*1 teaspoon sea salt*
*1½ lb onions, sliced*
*2 oz butter*
*1 large egg, beaten*

METRIC EQUIVALENTS:
*500 g wholemeal flour*
*15 g fresh yeast*
*just over 300 ml warm water*
*1 teaspoon sea salt*
*750 g onions, sliced*
*60 g butter*
*1 large egg, beaten*

*This onion bread is excellent with pâtés. It is best served within an hour of baking, while still warm.*

YEAST STARTER:
Put the yeast in a small jug with 2 tablespoons of the warm water. Stand in a warm place for 10 minutes.

THE MIX:
Put the flour in a large warm bowl. Dissolve the salt in a little very hot water, then make up to ½ pt (300 ml) with the warm water. When the yeast is ready, cream it with a teaspoon and pour into the centre of the flour. Add the warm water, beating with a wooden spoon, using just enough to make the dough cling together. Turn out and knead for 5 minutes, sprinkling with more flour as needed.

FIRST RISING:
When smooth and elastic, replace in a clean bowl which you have rubbed with oil, and cover with a cloth. Stand in a warm place for about 1½ hours, or until it has doubled in bulk.

SECOND RISING:
Punch down, knead again for 4 or 5 minutes, and lay on an oiled baking sheet in the shape of a round flat loaf. Put back in a warm place to rise again for 45 minutes.
While it is rising, cook the sliced onions gently in the butter, stirring now and then. Allow about 30 minutes for them to get soft without allowing them to brown. Drain for a few minutes in a colander, then spoon them on top of the bread just before putting it in the oven. Spread them evenly all over with a palette knife, and brush all over with the beaten egg.

PRE-HEAT OVEN
to 450°F (230°C) Gas 8.

BAKING TIME:
Bake for 45 minutes. After 15 minutes REDUCE HEAT to 425°F
(220°C) Gas 7. Halfway through, when the onions are a nice brown,
cover lightly with a piece of foil to prevent them becoming too
brown.

# Potato Rolls

*These rolls are especially good with soups, salads or hard cheeses.
They can be made with unbleached strong white flour instead of
wholemeal, if you prefer.*

*Makes 8 large or 16 small rolls*

THE FLOUR:
*¾ lb wholemeal flour*

YEAST STARTER:
Put the yeast and 1 teaspoon of the honey in a small jug with the
warm water. Stand in a warm place for 10 minutes.

THE STARTER:
*¼ oz fresh yeast*
*4 tablespoons warm water*

THE MIX:
Warm 2 large bowls. Heat the milk in a small pan until lukewarm,
then remove from the heat and add the butter, cut in small bits.
When the yeast is ready, pour it into one of the warm bowls and
add the milk and half-melted butter, the remaining honey, the salt,
and the beaten egg. Stir well until blended. Put the freshly mashed
potato in the second bowl, and pour the yeast mixture into this.
Stir again until blended, then gradually add the flour. When the
dough starts to cling together, turn out on to a floured surface and
knead, adding the remaining flour as needed. Knead for 6 to 8
minutes, until smooth and springy, then place in a clean bowl which
you have rubbed with oil, and cover with a cloth.

AND . . .
*3 teaspoons honey*
*4 fl.oz milk*
*3 oz butter*
*2 teaspoons sea salt*
*1 egg, beaten*
*3 oz freshly mashed potato*

METRIC EQUIVALENTS:
*350 g wholemeal flour*
*8 g fresh yeast*
*4 tablespoons warm water*
*3 teaspoons honey*
*100 ml milk*
*90 g butter*
*2 teaspoons sea salt*
*1 egg, beaten*
*90 g freshly mashed potato*

FIRST RISING:
Stand in a warm place for about 1½ hours, until doubled in volume.

SECOND RISING:
Punch down, turn out, and knead again for 5 minutes. Shape into
rolls—it will make 8 large rolls or 16 small ones—and lay them on
oiled baking sheets. Stand on top of the stove to rise again for 30
minutes.

PRE-HEAT OVEN
to 375°F (190°C) Gas 5.

BAKING TIME:
Bake large rolls for about 25 minutes, small ones for 20 minutes.
Test by knocking to see if they sound hollow; if not, leave for a few
more minutes. Cool briefly on a wire rack, and serve while still
warm, if possible. Alternatively, cool completely and re-warm before
serving.

# Bread Sticks

*Makes 16*

THE FLOUR:
*½ lb wholemeal flour*

THE STARTER:
*¼ oz fresh yeast*
*1 teaspoon honey*

AND . . .
*5 to 6 fl.oz warm water*
*1 teaspoon sea salt*
*1 tablespoon olive oil*
*1 egg, beaten*
*2 tablespoons sesame seeds*

METRIC EQUIVALENTS:
*250 g wholemeal flour*
*8 g fresh yeast*
*1 teaspoon honey*
*150 to 200 ml warm water*
*1 teaspoon sea salt*
*1 tablespoon olive oil*
*1 egg, beaten*
*2 tablespoons sesame seeds*

*This is a wholemeal version of a children's favourite—which adults adore.*

YEAST STARTER:
Crumble the yeast in a small jug with the honey and 3 tablespoons of the warm water. Stand in a warm place for 10 minutes, until it starts to bubble.

THE MIX:
Dissolve the salt in a little very hot water, then make up to 5½ fl.oz (175 ml) with the warm water. Put the flour into a warm bowl, make a well in the centre, and pour in the yeast mixture, then the oil. Add the salted water gradually, stirring, until the dough starts to cling together. Turn out and knead for 3 or 4 minutes, until smooth and elastic.

RESTING TIME:
Cover with a cloth and leave for 5 minutes, then knead again once or twice.

PRE-HEAT OVEN
to 325°F (170°C) Gas 3.

THE RISING:
Divide the dough into 16 pieces, and form each one into a stick about as thick as your middle finger. Place on oiled baking sheets and leave on the top of the cooker for 12 to 15 minutes, until they are just starting to rise. Brush them with beaten egg and sprinkle with sesame seeds.

BAKING TIME:
Bake for about 35 minutes until golden-brown. Cool on a wire rack for 10 minutes, then serve immediately, or keep slightly warm.

# Marika Hanbury-Tenison

Marika Hanbury-Tenison is married to an explorer, who every so often takes off to live with native tribes (most recently with the Yanoamas of Brazil for three months on a Time-Life book assignment).

Left to her own devices on their farm in Cornwall she throws herself into cookery. "It's either getting into trouble or writing cookery books," she says. She's written 28, from the *Sunday Telegraph Cookery Book* (she is their cookery editor), *Vegetable Cookery, Cooking from a Country Kitchen*, to books on freezing and slimming like *Eat Well and Stay Slim*.

On a few occasions, four to be precise, she has accompanied her husband on his journeys. In 1978 she went to Borneo with him and lived in a tribal long-house for two months baking the bread each day for 45 scientists. "I started cooking with a kerosene stove, with a tin oven on top. Then I made my own clay oven. It was fabulous."

She took masses of MacDougall's Bread Mix, and it seems its granular structure appealed to the local bees who mistook it for something like pollen and fell into it. "The results were sometimes like Garibaldi biscuits. But no-one seemed to mind. Bread was very important to morale. On these jungle expeditions it is very difficult to get anything home-made and fresh. It relieved tension and reduced strain while they were working extremely hard in almost intolerable conditions."

Marika started cooking as soon as she could prop herself up at the kitchen table. She was encouraged by her Swedish mother, glad to have some help in the house. "She'd been brought up in an era when people had endless cooks."

Among the first books Marika read were her mother's cookery books, which held out promise of great culinary delights. "I was always exceptionally greedy," she remembers.

When Marika was 11 she cooked a dinner party for her parents—for eight. "Starting with *moules marinières*, finishing with *crème brûlée*. The main course was escalopes of veal. There was a cockroach, unfortunately, in the *moules marinières* (it was a very big, very old house). It surfaced in the plate of a Mr. Heinz who was immensely important. I don't

know if it was *the* Mr. Heinz. Anyway, he left everything on his plate. I was terribly upset."

Schooling was interrupted when she contracted polio; the year she spent on her back, reading good books, spoilt her and she couldn't settle down to school-work again. She married when she was 20, and with her husband who was only 22, moved into their huge house in Cornwall, which they set out to restore while farming. It took ten years to do it.

It was then that she started to write about food. "I've always loved cooking. It's a relaxation and a therapy and an enjoyment. I started to bake bread for the first time; the Aga was crying out to be used for baking. I found it very distressing at first. I couldn't do it. I had to overcome it—being a cookery writer and not being able to make bread was a bit embarrassing. One day you just can't do it. Then overnight it comes.

"I think I was too frightened of leaving the dough to rise in a place warm enough. And the other thing is impatience. I'm very impatient by nature. You have to go at the pace the dough demands. I've actually got three different lots rising in different places at the moment. But when you've got the hang of it, you just can't go wrong again."

# Cumin and Poppy Seed Rolls

In colour—page 233

*Light brown bread rolls with an interesting flavour of cumin and poppy seed. I like these for breakfast, piping hot and split, with butter and honey, but they also go well with a good many soups both hot and cold.*

*Makes 12*

THE FLOUR:
½ lb strong white flour
½ lb wholemeal flour

THE STARTER:
1 oz fresh yeast
1 teaspoon honey
4 fl.oz milk
¼ pt water

AND...
2 teaspoons cumin seeds
1½ teaspoons salt
1 oz butter
2 tablespoons poppy seeds

METRIC EQUIVALENTS:
250 g strong white flour
250 g wholemeal flour
30 g fresh yeast
1 teaspoon honey
100 ml milk
150 ml water
2 teaspoons cumin seeds
1½ teaspoons salt
30 g butter
2 tablespoons poppy seeds

YEAST STARTER:
Cream the yeast and honey together. Warm the milk and the water to blood heat, add a little to the yeast and leave to stand for 5 minutes.

THE MIX:
Warm the flours, cumin seeds and salt in a low oven. Rub in the butter until the mixture resembles very fine breadcrumbs. Make a well in the centre. Gradually blend the rest of the liquid into the yeast mixture, then pour this into the well. Gradually draw the liquid into the flour and knead into a smooth dough.

FIRST RISING:
Place in an oiled bowl, cover with a damp cloth and leave to rise for about 1 hour, until double in bulk.

SECOND RISING:
Punch down, knead well and cut into 12 squares. Place on a baking sheet, cover and leave to rise for 30 minutes.

PRE-HEAT OVEN
to 400°F (200°C) Gas 6.

BAKING TIME:
Brush the top with lightly salted water, sprinkle with poppy seeds and bake for 20 minutes.

# Onion Bread

*I first had this bread in a small trattoria in Tuscany. When I returned home, I tried it myself and have found it a guaranteed success with guests and family ever since. Instead of the onions you can flavour the bread with chopped prosciutto or bacon.*

PREPARATION:
Peel and chop the onions very finely. Heat the oil in a frying-pan, add the onions and cook over a moderately low heat, stirring every now and then, until they are well browned and crisp. Drain the onions on kitchen paper.

YEAST STARTER:
Warm the milk to blood temperature. Cream the yeast with the honey, add the milk and stir until smooth. Leave to stand, covered, for 5 minutes.

THE MIX:
Warm the flour in a basin with the salt. Add the butter, cut into small pieces, and rub it into the flour until the mixture resembles fine breadcrumbs. Add the onions and mix well.
Make a well in the centre of the flour, add the yeast mixture and gradually draw the flour into the liquid until the mixture forms a firm dough. Turn on to a floured board and knead until smooth and elastic.

FIRST RISING:
Place in an oiled bowl, cover with a damp cloth and leave in a warm, draughtproof place to rise for 1 hour.

SECOND RISING:
Punch down, place in 2 oiled 1 lb (500 g) tins, cover with a damp cloth and leave to rise again for a further 45 minutes.

PRE-HEAT OVEN
to 450°F (230°C) Gas 8.

COOKING TIME:
Brush with beaten egg and bake for about 20 minutes until golden-brown and sounding hollow when tapped on the bottom. Turn on to a wire rack.
*Note:* You can also bake this dough in the form of 2 plaits, or make it into rolls.

*Makes 2 small loaves*

THE FLOUR:
*1¾ lb strong white flour*

THE STARTER:
*1 oz fresh yeast*
*½ pt milk*
*1 teaspoon honey*

AND . . .
*2 large onions*
*2 tablespoons sunflower oil*
*1½ teaspoons salt*
*½ oz butter*
*1 egg*

METRIC EQUIVALENTS:
*850 g strong white flour*
*30 g fresh yeast*
*300 ml milk*
*1 teaspoon honey*
*2 large onions*
*2 tablespoons sunflower oil*
*1½ teaspoons salt*
*15 g butter*
*1 egg*

# Claudia Roden

Claudia Roden is the author responsible for bringing the cuisines of the Middle East into British homes. Her *Book of Middle Eastern Food* published by Penguin not only teaches the home cook how to add variety to her table, it also explains the traditions and eating habits of the Middle East.

There are many different types of Arab bread; leavened and unleavened, some thick, some paper thin, some hollow. They are cooked over a metal dome on an open fire or baked in charcoal ovens. The most common everyday bread is *khubz*, known here as pitta. It is round, flat, soft and hollow. Some people prepare their own dough, but send it to the bakery to be baked. They eat bread with every meal, often folding it and using it as a scoop to pick up morsels of food.

Strong superstitious feeling is attached to bread in some countries of the region: for example, a hungry man may kiss the bread given to him as alms, a cook may invoke God before kneading the dough or placing it in the oven.

The simple pitta is easily transformed into a meal by cutting it in half and filling the hollow pocket of the centre with hot shish kebab and salad. Sometimes a fried egg is opened on top of the bread or the pitta may be topped with a mincement mixture. There follows a basic unleavened bread and a delicious Arab type of pizza.

## Unleavened Bread

*Serves 6 to 8*

THE FLOUR:
½ lb wholemeal or fine maize
   flour
½ lb strong white flour

AND...
*about ½ pt water*

METRIC EQUIVALENTS:
*250 g wholemeal or fine maize flour*
*250 g strong white flour*
*about 300 ml water*

*This typical Arab peasant bread uses no leavening. In a modern kitchen it is best cooked under the grill, where it puffs up nicely. If you like, you can use fine maize flour, available from Greek shops, instead of the wholemeal flour. Brush the hot bread with melted butter and spread with honey. Or eat it hot with soup, or use to dip in a stew or sauce.*

THE MIX:
Mix the flours together well and add enough water to make a firm dough. Knead vigorously for at least 8 minutes, until elastic and resilient.

THE RESTING:
Leave, covered with a damp cloth for 30 minutes.

THE SHAPING:
Pull off small lumps of dough (a little larger than a large egg). Flatten each lump between floured palms and pull out or roll out very thin.

PRE-HEAT GRILL
and grill pan to very hot.

COOKING TIME:
When the grill pan is very hot, lay the thin cakes of dough on it and grill for 2 to 3 minutes until they puff up. Turn over and grill the other side for 2 to 3 minutes until light brown spots appear.

# Lahma Bi Ajeen

In colour—page 232

*This elegant savoury is the Arab version of the pizza. A
cucumber and yoghurt salad goes well with this dish.*

*Serves 8 to 10*

THE FLOUR:
*6 oz wholemeal flour*
*10 oz strong white flour*

YEAST STARTER:
Dissolve the yeast and honey in 3 to 4 tablespoons of the warm
water and set aside for about 10 minutes until bubbly.

THE STARTER:
*½ oz fresh yeast*
*½ teaspoon honey*

THE MIX:
Put the flours and salt in a large warmed mixing bowl. Add the oil
and yeast mixture and enough of the remaining warm water to
make a soft dough. Knead vigorously for about 15 minutes. The
dough should be pliable and elastic. Put a little oil in the bottom of
the bowl and roll the ball of dough in it, coating the whole surface.
This prevents it from forming a dry crust as it rises.

AND . . .
*scant ½ pt lukewarm water*
*1 teaspoon salt*
*2 tablespoons oil*

THE RISING:
Cover with a damp cloth and set aside in a warm place for 2 to 3
hours, until double in bulk.

THE FILLING:
*1 lb onions, finely chopped*
*2 tablespoons olive oil*
*1½ lb lean lamb or beef, minced*
*1 lb fresh tomatoes, skinned and
   chopped, or 14 oz can tomatoes*
*1 small (2¼ oz) can tomato purée*
*½ teaspoon honey*
*¾ teaspoon ground allspice*
*1 to 2 tablespoons lemon juice*
*salt and pepper*
*3 tablespoons finely chopped
   parsley (optional)*
*pinch of Cayenne pepper
   (optional)*

THE FILLING:
Soften the onions in the oil but do not let them colour. Mix together
the meat, tomatoes and tomato purée in a large bowl. (Crush fresh
tomatoes to a pulp. Drain canned tomatoes, or the mixture will be
too wet.) Add the honey, allspice and lemon juice and season with
salt and pepper. Drain the oil from the onions and add them to the
mixture. Knead well by hand and add chopped parsley and Cayenne
pepper, if liked.

PRE-HEAT OVEN
to 450°F (230°C) Gas 8.

METRIC EQUIVALENTS:
*175 g wholemeal flour*
*300 g strong white flour*
*15 g fresh yeast or 8 g dried yeast*
*½ teaspoon honey*
*scant 300 ml lukewarm water*
*1 teaspoon salt*
*2 tablespoons oil*
The filling:
*500 g onions, finely chopped*
*2 tablespoons olive oil*
*750 g lean lamb or beef, minced*
*500 g fresh tomatoes, skinned and
   chopped, or 400 g can tomatoes*
*1 small (65 g) can tomato purée*
*½ teaspoon honey*
*¾ teaspoon ground allspice*
*1 to 2 tablespoons lemon juice*
*salt and pepper*
*3 tablespoons finely chopped
   parsley (optional)*
*pinch of Cayenne pepper (optional)*

THE SHAPING:
Knead the risen dough several times and divide it into many
walnut-sized balls. Leave to rest for a few minutes. Then roll out
each piece on a lightly floured board until it measures 5 to 6 in (13
to 15 cm) in diameter. Spread the filling very generously over each
piece, covering the surface completely. Place each prepared round on
a lightly oiled baking sheet.

BAKING TIME:
Bake for 8 to 10 minutes. They should be well done, but still soft
enough to roll up or fold in the hand and be eaten like this, as many
people do.

VARIATION:
To vary the filling, leave out the tomatoes and add 2 oz (60 g) pine
nuts and 2 to 3 tablespoons tamarind instead.

# Anton Mosimann

Off the large kitchens, echoing with the clatter of dishes, beneath London's Dorchester Hotel, there's a small, warm bakery. Until last year this bakery produced 16,000 rolls a day. It supplied bread to Harrods and the Houses of Parliament, to the Hilton and Intercontinental hotels and to several London night-clubs.

Now, Anton Mosimann, the youngest chef ever to run the kitchens, has decided that the bakery should supply only the needs of this famous hotel: "That way," he says with his soft Swiss-German accent, "we produce less quantity, but better quality. And we still have lots of variety. We bake white rolls and wholemeal rolls, French *baguettes*, small round flutes for canapés, sandwich loaves, brioches, croissants and Danish pastries". This is one of many decisions in favour of quality that Anton has made since he took over the running of the kitchens in 1976.

Anton is 33. His career began in his parents' restaurant in the village of Nidau in Switzerland. By the time he was eight years old he was inviting friends to sample his own dishes. At 15 he became an apprentice at the Hotel Baeren in Twann. At 17 he won his *Diplômé de Cuisinier*, which most people don't take until they're 19, and at 18 he got his first job at the Palace Hotel at Villars.

Since then he has climbed quickly to the top of the cookery world. He chose his masters carefully: in Rome he worked under René Rastello at the Cavalieri Hotel: in St. Moritz under M. Defrance, who had worked under the great Auguste Escoffier.

He worked in Canada and Japan and returned to Switzerland to win the highest cookery award, *Chef de Cuisine Diplômé*. Eugene Kaufeler, celebrated chef of London's Dorchester Hotel for 25 years, asked Anton to join him: and he took over a year later at the age of 29, handling with maturity a staff of 110, many of them older than himself.

Anton has created many new dishes in the spirit of the "*Nouvelle Cuisine*": with the emphasis on delicacy, freshness and simplicity. The simplicity of bread appeals to him: "It has always been a wonderful experience," he says.

At home, when he was a child, Sunday was the day set aside for making bread; the loaf was the traditional Swiss *Zopf:* "It was wonderful—a white bread with eggs and a lot of butter, similar

to cholla, but with more twists and curves. Like ladies' hair."

He made his first *Zopf* when he was 11: "It was a success, but not quite even. Actually, it was very uneven. You need a lot of practice to make the twists. But the taste was OK."

His parents did not bake for the restaurant, because the local baker produced such good bread. This local bakery, which was run by the father of Anton's school-friend, was a great source of enjoyment and learning to Anton: "It had a wood-burning stove. The smell was beautiful. You could smell it for half a mile around the shop."

Early in the morning, from 6 am onwards, on his free afternoons and during the holidays, Anton was to be found helping out in the bakery. He collected wood and shovelled it into the stove, watching the bricks, on which the bread baked, get hotter and hotter. "It was great fun."

It also had its serious side: "Sometimes there were accidents. We put too much wood in the stove and the bread came out very dark. But the baker said, 'Don't worry, some people like it like that'." And he was right. By seven that evening it had all been sold. "That day I learned something very important. I learned that if you make a mistake, it may be to somebody's liking."

The combination of good fun and learning that Anton experienced as a young boy in the bakery, was what he sought to recapture in his early working career. On several occasions, the kitchens he supervised had their own bakeries. At the Kulm Hotel, St. Moritz, "They worked very hard. They made everything—brioches, rolls, sandwiches, everything. The work never stopped."

Everyone was out on the slopes skiing in the daylight and drinking and enjoying themselves until late at night. The chefs wanted to enjoy themselves too, and why not the baker? "Sometimes, he would find us in a bar and drink with us until two or three in the morning. Then he had to go straight back to work and start making the bread." Once or twice Anton found him at eight in the morning fast asleep in the flour: "And there was no bread. So, then, we all made bread." Was Anton annoyed? "No, oh no. He was a very good baker. He was Italian, and Italians have a gift for making bread."

At the Palace Hotel, also in St. Moritz, the baker was Swiss. "This baker was 70 years old. He was very serious, very conscientious and well organised. He made beautiful bread. He would allow no-one into the bakery, so it was a special privilege that he allowed me to watch him work." And he gave Anton some time-old secrets: "Usually a chef's secret is something quite small— the temperature of the oven, a tiny bit more salt, perhaps having the water a little warmer. This baker mixed his own flours. There was a lot of detail and feeling. A good baker works a lot with feeling. That, and know-how."

In Japan, where Anton was head chef at the Swiss Pavilion for Expo 70, he again organised the bakery. Twenty-five of the 35 chefs working for him were Japanese. The Japanese do not eat bread, so he made sure that Europeans— French and Swiss—ran the bakery. Here, once more, the importance of flour was reinforced: "It was imported from all over Europe. You need the right flour. If you're used to making a specific recipe, it must have the same flour all the time."

The knowledge he gained from his experiences abroad Anton has now brought to the Dorchester. But in his private life, it's his Swiss wife Kathrin who does the baking: "Every Sunday Kathrin

makes a *Zopf*. It's like being at home again, when I was a child." Kathrin has taught their two sons Philip and Mark to bake. The youngest, three-and-a-half-year-old Mark enjoys it most: "He plays with the dough and bakes a tiny *Zopf* for himself. He's very proud and will eat only his own bread. I'm not allowed to touch his loaf, but occasionally he gives me a bit."

The family take their holidays in Switzerland, at their chalet in Emmenthal. The only bakery for 12 miles around with a wood-burning stove is not far away. Every day Anton drives five miles to this bakery for bread: "I always put on weight because I eat double the amount of bread I eat in England. The wood stove gives it such a special flavour. It reminds me of my childhood in my friend's bakery."

He always brings a few loaves back to England with him: "I'm in love with that bread. No-one can do me a bigger favour than to bring me one of those loaves from Switzerland." Many of his friends do just that.

Here are some recipes for breads that they bake at the Dorchester.

# Brioches

*These have a light, soft centre with a golden crisp outside, and were made famous by the French for breakfast.*

*Makes about 20*

THE FLOUR:
*1 lb strong white flour, sifted*

THE STARTER:
*½ oz fresh yeast*

AND...
*4 fl.oz lukewarm water*
*½ lb butter*
*1 teaspoon honey*
*1 teaspoon salt*
*4 eggs*

METRIC EQUIVALENTS:
*500 g strong white flour, sifted*
*15 g fresh yeast*
*100 ml lukewarm water*
*250 g butter*
*1 teaspoon honey*
*1 teaspoon salt*
*4 eggs*

YEAST STARTER:
Cream the yeast in the lukewarm water and add 3½ oz (100 g) of the flour. Mix into a thin batter.

RESTING TIME:
Cover and set aside in a warm place for about 1 hour.

THE MIX:
Knead the butter until soft, and cream with the honey until smooth. Add the rest of the flour, the salt and the eggs and make into a dough. Add the batter and knead the sticky dough vigorously.

CHILLING TIME:
Chill for 30 to 40 minutes.

SHAPING:
Divide into 2 oz (60 g) pieces, and using a lightly floured surface shape each piece into a roll, allowing two-thirds for a base and balancing one-third in a ball on top.

THE RISING:
Cover and allow to rise in a warm place for about 1 hour.

PRE-HEAT OVEN
to 400°F (200°C) Gas 6.

BAKING TIME:
Bake for about 15 minutes until golden-brown.

OPPOSITE:
*Lahma Bi Ajeen (Claudia Roden) p.229. Serve with cucumber and yoghurt salad.*
OVERLEAF LEFT:
Top: *Maize and Millet Bread (Alan Long) p.244.* Below left: *Zopf (Anton Mosimann) p.235.* Below right: *Muesli Loaf (Adrian Bailey) p.207.*
OVERLEAF RIGHT:
Top: *Brioche/Savarin (Len Deighton) p.260.* Below left: *Special Four-Cereal Bread decorated with sesame seeds (Alan Long) p.239.* Below right: *Wholemeal Apple Scones (Jordans) p.248.*

# Bread Rolls

*A simple, traditional roll to serve at any time of the day. If possible, bake with steam (see p.289).*

**YEAST STARTER:**
Cream the yeast with a little of the warm water and set aside for about 10 minutes.

**THE MIX:**
Add the salt to the flour and rub in the butter. Make a well in the centre, add the yeast mixture, and enough of the remaining warm water to make a pliable dough. Knead well.

**FIRST RISING:**
Cover and set aside in a warm place for at least 30 minutes.

**SECOND RISING:**
Knock back and shape into rolls. Place on a greased baking tray, cover and leave for about 30 minutes.

**PRE-HEAT OVEN**
to 500°F (260°C) Gas 9.

**BAKING TIME:**
Bake for about 15 to 20 minutes until golden brown.
This dough can also be shaped into loaves which should bake for about 25 minutes.

*Makes 45*

THE FLOUR:
*2 lb wholemeal flour*

THE STARTER:
*2 oz fresh yeast*

AND . . .
*about 1 pt lukewarm water*
*2 teaspoons salt*
*1½ oz butter*

METRIC EQUIVALENTS:
*1 kg wholemeal flour*
*60 g fresh yeast*
*about 600 ml lukewarm water*
*2 teaspoons salt*
*40 g butter*

OPPOSITE:
Top left: *Cumin and Poppy Seed Rolls (Marika Hanbury-Tenison) p.226.* Centre: *Irish Bran Loaf (Alan Long) p.242.* Front and top right: *Boxty Bread (Theodora FitzGibbon) p.220.*

# Walnut and Raisin Bread

*Makes 2 large loaves*

*A very good bread to serve with cheese at the end of a meal.*

THE FLOUR:
*2 lb wholemeal flour*

YEAST STARTER:
Cream the yeast in a little of the water and set aside for about 10 minutes.

THE STARTER:
*2 oz fresh yeast*

THE MIX:
Add the salt to the flour and rub in the butter. Make a well in the centre and pour in the yeast mixture and enough of the remaining water to make a workable dough. Knead well.

AND . . .
*about 1 pt lukewarm water*
*2 teaspoons salt*
*2 oz butter*
*2 oz chopped walnuts*
*1 oz sultanas or raisins*

FIRST RISING:
Cover and put in a warm place for about 30 minutes.

SECOND RISING:
Knead in the chopped walnuts and raisins. Shape into 2 loaves. Cover with a cloth and leave to rise for about 30 minutes.

METRIC EQUIVALENTS:
*1 kg wholemeal flour*
*60 g fresh yeast*
*about 600 ml lukewarm water*
*2 teaspoons salt*
*60 g butter*
*60 g chopped walnuts*
*30 g sultanas or raisins*

PRE-HEAT OVEN
to 450°F (230°C) Gas 8.

BAKING TIME:
Bake for about 25 minutes.

# Banana Bread

*Makes 2 small loaves*

*A moist tea-time bread which is delicious to eat hot from the oven in thick slices, with or without butter.*

THE FLOUR:
*10 oz wholemeal flour*
*10 oz white flour*

THE MIX:
Blend the bananas, honey, baking powder and salt. Mix the flours together, then gradually add them to the banana mixture. Add the eggs, then the oil and buttermilk. Mix well together.
Pour into two 1 lb (500 g) greased baking tins.

THE RAISING AGENT:
*½ tablespoon baking powder*

PRE-HEAT OVEN
to 350°F (180°C) Gas 4.

AND . . .
*1¼ lb very ripe bananas*
*½ lb honey*
*½ teaspoon salt*
*3 eggs, beaten*
*2 fl.oz vegetable oil*
*¼ pt buttermilk, or soured cream*

BAKING TIME:
Bake for ¾ hour. Remove from tins, turn over and bake for 5 more minutes.

METRIC EQUIVALENTS:
*300 g wholemeal flour*          *250 g honey*
*300 g white flour*              *½ teaspoon salt*
*½ tablespoon baking powder*     *3 eggs beaten*
*½ kg very ripe bananas*         *50 ml vegetable oil*
                                 *150 ml buttermilk, or soured cream*

# Zopf

*The traditional Swiss Sunday loaf, similar to Jewish cholla, but plaited differently.*

**YEAST STARTER:**
Cream the yeast with the honey in about 2 tablespoons of the warm milk and set aside to froth.

**THE MIX:**
Add the melted butter, the salt and the rest of the milk to the yeast mixture. Gradually mix this liquid into the flour. Add the egg and knead well for about 5 minutes.

**FIRST RISING:**
Cover and leave to rise in a warm place for about 1½ hours.

**THE SHAPING:**
Knock back the dough and divide into 3 equal pieces. Shape each piece into a long thin strip. Start to plait from the centre. Turn loaf around and plait from the other end (as shown in the diagram).

**SECOND RISING:**
Cover and set to rise a second time for about 30 minutes. Then before baking put in a cool place for 10 minutes.

**PRE-HEAT OVEN**
to 375°F (190°C) Gas 5.

**BAKING TIME:**
Brush with the egg yolk and bake for 45 minutes.

In colour—page 232

*Makes 1 large loaf*

THE FLOUR:
*1 lb strong white flour*

THE STARTER:
*½ oz fresh yeast*
*1 teaspoon honey*

AND . . .
*8 fl.oz lukewarm milk*
*2 oz butter, melted*
*1 teaspoon salt*
*1 egg*

THE GLAZE:
*1 egg yolk*

METRIC EQUIVALENTS:
*500 g strong white flour*
*15 g fresh yeast*
*1 teaspoon honey*
*250 ml lukewarm milk*
*60 g melted butter*
*1 teaspoon salt*
*1 egg*
*1 egg yolk, for glazing*

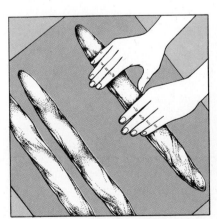 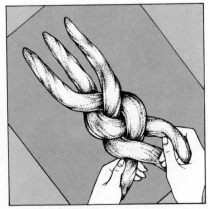 

## Alan Long

Bread-making has become a Sunday occupation for men, according to Alan Long, a scientist and honorary Research Adviser of the Vegetarian Society: "It's satisfying and, with freezers, it's very practical."

Alan is in the fortunate position of not often needing to bake his own; people give it to him: "I'm the dustbin," he says; bread bin would be more exact. People like to impress him. He's a judge of bread at horticultural shows around the country, so his praise carries a lot of weight: "I like a robust loaf. Many people judge bread according to its whiteness, evenness and fine crumb. I make allowances for wholemeal; it needn't necessarily be completely even, though it shouldn't have big holes."

He cuts the loaf to examine the inside and he looks closely at the weight: "If it's too heavy, it's because there's too much moisture. I judge it for taste and texture and mouth feel, as well as crust, shape and novelty."

Alan became a vegetarian when he was eight years old, and as a result the whole family changed their diet. His pharmacist mother baked a brown loaf. She was involved in a nature-cure clinic, developing cosmetics for beauty without cruelty. When she wasn't testing these out on Alan, she tested out wholemeal recipes, using Allinson flour.

Alan joined the Vegetarian Society and gravitated towards the nutrition and farming side: "Between the wars and during the fifties, before wholemeal really took a grip, the vegetarian movement kept Allinson and Prewett's going. Health food stores that didn't have their own bakery persuaded small bakers to bake with Allinson flour."

The Vegetarian Society has its own nutritional research centre, started by the late Dr. Frank Wokes. "Towards the end of the sixties we had put a lot of thought into the relevance of vegetarianism to the world food crisis. By 1976 we had put together a green plan for Britain's farming, land, food and health."

The green plan was launched with dishes based on "Best of British" goods. "We made wholemeal loaves in flowerpots. We emphasised the use of home-grown grists (raw materials). We presented a loaf to the Minister of Agriculture and to the

then Prime Minister, Harold Wilson. We offered a loaf to the Farmers' Union, but they asked us to send it by post. Obviously they like their bread stale."

The movement's aim was to increase the consumption of unrefined cereals and reverse the declining sales of bread by encouraging the increased consumption of wholemeal loaves. CAMREB, their own Campaign for Real Bread, developed from this: "The Campaign for Real Ale had shown that the consumer was prepared to go to some trouble and pay a premium to get what he wanted. Good food costs money, and so does good bread. You pay more for a Rolls Royce than a Ford, because craftsmen are making it."

Alan is interested in the historic side of what we eat: "Yeast is alleged to have been discovered by the Greeks or Egyptians. It's only a few thousand years old. And wholemeal bread only goes back about ten thousand years, to the second half of the agricultural revolution." Yet bread has such an important place in man's history: "There's a luxury about risen bread.

Jews, when they're doing penance, eat unleavened bread. Ascetics go for sourdough—because it's less luxurious."

Alan tried cutting down on the luxury, but prefers not to: "Unleavened rolls are fine when you're in a hurry, but they're only good for one day. After that they go rock hard."

Vegetarians usually bake with wholemeal flour. Alan's association with a medical team at Oxford reinforces this choice: "Vegetarians eat more dietary fibre than the general population, and this high consumption is related to a lower risk of incurring diverticular disease."

He prefers the flavour and robustness of wholemeal: "I buy home-grown flour to support the British farmer. Usually Pimhill or Doves Farm. But you shouldn't keep it for more than six months—the weevils like it. White flour lasts a little longer. Weevils have good taste."

During the bread strikes, hundreds of people rang the Vegetarian Society for recipes. They were even put out over the radio. Next time there's a strike, you need look no further than here. Below is Alan's selection of favourite recipes, adapted from *Betty's Bakery Cookbook*, and the millers W. & G. Brown in Derby. When adding fat, however, Alan always uses poly-unsaturated oil or margarine instead of butter.

A final word from Alan: "Bread is like friends and lovers. If you aren't prepared to spend time and money on it, you get a pretty low level of gratification."

# Potato Bread

*A good bread for toasting, adapted from* Betty's Bakery Cookbook.   *Makes 2 large or 3 small loaves*

YEAST STARTER:
Dissolve the yeast in a little warm water.

THE MIX:
Allow the mashed potatoes to cool in a large mixing bowl. Then add the flour and salt. Knead into a soft and elastic dough, adding enough warm water as necessary.

FIRST RISING:
Return to the cleaned bowl, cover with a damp cloth and put to rise in a warm place for about 1 hour. Shape into 2 or 3 loaves and place on greased baking trays.

SECOND RISING:
Leave, covered, for about 30 minutes.

PRE-HEAT OVEN
to 400°F (200°C) Gas 6.

BAKING TIME:
Bake for about 30 minutes.

THE FLOUR:
*1 lb wholemeal flour*

THE STARTER:
*1 oz fresh yeast*

AND . . .
*warm water, as needed*
*1 lb potatoes, cooked and*
   *mashed*
*pinch of salt*

METRIC EQUIVALENTS:
*500 g wholemeal flour*
*30 g fresh yeast*
*warm water, as needed*
*500 g potatoes, cooked*
   *and mashed*
*pinch of salt*

In colour—page 120

*Makes about 12*

THE FLOUR:
*12 oz wholemeal flour*

THE STARTER:
*½ oz fresh yeast*
*1 teaspoon honey*

AND . . .
*1 small potato, peeled*
*12 fl.oz lightly salted water*
*1 teaspoon salt*

METRIC EQUIVALENTS:
*350 g wholemeal flour*
*15 g fresh yeast*
*1 teaspoon honey*
*1 small potato, peeled*
*350 ml lightly salted water*
*1 teaspoon salt*

# Crumpets

*Betty's Bakery's version of a traditional tea-time treat.*

PREPARATION:
Boil the potato in the water for 15 minutes, until soft. Drain and keep the water. Mash the potato.

YEAST STARTER:
Dissolve the yeast and honey in 4 fl.oz (100 ml) of the potato water.

THE MIX:
Add the remaining potato water and the salt to the yeast mixture and stir in the mashed potato and flour to make a heavy batter.

FIRST RISING:
Cover with a damp cloth and put in a warm place to rise for 1 hour.

SECOND RISING:
Beat rapidly for 5 minutes with a wooden spoon. Cover and leave to rise again for 1 hour.

THIRD RISING:
Beat again for 5 minutes and put to rise for 30 minutes.

FOURTH RISING:
Beat again and put to rise for a final 30 minutes.

THE COOKING:
Grease the inside of 4 crumpet rings (you can use well-washed small cans with the tops and bottoms removed).
Grease a griddle or heavy based frying-pan lightly and keep it at a low even heat. Place the rings around the sides, half fill with batter and cook for 15 minutes on one side. Turn over and cook the second side for 5 minutes.

*Makes 12*

THE FLOUR:
*1 lb wholemeal flour*
*8 oz strong white flour*

THE STARTER:
*1 oz fresh yeast*

AND . . .
*¾ pt mild or brown ale*
*2 tablespoons vegetable oil*
*2 level teaspoons salt*

# Ale Buns

*A prize-winning recipe for Mrs. Linda Jones: delicious buns made with real ale.*

YEAST STARTER:
Dissolve the yeast in 6 tablespoons of the ale and leave in a warm place until frothy.

THE MIX:
Bring the remaining ale and the oil to the boil, then cool to lukewarm. Mix the flours and salt together in a large mixing bowl. Add the warm ale and the yeast mixtures and make a dough. Knead for about 10 minutes until smooth.

**FIRST RISING:**
Cover and leave to rise in a warm place until double in size.

**SECOND RISING:**
Knead for a further 2 to 3 minutes. Shape into 12 balls and place with the sides touching in a greased roasting tin. Cover and leave to rise a second time for about 30 to 35 minutes until double in size.

**PRE-HEAT OVEN**
to 400°F (200°C) Gas 6.

**BAKING TIME:**
Bake for about 35 minutes. Cool. Break apart into small buns.

METRIC EQUIVALENTS:
*500 g wholemeal flour*
*250 g strong white flour*
*30 g fresh yeast*
*400 ml mild or brown ale*
*2 tablespoons vegetable oil*
*2 level teaspoons salt*

# W. & G. BROWN

*The following eight recipes have been adapted from pamphlets published by the old-established millers, W. & G. Brown of Derby. They specialise in whole flours from wheat, brown rice, soya, millet and maize. Some of their recipes are of value to people on special diets: they include gluten-free loaves, high-fibre bread, a slimming loaf and one of Alan Long's favourites, a high nutrition loaf, Special Four-Cereal Bread.*

## Special Four-Cereal Bread

In colour—page 232

*This mixture will make either rolls or 3 loaves of bread. If you are making rolls, they will prove on top of the oven while it is pre-heating.*

*Makes 3 loaves*

**YEAST STARTER:**
Add the yeast to the warm water and leave for 10 minutes to dissolve.

**THE MIX:**
Gradually add the wholemeal flour, the wheat, rye and millet flakes, and mix in the ground sesame seeds, oil and salt. Knead well.

**THE RISING:**
Leave in a warm place to rise for 30 minutes.

**PRE-HEAT OVEN**
to 400°F (200°C) Gas 6.

**BAKING TIME:**
Bake for 15 minutes.

THE FLOUR:
*6 oz wholemeal flour*
*6 oz wheat flakes*
*6 oz rye flakes*
*6 oz millet flakes*

THE STARTER:
*1 teaspoon dried yeast*
*scant 1½ pt tepid water*

AND . . .
*4 oz ground sesame seeds*
*2 tablespoons vegetable oil*
*1 teaspoon sea salt*

METRIC EQUIVALENTS:
*175 g wholemeal flour*
*175 g wheat flakes*
*175 g rye flakes*
*175 g millet flakes*

*1 teaspoon dried yeast*
*scant 900 ml tepid water*
*125 g ground sesame seeds*
*2 tablespoons vegetable oil*
*1 teaspoon sea salt*

# High Protein Low-Calorie Bread

*Makes about 2 loaves*

THE FLOUR:
*8 oz wholemeal flour*
*4 oz soya meal*
*4 oz brown rice flour*

THE STARTER:
*1 oz fresh yeast or ½ oz*
 *dried yeast*
*¾ pt lukewarm water*

AND . . .
*2 tablespoons corn oil*
*3 tablespoons honey*
*2 oz skimmed milk powder*
*2 teaspoons salt*
*oil for brushing*

METRIC EQUIVALENTS:
*250 g wholemeal flour*
*125 g soya meal*
*125 g brown rice flour*
*30 g fresh yeast or 15 g dried yeast*
*400 ml lukewarm water*
*2 tablespoons corn oil*
*3 tablespoons honey*
*60 g skimmed milk powder*
*2 teaspoons salt*
*oil for brushing*

*The perfect bread to eat when you're on a slimming diet.*

YEAST STARTER:
Dissolve the yeast in the water in a bowl and add 1 tablespoon of the honey. Let this mixture stand, rise and bubble.

THE MIX:
Add the oil and the remaining honey to the yeast mixture. Stir in the wholemeal flour, mix well, then stir in the soya meal, rice flour, milk powder and salt, and cover.

FIRST RISING:
Leave the dough in a warm place to rise until it has doubled in bulk, about 1 hour.

SECOND RISING:
Add more soya meal, if necessary, to make a stiff dough. Knead well for 5 minutes, place in well-greased bread tins, and leave to rise again, for about 40 minutes.

PRE-HEAT OVEN
to 400°F (200°C) Gas 6.

BAKING TIME:
Bake for 55 minutes. After 15 minutes, REDUCE HEAT to 350°F (180°C) Gas 4. Brush the tops of the loaves with some oil before placing on a rack to cool.

# Nutritional Loaf

*Makes 2 loaves*

THE FLOUR:
*2 lb wholemeal flour*
*2 tablespoons soya flour*
*1 tablespoon fine oatmeal*

THE STARTER:
*1 oz fresh yeast*

AND . . .
*1 heaped tablespoon honey*
*about ½ pt warm water*
*2 tablespoons dried milk*
*1 tablespoon ground almonds*
*½ teaspoon salt*
*6 tablespoons corn oil*
*about ½ pt milk*

*A rich combination of flavours and textures are contained in this highly nutritious bread.*

METRIC EQUIVALENTS:
*1 kg wholemeal flour*
*2 tablespoons soya flour*
*1 tablespoon fine oatmeal*
*30 g fresh yeast*
*1 heaped tablespoon honey*
*about 300 ml warm water*
*2 tablespoons dried milk*
*1 tablespoon ground almonds*
*½ teaspoon salt*
*6 tablespoons corn oil*
*about 300 ml milk*

YEAST STARTER:
Dissolve the yeast with 1 teaspoon of the honey and a little of the warm water, and set aside.

THE MIX:
Mix the flours, dried milk, ground almonds and salt in a mixing bowl, and keep them warm. Put the oil, milk, and the remaining honey and water in a pan to warm through. Add the yeast mixture to the flour mixture, then add the liquids and knead well.

FIRST RISING:
Leave in a warm room for at least 1 hour or until double in size.

SECOND RISING:
Knead again, divide and put into 2 greased loaf tins, not more than half full. Leave to rise again until double in size, about 40 minutes.

PRE-HEAT OVEN
to 400°F (200°C) Gas 6.

BAKING TIME:
Bake for 45 minutes. After 15 minutes REDUCE HEAT to 375°F (190°C) Gas 5.

# Corn Bread

*This is a golden-yellow, gluten-free loaf with a crisp crust.*

PRE-HEAT OVEN
to 400°F (200°C) Gas 6.

THE MIX:
Mix the flours and the baking powder together, then add the honey, milk and beaten egg. Mix to a smooth batter, add the corn oil or melted butter, and stir well. Pour the batter into a greased baking tin 8 x 10 x 1 in (200 x 255 x 25 mm).

BAKING TIME:
Bake until the top is just brown, about 40 to 45 minutes.

METRIC EQUIVALENTS:
*250 g maize meal or cornmeal*
*1 tablespoon soya flour*
*1 teaspoon baking powder*
*1 teaspoon honey*

*200 ml milk*
*1 free-range egg, beaten*
*1 tablespoon corn oil or 15 g*
*    melted butter*

*In colour—page 216*

*Makes 1 large corn bread*

THE FLOUR:
*8 oz maize meal or cornmeal*
*1 tablespoon soya flour*

THE RAISING AGENT:
*1 teaspoon baking powder*

AND . . .
*1 teaspoon honey*
*7 fl.oz milk*
*1 free-range egg, beaten*
*1 tablespoon corn oil or ½ oz*
*    melted butter*

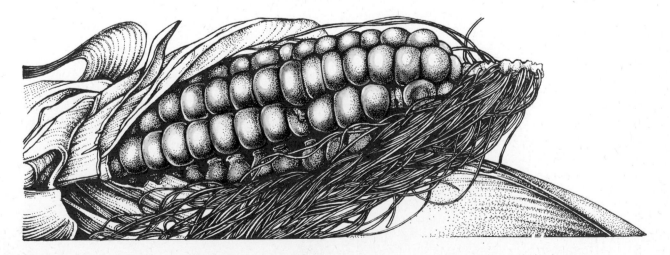

# Irish Bran Loaf

In colour—page 233

*Makes 1 large loaf*

THE FLOUR:
*8 oz wholemeal flour*
*8 oz bran*

THE RAISING AGENTS:
*1 teaspoon bicarbonate of soda*
*1 teaspoon cream of tartar*

AND . . .
*about 1 pt buttermilk or sour*
*milk or 1 pt milk with*
*1 tablespoon cider vinegar*

METRIC EQUIVALENTS:
*250 g wholemeal flour*
*250 g bran*
*1 teaspoon bicarbonate of soda*
*1 teaspoon cream of tartar*
*about 600 ml buttermilk or sour*
*milk or 600ml milk with*
*1 tablespoon cider vinegar*

*This high-fibre dough can be rolled out into a circle, then cut into triangular wedges or farls and cooked on a griddle or in a non-stick frying-pan.*

THE MIX:
Mix together the flour, bran, bicarbonate of soda and cream of tartar, then blend them together with enough buttermilk to make a soft dough.

THE RISING:
Put the dough into a greased bread tin and leave in a warm place for 15 minutes.

PRE-HEAT OVEN
to 375°F (190°C) Gas 5.

BAKING TIME:
Bake for 1 hour. After 30 minutes REDUCE HEAT to 300°F (150°C) Gas 2.

# Soya Rice Raisin Bread

*Makes 1 loaf*

THE FLOUR:
*6 oz ground rice*
*2 oz soya flour*

THE STARTER:
*1 teaspoon baking powder*

AND . . .
*4 tablespoons milk*
*2 free-range eggs, beaten*
*4 tablespoons honey*
*4 tablespoons vegetable oil*
*2 oz raisins*
*1 oz chopped nuts*

*This delightful soft, light, gluten-free loaf is made with an unusual combination of flours.*

THE MIX:
Mix together the milk, eggs, honey and oil. Sift the ground rice, soya flour and baking powder together and slowly add them to the egg mixture. Stir in the raisins and nuts. Mix well. Spoon into a well-greased 1 lb (500 g) baking tin.

THE RISING:
Let it stand for 1 hour.

PRE-HEAT OVEN
to 350°F (180°C) Gas 4.

BAKING TIME:
Bake for 40 to 45 minutes.

METRIC EQUIVALENTS:
*175 g ground rice*
*60 g soya flour*
*1 teaspoon baking powder*
*4 tablespoons milk*
*2 free-range eggs, beaten*
*4 tablespoons honey*
*4 tablespoons vegetable oil*
*60 g raisins*
*30 g chopped nuts*

# Rice Bread

*This gluten-free loaf is based on a rice sourdough, which should be made at least a day before required.*

PREPARE SOURDOUGH:
Mix the honey, water and ground rice to a beatable consistency, add the yeast and beat for 5 minutes. Leave overnight in a warm place.

YEAST STARTER:
Dissolve the yeast and honey in the 5 tablespoons of warm water and allow to sponge.

THE MIX:
Mix the ground rice, soya flour, soya meal, rice flakes and bran together, mix in the vegetable oil, then make a well and sprinkle in the salt. Beat the rice sourdough for 5 minutes. Add it to the flour mixture with the beaten egg and yeast mixture, adding more water if necessary. Knead for 5 minutes, using more soya or rice flour as required. Press into a loaf tin, well greased and dusted with rice flour.

PRE-HEAT OVEN
to 350°F (180°C) Gas 4.

BAKING TIME:
Bake for 1 hour. If the base is not firm to the touch, turn the loaf out and return it to the oven for 10 to 20 minutes.

*Makes 1 loaf*

RICE SOURDOUGH:
*½ teaspoon honey*
*3 tablespoons warm water*
*3 tablespoons ground rice*
*pinch of fresh yeast*

THE FLOUR:
*4 tablespoons ground rice*
*4 tablespoons soya flour*
*2 tablespoons soya meal*
*2 tablespoons rice flakes*
*2 tablespoons bran*

THE STARTER:
*½ oz fresh yeast*
*1 teaspoon honey*
*5 tablespoons warm water*

AND . . .
*2 tablespoons vegetable oil*
*pinch of salt*
*1 free-range egg, beaten*

METRIC EQUIVALENTS:
*½ teaspoon honey*
*3 tablespoons warm water*
*3 tablespoons ground rice*
*pinch of fresh yeast*
*4 tablespoons ground rice*
*4 tablespoons soya flour*
*2 tablespoons soya meal*

*2 tablespoons rice flakes*
*2 tablespoons bran*
*15 g fresh yeast*
*1 teaspoon honey*
*5 tablespoons warm water*
*2 tablespoons vegetable oil*
*pinch of salt*
*1 free-range egg, beaten*

In colour—page 232

# Maize and Millet Bread

*Makes 1 loaf*

*A pretty-coloured, gluten-free loaf, speckled with orange, which rises well without the use of the usual raising agent or yeast starter.*

THE FLOUR:
*2 oz maize flour or cornmeal*
*2 oz millet meal*

PRE-HEAT OVEN
to 400°F (200°C) Gas 6.

AND . . .
*2 oz grated carrot*
*1 teaspoon honey*
*¼ pt boiling water*
*2 free-range eggs, separated*
*3 teaspoons cold water*

THE MIX:
Mix the maize flour, millet meal, grated carrot and honey together and add the boiling water. Mix again.
Beat the egg yolks, add the cold water then add them to the flour and carrot mixture. Beat the egg whites stiffly and fold into the mixture. Pour into a well-greased loaf tin.

METRIC EQUIVALENTS:
*60 g maize flour or conrmeal*
*60 g millet meal*
*60 g grated carrot*
*1 teaspoon honey*
*150 ml boiling water*
*2 free-range eggs, separated*
*3 teaspoons cold water*

BAKING TIME:
Bake for 30 to 35 minutes.

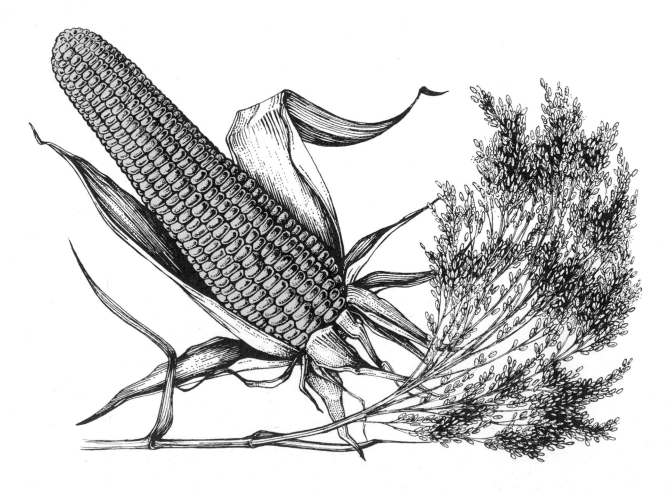

# Jordan's

In the Sixties when Joseph Rank, Garey Weston and Spillers were buying every bakery and mill in sight, Jordan's was a prime target. "Come and join us," said the Big Three. "Remember what happens to the odd banana in the bunch." But Jordan's resisted. And this particular banana turned out to be the pick of the bunch.

"There is an obstinate streak in our family," grins Bill Jordan, 32, who runs the business with his brother, David, who's only 31. It was their father who resisted the big millers; and the sons who have reaped the benefits, turning one of the country's oldest roller mills into the second biggest producer of wholemeal flour—to say nothing of a prestigious cereal business which includes *Original Crunchy*, (Britain's answer to *Granola*), *Crunchy Bars* and Muesli mixes.

Jordan's mill at Biggleswade lives up to the romantic marketing image you see on their flour packets: there's the Victorian mill, the mill-race, the trees overhanging it; it's still a family business, with father John, who manages the animal feeds side: his wife who set up the attractive farm shop at the mill: their children Bill and David as well as daughter Lindsay, who has been roped in to test and prepare recipes for their booklets.

The history of the mill which goes back to the Domesday Book is a stirring tale, but Bill and David are very modern and abreast of changes in custom and diet. They were only 20 when they went to America and discovered that the roasted and toasted honey cereals with nuts and dried fruits such as *Granola*, were the new big thing.

Bill is an athlete, and runs in the steeplechase, and David water-skis; the whole family goes walking; so their fitness fanatacism is matched by an interest in diet. This is partly why they were attracted to nutritious breakfast foods. "We experimented with puffed wheat. Puffed wholewheat. It really is shot from guns. And we experimented with them, huge phosphor-bronze cannons. You put in ten pounds at a time and fire it. Bang! We couldn't get anyone to work it because of the noise. We tried wheat without the husk and organic brown rice." It was David who eventually came up with the recipe and techniques for their toasted cereals, which they called *Original Crunchy*—since *Granola* is a trade name.

They were also quick to respond to the wholefood movement when it brought wholemeal bread into the limelight. Then at last the Royal College of Physicians endorsed fibre in the diet, and now everyone wants wholemeal. "Belatedly," says Bill Jordan. "The doctors should have been there years ago."

The Jordans' flour is not stoneground. Bill Jordan doesn't knock it, but he suggests that roller mills like his are very different from the modern roller mills at the big millers which work at three times the speed. "Slow speed milling prevents overheating of the flour," says Bill. "This means the enzyme and vitamin content is retained at a high level."

The wheel, in this case a water-wheel, has gone full circle. In 1896 Holme Mills were among the most modern in the country. It was described in *The Miller* of the day as "one of the best planned and most efficient country roller mills." It was grinding wheat at a speed of 250 revolutions a minute, terribly, terribly fast. But gradually the mills got faster and faster and today a modern mill runs at at least 600 r.p.m. Now Holme Mills is terribly, terribly slow, but still in the forefront of milling.

The quality of grain is vital to milling good flour. And Bill Jordan has tried every grain to get the ideal blend for both baker and housewife. He even approached the Chorleywood government research station to see if they could help, and they couldn't. "'We can put men on the moon,' they said, 'but we don't know about the amino-acids in wholemeal.' In the end they said, 'select the wheats you like best and stick to them'. We use 50 per cent Canadian Red Western Spring (from Manitoba), and half local farmers' wheats."

"The wheat's important to us. Some people may be able to grind any old paltry wheat and subject it to bucket chemistry. A bit of this and a bit of that to give the flour lift. We can't do that."

Bill and David came to eating wholemeal bread by chance, in spite of living on a mill. "The local baker packed up, and we had to start making our own. We soon lost interest in eating white bread."

Lindsay, their younger sister, who's married with two small children, only joined the family business when the wholemeal flour side started to expand. "The idea is to encourage people to use wholemeal flour in pastry and biscuits and not only in bread," says Bill Jordan.

Lindsay: "I cooked my way through hundreds of recipes; the family would eat them at tea-time and criticise. We tried a lot of American recipes; they were foul. Do you know the walking loaf? Walkers and hikers take it with them; we made two loaves for a week-end walking in the Lake District. It's a high energy loaf, packed with everything: all kinds of cereals and molasses, soya flour, sesame seed, millet, dried fruit. You need a hacksaw to get into it. But it does sustain you, bejesus. It's supposed to be a totally balanced meal. Actually it's a totally balanced rock."

The recipes below were developed by Lindsay: "You'll be using Jordan's flour, of course," she says.

# Wheat Germ Loaf

*Makes 3 small loaves*

*Wheat germ contains B vitamins and gives the loaf a nutty flavour.*

THE FLOUR:
*1 lb 13 oz wholemeal flour*
*3 oz wheat germ*

THE STARTER:
*1 level tablespoon dried yeast*
*1 level tablespoon malt extract*
*1 pt warm water*

AND . . .
*3 level teaspoons salt*
*2 oz butter*

METRIC EQUIVALENTS:
*875 g wholemeal flour*
*90 g wheat germ*
*1 level tablespoon dried yeast*
*1 level tablespoon malt extract*
*600 ml warm water*
*3 level teaspoons salt*
*60 g butter*

YEAST STARTER:
Dissolve the malt extract in the warm water. Sprinkle on the dried yeast and set aside for about 10 minutes, until frothy.

THE MIX:
Mix together the flour, wheat germ and salt, and rub in the butter. Pour on the yeast mixture and mix well. Turn out on to a floured board and knead for 10 to 15 minutes. Divide into 3 parts, shape and place in 3 greased 1 lb (500 g) loaf tins.

THE RISING:
Cover with oiled polythene, put in a warm place and leave to rise until double in size, about 1 hour.

PRE-HEAT OVEN
to 400°F (200°C) Gas 6.

BAKING TIME:
Bake for 35 to 45 minutes. After 10 minutes REDUCE HEAT to 350°F (180°C) Gas 4.

# Oatmeal Bread

*The oatmeal gives a chewy texture to this bread.*

*Makes 2 small loaves*

PREPARATION:
Pour the warm milk over the rolled oats or oatmeal and leave for 30 minutes.

YEAST STARTER:
Dissolve the honey in the warm water, sprinkle the dried yeast on top and set aside for about 10 minutes until frothy.

THE MIX:
Mix together the flour and salt in a bowl, add the oil, yeast liquid and oat mixture. Mix well, turn on to a floured board and knead for about 10 minutes.

FIRST RISING:
Wash the bowl, then oil it and replace the dough. Cover with oiled polythene and leave to rise in a warm place until double in size, about 1 hour.

SECOND RISING:
Knead the dough again for about 3 minutes. Divide into 2 pieces and shape into loaves. Place in 2 well-greased 1 lb (500 g) bread tins. Cover with oiled polythene and leave to rise again in a warm place for about 40 minutes.

PRE-HEAT OVEN
to 400°F (200°C) Gas 6.

BAKING TIME:
Bake for 30 minutes. Cool on a wire rack.

THE FLOUR:
*12 oz wholemeal flour*
*8 oz rolled oats or medium oatmeal*

THE STARTER:
*2 teaspoons dried yeast*
*1 teaspoon honey*
*¼ pt warm water*

AND . . .
*½ pt warm milk*
*2½ level teaspoons salt*
*1 tablespoon vegetable oil*

METRIC EQUIVALENTS:
*350 g wholemeal flour*
*250 g rolled oats or medium oatmeal*
*2 teaspoons dried yeast*
*1 teaspoon honey*
*150 ml warm water*
*300 ml warm milk*
*2½ level teaspoons salt*
*1 tablespoon vegetable oil*

# Wholemeal Apple Scones

*In colour—page 232*

*Makes about 8 to 10*

THE FLOUR:
*8 oz wholemeal flour*

THE RAISING AGENT:
*4 level teaspoons baking powder*

AND...
*pinch of salt*
*2 oz butter*
*2 tablespoons grated apple*
*about ¼ pt milk*
*1 egg*

METRIC EQUIVALENTS:
*250 g wholemeal flour*
*4 level teaspoons baking powder*
*pinch of salt*
*60 g butter*
*2 tablespoons grated apple*
*150 ml milk*
*1 egg*

*The apple gives these scones a slightly tart flavour.*

PRE-HEAT OVEN
to 400°F (200°C) Gas 6.

THE MIX:
Mix together the flour, baking powder and salt. Rub in the butter and stir in the grated apple. Beat the milk and egg together and add enough of this mixture to the flour to form a manageable dough. Turn on to a floured board and knead very lightly.

THE SHAPING:
Either roll out the dough to ½ in (1.5 cm) thick and cut into 2 in (5 cm) fluted rounds, or shape the dough into one large flat round and mark into 8 pieces. Place on a greased baking tray and brush with the remaining egg and milk mixture.

BAKING TIME:
Bake individual scones for 10 to 12 minutes and 1 large round scone for 15 to 20 minutes.

VARIATIONS:
To make spiced scones, omit the apple and stir in 1½ teaspoons mixed spice before rubbing in the butter. To make bran or wheat germ scones, omit the apple and add 2 to 3 level tablespoons bran (or wheat germ) to the flour before rubbing in the butter.

# Wholemeal Pancakes

*Serves 4*

THE FLOUR:
*4 oz wholemeal flour*

AND...
*½ level teaspoon salt*
*2 eggs*
*½ pt milk*
*a little vegetable oil*

METRIC EQUIVALENTS:
*125 g wholemeal flour*
*½ level teaspoon salt*
*2 eggs*
*300 ml milk*
*a little vegetable oil*

*More filling than ordinary pancakes: try these wholemeal ones with honey and lemon.*

THE MIX:
Mix the flour and salt in a bowl. Beat the eggs and milk together. Pour the liquid over the flour and beat well.

RESTING TIME:
Cover and leave to stand for 1 hour.

PRE-HEAT
a heavy based frying-pan brushed with a little vegetable oil over a medium heat, until a blue flame can be seen rising from the pan.

COOKING TIME:
Remove the pan from the heat, pour in a little batter and shake the pan to distribute it all over the base. Replace on the heat and cook until the pancake leaves the sides of the pan easily. Turn with a fish-slice and cook the other side until golden-brown.

# *Allinson*

Allinson are the largest millers of stoneground wholemeal flour in Europe, and are part of the Booker McConnell Group which owns a large chain of health food stores.

The company is named after Dr. Thomas Allinson, a Victorian pioneer of medicine and nutrition. His notion that flour from the whole grain was more nutritious than white flour from the new roller millers was considered revolutionary in his day. In early days the bran in wholemeal bread had been thought to neutralise the goodness in bread.

Dr. Allinson led a nationwide campaign to educate people into the new way of thinking. In 1895 he went to the extraordinary lengths of buying his own flour mills to mill stoneground flour. He founded the Natural Food Company which was later named Allinson. Here are two extracts from his pamphlet *The Advantages of Wholemeal Bread*, which give the characteristic flavour of his crusading style. A hundred years later modern nutritionists do not find much to disagree with.

"We will now consider the advantages of wholemeal bread over the white loaf. The first solid food a child should have is wholemeal bread and milk, as such will aid the teeth in coming through, and if a child is given no other bread but this, he can grow up tall, strong, well, and cheerful. By acting as a corrector and regulator of the bowels it prevents children from being troubled with falling of the bowel or similar complaints. Growing children should all have it, as it helps to prevent their teeth from decaying early, supplies their systems with bony matter, so that they grow up of proper height. Moreover, they will learn lessons more readily, as wheat contains valuable and soluble phosphates for the brain and nervous system. When babies and children are fed on white bread they are apt to become rickety, bow-legged, and pigeon-chested. Such rarely happens if fed on good wholemeal bread. Grown-up persons must eat this bread always, as it gives more satisfaction; hunger is not felt so readily, and it 'stays' the body better. Constipation is almost unknown amongst regular eaters of it; this complaint is accompanied by indigestion, want of energy, backache, lassitude, weariness, dullness, depression, and a dozen little ail-

*T. R. Allinson Ex L.R.C.P. Edin*

ments that do not make us ill, but yet life is not as pleasant as it might be if these were not present. Wholemeal bread, by curing this condition, does away with these distressing symptoms. Piles, or haemorrhoids, varicose veins, varicocele, and other like ailments are banished by it, as these are caused in a great measure by costive bowels.

"Wholemeal bread is a necessity for all classes of the community. The rich should eat it, so that it may carry off some of their superfluous foods and drinks; and the poor must eat it, then they will not need to buy so much flesh foods and other expensive articles of diet. If a law could be passed forbidding the separation of the bran from the fine flour, it would add very greatly to the health and wealth of our nation, and lessen considerably the receipts of the publican, tobacconist, chemist, dentist, doctor, and undertaker. Weight-for-weight chemists prove that white bread is more soluble than brown, but, when we examine in detail the influence of the two on the body, we find that, whilst wholemeal perfectly nourishes all the fluids, tissues, and structures of the body, white bread starves the muscles and bones, and makes a physical wreck of it. Dogs can be fed an indefinite time on wholemeal bread and water, but they soon die of starvation if fed on white bread and water only. Readers are requested to take warning in time, and eat only wholemeal bread. To banish the white flour loaf from his home is the duty of every good citizen." Here are two healthy Allinson recipes.

# Basic Wholemeal Bread

*Makes 4 loaves*

*One of the most widely baked loaves in Britain.*

THE FLOUR:
*3 lb stoneground wholemeal flour*

THE STARTER:
*1 oz dried yeast*
*2 teaspoons honey*

AND . . .
*about 1½ pt lukewarm water*
*1 oz butter*
*1 level tablespoon salt*
*2 teaspoons honey*

METRIC EQUIVALENTS:
*1½ kg stoneground wholemeal flour*
*30 g dried yeast*
*2 teaspoons honey*
*about 900 ml lukewarm water*
*30 g butter*
*1 level tablespoon salt*
*2 teaspoons honey*

YEAST STARTER:
Dissolve 2 teaspoons honey in ½pt (300 ml) of the warm water. Add the dried yeast and whisk in thoroughly with a fork. Leave to stand in a warm place for 10 to 15 minutes, until frothy.

THE MIX:
Rub the butter into the flour. Dissolve the salt and 2 teaspoons honey in the remaining water. Add this and the yeast mixture to the flour. Mix thoroughly to form a smooth dough. Turn on to a lightly floured board and knead for 10 minutes.

FIRST RISING:
Put the dough into a greased or floured polythene bag and leave in a warm place to prove for 30 minutes.

PRE-HEAT OVEN
to 475°F (240°C) Gas 9.

SECOND RISING:
Grease four 1 lb (500 g) loaf tins, and put the tins to warm. Divide the dough into 4 pieces. Flatten each piece into an oblong (the same width as the tin). Fold each piece in three, smooth the top, tuck in the ends and place in the tins. Cover and leave to rise for about 30 minutes.

BAKING TIME:
REDUCE HEAT to 450°F (230°C) Gas 8. Put the loaves on the centre shelf and bake for 30 to 40 minutes. If the loaves brown too quickly, REDUCE HEAT to 425°F (220°C) Gas 7 after 20 minutes.

VARIATION:
To speed up the proving time, add 1 Vitamin C tablet (50 mg) to the yeast starter. Mix the dough well, allow it to rest for 5 minutes, then divide into four and put straight into the greased bread tins. Allow to prove for 30 minutes and bake. There is no need for a second rising when you add Vitamin C.

# Fruity Tea Bread

*A basic tea bread enriched with dried fruit.*

*Makes 2 loaves*

### YEAST STARTER:
Dissolve the ½ tablespoon honey in the warm water and sprinkle the dried yeast on top. Leave until frothy, about 10 minutes.

### THE MIX:
Mix the flour and salt and rub in the butter. Dissolve the tablespoon of honey in the warm milk and add this to the flour, together with the yeast mixture. Work to a dough. Turn on to a lightly floured board and knead until smooth and elastic, about 5 minutes.

### FIRST RISING:
Put the dough in a lightly greased polythene bag lightly tied or a saucepan with a lid. Leave to rise until the dough doubles its size and springs back when lightly pressed with a floured finger, about 1 hour.

### SECOND RISING:
Turn out the dough and work in the dried fruit. Divide the dough in two, flatten each piece and roll up like a Swiss roll to fit 2 greased 1 lb (500 g) loaf tins.
Place the tins in polythene bags and leave to rise until the dough reaches the tops of the tins or springs back when lightly pressed.

### PRE-HEAT OVEN
to 375°F (190°F) Gas 5.

### BAKING TIME:
Bake on the middle shelf of the oven for 30 to 40 minutes. Brush the tops of the hot loaves with a wet brush dipped in honey. Cool on a wire rack.

### THE FLOUR:
*1 lb wholemeal flour*

### THE STARTER:
*1½ teaspoons dried yeast*
*½ tablespoon honey*
*¼ pt warm water*

### AND . . .
*2 teaspoons salt*
*1 oz butter*
*1 tablespoon honey*
*¼ pt warm milk*
*4 oz seedless raisins*
*4 oz currants*
*4 oz mixed peel*
*honey for glazing*

### METRIC EQUIVALENTS:
*500 g wholemeal flour*
*1½ teaspoons dried yeast*
*½ tablespoon honey*
*150 ml warm water*
*2 teaspoons salt*
*30 g butter*
*1 tablespoon honey*
*150 ml warm milk*
*125 g seedless raisins*
*125 g currants*
*125 g mixed peel*
*honey for glazing*

# Craig Sams

Craig Sams owns Ceres Bakery, one of the first, and still the most famous of the wholefood bakeries in Britain.

His purist attitude towards bread is almost monastic; he believes in a Holy Trinity of flour, yeast, salt; no sugar to feed the yeast. The flour must be freshly milled wholemeal, the salt must be crystals of sea salt, and even the water must be filtered, to leach off chlorine, so as to remove its unpleasant taste, and also because it has a retarding effect on yeast. You need less yeast to make bread rise when chlorine is removed. "Filtering also removes the lead," Sams adds.

Ceres customers are dreamy idealists, driven towards purer and purer concepts of wholefoods and Sams manages to satisfy them. What could be purer than the wholemeal loaf just described? There is an answer; a sourdough bread. He provides them with sourdough too.

Sams is an American from Nebraska in the Mid-West of the United States. His grandparents were immigrants from Syria who gave their name at the Customs as Abood-Saba. The immigration official christened him Sam. Craig Sams' own parents were converted to wholefood when his father suffered an intestinal illness. "He wasted to eight stone. They tried everything, antibiotics, every kind of medical drug without success. Then he went to a Japanese doctor by the name of Nakadadi who put him onto wholegrain foods, stopped him eating sugar and refined foods. The illness cleared up immediately."

The Sams family moved to London when Craig was nine, and they settled in London's Notting Hill Gate. He remembers being sent to buy wholemeal bread at a Heath and Heather shop. He didn't like any other kind of bread; and when he and his brother, Greg, realised many others would respond to a real food philosophy, they decided to start their own wholefood restaurant called Seed. It opened in 1967—"the Summer of Love"—Craig Sams recalls. People loved the food but couldn't get the ingredients to cook it at home. They started selling to customers from the pantry, then opened a retail shop, and when other shopkeepers started buying there, they went wholesale, starting Harmony Foods in 1970: they soon became famous for their boisterously hearty flavours—including a spectacularly crunchy peanut butter.

Craig's wife Anne used to bake a batch of 20 to 30 wholemeal loaves each night, and they sold out every day by 11 o'clock. And then in 1972 she became pregnant. Two days before their son Karim was born Craig opened the bakery in a former pie and eel shop next door. It already had ovens for baking pies; they bought £1,000 worth of second-hand equipment, found a baker and started baking. One of their specialities is sourdough.

According to Craig there's San Francisco sourdough, and the true sourdough. "San Francisco is a white bread with yeast and some souring agent."

Jewish bakers make a sourdough in London. If they are making, say 150 loaves, and they have made enough dough for 200, they chuck the left-over dough in a bucket. Within a day it has gone lactic."

Lactic acid gives the bread its pleasantly sour flavour and conditions the dough. "Yeast and micro-bacilli each have their own acidity of environment. Yeast multiplies faster in the early stages in a dough, then it dies in its own carbonic acid. Then the lacto-bacilli take over. Interestingly these bacilli live on the skin, and in the stomach, anywhere where there is life—and they ultimately gain control. When the yeast dies, these bacilli keep on growing."

If you're making a sourdough the yeast is most active during the first rising. "Then, when you knock it back, the lacto-bacilli assume a dominance," explains Sams. The mixture produces a satisfying, tasty, well-risen bread, imparting all the healthy benefits attributed to lactic acid.

"Some sourdoughs are almost unprintable, they sound like adulteration, but they are not. Some bakers introduce stale or left-over breadcrumbs into the dough. Or they soak the bread in water to make a mash. It gives a faster fermentation because the starch in the flour has already been turned to dextrin by the first baking, and the yeast feeds on this. It's like using malt. It makes for a sweeter loaf. It is *Zweiback*, twice baked. It produces the sweetened effect you get in French *biscottes*, rusks, Melba toast."

Craig Sams doesn't use this method, but he does make bread from natural leaven. It's perhaps the purest method of all, and is only used in one other serious bakery he knows, the Lima bakery in Belgium. The loaf is well-risen, moist, nutty, teasingly sweet and sour at the same time. It's a bread you can eat plain or with butter. It seems a pity to spoil it by adding anything more.

No commercial yeast is used to make this "starter". But once made, it is treasured, and stored indefinitely in a glass, earthenware or stone container in a cold place (the fridge is fine). When any is used, it is replaced with the same volume of flour and water, stirred, and left to mature.

By an old American tradition, men who travelled to the Yukon in Alaska during the Gold Rush were known as Sourdoughs, because they carried their own natural leavens with them, some of them keeping it alive by taking it under the covers with them in their bedrolls.

Sams knows the date of his own leaven as parents know the birthday of their children. "Ours was made on February 14, 1977," he says promptly. It was very simple. He took a cup of rye flour, adding two cups of lukewarm water. He mixed it well, and left it, covered, in a warm place, for three days. As any home brewer knows, natural bacteria in the air find their way to any nice damp mixture, and start to activate it into a ferment; these are wild yeasts. At the same time, bacteria which are on the wholewheat grain also start to act. The end result is a leaven, which raises bread: it acts slower than yeast, but because of this, it has its own characteristic texture and flavour. Sams didn't keep his in a jar: it went straight into the dough: and a piece of old dough is held over each day for the next batch.

Old books give very many suggestions and recipes for making leavens at home. The housewife in a remote country cottage was utterly dependent on the trick of making them. So too were ships' cooks at sea. In some, boiling water is poured on to a mixture of wheat flour and potato flour; or wheat flour and rye flour: or on grated potatoes; sometimes barley is included, or crushed malt flakes. In each case the object is to expose starches and sugars to the wild yeasts in the air. If boiled hops are used, it is to limit the incoming yeasts—police them, keep them under control.

But Sams' method is rare because he specifies the fresh milling. "The bacteria which are present on the skins of the wheat berry die after a few days when the grain is milled into flour." His mixture produces a certain blend of bacilli and enzymes which you can only get from fresh wheat.

"Fresh wheat is the bane of most bakers," says Sams. "It contains these organisms which have a mind of their own. They won't behave. So bakers and millers use chemical agents to age the flour, kill off the bacteria. But the bacteria also have an ageing effect—the bacteria are in effect agents of decay—but they are unpredictable and this obviously upsets conventional bakers. But we can utilise their qualities when we use a natural leaven. We've found that these bacteria are effective at digesting bran in wholemeal. This is important where people are choosing to eat wholemeal because of the dietary fibre content—the bran.

"The usual fast, mechanical commercial processes for making wholemeal bread don't soften the bran," says Sams. "The bran isn't getting soft, and if it isn't, it has an abrasive effect. It's like hundreds of tiny little razor blades going through you. All right for rabbits, who have a special stomach. We don't."

This is where natural leaven has the edge. In the long, slow fermenting process the bran is broken down by the bacteria, and softened. "They break down the cellular structure, making the bran more accessible, and giving you a natural softer bread."

Sourdoughs. Natural leavens. He hasn't yet started a barrel of barm in the bakery. "A Scottish baker told me how every baker had his own barm, a barrel half full of water, into which he threw any pieces of unused dough. They still continued to ferment, and produced a highly alcoholic soup. The mixture would be stirred and added to flour instead of yeast.

"The liquid tasted rather nice, and I think it must have been like a rather sweet beer with a bready flavour. The baker told me that it was the origin of the word barmy, and when the bakers drank it, it really made them crazy."

# Sourdough Starter

1 teaspoon dried yeast
8 fl.oz warm water
4 oz wholemeal flour
   (freshly milled is best)

METRIC EQUIVALENTS:
1 teaspoon dried yeast
¼ litre warm water
125 g wholemeal flour

Once you have made this yeasty mixture, you can keep it indefinitely: but some of it should be used at least every 10 days. Each time you use some of it, replenish it with flour and water (see TO FEED YOUR STARTER below) to make up what you have removed. It will continue to work in the fridge.

Dissolve the yeast in the warm water and leave for 10 minutes. Slowly mix in the flour. Leave at room temperature for several days, but not in a cold place. The starter is ready when it is fermented and bubbly. The yeast will have died down and been replaced by lacto-bacilli. Stir and refrigerate. The starter can be kept indefinitely, but should ideally be used at least every 10 days.

In colour—page 256

Makes 2 loaves

THE FLOUR:
1½ lb wholemeal flour

THE STARTER:
8 fl.oz sourdough starter
   (see above)

AND...
16 fl.oz warm water
1 tablespoon sea salt
3 fl.oz vegetable oil (optional)

METRIC EQUIVALENTS:
750 g wholemeal flour
¼ litre sourdough starter
   (see above)
½ litre warm water
1 tablespoon sea salt
80 ml vegetable oil (optional)

# Sourdough Bread

THE MIX:
Mix the starter, warm water, salt and vegetable oil together. Add the flour. Knead until a dough is formed. Different kinds of flour have different degrees of water absorption. Hard wheats soak up more, soft wheats less, so don't follow recipes blindly. Make a dough that has the texture that you feel is best.

FIRST RISING:
Put in a non-metallic bowl and leave to rise for 2 to 4 hours or until double in size.

SECOND RISING:
Form 2 loaves from the dough and place in oiled bread tins. Leave to rise for 1 to 3 hours or until 1½ to 2 times larger.

PRE-HEAT OVEN
to 350°F (180°C) Gas 4.

BAKING TIME:
Bake for about 40 minutes. Cool on wire racks.

TO FEED YOUR STARTER:
When you have removed the 8 fl.oz (¼ litre) of the sourdough starter to make bread, remember to feed the remainder of the starter—ready for your next loaf. This is done by adding 1 part flour to 2 parts lukewarm water, for example: 4 oz (125 g) wholemeal flour to 8 fl.oz (¼ litre) lukewarm water. Mix with the starter, stir well and refrigerate until ready to use.

ALTERNATIVE SOURDOUGH STARTER
The best starter has the ability to raise 30 times its own weight of dough. Swap starters with others to develop strong mixed strains. Inbreeding is bad for lacto-bacilli too.
Mix the flours and water with the remaining sourdough starter. Stir well and refrigerate until ready for use.

*2 oz rye meal*
*2 oz wholemeal flour*
*8 fl.oz lukewarm water*

METRIC EQUIVALENTS
*60 g rye meal*
*60 g wholemeal flour*
*¼ litre lukewarm water*

# Natural Leaven Bread

*Chlorinated water can inhibit the delicate rising action of this dough. You should use spring water for best results. Natural leaven bread is made by making a slack batter which ferments by attracting wild yeasts. It is a long, slow relaxed process.*

THE MIX:
Mix the warm water and 1 lb (500 g) of the flour to form a batter.

STANDING TIME:
Cover with a damp towel and stand in a warm place overnight to attract the wild yeasts. Add the remaining flour and the salt the following day and form a dough. Knead well.

THE RISING:
Place in oiled bread tins and leave to rise for at least 4 hours, or even up to 12 hours.

PRE-HEAT OVEN
to 350°F (180°C) Gas 4.

BAKING TIME:
Bake for 45 minutes. Cool on a wire rack.

*Makes 2 loaves*

THE FLOUR:
*about 2 lb wholemeal flour*

THE STARTER:
*No traditional starter*

AND . . .
*1¼ pt warm water*
*1 teaspoon sea salt*

METRIC EQUIVALENTS:
*about 1 kg wholemeal flour*
*750 ml warm water*
*1 teaspoon sea salt*

# Cranks

Cranks was the first serious vegetarian wholefood restaurant in the country when it opened only 20 years ago. Now they are branching out all over the place, and are much copied; Cranks' main branch is now in Marshall Street and the latest branch is in the new Covent Garden complex. There are also branches in Heal's and Peter Robinson, and in Dartington, and Totnes in Devon, as well as in Copenhagen.

It is run by three partners, David Canter and his wife Kay, and Daphne Swann, a trio who were conscious that they were creating an alternative lifestyle rather than sticking out for a fad. "We poked fun at ourselves with the name Cranks," says David Canter, "because the vegetarian image was a bit stuffy. We wanted to create a light-hearted atmosphere."

The lifestyle is reflected in the design of the pottery—David is an amateur potter, and he chose Ray Finch to make their ceramics. Edward Bawden, the artist, designed their first card. John Lawrence did the illustrations. Donald Jackson, who is the Queen's Scribe and makes out Patents of Nobility, still does all their calligraphy. The arts side has eventually given birth to Craftwork Gallery.

They had a bakery from the beginning, although early loaves hardly rose at all. "We made all sorts of bricks to begin with," says Kay Canter. "We'd recommend home bakers not to be put off by failures. If you persevere with a good recipe, you will get it right in the end. When you've got one recipe right, you can branch out, and make other kinds of loaves."

People who enjoy the Cranks loaves often write to say they try to get the same result at home and it doesn't work. So Cranks now run a Free Home Baking Service. Send a stamped addressed envelope to Kay Canter, Baking and Cookery Advisory Service, Cranks Health Foods, Marshall Street, London W.1, if you'd like their help.

The most common problems: bread not rising properly, yeast not frothing enough, crust on the finished loaf too hard, too thick or too soft. Some people don't realise that fresh yeast goes off. If in doubt, use dried yeast.

For people who ask the secret of Cranks' renowned cheese baps (winners of the *Evening Standard* Sandwich Award), the answer is; use a lot of good, well-flavoured cheese. Here is the recipe for making these delicious baps.

OPPOSITE:
Top left: *Sourdough Bread (Craig Sams) p.254.* Top right: *Fouace (Walnut Hearth Cake) from Elisabeth Lambert Ortiz p.170.* Below right: *Monastery Oat Bread (Ursel Norman) p.200.*

# Cranks' Cheese Baps

*One of the most popular of all Cranks' recipes—serve split, buttered and filled with mustard and cress.*

YEAST STARTER:
Mix the yeast and honey in a small bowl with ¼ pt (150 ml) of the warm water. Leave in a warm place for about 10 minutes to froth.

THE MIX:
Mix the flour with the salt. (In very cold weather, warm the flour slightly.) Pour the yeast mixture into the flour, add the egg, and gradually add the remaining water, mixing well by hand. Knead for about 5 minutes.

FIRST RISING:
Cover with a cloth and leave in a warm place for about 1 hour to double in size.

THE SHAPING AND SECOND RISING:
Knock down the dough and knead lightly. Roll out on a lightly floured surface to a rectangle 15 x 10 in (38 x 25 cm). Sprinkle a third of the cheese over the centre one-third of the dough. Fold the left-hand third of the dough over the cheese. Sprinkle another third of the cheese over the double thickness of dough, then fold the right-hand side of the dough over to completely cover the cheese. Press down well into a greased tin for making a loaf. Or roll out and cut out 4 in (10cm) rounds. Place on a floured baking sheet and brush lightly with milk. Sprinkle with the remaining cheese. Leave for about 30 minutes.

PRE-HEAT OVEN
to 400°F (200°C) Gas 6.

BAKING TIME:
Bake for about 25 minutes. Cool on a wire tray.

*Makes 6 baps or 1 loaf*

THE FLOUR:
*1 lb wholemeal flour*

THE STARTER:
*½ oz fresh yeast*
*1 teaspoon honey*

AND . . .
*½ to ⅔ pt warm water*
*1 teaspoon sea salt*
*1 free-range egg, beaten*
*9 oz Cheddar cheese, grated*

METRIC EQUIVALENTS:
*500 g wholemeal flour*
*15 g fresh yeast*
*1 teaspoon honey*
*300 to 360 ml warm water*
*1 teaspoon sea salt*
*1 free-range egg, beaten*
*275 g Cheddar cheese, grated*

OPPOSITE:
Top: *Two loaves Wholemeal Bread with Eggs (Barbara Cartland) p.267.* Bottom left: *Yoghurt Bread (Jane Asher) p.272.* Bottom centre: *Two loaves Mixed Wholemeal Bread (Len Deighton) p.259.* Centre right: *Wholemeal, Weetabix and Grapenut Loaf (Clement Freud) p.258.*

# Clement Freud

Clement Freud, the Liberal MP. Clement Freud, the humorist. Clement Freud, the inspired cook and journalist. Unfortunately the roles do not run concurrently and you can't have them all together. Clement Freud, the cookery writer is badly missed.

Few people have written more wittily about food, and his early career (thanks to a start in the hotel business) included a string of credits from *The Observer* to *Time and Tide,* and a book which accrued from the articles, *Freud on Food.*

This recipe below, in response to a request for something healthy, may sound rather casual. But those who know him will not be surprised to find the technique is impeccable, and the result marvellous.

In colour—page 257

## Wholemeal, Weetabix and Grapenut Loaf

*A delicious loaf of unusual texture and flavour.*

*Makes 1 large loaf*

THE FLOUR:
*about 1½ lb wholemeal flour*
*2 to 3 (or more) Weetabix,*
*   crumbled up*

THE STARTER:
*½ oz dried yeast*
*1 tablespoon black treacle*

AND . . .
*generous 1 pt warm water*
*1 tablespoon vegetable oil*
*½ level teaspoon salt*
*liquidized grape nuts—as many*
*   as you like*

YEAST STARTER:
Put the yeast, treacle and 2 tablespoons of the flour in a basin with the warm water. Wait 5 minutes.

THE MIX:
Add the oil, salt and as much crumbled-up *Weetabix*, wholemeal flour and liquidized grape nuts as makes the sort of consistency you can knead. Knead well.

THE RISING:
Place in a buttered tin, cover and leave to rise to twice its volume.

PRE-HEAT OVEN
to 400°F (200°C) Gas 6.

BAKING TIME:
Bake for about 50 minutes.

METRIC EQUIVALENTS:
*750 g wholemeal flour*
*2 to 3 Weetabix, crumbled up*
*15 g dried yeast*
*1 tablespoon black treacle*

*generous 600 ml warm water*
*1 tablespoon vegetable oil*
*½ level teaspoon salt*
*liquidized grape nuts*

# Len Deighton

Len Deighton is the successful spy and thriller writer and military historian; author of *Funeral in Berlin, The Billion Dollar Brain, An Expensive Place to Die,* (he created Harry Palmer, the insolent rebel spy), *Horse Under Water, The Ipcress File, XPD, Bomber,* and *Only When I Larf.*

He still has time to cook, and he bakes his own bread every week. He is a cockney who went to art school, worked as a pastry-cook and airline steward, became a graphic designer, founded the best cookery strip in newspapers, *Action Cook* (out of which came two books), before settling down to be simply one of our best writers.

Now he lives in Ireland, with his second wife, and enjoys a peaceable life, writing seven days a week. He finds time for international excursions which are quite likely to take him to the great gastronomic centres of the world, like Paul Bocuse's restaurant at Collonges-au-Mont-d'Or. The recipe overleaf was inspired by such a visit.

## Mixed Wholemeal Bread

*A crumbly wholemeal loaf with a difference, that melts in your mouth.*

In colour — page 257

*Makes 2 loaves*

YEAST STARTER:
Dissolve the yeast in a little warm water and set aside for 5 minutes.

THE MIX:
Mix the flours and the other dry ingredients, except the nuts in a large bowl. Add the melted butter and some warm water (very warm water if you're in a hurry). Add the yeast mixture. The amount of water you need depends on the absorbency of the flour. The resulting dough should be like putty.
Knead, tearing at the dough to stretch it any way you like. We use a Kenwood Mixer with a dough hook, but if you've never made bread before knead it by hand because it helps you to judge how much water to add to the flour mixture. It takes about 5 minutes for the pastry-like texture to change into soft, shiny dough.

THE RISING:
Leave in a warm place to double in size. It will take about 1 hour. If using nuts, add them now. Knead briefly. Put the dough into 2 well-greased and floured bread tins. Leave for 30 minutes.

PRE-HEAT OVEN
to 400°F (200°C) Gas 6.

BAKING TIME:
Bake for about 50 minutes. After 20 minutes REDUCE HEAT to 350°F (180°C) Gas 4. Remove from the tins. Cool for 2 hours before cutting.

NOTE
*A heaped tablespoon of finely chopped raw onion or shallot added to the dough when you knock it down makes a delicious savoury bread to serve with terrine.*

THE FLOUR:
*1 lb wholemeal flour*
*¼ lb white flour*
*¼ lb made up from all or any of the following: porridge oats, cornmeal, barley flakes, rye flakes, wheat germ, bran, walnuts, almonds or hazelnuts (whole, chopped or flakes)*

THE STARTER:
*1 oz fresh yeast or 2 teaspoons dried yeast*
*a little warm water*

AND . . .
*3 oz melted butter*
*1 teaspoon salt dissolved in a little warm water*

METRIC EQUIVALENTS:
*500 g wholemeal flour*
*125 g white flour*
*125 g made up from all or any of the following: porridge oats, cornmeal, barley flakes, rye flakes, wheat germ, bran, walnuts, almonds or hazelnuts (whole, chopped or flakes)*
*30 g fresh yeast or 2 teaspoons dried yeast*
*a little warm water*
*90 g melted butter*
*1 teaspoon salt dissolved in a little warm water*

In colour—page 232

# Brioche/Savarin

*This recipe will make one small brioche, enough for breakfast for a small family. The same bread can be soaked in a rum mixture to make a dessert. Dried fruit can be added to the mixture.*

*Serves 4*

THE FLOUR:
*8 oz white flour*

THE STARTER:
*½ oz fresh yeast*
*3 to 4 tablespoons warm water*

AND . . .
*2 oz butter*
*2 fl.oz milk*
*2 eggs, beaten*
*¼ teaspoon salt*

METRIC EQUIVALENTS:
*250 g white flour*
*15 g fresh yeast*
*3 to 4 tablespoons warm water*
*60 g butter*
*50 ml milk*
*2 eggs, beaten*
*¼ teaspoon salt*

YEAST STARTER:
Dissolve the yeast in the warm water.

THE MIX:
Warm the butter in the milk until it melts. Put in a large bowl with the rest of the ingredients and the yeast mixture. Beat everything together using a wooden spoon or your fingers. The mixture must be sticky and rather wet. (You might need to adjust the texture by adding more warm water or flour.) Put the mixture into a greased ring baking tin.

THE RISING:
Leave to rise until double in size, at least 30 minutes.

PRE-HEAT OVEN
to 325°F (170°C) Gas 3.

BAKING TIME:
Bake for about 20 minutes. Test with a skewer to make sure the inside is not wet. Cool and serve.

VARIATION:
You can make a simple version of *Saucisson en brioche* that the French chef, Paul Bocuse, used to provide as a free titbit for his customers. (This year, I noticed, it appeared on the bill.) To make it yourself, bury a cooked sausage in the mixture before letting it rise in the tin. If you do this you must flour the sausage and paint it with raw egg, otherwise the sausage will be loose inside the bread.

# Barbara Ronay

Barbara Ronay is married to Egon Ronay and helps her husband prepare his restaurant guide.

She eats out often and is constantly surprised that more restaurants don't take trouble to provide good bread. "The Connaught Hotel do nice bread rolls. But you have to go abroad to get good bread in restaurants. French bread in France; Italian bread is good; and in New York there's tremendous variety, rye bread and black bread."

Barbara Ronay was born into a musical family in Melbourne, Australia, and became a concert pianist. She came to England to visit in 1960, started the journey back by sea, and hopped off at Naples. "I though if I got back to Australia I'd never be able to afford to come here again."

She saw a job advertised with the Egon Ronay organisation. She got the job, then the boss. When the guide breaks into a recipe section—that's her: all her own recipes, developed at home.

Here is her basic bread recipe.

# Everyday Loaf

*This is the Ronay family favourite.*

*Makes 2 loaves*

THE MIX:
Pour the milk into a large bowl and stir in the yeast, butter and molasses until well mixed. Slowly add the flour and salt, mixing all the time until a dough is formed. Add a little extra milk if the mixture is too dry. Knead the dough on a floured board until smooth, or with an electric dough hook for about 3 minutes.

THE RISING:
Place in a clean bowl and cover with a damp cloth. Leave in a warm spot until the dough has risen to almost double its bulk, about 1 hour. Remove from the bowl and knead once more.

PRE-HEAT OVEN
to 450°C (230°C) Gas 8.

BAKING TIME:
Divide the dough in half. Place in 2 greased baking tins, 9 x 4 in (23 x 10 cm). Bake for 30 to 35 minutes.

THE FLOUR:
*2 lb 81% or 85% wholewheat flour*

THE STARTER:
*2 oz fresh yeast*

AND . . .
*18 fl.oz lukewarm milk*
*1 oz butter, melted*
*2½ tablespoons molasses*
*2 teaspoons salt*

METRIC EQUIVALENTS:
*1 kg 81% or 85% wholewheat flour*
*60 g fresh yeast*
*500 ml lukewarm milk*
*30 g butter, melted*
*2½ tablespoons molasses*
*2 teaspoons salt*

# Fay Maschler

Every day for breakfast Fay Maschler eats a poached egg with a piece of lightly toasted wholemeal bread; quite plain, no butter or jam.

She seems rather surprised about this herself. As the restaurant critic of the London evening paper, *The New Standard*, she will have had the pick of the capital's best dishes the evening before.

Nothing could contrast so sharply as plain wholemeal bread. Indeed, until a year ago, Fay thought it was a ridiculous idea to eat bread at all. "I'd always been taught that bread and potatoes were fattening," she says.

The biggest worry of a restaurant critic is the spectre of the expanding waistline; and whenever she ate out she carefully avoided the baskets of bread and breadsticks, holding back her calorie reserves for morsels of the chef's delicacies, which she knows too well from experience contain all those goodies the modern doctor tells you are so bad for health—butter, cream and so on. In fact, bread wasn't such a temptation; she explains that it was unusual until recently to find good bread in restaurants. "You usually got cut-up pieces of French bread, and stale too. But now restaurants are trying hard to offer you a selection of breads. I have often wondered why they haven't always done this. Now there is often a choice of white, wholemeal, and black rye. It seems obvious that a restaurant should provide good bread. Especially if service is indifferent . . . and you have nothing else to eat while you wait."

Fay Maschler has been a restaurant critic for eight years, and in 1979 won the Critic of the Year award—the first time a food critic had been put before critics of drama, TV, painting, ballet, poetry. It is a tribute not only to her wit and style, but to her integrity.

She has also written cookery books and a food column for the magazine *Over 21* where she once described her interest in food as pathetic. "The story of why I started cooking has been known to bring tears to the eyes of the listener." While her older sister was dating the best-looking player in an American East Coast football team, the young Fay stumbled through an interminable summer vacation cooking meringues, soufflés and puff pastries from a heavy kitchen book—noticing that this activity brought approval and praise; a consequence she never quite forgot.

In London, to supplement a secretary's income, she worked in Nick's Diner, one of the first good restaurants to emerge from the Sixties, and run by an Etonian and Guardsman, Nick Clarke.

In 1970 she married Tom Maschler, the publisher, who runs Jonathan Cape; wooing him, she says, with food. Their honeymoon provided a happy experience of bread, which she has only recently converted into hard currency.

"We married in Wales, but I'd always wanted to go to Ireland. Len Deighton (the thriller writer, who is also a gourmet and cook) was staying at the Gate House at Ballymaloe, which is run by Myrtle Allen and we stayed there and ate some wonderful bread. It was lovely, bready, nutty, moist and delicious. You could make a meal of the bread alone. The secret is to use black treacle with the yeast as a starter. Myrtle uses locally ground flours, and makes the bread fresh every day.

Her conversion to wholemeal bread was the result of reading a healthy bestseller, *The Scarsdale Diet*. "I'm not obsessed with slimming, but I used to think you ought to leave bread out if you want to be thin, and it was easy to do so. Now I'm a convert. Wholemeal bread is full of Vitamin B1 and other good things. I eat bread for good health. And I discovered that if you eat a couple of slices of good wholemeal, it overcomes the constipation problem."

At week-ends, in the country, Fay bakes her own bread as closely to the Ballymaloe recipe as possible ("it's never quite as good"), but in London she doesn't because she's got a Ceres store on her doorstep. But her favourite loaf is the wholemeal bread from Neal's Yard, the stunning complex in Covent Garden which is an inspiration to the wholefood movement. "It's the nicest wholemeal loaf I know. It's the best."

Fay Maschler's own bread is made very rapidly. "The minute you understand how yeast works you can't go wrong. Get the dough started—and leave it in the fridge until you want to bake it, if you like. Leave it out a couple of hours to rise. When you think about it, it's only a few minutes of actual activity, making the dough." With wholemeal bread she doesn't put it to rise a second time. "All that business of knocking back. I get good results working very quickly. People are put off by the mystery of bread. They think it must take a long time."

# Ballymaloe Brown Bread

*Fay Maschler bases her own loaf on the one described below. The treacle or molasses imparts richness and a moist quality. The dough is made quite wet.*

**YEAST STARTER:**
Mix the treacle or molasses with ¼ pt (150 ml) of the lukewarm water in a small bowl and crumble in the yeast. Put the bowl in a warm place and leave for about 5 minutes.

**THE MIX:**
Put the flour in a large bowl, add the salt, and warm in a cool oven. Grease four 1 lb (500 g) bread tins and put them to warm. Stir the yeast mixture well and pour it with the rest of the water into the flour gradually, to make a wettish dough. Warm a tea towel. Put the dough into the warm, greased bread tins.

**PRE-HEAT OVEN**
to 450°F (230°C) Gas 8.

**THE RISING:**
Cover the tins with the warm tea towel and leave in a warm place for about 20 minutes when the loaves should have risen by about a third of their original size.

**BAKING TIME:**
Bake for 45 minutes until loaves are nicely browned and sound hollow when tapped.

*Makes 4 small loaves*

**THE FLOUR:**
*3½ lb wholemeal flour*

**THE STARTER:**
*3 oz fresh yeast*
*   or 1½ oz dried yeast*
*2 to 4 tablespoons black treacle*
*   or molasses*

**AND . . .**
*about 2¼ pt water at blood heat*
*1 tablespoon salt*

**METRIC EQUIVALENTS:**
*1½ kg wholemeal flour*
*90 g fresh yeast*
*   or 40 g dried yeast*
*2 to 4 tablespoons black treacle or*
*   molasses*
*about 1¼ litres water at blood heat*
*1 tablespoon salt*

**FOR ONE LOAF:**
*Allow 1 lb wholemeal flour*
*about 10½ fl.oz water at blood*
*   heat*
*3 teaspoons black treacle*
*2 teaspoons salt*
*1 oz yeast*

**METRIC EQUIVALENTS:**
*500 g wholemeal flour*
*about 315 ml water at blood heat*
*3 teaspoons black treacle*
*2 teaspoons salt*
*30 g fresh yeast*

# John Seymour

John Seymour virtually invented self-sufficiency, and a way of life for many hundreds of people who were sickened by modern methods of food production.

When he wrote his book, *Self-Sufficiency,* in 1973, he had been practising self-sufficiency with his wife Sally for some 18 years. But suddenly the time was right, and there was a headlong rush of willing guinea-pigs, ready to go back to the land. Of course, no-one found it the way John wrote, which is rich and funny and robust and romantic.

But he was the first in our time to put a finger on the fun in farming, and to write entertainingly and informatively about growing crops, making cheese, smoking fish, breeding farmyard animals.

Here, in typical style, are his instructions for making a loaf of bread, joyfully inexact, equally inspiring.

## No-Quantity Bread

THE FLOUR:
*Wholemeal—as much as you
   think you need.*

THE STARTER:
*Fresh baker's yeast, but dried
   yeast is quite OK. Brewers
   yeast (a different species) is
   always all right, too—I have
   often used half a cupful of the
   yeast one skims off the top of
   the brewing beer.
A little honey*

AND . . .
*Water and salt*

*Why do I give no quantities? Because I think writers of recipes or givers of advice should allow their readers or listeners some common sense of their own. If, for example, a person hasn't got the sense to judge roughly how much salt to put into a batch of dough he deserves to eat over or under salty bread. I never weigh anything but I always make superb bread.*

THE MIX:
Mix up a sloppy mush of wholemeal flour, water, a tiny bit of honey (for the yeast), salt and baker's yeast. Do this before you go to bed at night. Cover it over and leave in a warm place.

NEXT MORNING:
Next morning come down (it will probably have overflowed its container messily), dump a large amount of dry flour on a table, dump the mash onto this, and mix it together and knead. Knead well—there are good reasons for this—such as that it makes better bread. Do not believe the siren song of the no-kneaders.

THE RISING:
When the stuff has a really stiff consistency shape it into loaves, fling these into well-greased bread tins, leave covered up near the stove for an hour or so, so that the dough rises spectacularly above the tins.

PRE-HEAT OVEN
to 400°F (200°C) Gas 6.

BAKING TIME:
Without shaking or bumping—place the tins in the oven. After the initial "blast", drop the heat to 350°F (180°C) Gas 4. Leave the bread in for an hour to an hour and a half, changing from top to bottom of oven as required. You know when they're done, if you are a beginner, by shoving a skewer through them (it should come out clean); if experienced, well—you just know they are done. Take 'em out—and remove from the tins at once, so they can let out steam.

# Tessa Traeger

Tessa Traeger is a celebrated photographer who exploits the sensual qualities of food to produce pictures which are like oil paintings. She also enjoys eating. And she's very particular that food should be fresh and wholesome.

Bread, for her, is about the most important food of all. "It's the most basic food there is. It's good for you and it's not fattening. You can eat a lot of it and feel that it's doing you good."

Tessa lives and works in London, but whenever she can, she hurries away to her Devon farmhouse.

Tessa makes her bread at a large wooden table in the kitchen. She leaves it to rise overnight on top of the Raeburn. Next day she kneads it again: "It's hard work physically, but good for getting rid of aggression, especially in the morning. And it's magical and fascinating. The way it rises to the top of the bowl. And it changes suddenly. It's good entertainment." She bakes it in the Raeburn: "It's a terrifically good way of cooking bread. It's quite dry, like the old ovens, and it gives the bread a nice crust." She makes toast on the top plate of the Raeburn: "It crisps up nicely. And if I've made an error and undercooked the bread, it's a good way of finishing it off."

She and her guests sometimes eat a whole loaf of bread for breakfast. "I don't feel guilty about eating too much bread, like I do with cakes. If I make too much, I freeze it and take it back to London. But you can buy lots of good bread in London. Making bread is for the country."

The country is relaxation and simple food. It's also the satisfaction of all the senses, not least the sense of smell. And bread, is the ultimate smell: "The smell of yeast, when the bread is cooking, is the best. It fills the whole house. It's a great smell. Deep and emotional. A smell that people respond to."

# Basic Bread

*A basic loaf to leave overnight on the Aga or in any warm place.*

YEAST STARTER:
Put the yeast and honey in half of the warm water and leave in a warm place until it becomes frothy.

THE MIX:
Put half the flour in a large bowl. Add the salt, oil and enough warm water to make the mixture wet. Mix in the frothy yeast.

FIRST RISING:
Cover the bowl with a cloth and leave overnight in a warm place.

SECOND RISING:
Next morning, add enough of the remaining flour to the mixture so that it is dry enough to handle and turn it out on to a floured surface. Now start kneading the dough. Add the rest of the flour gradually and knead for 10 to 20 minutes. Then cut into 2 large and 2 smaller pieces. Put them into 2 large and 2 small greased bread tins, cover and leave to rise a second time, for about 40 minutes.

PRE-HEAT OVEN
to 400°F (200°C) Gas 6.

BAKING TIME:
Bake for about 30 minutes.

*Makes 2 large and 2 small loaves*

THE FLOUR:
*about 3 lb wholemeal flour*

THE STARTER:
*1 oz fresh yeast or ½ oz dried yeast*
*1 teaspoon honey*

AND . . .
*about 2 pt warm water*
*1 teaspoon salt*
*1 tablespoon vegetable oil*

METRIC EQUIVALENTS:
*1½ kg wholemeal flour*
*30 g fresh yeast or 15 g dried yeast*
*1 teaspoon honey*
*about 1¼ litres warm water*
*1 teaspoon salt*
*1 tablespoon vegetable oil*

# Barbara Cartland

Barbara Cartland keeps fit and well by following her own advice. Her book, *The Magic of Honey*, and four other cookery books contain her philosophy on good nutrition which embraces a love of wholefoods, including wholewheat; of vitamins, trace elements and other nutrients which are lacking in supermarket food.

She is President of the National Society of Health which she helped to form over 20 years ago: through her various columns she says she answers some 200 letters a week—10,000 a year—on health: It is a labour of love which she fits in between writing her romantic novels. *The Guinness Book of Records* lists her as the best-selling author in the world, and readers have bought over 200 million copies of her books. She was writing her 305th when she contributed the recipes which follow.

Barbara Cartland is also a Dame of Grace of the Order of St. John, and deputy president of the St. John's Ambulance Brigade in Hertfordshire, the county in which she lives.

## Nutritional Wholemeal Bread

*Makes 2 loaves*

*Our favourite loaf.*

THE FLOUR:
*about 2 lb wholemeal flour*

THE STARTER:
*1 tablespoon dried yeast*

AND . . .
*generous 1½ pt warm water*
*3 tablespoons vegetable oil*
*1 tablespoon salt*
*6 tablespoons honey*
*½ cup Brewers yeast*

METRIC EQUIVALENTS:
*about 1 kg wholemeal flour*
*1 tablespoon dried yeast*
*generous 900 ml warm water*
*3 tablespoons vegetable oil*
*1 tablespoon salt*
*6 tablespoons honey*
*½ cup Brewers yeast*

YEAST STARTER:
Dissolve the yeast in 3 tablespoons of the warm water.

THE MIX:
Put just over half the flour in a mixing bowl and blend in the yeast liquid with the oil, salt, honey, Brewers yeast and the rest of the water. Mix well.

FIRST RISING:
Cover. Keep in a warm room and leave to rise for at least 2 hours.

SECOND RISING:
Blend in the remaining flour and knead until the dough is stiff. Oil the dough. Return it to the bowl, cover and leave to rise for 1 hour.

THIRD RISING:
Punch down and knead. Divide the dough into 2 loaves and shape to fit 2 greased bread tins. Cover and leave to rise again until double in bulk.

PRE-HEAT OVEN
to 325°F (170°C) Gas 3.

BAKING TIME:
Bake for 40 to 50 minutes.

# Wholemeal Bread with Eggs

In colour—page 257

*My chef, Nigel Gordon, makes this for invalids or guests who are very tired.*

*Makes 3 loaves*

YEAST STARTER:
Dissolve the 2 tablespoons dried yeast in 3 tablespoons of the water.

THE FLOUR:
*about 2 lb wholemeal flour*

THE MIX:
Warm the milk with the salt, remaining water, Brewers yeast, vegetable oil and honey, then cool to lukewarm. Add the eggs to the dried yeast liquid and then mix with the milk mixture. Add 1½ lb (750 g) of the flour and blend thoroughly. Let it stand for 10 minutes. Then add enough of the remaining flour to knead easily. Knead for 10 minutes.

THE STARTER:
*2 tablespoons dried yeast*

AND . . .
*⅓ pt water*
*generous ¾ pt milk*
*1 tablespoon salt*
*3 tablespoons Brewers yeast*
*5 tablespoons vegetable oil*
*3 tablespoons honey*
*3 eggs, beaten*

FIRST RISING:
Oil the dough, place in a bowl and cover. Leave to rise until double in bulk.

SECOND RISING:
Punch down. Knead and leave to rise until again double in bulk.

METRIC EQUIVALENTS:
*1 kg wholemeal flour*
*2 tablespoons dried yeast*
*175 ml water*
*generous 400 ml milk*
*1 tablespoon salt*
*3 tablespoons Brewers yeast*
*5 tablespoons vegetable oil*
*3 tablespoons honey*
*3 eggs, beaten*

THIRD RISING:
Punch down. Shape into 3 loaves, place in oiled bread tins and leave to rise for the third time, about 30 minutes.

PRE-HEAT OVEN
to 400°F (200°C) Gas 6.

BAKING TIME:
Bake for 45 minutes. After 15 minutes REDUCE HEAT to 375°F (190°C) Gas 5.

# Stuart Hall

Stuart Hall is the broadcaster and extrovert tele-star of the BBC's Look North-West. His father was a baker, and he remembers that as a two-year-old he prodded six dozen walnut loaves with a pencil, to give a decorative effect.

He has enjoyed cooking as long as he can remember, but became a bakery star overnight when his studio director asked him to bake bread on TV during a bakers' strike and he produced his Aphrodisiac loaf. Two thousand viewers wrote for the recipe. He has since published his own cookery book, *Cook the 'Look North' Way*, which is largely about coping with Aunt Glad—25 stone, bow-front chest, billiard table legs, half a dozen chins that quiver with excitement at the mere suggestion of food, and an appetite like a herd of buffalo.

## Aphrodisiac Milk Bread

*Makes 3 to 4 loaves*

THE FLOUR:
*3 lb strong white flour*

THE STARTER:
*1 oz fresh yeast*

AND...
*3 oz butter*
*¾ oz salt*
*about ¾ pt warm water*
*about ¾ pt warm milk*

METRIC EQUIVALENTS:
*1½ kg strong white flour*
*30 g fresh yeast*
*90 g butter*
*20 g salt*
*about 400 ml warm water*
*about 400 ml warm milk*

*To get the full effect of this simple recipe, invented by "Small Hall Himself", add the merest sensation of rhinohorn!*

YEAST STARTER:
Dissolve the yeast in a little of the warm water.

THE MIX:
Rub the butter into the sieved flour and salt and make a well in the centre. Add enough of the water and milk to make a dough. Mix well and knead for at least 5 minutes.

FIRST RISING:
Cover the bowl with a damp cloth. Let the dough rise in a warm place for about 1 hour.

SECOND RISING:
Knock down the dough and knead lightly. Return to the bowl for a further 30 minutes.

PRE-HEAT OVEN
to 475°F (240°C) Gas 9.

THE RISING:
Weigh into 1 lb (500 g) pieces. Shape and place in greased tins. Allow to rise for about 20 minutes.

BAKING TIME:
Bake for 30 minutes.

# Cheshire Cheese Scones

*These smooth-textured scones have a deliciously sharp flavour.*

*Makes 12*

THE MIX:
Sieve the flour with the salt, bicarbonate of soda and cream of tartar and rub in the butter. Mix in the grated Cheshire cheese. Make a well in the flour mixture and pour in the buttermilk or soured cream and two-thirds of the beaten egg. Mix until you have a soft spongy dough.
Turn out on to a lightly floured surface and divide into two. Lightly knead each piece to a ball, flatten to a thickness of about ¾ in (2 cm), and cut each round into 6 triangles or 6 portions.

PRE-HEAT OVEN
to 450°F (230°C) Gas 8.

RESTING TIME:
Brush scones with the remainder of the beaten egg and leave to rest for 15 to 20 minutes before baking.

BAKING TIME:
Bake near the top of the oven until the scones have risen well and turned brown, about 10 minutes.

THE FLOUR:
*½ lb white flour*

THE RAISING AGENTS:
*1 level teaspoon bicarbonate of*
*    soda*
*1 level teaspoon cream of tartar*

AND...
*½ level teaspoon salt*
*2 oz butter*
*2 oz Cheshire cheese, grated*
*4½ tablespoons buttermilk or*
*    soured cream*
*1 large egg, well beaten*

METRIC EQUIVALENTS:
*250 g white flour*
*1 level teaspoon bicarbonate of soda*
*1 level teaspoon cream of tartar*
*½ level teaspoon salt*
*60 g butter*
*60 g Cheshire cheese, grated*
*4½ tablespoons buttermilk or*
*    soured cream*
*1 large egg, well beaten*

# Fay Godwin

Fay Godwin, the photographer, bakes her own bread because she can't buy loaves which are interesting enough. "I used to buy rye bread and wholemeal, but they were always the same and predictable."

At first her breads were so crumbly you had to eat them with a spoon, and she assumed that it was something to do with the way she mixed the grains and seeds. "Then I bought Elizabeth David's book on bread and learnt how to make bread properly."

She makes three pounds at a time, using recipes as a starting point, and tipping generous amounts of roasted spices or sesame seeds into them. "The best breads are made from doughs which I leave overnight. I always find it better to use half the dried yeast recommended in the packet instructions." She says quite happily that she's had many failures and they don't discourage her at all; just as long as it tastes good. Here are two recipes from her repertoire of unusual bread.

## Wholemeal Barley Loaf

*Makes about 4 loaves*

THE FLOUR:
*3 lb wholemeal flour*
*½ lb barley flour*

THE STARTER:
*2 oz fresh yeast or 3 scant level*
*teaspoons dried yeast*

AND . . .
*2 teaspoons salt*
*8 oz roasted sesame seeds*
*3 to 4 fl.oz buttermilk*
*or soured cream*
*about 1½ pt warm water*

METRIC EQUIVALENTS:
*1½ kg wholemeal flour*
*250 g barley flour*
*60 g fresh yeast or 3 scant*
*level teaspoons dried yeast*
*2 teaspoons salt*
*250 g roasted sesame seeds*
*80 to 100 ml buttermilk or soured*
*cream*
*about 900 ml warm water*

*The sesame seeds give this bread a distinct crunchy flavour which combines well with the smooth texture of the barley flour.*

YEAST STARTER:
Cream the yeast in a little of the warm water and set aside for about 10 minutes.

THE MIX:
Mix the flours well in a large bowl. Add the salt and make a well in the centre. Add the sesame seeds, pour in the yeast liquid, the buttermilk, and enough of the warm water to make a workable dough. Knead well.

FIRST RISING:
Cover with polythene and put in a warm place to rise overnight.

SECOND RISING:
Knock back and knead lightly. Divide the dough up and place in greased baking tins, filling them half full. Cover and leave to rise again for about 45 minutes.

PRE-HEAT OVEN
to 450°F (230°C) Gas 8.

BAKING TIME:
Bake for about 40 minutes. After 15 minutes, REDUCE HEAT to 400°F (200°C) Gas 6. Remove the loaves from their tins and turn over for the last 10 minutes of baking. Cool on a wire rack.

# Potato Bread

*Delicious, especially when toasted.*

*Makes 1 large loaf*

YEAST STARTER:
Cream the yeast in a little of the warm milk and water set aside.

THE FLOUR:
*1 lb wholemeal flour*

THE MIX:
Add the salt to the flour and rub in the mashed potato, while still warm, until completely mixed. Add the yeast mixture and enough of the warm milk and water to make a dough.

THE STARTER:
*¾ oz fresh yeast*

AND...
*about ½ pt warm milk and
    water, mixed*
*1 teaspoon salt*
*4 oz cooked potato, mashed*

FIRST RISING:
Cover and leave in a warm place until well risen, up to 2 hours.

SECOND RISING:
Knock back, knead lightly and place in a greased 2 lb (1 kg) baking tin. Cover with a damp cloth and leave until the dough rises to the top of the tin, about 45 minutes.

METRIC EQUIVALENTS:
*500 g wholemeal flour*
*20 g fresh yeast*
*about 300 ml warm milk and water,
    mixed*
*1 teaspoon salt*
*125 g cooked potato, mashed*

PRE-HEAT OVEN
to 425°F (220°C) Gas 7.

BAKING TIME:
Bake for about 45 minutes.

## Jane Asher

Jane Asher, the actress (she played Celia in TV's *Brideshead Revisited*) is an enthusiastic home baker. She bakes her own bread simply for the good taste: "But I occasionally go on health binges. I've been specially affected by the high fibre diet of the last few years."

She bakes bread in batches and freezes the loaves until they are needed. "But I love it best when it's warm. And thoroughly indigestible."

Her mother was a good cook and Jane has enjoyed cooking all her life. She's currently completing a fanciful book on cake decoration. "The opposite of healthy eating, of course; all that sugar. Wicked. But I don't actually like eating the cake. Only decorating."

Here is one of her favourite recipes.

*In colour—page 257*

## Yoghurt Bread

*Makes 1 loaf*

*This healthy, nutritious bread is enriched with yoghurt and eggs.*

THE FLOUR:
*10 oz wholemeal flour*
*6 oz strong white flour*
*(or 4 oz strong white flour plus*
*2 oz bran or wheat germ)*

PRE-HEAT OVEN
to 350°F (180°C) Gas 4.

THE RAISING AGENT:
*1½ teaspoons baking powder*

THE MIX:
Mix the wholemeal and white flours, salt and baking powder together in a bowl. Mix the yoghurt, eggs and honey together and add the flour. Put in a well-greased tin.

AND...
*1 teaspoon salt*
*8 fl.oz natural yoghurt*
*2 eggs*
*1 tablespoon honey*

BAKING TIME:
Bake for 1 hour.

METRIC EQUIVALENTS:
*300 g wholemeal flour*
*175 g strong white flour*
*(or 125 g strong white flour plus*
*60 g bran or wheat germ)*
*1½ teaspoons baking powder*
*1 teaspoon salt*
*250 ml natural yoghurt*
*2 eggs*
*1 tablespoon honey*

OPPOSITE:
Top right: *Flower Pot Loaves (Renny Harrop) p.98.*
Centre left: *Potato Scones (Olive Odell) p.141.* Below: *Ruth's Raisin Scones (Doris Grant) p.72* and top left: *a variation made with dates.*

OVERLEAF:
Left: *Basic Wheat Germ Brown Bread (Ursel Norman) p.205.*
Right: *Oat Cakes (Bobby Freeman) p.195.*

## Using up Bread

When you make good home-made bread it's too good to throw away. It's good for bread-crumbs of course: make them in the blender and store in the deep freeze wrapped in plastic bags.

Or consider some of these traditional recipes: they are quite special when the essential ingredient —your own home-made bread—is the basis.

## Bread Sauce

THE METHOD:
Stick the clove in the onion, place this and the mace in the milk in the top of a double boiler. Heat to scalding. Remove the mace. Sprinkle in the breadcrumbs, stirring and beating as you do so. Add salt and pepper to taste and half the butter.

COOKING TIME:
Cook, beating often, for 20 minutes. Add the cream and the rest of the butter. Remove the onion with its clove and serve the sauce at once with roast chicken, turkey or game.

METRIC EQUIVALENTS:
*60 g fresh soft breadcrumbs*
*1 clove*
*1 small onion*
*1 blade mace*

*300 ml milk*
*salt and pepper*
*15 g butter*
*1 tablespoon cream*

THE BREAD:
*2 oz fresh soft breadcrumbs*

AND . . .
*1 clove*
*1 small onion*
*1 blade mace*
*½ pt milk*
*salt and pepper*
*½ oz butter*
*1 tablespoon cream*

## Eggy Bread, also known as French Toast

THE METHOD:
Dip each slice of bread in the egg and hold on the end of a fork to drain off any excess egg.

THE COOKING:
Fry in the heated butter or vegetable oil until golden-brown on both sides.
Serve hot with savoury sauce or honey.

THE BREAD:
*slices of any day-old bread*

AND . . .
*beaten egg*
*butter or vegetable oil*

## Bread Sippets

THE COOKING:
Fry the "sippets" in the hot vegetable oil or butter. Drain well. Use as a garnish.

THE BREAD:
*Any stale bread cut into small pieces the shape of stars, triangles, diamonds or anything else*

AND . . .
*Vegetable oil or butter*

## Cheesy Bread and Butter Pudding

*A delicious savoury dish from Allinson using stale wholemeal bread.*

THE BREAD:
*7 or 8 slices stale wholemeal bread*

AND . . .
*butter*
*about 6 oz Cheddar cheese*
*1 egg*
*½ pt milk*
*sea salt*

METRIC EQUIVALENTS:
*7 or 8 slices stale wholemeal bread*
*butter*
*about 175 g Cheddar cheese*
*1 egg*
*300 ml milk*
*sea salt*

THE METHOD:
Spread the slices of stale bread with butter and cut into triangles. Line the base of a medium-sized casserole dish with some of the bread. Cut thin slices of Cheddar cheese to cover the bread, top with another layer of bread.
Lightly beat the egg and milk together and season with salt. Pour over the bread.

PRE-HEAT OVEN
to 350°F (180°C) Gas 4.

BAKING TIME:
Bake for 45 minutes.

## Barbecued Bread

*Another good idea from Allinson for using up stale bread.*

THE BREAD:
*thick slices wholemeal bread*

AND . . .
*butter*
*grated cheese*
*mustard*
*chopped onion*
*Worcester sauce*

THE METHOD:
Spread the slices of bread with the butter. Mix grated cheese, mustard and chopped onion together and season with Worcester sauce. Put the slices together to make a loaf shape and wrap in kitchen foil.

BAKING TIME:
Bake in a hot oven for about 15 minutes.

## Summer Pudding

THE BREAD:
*¼ in (5mm) thick slices of bread, crusts removed, enough to line and cover a basin.*

AND . . .
*soft fruit such as raspberries, blackberries, redcurrants, blackcurrants or soft strawberries, or a combination of 2 or 3 of these.*
*honey*

THE METHOD:
Stew the fruit with some honey to sweeten it, in a small saucepan. Do not overcook.
Butter a basin and line it with the slices of bread, being careful not to leave any gaps. Pour in the hot fruit so that it immediately softens the bread. When the basin is almost full, stand it on a plate to catch any escaping juice. Place slices of bread on top to cover. Fit a saucer or small plate over the top of the basin and press it down on to the pudding. Place a heavy weight or jar on top.

STANDING TIME:
Leave overnight in the fridge.

TO SERVE:
Turn out upside-down on to a plate and serve with whipped cream or ice-cream.

# Torriga

*The Spanish version of* Pain Perdu.

THE METHOD:
Dip the squares of bread in the milk, but do not soak too long. Then dip into beaten egg.

THE COOKING:
Heat the oil to 375°F (190°C). Drop in the squares and fry until golden-brown—a dry bread cube dropped into the oil should brown in about 1 minute. Serve with warmed honey.

THE BREAD:
*squares of crustless bread about ½ in (1.5 cm) thick*

AND . . .
*milk*
*beaten egg*
*vegetable oil*
*warmed honey*

# Pain Perdu

THE METHOD:
Mix the milk, honey and flavouring together and boil until reduced to half the quantity. Soak the bread in the milk until the milk has been absorbed and the bread is half dry. Sprinkle with sultanas.

THE COOKING:
Fry the slices in butter until both sides are golden-brown. Serve hot and, if liked, spread with warmed honey.

THE BREAD:
*small, crustless slices of any wholemeal, brown, white or fruit bread*

AND . . .
*milk          sultanas*
*honey         butter*
*flavouring,*
*    such as vanilla essence*

# Printer's Pudding

THE METHOD:
Grease a 1½ pt (900 ml) ovenproof dish. Sprinkle in the breadcrumbs, coconut and lemon rind. Whisk the eggs with the honey until creamy, then stir in the milk. Pour this into the dish and stir until thoroughly mixed.

STANDING TIME:
Leave to stand for about 1 hour so that the crumbs and coconut absorb the liquid.

PRE-HEAT OVEN
to 325°F (170°C) Gas 3.

BAKING TIME:
Bake on the middle shelf for 1½ hours, until a knife or skewer comes out clean. Serve hot or cold with cream or ice-cream and stewed fruit.

THE BREAD:
*3 heaped tablespoons fresh*
*    breadcrumbs*

AND . . .
*2 heaped tablespoons desiccated*
*    coconut*
*grated rind of ½ lemon*
*2 eggs*
*1 tablespoon honey*
*1 pt cold milk*

METRIC EQUIVALENTS:
*3 heaped tablespoons fresh*
*    breadcrumbs*
*2 heaped tablespoons desiccated*
*    coconut*
*grated rind of ½ lemon*
*2 eggs*
*1 tablespoon honey*
*600 ml cold milk*

# Mr. A. D. May's Bread and Butter Pudding

*Serves 4*

THE BREAD:
*4 slices white bread
(2 or 3 days old)*

AND . . .
*2 eggs
½ pt milk
2 oz double cream
1 oz honey
2 oz unsalted butter
2 to 3 oz raisins
pinch or two grated nutmeg*

METRIC EQUIVALENTS:
*4 slices white bread
2 eggs
300 ml milk
60 g double cream
30 g honey
60 g unsalted butter
60 to 90 g raisins
pinch or two grated nutmeg*

*The Maypole English Restaurant in Leather Lane, London WC1, is stylishly unstylish. Every bit of Mr. May's expertise goes into delivering a small selection of fine English roasts and sweets; absolutely none is spent on decor and ambience. Diners share a cameraderie, the relish of good old-fashioned English cooking. Here is his traditional bread and butter pudding.*

THE METHOD:
Beat the eggs, milk, cream and honey to make a custard mixture. Melt the butter and dip the slices of bread in it on both sides. Put two slices of the bread in a small shallow dish, strew with the raisins and a pinch of nutmeg. Cover with the other two pieces of bread. Pour the custard mixture over the slices of bread, pushing them well down to cover. Sprinkle with more nutmeg. Leave for half an hour to soak in.

PRE-HEAT OVEN
to 325°F (170°C) Gas 3.

BAKING TIME:
Bake for 30 minutes. Raise the heat to 375°F (190°C) Gas 5 for 5 minutes to colour the top and serve.

# Spicy Bread Pudding

THE BREAD:
*4 oz wholemeal bread*

AND . . .
*cold water or milk
2 tablespoons honey
2 oz dried fruit, such as
   sultanas, raisins, dates
1 egg
1 oz butter, melted
½ teaspoon mixed spice
½ teaspoon ground cinnamon
½ teaspoon grated lemon rind*

THE METHOD:
Remove the crusts and soak the bread in enough cold water or milk to cover it, then squeeze out the excess moisture. Mash with a fork and combine with all the other ingredients, mixing well. Butter a baking dish.

PRE-HEAT OVEN
to 400°F (200°C) Gas 6.

BAKING TIME:
Bake for 45 minutes. Serve on its own or with home-made custard or cream, or orange sauce.

METRIC EQUIVALENTS:
*125 g wholemeal bread
cold water or milk
2 tablespoons honey
60 g dried fruit, such as sultanas,
   raisins, dates*

*1 egg
30 g butter, melted
½ teaspoon mixed spice
½ teaspoon ground cinnamon
½ teaspoon grated lemon rind*

# Bread Pudding

THE METHOD:
Remove any hard crusts from the bread. (This can be used to make breadcrumbs, if you like.) Pour some milk into a flattish dish and place each slice of bread in it, until saturated. Add more milk as you go. Then dip the bread, slice by slice into the beaten egg, drain off any excess egg, and finally dip in the oatmeal, wholemeal flour or baked breadcrumbs. Fry in butter.
You can spread the fried bread with jam or honey and serve like this. Or you can butter an ovenproof dish and place the bread slices in this with a little honey between the layers. Whisk an egg white until stiff and pour this on top.

PRE-HEAT OVEN
to 400°F (200°C) Gas 6.

TO BAKE:
Bake until the white of egg goes brown, about 10 minutes.

THE BREAD:
*slices of any bread ¼ to ½ in (0.5 to 1.5 cm) thick*

AND . . .
*milk*
*beaten egg*
*oatmeal, wholemeal flour or baked breadcrumbs*
*butter*
*jam or honey*
*white of an egg*

# Light Christmas Pudding

*A variation on the usual Christmas pudding, from Caroline Conran. The pudding needs no maturing, but if made in advance, needs 1 hour more steaming on the day.*

THE METHOD:
Pour some boiling water over the candied peel and soak for 3 to 4 minutes. Drain and cut in slivers. Mix the large raisins with the sultanas, candied peel, ground almonds, breadcrumbs and salt. Stir or rub in the butter. Add the honey, grated lemon rind and juice. Beat the eggs well with the brandy if used, and milk. Add to the breadcrumb mixture and mix well. Add the spices. Stir the pudding well. Butter a 1¾ pt (1 litre) basin and pour in the mixture. Cover with buttered greaseproof paper, then kitchen foil tied with string, making a handle to hold the pudding.

THE COOKING TIME:
Steam for 4 hours. Steam for 1 more hour on the day.

METRIC EQUIVALENTS:
*90 g fine fresh wholemeal bread, without crusts, made into breadcrumbs*
*60 g whole pieces of candied peel*
*250 g large seedless raisins*
*250 g sultanas*
*90 g ground almonds*
*pinch of sea salt*
*90 g softened unsalted butter*
*2 tablespoons honey*
*juice and rind of ½ large or 1 small lemon*
*2 eggs*
*3 tablespoons brandy (optional)*
*1 tablespoon milk*
*¼ teaspoon freshly grated nutmeg*
*½ teaspoon ground cinnamon*
*½ teaspoon mixed spice*

*Serves 6 to 8*

THE BREAD:
*3 oz fine fresh wholemeal bread, without crusts, made into breadcrumbs*

AND . . .
*2 oz whole pieces of candied peel*
*8 oz large seedless raisins*
*8 oz sultanas*
*3 oz ground almonds*
*pinch of sea salt*
*3 oz softened unsalted butter*
*2 tablespoons honey*
*juice and rind of ½ large or 1 small lemon*
*2 eggs*
*3 tablespoons brandy (optional)*
*1 tablespoon milk*
*¼ teaspoon freshly grated nutmeg*
*½ teaspoon ground cinnamon*
*½ teaspoon mixed spice*

# A Step-by-step Children's Recipe

*Bread is magic—And it is simple to make.*

*You only need flour, water, salt, a little honey and yeast. Mix them together. If the mixture is warm enough it will grow bigger and bigger. (If it gets cold it sinks.)*

*When you put it to bake in a very hot oven, it stays large and the outside crust becomes crisp and tasty.*

*This can be better bread than you can buy in any shop.*

THE FIRST BIT is messy and fun: You just make a dough by mixing the ingredients together.

THE SECOND BIT is easy: The bread just rises and rises.

THE THIRD BIT is easiest: The bread bakes until golden brown.

# Making Bread

**YOU NEED:**

**THE FLOUR:**
8 oz wholemeal flour
8 oz strong white flour

**THE STARTER:**
to make the bread rise: 1 oz fresh
    yeast or 1½ level teaspoons
    dried yeast

**AND . . .**
½ pt warm water
1 teaspoon salt
1 teaspoon honey

**YOU ALSO NEED:**
scales
measuring jug
cup
teaspoon
large mixing bowl

wooden spoon
tea-cloth
baking tin or baking tray
oven gloves

**METRIC EQUIVALENTS:**
250 g wholemeal flour
250 g strong white flour
30 g fresh yeast or 1½
    level teaspoons dried yeast
300 ml warm water
1 teaspoon salt
1 teaspoon honey

**YEAST STARTER:**
1. Measure the warm water in a measuring jug. Add the salt and honey. Stir well.

3. Pour the yeast mixture into the water in the measuring jug. Stir well.

2. Put the fresh yeast in a cup. Pour a little of the warm water on to the yeast—just enough to cover it. Cream it with a teaspoon. (If you use dried yeast, do what it tells you on the packet.) Leave for 5 minutes.

**THE MIX:**
4. Mix the wholemeal and white flour together in a large mixing bowl.

**5.** Add the warm water to the flour in 3 stages. Mix in first with a wooden spoon and then with your hands. You have now made the dough.

**8.** Wash and dry the mixing bowl. Sprinkle it with a little flour. Place the dough in it. Cover the bowl with a tea-cloth.

**6.** Sprinkle a little flour on to a board or table top. Turn out the dough. If it is too dry, add a little more water. If it is too sticky, add some more flour.

FIRST RISING:
**9.** Put the bowl in a warm place, like an airing cupboard, for 1 hour. The dough will rise to double its size.

**7.** Knead the dough for 15 minutes. Roll it out and fold it over and press the palms of your hands into it. This is hard work, but keep going, until the dough feels springy and is smooth and shiny in your hands.

**10.** After 1 hour "knock back" the dough by lifting it from the bowl and kneading it for a few minutes, but only a few minutes.

**11.** Grease a baking tin or tray with a little butter on a piece of paper. Shape the dough into a round and place it on the tray OR shape it into a rectangle and push it into the tin.

BAKING TIME:
**14.** Bake for 25 minutes. Turn the loaf upside down and bake for a further 5 minutes. Ask mummy or daddy again to help you do this.

SECOND RISING:
**12.** Cover again with the tea-cloth and leave to rise a second time for 30 minutes.

**15.** Remove from the tin or tray and place on a wire rack to cool.

PRE-HEAT OVEN
to 425°F (220°C) Gas 7.
**13.** When the bread has risen to almost double its size put it in the oven. Wear oven gloves and make sure mummy, daddy or an elder brother or sister helps you.

# Part III
# All About Bread

# How To Bake

People think that making bread is time-consuming and therefore don't attempt it. It is not. It is a bit like being a goalkeeper: there are sudden bursts of energetic activity, then long periods when you have nothing to do at all.

It is particularly delightful for the beginner, because it doesn't require any of the traditional skills of the home cook. That is one of the reasons it appeals to men, who do not normally venture into the kitchen. Baking is baking, not cooking. And all can enjoy the therapeutic experience of working a piece of dough energetically.

You can make bread fit in with your other activities, even if these encompass days at the office. You can speed up the process, or you can slow it down. Bread is responsive to *your* needs. It can rise to suit any occasion.

You can go straight into the kitchen now, dissolve some yeast in warm water and mix it with flour and water in a bowl. Knead it for ten minutes, put it in a covered bowl, leave it to rise—while you go away—for 1 hour (in a warm place) or 2 hours (in a cooler place) or 4 hours (in the fridge) or overnight (in the fridge).

When you come back, you are less than 1½ hours from producing a finished loaf. You will find the dough has risen like a balloon to twice its size. You put it on a floured surface and knock all the gas out of it (knocking back) and shape it into loaves or put it into greased tins, and leave it to double in size again, usually 30 minutes (or longer if you prefer). Turn on the oven and get it as hot as you can.

And now the easiest bit. Put the loaves in the oven and bake until they're done, usually 10 minutes for rolls, 25 to 30 minutes for small loaves, 40 to 45 minutes for a larger loaf.

The dough is so obliging, that if you weren't ready to bake it after it had risen the second time, you could keep on knocking it back and putting it to rise until you were ready.

The bread will be superb. And you can get extraordinary professional results by brushing the bread with a little diluted egg yolk, cream or even milk to give it a sheen, like varnish.

It takes only a few seconds more to sprinkle a few poppy seeds or sesame seeds onto the glaze. You have a loaf worthy of cries of admiration from friends and family.

# Kneading

When you've mixed the flour with the yeast and liquid, the dough must be kneaded, until smooth. This is the part that most home bakers relish and enjoy. The object is to stretch the gluten in the flour, so that as the yeast works it will eventually trap the gas bubbles, and cause the loaf to rise. You should knead white flour for at least 10 minutes. The more you knead it, the better a loaf will rise.

The idea is to flatten out the dough, fold it over on itself, flatten again and roll. You do this by pushing the dough forward with the palm and heel of the hand and then pulling it back with the fingers. Push and pull the dough as forcefully as you can. Sometimes you'll see bakers pick up a roll of dough by each end and bang it up and down on the work-surface, stretching it as they do so.

## The texture
It's unlikely that you will get exactly the right texture from the measurements in a recipe, because flour differs in its absorbency. Don't be afraid to add a little more liquid if the dough mixture seems stiff and difficult to work. If the mixture is wet and sticky, add some more flour: place a handful of flour at the back of the work-surface and with floured hands introduce it bit by bit into the dough. Don't incorporate too much extra flour; the dough

*To knead the dough, flatten it out, fold it over on itself, flatten again and roll.*
Above left: *Do this by pushing the dough forward with the palm and heel of the hand.*
Above: *Then pull it back with the fingers.*
Opposite above: *You can be as rough as you like with the dough as you knead it.*
Opposite below: *When the dough is ready it should be elastic and springy.*

must be elastic and springy.

After kneading for 8 to 10 minutes you'll feel a change come over the mass in your hands. Its elasticity will become pronounced. It is now ready to put aside to rise: but you can do no harm if you knead it more.

You can cut down the time involved—but also some of the pleasure—by using an electric mixer with a dough hook. Set it at slow speed or you'll damage the machine. Follow instructions from the booklet provided.

## Keeping the dough warm
In winter especially take care that the dough does not get cold while you are working it. It helps if you first warm the flour in a low oven for a few minutes, and warm all utensils including the mixing bowl and baking tins. If you have to leave the dough for any reason while you are working it, cover it with a tea-towel or plastic bag to keep out draughts.

# Rising

Dough can be left to rise and be knocked back any number of times. If you add Vitamin C to wholemeal flour you need only leave it to rise once in its baking tin, because the vitamin accelerates the action of the gluten in the dough.

## First Rising

It is most usual to put dough to rise first in the mixing bowl, covered with a damp cloth or a plastic bag. This keeps it warm and moist and enables it to double in size without forming a skin or a crust.

In a warm place it will double in size in 1 hour: for example in an airing cupboard, near a fire or on top of a boiler insulated with a folded towel underneath it to prevent direct heat. At room temperature away from the heat it will double in size in 2 hours. In a cool larder or pantry it will double in size in about 4 or 5 hours. It will rise in a cold refrigerator within 6 to 12 hours depending on how cold it is. In recipes in this book shorter times are given: you can vary the times to suit your convenience by leaving the dough to rise in warmer or colder places.

Below: *Leave the dough to rise first in the mixing bowl. Cover the bowl with a damp cloth or a sheet of polythene to prevent a skin forming.*

## Knocking Back

After the first rise, the dough is ready to be shaped into loaves or put into tins. Remove the dough from the bowl, place it on a floured surface and punch it down to knock out all the gas. This is called knocking back. Roll and knead the dough briefly. It is now ready to prove, that is, to rise again, preparatory to baking.

## Second Rising

Shape the dough as desired and place on a greased baking tray, cover and put to rise. The second rising usually takes about 30 minutes. Or, if using a tin, grease it and roll the dough into a sausage shape. Tuck the ends underneath, and press down so that it half fills the tin. When it rises to the top it is ready to bake.

# Decorating

## Cuts

Some recipes call for decoration. Decorating often takes the form of cuts which open up attractively during the baking. These effects can be produced quite simply. Use a razor or your sharpest knife to slash the dough making cuts at least ¼ in (5 mm) deep. Not only are the cuts decorative, they also serve a useful purpose: they leave space for the dough to expand, sometimes dramatically. You can make a simple cross to produce the Coburg effect, or cut evenly spaced diagonals, or even do a criss-cross lattice pattern to create a famous old English bread.

## Finishing Touches

See glazes, pages 300-301.

# Baking

## Pre-Heat Oven

As a general rule 15 minutes or so before you're ready to bake, put the oven on at its hottest temperature. When you're ready to put the loaves in, you can turn down the heat to the required temperature. This way you're sure to get the bread off to a good start. Some fruit breads and sweet breads, however, are cooked at quite a low temperature, in which case do not over-heat the oven.

## Heat

All ovens vary slightly and you will learn to adjust temperatures to suit the needs of your own. Ovens are usually hottest at the top and coolest on the lowest grid. Electric fan ovens, however, are even in temperature. Most breads cook best in the middle of the oven with the heat circulating around them. It may be necessary to make a half turn during the baking to get an even finish. If you put loaves high in the oven the heat seals the top of the loaf forming a hard crust which prevents the bread rising. This may result in the top coming away or the bottom tearing. The result may not look professional, but the bread should taste just as good. Some of our recipes give lower heats because this is how they work best for the cooks who gave them. Experiment.

Start with a very hot oven to give the yeast a 10 to 15 minute boost to keep the dough rising; after that time the heat kills the yeast, so you can gradually lower the temperature. In this way you will find you are baking to a long tradition: the old brick ovens used to be heated for half an hour with burning bunches of faggots of twigs, then they were raked out, and the dough pushed in rapidly. With the oven door closed, and no extra heat, the temperature would fall evenly and gradually.

For a bread that's crisp all over, towards the end of the cooking time, turn over free-form loaves and remove bread from tins. Place upside down on the shelf for a final 5 minutes' cooking. The bread is done when you can tap it with your knuckle and it makes a hollow sound. If in doubt, test it with a skewer. The loaf is done when a skewer inserted in the middle comes out clean.

If you notice that the bread is beginning to scorch before the cooking time is up, cover the top with foil.

If you put a lot of bread into an oven at one time, the oven temperature will fall quite noticeably, so professional bakers use higher oven temperatures than home cooks need. The recommended initial heat is between 450°F (230°C) Gas 8 and 500°F (260°C) Gas 9 (plus). For home cooking the government's bakery research station suggests an initial 425°F (220°C) Gas 7. Unfortunately ovens are not all as accurate as they should be, and it may be a matter of trial and error to find the best results. You can tell when your bread is over or under-cooked and adjust the temperature accordingly.

## Baking times

Rolls: 10 to 15 minutes in a very hot oven.
14 oz to 1 lb (400 to 500 g) loaves: 30 to 35 minutes.
28 oz to 2 lb (850 g to 1 kg) loaves: 35 to 40 minutes.
Larger loaves: Up to 50 minutes—to enable heat to penetrate to the very centre and cook it. Lower the heat slightly so that the outside crust doesn't become too hard and burn.

## Steam in baking

(See page 303)
If you can introduce steam into the oven in the early stages, it helps even rising. It gives a good shape to oven bottom bread (as opposed to bread baked in tins). The steam also glazes the crust, because it first gelatinises the starch to sugar, and the heat of the oven seals it.

# Cooling

Put the baked bread on wire trays or racks out of the way of draughts to avoid too rapid cooling. If you put hot bread directly on to a surface, the bottom will go soggy. Rolls are for eating within the hour, but let white breads cool completely before trying to cut them. Wholemeal breads need longer to settle down. Rye breads should be cooled, then wrapped in cling film and not eaten for 24 hours. They keep moist and fresh for at least a week.

# Storing

Don't store bread until it is cooled. Keep white bread in tins. Many people like to keep wholemeal bread wrapped in a cloth on a kitchen shelf. Wrap rye bread in cling film. If you leave bread out it stales quickly because of gradual evaporation of moisture, as well as chemical changes. (Hence the big bakers' determination to get the bread to hold as much water as possible, to keep it "fresh" and give it shelf life in supermarkets.) The home baker with a ready and appreciative audience may not be concerned with its keeping qualities, and many of the marvellous breads in this book will be unlikely to hang around on shelves or in bread bins all week.

# Freezing

The freezer is a marvellous aid to baking. If there's any space in it, fill it up with bread. It keeps well for four to six weeks. Loaves thaw out at room temperature within two hours. Before your bread goes stale, put left-over pieces through a food processor, and store the breadcrumbs in the freezer.

Freeze a mixture of unrisen dough, if you need to, but add 50 per cent more yeast. Roll into a ball, seal in a polythene bag and label it To use, thaw it at room temperature, in its bag, loosely opened for up to six hours, when it will have risen nicely. Knock down, put in greased tins, and leave for half an hour more before baking. You can also freeze a dough after it has risen, whether it's the first, second or umpteenth time. Simply knock it back, roll into a ball, wrap in a polythene bag, and freeze. Tea-breads which are moist and sweet keep well for a very long time; and savoury breads, up to six months. Wrap in polythene bags first.

# Ingredients

This book is about breads which are tasty as well as healthy. Below we list the most common ingredients with notes on their health value.

## *Flours*

Wheat is the grain most used for baking bread; it gives the lightest, best-risen loaves. This is because it contains a substance called gluten which stretches, and so traps air bubbles during fermentation. Other grains have less gluten, or almost none at all. They make dense loaves, but people who use them prefer their marked taste to the blandness of bread made with plain white flour.

Wheat is milled to produce wholemeal flour or white flour.

### Wholemeal flour

Also known as 100% wholewheat flour. This is made from the whole wheat grain, including the outside skin—the bran, as well as the wheat germ, the berry's own tiny "seed". It can be bought stoneground or ground by steel roller mills.

### 85% and 81% Wholewheat flour

This is a wholemeal flour which has had 15 to 19% of the coarser bran extracted, to make it a lighter flour.

STONEGRINDING
This produces the best flavoured wholemeal: the bran, wheat germ, and endosperm (which contains the bulk of the flour) are crushed together.

STEEL ROLLER MILLING
The elements of the grain are separated and the bran and wheat germ are sieved away. This "offal" usually goes for animal feed. The wheat germ is flattened, not broken. For wholemeal flour, the separated elements are brought together again.

STORING STONEGROUND WHOLEMEAL FLOUR AT HOME
Use as soon as possible, and do not keep for more than two months. After that the oil in the wheat germ starts to go off, and gradually turns rancid. Store in a cool place. Stoneground flour keeps best refrigerated. Storing is not a problem if you mill your own wholemeal flour freshly at home from the whole grain, or buy small amounts regularly.

## FIG. 4: NUTRITIONAL CONTENT OF FLOURS PER 100g

| FLOURS | CALORIES | PROTEIN g | CARBOHYDRATE g | FAT g | FIBRE g | NOTES |
|---|---|---|---|---|---|---|
| BARLEY | 360 | 7.9 | 83.6 | 1.7 | 6.5 | |
| BRAN | 206 | 14.1 | 26.8 | 5.5 | 44.0 | |
| OATMEAL | 401 | 12.4 | 72.8 | 8.7 | 7.0 | |
| PLAIN WHITE | 350 | 9.8 | 80.1 | 1.2 | 3.4 | |
| RYE | 335 | 8.2 | 75.9 | 2.0 | 0.8 | |
| SOYA (FULL FAT) | 447 | 36.8 | 23.5 | 23.5 | 11.9 | |
| STRONG WHITE (72%) | 337 | 11.3 | 74.8 | 1.2 | 3.0 | |
| WHOLEMEAL (100%) | 318 | 13.2 | 65.8 | 2.0 | 9.6 | Allinson stoneground wholemeal flour has 12.00g/100g dietary fibre |
| 85% WHOLEWHEAT | 327 | 12.8 | 68.8 | 2.0 | 7.5 | |

Note: 100g=3½oz approximately
Table compiled from: Geigy Scientific Tables, Allinson, and McCance & Widdowson's *The Composition of Foods,* HMSO 1978

## FIG. 5: MINERAL CONTENT OF FLOURS PER 100g

| FLOURS | SODIUM (SALT) mg | POTASSIUM mg | CALCIUM mg | MAGNESIUM mg | PHOSPHORUS mg | IRON mg | COPPER mg | ZINC mg | SULPHUR mg | CHLORIDE mg |
|---|---|---|---|---|---|---|---|---|---|---|
| BARLEY | 3 | 120 | 10 | 20 | 210 | 0.7 | 0.12 | (2.0) | 110 | 110 |
| BRAN | 28 | 1160 | 110 | 520 | 1200 | 12.9 | 1.34 | 16.2 | 65 | 150 |
| OATMEAL | 33 | 370 | 55 | 110 | 380 | 4.1 | 0.23 | (3.0) | 160 | 73 |
| PLAIN WHITE | 2 | 140 | 150 | 20 | 110 | 2.4 | 0.17 | 0.7 | — | 45 |
| RYE | (1) | 410 | 32 | 92 | 360 | 2.7 | 0.42 | (2.8) | — | — |
| SOYA (Full Fat) | 1 | 1660 | 210 | 240 | 600 | 6.9 | — | — | — | — |
| STRONG WHITE (72%) | 3 | 130 | 140 | 36 | 130 | 2.2 | 0.22 | 0.9 | 110 | 62 |
| WHOLEMEAL (100%) | 3 | 360 | 35 | 140 | 340 | 4.0 | 0.40 | 3.0 | — | 38 |
| 85% WHOLEWHEAT | 4 | 280 | 150 | 110 | 270 | 3.6 | 0.35 | 2.4 | — | 45 |

Note: 100g=3½oz approximately. Figures in brackets are estimates; dashes indicate that no information is available.
Table compiled from McCance & Widdowson's *The Composition of Foods.*

## FIG. 6: VITAMIN CONTENT OF FLOURS PER 100g

| FLOURS | VIT A µg | THIAMIN mg | RIBOFLAVIN mg | NICOTINIC ACID mg | B6 mg | B12 µg | FOLIC ACID µg | PANTOTHENIC ACID mg | BIOTIN µg | VIT C mg | VIT D µg | VIT E mg |
|---|---|---|---|---|---|---|---|---|---|---|---|---|
| BARLEY | 0 | 0.12 | 0.05 | 2.5 | 0.22 | 0 | 20 | 0.5 | 0 | 0 | 0 | 0.2 |
| BRAN | 0 | 0.89 | 0.36 | 29.6 | 1.38 | 0 | 260 | 2.4 | 14 | 0 | 0 | 1.6 |
| OATMEAL | 0 | 0.50 | 0.10 | 1.0 | 0.12 | 0 | 60 | 1.0 | 20 | 0 | 0 | 0.8 |
| PLAIN WHITE | 0 | 0.33 | 0.02 | 2.0 | 0.15 | 0 | 22 | 0.3 | 1 | 0 | 0 | Tr |
| RYE | 0 | 0.40 | 0.22 | 1.0 | 0.35 | 0 | 78 | 1.0 | 6 | 0 | 0 | 0.8 |
| SOYA (Full Fat) | 0 | 0.75 | 0.31 | 2.0 | 0.57 | 0 | — | 1.8 | — | 0 | 0 | — |
| STRONG WHITE (72%) | 0 | 0.31 | 0.03 | 2.0 | 0.15 | 0 | 31 | 0.3 | 1 | 0 | 0 | Tr |
| WHOLEMEAL (100%) | 0 | 0.46 | 0.08 | 5.6 | 0.50 | 0 | 57 | 0.8 | 7 | 0 | 0 | 1.0 |
| 85% WHOLEWHEAT | 0 | 0.42 | 0.06 | 4.2 | (0.30) | 0 | 51 | (0.4) | (3) | | 0 | Tr |

Note: 100g=3½oz approximately. 0 means that this vitamin is not present; Tr means a trace is present; figures in parentheses are estimates; a dash indicates that no information is available.
Table compiled from McCance & Widdowson's *The Composition of Foods,* HMSO 1978.

## BAKING QUALITIES

Wholemeal flour does not rise as well as white flour; the bran content makes it heavy and moist. But it has more flavour and contains more nutrients than white flour, particularly all the B vitamins, Vitamin E, magnesium, potassium and iron. A well-balanced modern mixed diet should not be deficient in these nutrients but it is good that bread should provide them as it is everyone's basic food.

## White flour

White flour is made by sieving wholemeal flour. The percentage of white flour extracted from the sieving is called the extraction rate. White flour sold in High Street shops has an extraction rate of about 72 per cent.

Commercial white flour is made on roller mills. The bran and wheat germ are sifted out, and the flour is treated with a bleach to whiten it and mature it. Some nutrients are lost in this process, but the government requires 2 B vitamins (thiamin and nicotinic acid) and some iron to be returned.

### WHITE FLOUR MAY BE SOFT OR HARD

**Soft flour** from soft wheats has a low protein content and is ideal for making biscuits. But, in this country it is not considered suitable for making well-risen bread. (In France they do manage to make good breads using soft wheats.) Soft flour takes up less water and apparently because of this stales quickly.

**Hard flour,** from hard wheat, takes up more water and is better for bread you want to keep for more than a day. "Strong white flour" is milled from hard wheat.

## Unbleached white flour

This comes from the stoneground millers and consists of up to 80% extraction, which means that about 20% of bran and wheat germ have been removed by sieving. Unbleached white flour has some traces of finely crushed wheat germ in it, which adds to the flavour, but, like wholemeal flour, will go off after about two months. It has a pleasing creamy yellowish colour. White loaves made with it will resemble bread eaten on holiday in Spain, Italy and the Balkans, and the French *pain de compagne.*

Some millers and health food stores sell unbleached white flour. If you can't buy it you can make it yourself by sieving wholemeal flour, to remove about one-fifth of the coarser material.

## Brown flour (or wheatmeal)

The term wheatmeal is misleading, and must not be confused with wholemeal (wholewheat) flour, which includes the whole berry. Wheatmeal is really brown flour, or in fact white flour with a small quantity of finely milled bran returned to it. Any recipes which call for wheatmeal flour can be improved by substituting white flour and wholemeal. The government is phasing out the use of the word wheatmeal in the baking industry.

## Graham flour

An American wholemeal flour which is coarsely milled and contains larger bran fragments. It is named after Dr. Sylvester Graham, the food reformer, who was campaigning for wholemeal flour about a century ago. Not generally available in the U.K.

## Granary flour

A proprietary brand of flour which includes some bran, some malt flakes and cracked wheat. It makes a particularly nutty well-flavoured loaf and has sufficient gluten to make an attractive well-risen loaf.

## Self-raising flour

White flour to which some baking powder has been added. Not recommended : you have no way of telling how old the flour is. The efficiency of baking powder deteriorates with time. Instead of self-raising flour use plain flour with a baking powder which contains no aluminium salts.

## Rye flour or meal

This greyish-brown flour, has a rich, slightly sweet flavour. It is usually combined with differing proportions of wheat flour to make solid breads characteristic of Middle and Eastern Europe.

Rye contains less gluten than wheat and makes a dense, moist loaf. The more rye flour added, the stickier the bread. A loaf entirely made with rye, like pumpernickel, produces a bread of a dark pudding-like texture. A mixture of 50% rye and 50% unbleached white flour gives a good bread which slices thinly. The rye breads sold at bakeries, which are well risen, contain around 80% white flour and 20% or even less rye flour. They do not

usually have the special sour flavour which marks traditional rye bread.

Rye flour has very little gluten and so requires less rising time than wheat flour because the fermenting yeast meets less resistance.

Sourdough rye breads owe their flavour to lactic acid which is produced in the dough by the action of lacto-bacilli. You mix equal weights of rye flour and warm water, for example 1 lb (500 g) rye flour and 1 lb (450 ml) warm water, and leave covered in a warm place for two or three days. The mixture first of all attracts micro-organisms like lacto-bacilli in the air. At first the yeast starts the fermentation process and then the lacto-bacilli take over, producing lactic acid and giving the paste a pleasant sour smell, like apples. The lactic acid inhibits undesirable micro-organisms from turning the dough mouldy.

Use this paste as a starter, instead of yeast. After three days or longer, you can use it to make an ordinary dough by adding a 1 lb (500 g) of wheat flour and 8 fl. oz (250 ml) water. Any flour can be added; white or wholemeal or more rye, but it is always the rye flour which is soured and never the wheat.

Keep back one-fifth of each batch of dough to add to the next batch as a starter. In this way, each new mixture of rye and wheat flour includes one-fifth of its weight in soured dough.

### Barley flour (or meal)

Best combined with wheat flour, to give a slightly sweet and nutty flavour with a cake-like quality. Warm the dry flour before making the dough. Do not use barley flour on its own, it has a low gluten content, and doesn't rise.

### Pearl Barley

The whole grain which has been soaked in water to soften the tough husks. These are then rubbed off. It is usually used to thicken soups, but can be milled at home to make barley flour.

### Oats

The only grain which grows well in Scotland and forms the basis of their national dishes, porridge and oat cakes.

### Rolled Oats

The de-husked grains which have been flattened. They are sometimes used for porridge, and are added to wheat flour doughs to give texture and sweetness, and make the bread chewy.

### Oatmeal

The de-husked grain milled into a variety of textures, coarse, medium and fine. Real Scottish porridge is made with oatmeal rather than rolled oats. Use oatmeal in parkins and scones and oat cakes. Oatmeal adds texture to bread.

### Cornmeal or maize flour

Cornmeal is made from the roughly milled grain of maize (sweetcorn). It comes in various textures and can be added to bread to make it crunchy. Buy it from health food shops or as matzo meal from Jewish shops or delicatessens. (Not to be confused with cornflour which is used as a thickening agent.)

Cornmeal is the basis of many American Southern breads, such as spoon bread, so called because it is so soft you can eat it with a spoon. The Balkan bread, *mamaliga,* is made with yellow cornmeal.

### Buckwheat flour

Used in Eastern Europe to make yeast-risen *blinis,* small dark grey pancakes, the perfect accompaniment to caviar, smoked salmon and soured cream. An earthy and warm flavoured flour flecked with charcoal coloured specks. Makes good pancakes and scones too.

### Millet

Add a handful of millet grains to the dough to give a pleasant crunchiness of texture. In Roman times, wheat flour was combined with millet meal to make bread. In Britain we traditionally feed it to birds; but for people who live nearer the equator it is a staple grain and as important as wheat. Good sprinkled on breakfast cereals too.

### Wheat germ

The tiny seed of the wheat berry which is removed in milling to make white flour. It contains natural oils, is rich in essential fatty acids and Vitamin E. It can be bought fresh from wholefood stores and used to enrich dough mixtures. If you toast it first in a dry frying-pan, it enhances the nutty flavour and gives added character. Keep fresh in the refrigerator; it does not have a long life. Wheat germ which has been heat-treated is also available, but there is some loss of nutrients.

### Soya Flour
High in protein and used in baking to improve bread texture. A small proportion makes for a softer dough which structures well and takes up more water and air.

# Yeast

Yeast, barm, leaven, starter, ferment: all these words are bandied about in baking. They are much the same thing, and here are some definitions. If you want to know what function yeast has in baking, read on.

### Yeast
A micro-organism, one of the tiniest forms of life. The air is full of thousands of different kinds all around you. Give it warm, damp surroundings and starchy or sweet matter and it will start to breed. As it multiplies, it turns starches and sugars to alcohol, breathing out carbon dioxide bubbles. Home-brewers and wine-makers know it well, since they are after the alcohol. But bakers are interested in the bubbles. Put them into a dough, and you can double its size.

### Baker's yeast
Of all the hundreds of thousands of different yeasts, this one is called *saccharymosa cereviserae.* It was originally a by-product of brewing beer. Now it is cultivated commercially in laboratory conditions, and sold as fresh yeast, compressed yeast or dried yeast.

### Leaven (see page 298)
Anything which makes bread lighter, i.e. aerated, but usually referring to yeast.

### Starter
Anything which gets the dough to begin to rise, such as a leaven, barm, yeast or "mature" dough, known as sourdough.

### Barm (see page 298)
Any form of yeast starter. It can grow from anything starchy, particularly wheat, rye, and other grains, or potato. Yeast will also grow on root vegetables and fruits, as home wine-makers know.

### Ferment
Another name for a barm. It comes from the description of the activity of wild (or cultured) yeasts working on the sweetener to produce alcohol, and carbon dioxide gas.

### Batter (or sponge)
A mixture which is half flour and half liquid, to which yeast is added, and then left to ferment 8 to 12 hours. Enough flour is then added to make a firm dough.

# Bringing Yeast To Life

Yeast must be mixed with a warmed liquid to dissolve it, before adding it to the flour. It is vital that the liquid is not too hot. If it is hotter than 110°F (43°C) it begins to kill the yeast cells (see liquids). It is not essential to add a sweetener to the yeast starter. Some people do to "prove" that the yeast is working, before adding it to the flour. If the yeast is very stale it will not "prove".

### Kinds of yeast
There are two kinds of basic commercial yeast and there are those which you make yourself and keep at home, called barms and natural leavens.

### Fresh yeast
Also known as compressed yeast, and sometimes as German yeast (because they invented this process of compressing yeast) can be bought by the ounce from some bakers, some wholefood shops and a number of small grocers. Purists cannot explain why they prefer fresh yeast but it does guarantee freshness and good rising qualities.

### Storing fresh yeast
Keep fresh yeast in a small polythene bag fastened at the top, or a screw-top jar in the refrigerator for six to ten days. To store a large amount, freeze it: cut it into 1 oz (30 g) cubes and wrap each individually in foil, then place them all in a polythene bag and freeze in the deep-freeze or freezing compartment. It keeps for at least three months, and usually a lot longer. If yeast is not well wrapped it dries out very quickly; it forms a dark crust, smells unpleasant and loses its potency.

If you do not keep it in the refrigerator it goes off very quickly.

To bring it back to life after deep freezing, cover it with lukewarm, but not hot, water and allow 15 minutes for it to start working. Then proceed with the recipe.

### Dried yeast

This is fresh yeast which has been dried to exclude all moisture. It merely needs liquid added to it to bring it back to life. Some say that dried yeast gives a beery smell to the bread. Dried yeast is often more convenient and it is always worth keeping in the house for emergencies. It comes in packets or air-tight tins. Once opened, it is important to make sure the tin is carefully sealed again.

To bring dried yeast to life, use water slightly hotter than for fresh yeast. Instructions on packets of yeast often suggest adding quite a lot of sugar to the starter mixture. This is unnecessary: we suggest adding a very small quantity of honey (see sweeteners).

### Barms

These are the yeast mixtures that were used by bakers centuries before modern compressed yeast was invented. If you don't want the inconvenience of buying fresh yeast every week, try making your own barm. It can be made of wheat flour or rye flour or a mixture of flours.

Use a jam jar or a stone jar with a loose-fitting lid. Dissolve 1 oz (30 g) of fresh yeast in 2 fl. oz (60 ml) warm water and fill the jar two-thirds full with equal quantities of lightly sieved wholemeal flour and water. Stir well and leave in the refrigerator for at least eight hours. Stir each day.

To make your dough, use three-quarters of the liquid in the jar and top up the jar again with equal quantities of flour and water for the next batch. Barms are not as fast or effective as commercial yeasts and need longer rising times.

If a recipe suggests 1 oz (30 g) fresh yeast, use at least 4 oz (125 g) barm.

The old-fashioned bakers stood their barms in large wooden barrels and returned any unused dough to them, which would disintegrate and thicken the mixture.

### Natural leavens

Natural leavens are also yeasts. But whereas the other mixtures are made from a commercial product, the natural leaven depends on attracting wild yeasts which are in the air. To make a leaven use about two tablespoons of freshly milled grain, usually wheat or rye. (It is easy to crush in a coffee blender.) Put the meal into a cup or small basin, pour on enough boiling water to cover. Stir well. The boiling water turns the starches in the grain into "sugar"; you will see it gelatanise (thicken like a jelly as in porridge). Then add a little warm water, until the mixture becomes a runny paste. Cover with a cloth and keep in a warm place until bubbly—three to five days. With any luck, the right kind of yeasts will be drawn to it, and start their activity.

Stir two or three times each day, and after three days and not more than five days, you should find the mixture is bubbly. It is then ready for use. Store in a loose-lidded jar in the fridge and use as for the barm above.

Traditionally, to inhibit unwanted bacteria in the air, some essence of hops was added: you can make this by gently boiling a tablespoon of dried hops in half a pint (300 ml) of water for half an hour and straining the liquid, before adding it to the leaven. The result is, of course slightly bitter. (You can get dried hops from any chemist's or store selling wine or beer-making kits).

In a natural leaven, you encourage a sour taste to develop. This is due to bacteria in the air called lacto-bacilli. At first the yeasts are active in the grain paste and then the bacteria become dominant, and produce a slightly acid taste, which gives natural leaven breads their characteristic flavour.

## *Liquids*

### Water

The usual medium for mixing flour. Flour varies in absorbency according to its age and the conditions in which it is kept. Wholemeal flour absorbs much more water than white flour, and some white flours which may have had a lot of calcium added may use a much smaller amount of water. The general rule for a dough is two parts flour to one part water, by weight. Some bakers prefer to use soft water rather than hard water for their bread. Use either rainwater or put a water purifier on your tap—and insure yourself against lead poisoning at the same time.

When mixing a dough, don't add all the water at once as you may not need it. If you have added too much, it doesn't matter—just add more flour until you get the texture right.

To get the dough off to a rolling start have the water at a temperature of 104°F (40°C). Measure it with a thermometer the first few times and you will soon get used to the right heat. Although hot you should be able to hold your hand in it for more than 10 seconds. An easy formula: use half boiling water and half cold water.

If the water is very cold the dough mixture will take a long time to start rising. If the water is too hot the dough will rise very fast, and indeed it is possible to kill the yeast cells completely.

## Milk

Milk improves the texture and flavour of white breads, adds to their keeping quality, and enriches the bread with extra protein and calcium. It's usual to boil (scald) milk and let it cool to room temperature before adding it to the dough. This kills bacteria; the yeast doesn't want any competition. If you use all milk, you have a milk loaf, but even a small quantity can make white breads tastier. Milk added to wholemeal bread can help replace the calcium which is "bound" by phytic acid in the bran.

## Buttermilk

Not buttery milk as it sounds, but a by-product of making butter. It tastes like pleasantly sour milk, which is exactly what it is. Buttermilk, and sour milk, are ideal for soda breads, which are made without yeast, but use bicarbonate of soda. The bicarbonate of soda which is alkali combines with lactic acid in buttermilk to produce the gas which aerates the dough.

## Sour milk

Used as buttermilk and in scone mixtures.

## Yoghurt

Can be thinned with water and used as buttermilk or sour milk.

## Beer, fruit juice, tea

Beer, fruit juice and tea are liquids too. Try them in your breads. Many people enjoy their special flavours.

# Salt

Excellent bread is made the world over from no other ingredients than flour, water, yeast and salt. Salt gives bread added flavour. But salt is also considered a factor in causing hypertension, which leads to hardening of the arteries and kidney failure, and is associated with stomach cancers. There is also a considerable amount of evidence that salt can cause fluid retention and even migraines in susceptible individuals. In the West people are taking between 3 and 30g of salt per day, when the body's needs are as low as 0.5g. This can be obtained without adding salt to any food.

Everyone likes a different amount of salt in their bread. Those who prefer to use less salt can cut down on the suggested amounts or leave it out altogether. Sometimes herbs and spices can be used instead of salt. Eliminating salt completely is difficult for many people but after an initial period foods—even bread—acquire new subtle flavours.

Bread with no salt at all has been considered tasteless and unacceptable to many people in this country, although in Italy, for example, little or no salt is the norm.

Salt has an inhibiting effect on yeast and in long rising doughs stops the fermentation from galloping away. On shorter-rising doughs you can use a minimal amount. It not only slows down the fermentation process, but can actually kill yeast, which is another good reason for not adding too much.

Never add salt to the yeast starter mixture and don't let salt come into direct contact with yeast, because the action of the salt draws out moisture from the yeast.

The recipes in this book, unless otherwise specified, use ordinary iodised table salt. If you have sea salt in crystals or flakes, you may like to substitute this: make sure that you do not exceed the right amount.

Table salt is usually sprinkled into the flour. Sea salt should be dissolved in the liquid before adding to the flour mixture.

# Sweeteners

It is common practice, though not essential, to add a sweetener to the starter mixture, because this gets the yeast working quickly. If you add too much, the yeast works too fast and can kill itself in its own gases.

The sweetener which is added to the starter is consumed by the yeast and gives little or no sweetening effect to the dough. Many authorities prefer to add the sweetener straight into the mix. The addition of a sweetener makes the dough rise more quickly.

Sugar is not used in these recipes. The excess of sugar in modern diets contributes to obesity, cardiovascular disease, diabetes and tooth decay. Where a sweetener is needed, honey is added; it has a similar effect, but you use less of it. Honey makes the dough softer and slacker, and, depending on the quality of the flour, it may be necessary to add a little more flour.

### Molasses or Black Treacle

This unrefined sweet syrup is a by-product of refining sugar cane and contains many good nutrients. The bitter, burnt taste adds character to rye breads in particular and loaves will be darker and more moist. Too much makes a loaf dense and spoils it. Treacles also accelerate the action of the yeast.

# Oils and Fats

Oils and fats are mixed with a dough to enrich it and to give a softer, finer crumb. They give bread a longer life, as they help the bread to resist staling.

Also used to grease baking tins and ceramic ware to prevent breads sticking to them in the oven.

The recipes in this book generally use natural animal fat such as butter or polyunsaturated vegetable oils. Hydrogenated fats such as margarine are not recommended because hydrogenation is a chemical process which changes unsaturated fats (liquid) to saturated fats (solid). Saturated fats have been shown to increase cholesterol levels, but unsaturated and polyunsaturated fats not only supply essential fatty acids but they may also actually lower cholesterol levels.

### Vegetable Oils

Safflower, corn and sunflower oil, are the lightest and best to use in home baking. Olive oil can be used but it imparts its own distinctive flavour and is heavier. Groundnut or soya oils are also heavy.

Oils may go off: store in a dry place away from heat and sun.

### Butter

A strong textured butter which doesn't cream too easily is needed for yeasted pastries like croissants and Danish pastries to hold the very thin sheets of bread dough apart. Butter gives a delicate flavour to breads. It is always used in a brioche.

### Margarine and lard

Margarine is not used in our recipes, although many homes use it because it is inexpensive. Lard is a hard saturated animal fat, and sometimes gives a greasy off flavour which is noticeable in the crust. We only use it for very traditional recipes such as Lardy Cake.

### Malt

A distinctive sweetener made from malting barley grain. Bakers use it in dried form, and the proprietary flour, *Granary,* includes flaked malted barley. You can more easily get malt in liquid form (from chemists). It adds a special flavour to bread, especially sweet breads. Yeast works on it very quickly, so be ready for shorter rising times.

# Glazes and Finishes

You can get a pretty finish to a loaf with a glaze: but just as unglazed pottery has its own beautiful colours and textures, a loaf can be as pleasing without a glaze. One of the nicest effects is the farmhouse loaf: the surface prodded with a fork, and then dusted with flour. The result is somehow cosy and reassuring.

Here are some of the glazes you can use. Hardware stores sell pastry brushes with nylon hairs but it's better to buy a good small house painter's brush about ¾ to 1 inch across and keep it for this purpose.

### Cream or milk

Glazing a loaf with cream or milk gives it a nice light yellow finish.

### Beaten whole egg

Brush on an egg beaten with 1 tablespoon of water just before baking to get a rich golden glow. But with long baking times and high oven setting it will blacken. If this is likely, brush loaves 10 minutes before taking them from the oven. It gives a superb burnished finish to a plaited loaf.

### Beaten egg yolk
This gives a darker, shiny glaze. Beat the yolk with a tablespoon of cold water. Good for rich white breads.

### Beaten egg white
This gives a crisp, polished light crust. Suitable for light rolls.

### Salt water
Half an ounce (15 g) salt to 8 tablespoons water gives a hard, dry pale crust; very crisp.

### Cornflour glaze
For a very hard finish, and polish. Dissolve 1 teaspoon of cornflour in a little cold water, then heat in a saucepan with 5 fl. oz (150 ml) water, stirring till it thickens. Leave to cool. Brush the loaf 10 minutes before baking time is up: it soaks into the surface and dries rock hard.

### Melted butter
Not exactly a glaze but if you brush the finished loaf, roll, bap or bun with melted butter, it leaves the surface soft and pliant, with a light colour and lovely texture. Suits sweetish breads.

### Oil
Oil, like melted butter, gives a soft finish and imparts its own flavour.

### Syrup
Gives a sticky bun result. Dissolve 1 oz (30 g) honey in 5 fl. oz (150 ml) water, and bring to boil. Use when cool. Brush on to dark rich spicy buns or fruit and malt loaves or rye bread 5 minutes before they leave the oven. If a sweet glaze is baked too long it will burn.

### Experimental Glazes
Invent your own. This one is from America, and makes a surprising finish, hard, crackly, shiny, mottled and streaked with colour. Make the mixture 10 minutes before putting your loaf into the oven. Dissolve ½ oz (15 g) fresh yeast and 1 teaspoon of

honey with 2 tablespoons of warm water; when it froths stir in 2 tablespoons of cornflour and 1 teaspoon of sunflower oil. Stir well and brush on loaf just before baking.

## Seeds and Garnishes

For centuries man has added every kind of seed from flowers and grasses to add interest, flavour and texture to his breads. The most enduring are:

### Poppy seed
Purple or white poppy seeds, crunchy and smoky, sprinkled on top of a glaze give a professional finish. Characteristic of Jewish and Middle European breads.

### Sesame seed
An oily white seed which toasts in the heat of the oven and gives an aromatic and chewy finish to the crust. Very popular on Middle East breads.

### Caraway seed
A searingly pungent seed which adds piquancy and bite to Polish and European breads, particularly sourdough breads. Also said to kill unwanted bacteria.

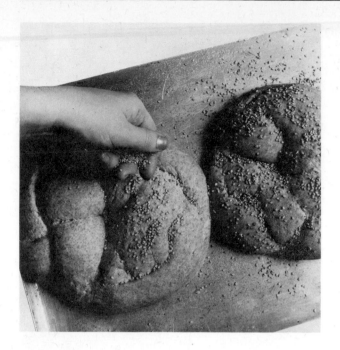

### Cumin seed
Cumin seed adds a haunting and mysterious scent and flavour to bread, and echoes the Middle East and India.

### Sunflower seed
A rich, ripe, crunchy and oily seed which can be added sparingly to a dough, especially a fruit bread. Can be sprinkled on top of the bread for a crude, rough finish.

### Celery seed
Sprinkle on savoury breads to give a spicy and slightly hot and bitter flavour.

### Cracked wheat and kibbled wheat
Sprinkle the loaf with the rough crushed grain to get a hard nutty, crisp shell to the loaf.

### Aniseed
Highly aromatic and pungent seeds to sprinkle on the top of breads; an echo of ouzo and Mediterranean holidays.

# Equipment

To start with you can manage perfectly well with utensils which you already have in the kitchen. You need:

1. The largest mixing bowl in the house, but you could use a plastic bowl or a large saucepan.
2. Scales to weigh the flour and yeast.
3. Measuring jug to measure liquids. If you haven't got a measuring jug; as a rough and ready measurement, the amount of liquid you add is usually half the weight of the flour, so you can weigh the liquid with your scales. (Wholemeal flour needs a little more than half its weight in liquid.)
4. Cup or soup bowl in which to dissolve the yeast.
5. A teaspoon for mixing the yeast.
6. A wooden spoon. This is best for mixing the flour and liquid, but any spoon will do, or you can use your hands.
7. A small saucepan: you may need this to warm liquids and melt fat, if used.
8. An uncluttered flat surface on to which you can turn out and knead the dough. Any work-surface or table top will do, but allow for the fact that flour likes to spread itself around. (As soon as you start mixing the dough, both hands will be sticky. You'll have flour on your sleeves and your elbows, and this is usually the moment the telephone rings or someone turns up at the front door. It is now too late to remind you that you should have rolled up your sleeves, put on an apron and taken the phone off the hook.
9. Baking sheet, bread tin, ceramic mould or even a flowerpot. If you don't have bread tins, it doesn't matter—you can make moulded, free-standing breads which are known as oven-bottom loaves. Stand them directly onto the greased baking sheet. An oven-bottom loaf gives you a good crust with plenty of flavour: bread in tins rises better and gives a better crumb inside.
10. Wire rack: There should be somewhere in the kitchen where you can stand loaves to cool after they've been baked. The air must circulate round them or the bottom becomes moist from generating its own steam.

That's all you need, but it will help if you have a clean tea towel or two, and oven gloves; either you're going to turn over very hot loaves quickly or take bread out of hot containers.

Below are some extras you might want once you've decided to be serious about this bread-baking business:

1. A kitchen thermometer: this is usually bought for jam-making, but can measure the critical temperature of the liquids in bread-making.

2. A plastic scraper: some doughs are very sticky, especially those with egg and sweet ingredients. A plastic scraper will help gather the dough and keep your hands free of some of the mess. It is also useful for cleaning up bowls and work-surfaces.

3. A pastry brush: a special pastry brush or a painter's brush ½ in (1.5 cm) across; useful for brushing on the egg wash glazes.

4. Food processer with dough hook: this cuts down the kneading time but denies you the satisfaction of handling the dough.

5. Special tins: you can buy all kinds of bread tins from specialist kitchen stores, but look out for old tins in second-hand shops. Conventional tins make 1 lb (500 g) and 2 lb (1 kg) loaves. Jordan's, the millers, sell ceramic pots which make good round loaves. You can use a clean new flowerpot or a well-washed one in the same way, but they need to be proved, ie, rubbed with oil or butter and baked empty two or three times, otherwise the bread will stick.

6. Tiles: large ceramic tiles can be placed on the middle grid of the oven to give loaves an extra boost of initial heat when you put them in to bake. You can bake rolls or free-form loaves directly on to tiles without using a baking sheet. The hot tiles need to be quickly dusted with a little cornmeal before you put the loaves on to them.

7. Plant spray: It is impossible to recreate in the home the effect of commercial ovens with steam sprays. But if you want to give a good crusty finish to rolls and French bread, you can introduce steam by spraying water from a plant spray into the oven immediately the loaves go in, again five minutes later, and then another five minutes later. Open and close the oven door very quickly to lose as little heat as possible.

8. Bricks: rather more complicated way of creating steam to make crusty bread and requiring confident dexterity. For the brick-in-the-tin method, you need an oven tin, about twice the size of a builder's brick. Place a brick on a high shelf in the oven while it is being pre-heated for baking. Before you put your bread in, put the tin half-filled with boiling water in the bottom of the oven. Carefully lower the red-hot brick into it, using fire tongs and wearing oven gloves. Be prepared for an explosion of steam and a tremendous hissing and bubbling. Without losing your nerve, slip the bread on a shelf and bang the oven door shut. Remove the pan with the brick after 15 minutes. Before attempting this manoeuvre with a red-hot brick and boiling water, practise with a cold brick and a tin of cold water. Great care should be taken with this manoeuvre to avoid burning yourself directly or with the steam.

# Where to Buy Good Flour

## Guide to British Mills

The label stoneground on a bag of flour can never be taken as an automatic guarantee that it will make good bread, but it is a guarantee that it has been ground slowly and that the grain is whole, with all its natural nutrients. The process by which most of today's commercial flour is made is not kind to wheat: modern high-speed roller mills overheat the grain and knock it flat, so that bran and wheat germ alike can be sifted out. Wheat germ is an enemy of modern millers, for it contains oil, and oil in time goes rancid. When you buy stoneground flour, the wheat germ is still there, broken up with the rest of the grain. For this reason it is important to buy the flour very fresh, and use it as soon as possible.

The vital factor in flour is the choice and blend of grain made by the miller, or his supplier. As Elizabeth David said in a letter to *The Sunday Times,* "Poor quality grain ultimately makes poor bread, whatever the method of milling, and the grain available varies season to season and year to year. When people find that their favourite brand of flour suddenly gives an erratic performance they usually either blame it on themselves, or on some imaginary defect in the yeast. It's more likely to be something to do with the flour. So it's always worth trying some from another mill."

The following mills are some of the many supplying stoneground wholemeal flour. Some also do a wheat flour of between 80 and 90% extraction with the coarsest bran removed, but with the wheat germ intact. You can often buy flour at the mills.

Many of the mills in our list have been saved from total dereliction by enthusiasts, and are well worth a visit just to see the old machinery working. The mills are listed by county.

AVON
**Bath**
Priston Mill, Priston, near Bath, Avon. Tel.
Bath (0225) 23894. *Owner:* Mr. J.R. Hopwood,
who runs the mill as an integral part of his
farming business.

Priston Mill is a watermill. It produces stoneground wholemeal flour and 81% wholewheat
flour.

It was first mentioned in the Domesday Book.
In AD 931, King Athelston passed the mill and
surrounding property to the monks of Bath Abbey.
The current 21 foot diameter pitchback water-
wheel was installed in 1850.

The flour is made from English spring wheat.
You can buy the flour from the mill at wholesale
prices in 25 kg (55.1 lb) sacks and at retail prices
in 1½ kg (3.3 lb) bags. It is also sold to local
bakeries, grocers and wholefood shops.

Open to the public from Easter to the end of
October from 2.15—5.00 pm, Tuesday to Friday,
and from 11.00 am—12.45 pm and 2.15—5.00 pm,
Saturdays, Sundays and on Bank holidays. Small
entrance fee. Coach parties, guided tours and farm
visits available, by appointment.


BEDFORDSHIRE
**Biggleswade**
Holme Mills, Biggleswade, Bedfordshire. Tel.
Biggleswade (0767) 312001. *Owner:* W. Jordan
& Sons.

Wheat and barley have been milled at Holme
Mills, on the River Ivel, for nearly 900 years. It
was first mentioned in the Domesday Book when,
together with its sister mill, it was valued at the
princely sum of 47 shillings as part of the estate
of a Ralph de Lisle. The mill remained in the hands
of the great landowners until 1611 when it was
bought by Edward Ferrers and Francis Philips,
two independent millers.

The Jordan family first took it over more than
200 years later when Holme Mills was one of 400
mills in Bedfordshire: today it is the sole remaining privately owned mill in the county.

William Jordan modernised the mill in 1896 and
replaced the old millstone with roller mills. Its
main source of power is the water-wheel and a
five foot fall of river water.

Holme Mills is one of the country's biggest suppliers of wholemeal flour to bakers, supermarkets

and wholefood shops. It mills 120 tons a week.
The flour includes 50 per cent imported Manitoba
whole grain wheat for strength, with 50 per cent
British spring wheat from local growers and the
Earl of Bradford's organic farms in Shropshire.
Jordan's also sell 85% wholewheat flour, and
strong white flour.

The mill is open by appointment on Wednesday
evenings after 5.00 pm.


BUCKINGHAMSHIRE
**Aylesbury**
Springhill Farm Mill, The Gatehouse Close,
Aylesbury, Bucks. Tel. Aylesbury (0296) 25333.
*Owners:* Springhill Rural Enterprises Ltd.
comprising Hugh Coates and family.

The bakery and mill have been operating since
1976, and the mill is an electric stoneground mill
which produces between four and five hundred
tons per annum. Flour is sold to visitors in small
quantities, but wheat is available to customers.

All the flour sold is wholemeal organic flour,
£6.50 for 55 lb. Wheat is £6.00 for 55 lb (1981
prices). They are supplied by their own farms in
the Vale of Aylesbury (they have three) and also
by organic farmers and growers.

The mill is not normally open to visitors, but
applications in writing can be made to The Country
Trust, Denham Hill Farm, Quainton, Aylesbury,
Bucks. which organises visits on the mill's behalf.


CAMBRIDGESHIRE
**Over**
The Mill, Over, Cambridgeshire CB4 5PP. Tel.
Swavesey (0954) 30742. *Owner:* G.C. Wilson, who

bought the mill derelict in 1960 and restored it to working order.

The mill buys wheat from local farmers or grain merchants. It is a windmill and produces stone-ground wholemeal flour and flour of 75% extraction which is sold mainly from the mill. Grain can be milled to order for individual customers.

The mill is open to visitors by appointment only. Customers are welcome at any time, but should telephone first to check on the availability of flour in stock.

### Soham

DOWNFIELD WINDMILL, Fordham Road, Soham, Cambridgeshire. Tel. Leicester (0533) 707625.
*Owner:* Nigel Moon.

The mill was originally built as a smock mill in 1720, but it was rebuilt 150 years later as a tower mill, after it had been extensively damaged in a gale. It is now fully restored and has been in production again since April 1980.

The flour is milled from locally grown wheat. They produce wholemeal flour, with added gluten if required. It is on sale on most Sundays, when the mill opens from 2.00—6.00 pm. There is a small admission fee. The mill always opens on the first Sunday of each month from April to December, and on Bank Holiday Mondays.

### CLWYD
**Colwyn Bay**

FELIN ISAF MILL, Llansanffraid, Glan Conway, Colwyn Bay, Clwyd LL28 5TE, Wales. Tel. Glan Conway (049 268) 646. It has been owned by Mostyn Estate Ltd. since 1856. The proprietors are Felin Isaf Millers.

Felin Isaf Mill is a watermill, producing stone-ground flour. It sells 200 tons of flour per annum to private customers and grocers. Its range of flour includes wholemeal, 85% wholewheat, plain and self-raising, and bran, and it will mill to a customer's requirements. It uses wheat grown by local farmers.

The mill has been in existence since 1680 and was in production until 1942. A tenant then lived in the mill for several years. The Estate decided to restore it in 1978 and it was reconditioned with the help of a job creation scheme. It subsequently won a commendation in the RICS/Times Award Scheme and Civic Trust Award Scheme.

Visitors and parties are welcome to the mill, and guide facilities are available. It is open from

April to October, Tuesday to Saturday, from 10.30 am—5.00 pm, and on Sunday from 2.30—5.00 pm. From November to April, it opens Monday to Friday, 10.30 am—5.00 pm. The entrance fee is 50p for adults, and 25p for children (1981).

Special produce made with stoneground flour from the mill is sold in the shop and refreshments are available. A museum of agricultural history and the development of the mill is also to be seen. Talks can be arranged for parties and societies.

## Pentrefoelas

FOELAS WATERMILL, Pentrefoelas, Clwyd, Wales. Tel. Pentrefoelas (069 05) 603. *Owner:* Foelas Estates, Bangor. Proprietor: Mrs. Margaret Horsfield, who has run the mill since 1950.

This watermill has a large water-wheel providing power for the millstones to grind the flour. It may be the only mill with a woman miller, who dresses the millstones. It is believed to be 250—300 years old. The millstones are original, 4 feet across and capable of grinding 2½ hundredweights an hour, but production is variable. There is also a bakery, which is actually a converted schoolhouse, where you can buy bread made with the mill's flour.

The mill uses wheat from organic farms, and produces stoneground wholemeal flour, as well as barley flour and rye meal. The flour is mainly sold to wholefood shops.

The mill is open to visitors, Monday to Friday.

## CUMBRIA
### Milnthorpe

HERON CORN MILL, Heron Corn Mill-Beetham Trust, c/o Henry Cooke Ltd., Waterhouse Mills, Milnthorpe, Cumbria. Tel. Carnforth (0524) 734858. Heron Corn Mill-Beetham Trust is a Charitable Trust owned by Henry Cooke Ltd., a subsidiary of the industrial group, J. Bibby & Sons Ltd.

This is a watermill, dating from about 1220. The mill is not commercially operated and is only used for demonstrations, so the flour sold is bought in. They sell 3 tons of stoneground wholemeal flour per annum to visitors to the mill and local customers.

The mill is open to the public from 1 April to the end of September, Tuesdays to Sundays, from 11.00 am—12.15 pm and 2.00—5.00 pm. It closes all day Monday.

### Penrith

THE WATERMILL, Little Salkeld, Penrith, Cumbria CA10 1NN. Tel. Langwathby (076 881) 523. *Owners:* Nicolas and Ana Jones, who restored the mill to working order six years ago.

This is a watermill producing stoneground flour. It dates from about 1750 although there has been a mill on the site for 500 years.

Using British wheat which has been organically grown, the mill produces 200 tons of stoneground flour per annum. It sells to bakeries, wholefood shops, grocers, supermarkets and through their own shop. A carrier service can be arranged. Wholemeal, rye flour and 85% wholewheat flour is for sale.

The mill is open to visitors from Easter to October on Wednesdays, Thursdays and Sundays from 2.30—5.30 pm.

### Ravenglass

MUNCASTER MILL, Ravenglass, Cumbria CA18 1ST. Tel. Ravenglass (065 77) 232. *Owners:* Ravenglass & Eskdale Railway Co. Ltd., who lease the mill to the Eskdale (Cumbria) Trust. The mill is served by the famous Ravenglass and Eskdale miniature railway.

This is a watermill with an overshot wheel which drives 3 pairs of stones.

The earliest record of the mill is in 1455, when it was leased to Thomas Senhouse at £3 per annum. It served the local manor of Muncaster. The present building dates from the eighteenth century and was renovated during 1977 and 1978.

Wheat is supplied by Organic Farmers and Growers Ltd., Suffolk. The mill produces 20 tons of stoneground flour per annum: coarse and fine wholemeal flour, unbleached white flour, semolina, bran and cracked wheat.

The mill is open daily (except on Saturdays) in April, May and September (11.00 am—5.00 pm) and June, July and August (10.00 am—6.00 pm). Visits at all other times of the year should be by appointment. Flour is available all the year round.

DEVON
**Ilfracombe**
THE OLD CORN MILL, Hele Bay, Ilfracombe, North Devon. Tel. Ifracombe (0271) 63162.
*Owners:* Mr. and Mrs. C.L. Lovell, who restored the mill and opened it in 1978. It was built in 1525.

This is a watermill producing four grades of stoneground wholemeal flour (fine, medium, coarse and granary), wheatflakes and kibbled wheat from

locally grown English wheat. It is open to visitors from Easter to the end of September, Monday to Friday 10.00 am—5.00 pm and Sunday 2.00—500 pm.

The wholemeal flour produced here is available in many shops in Devon, Cornwall and Somerset.

DORSET
**Shaftesbury**
CANN MILLS, Shaftesbury, Dorset SP7 OBL. Tel. Shaftesbury (0747) 2475. Has been owned for 32 years by Norman R. Stoate.

There is a watermill and a windmill and horizontal millstones are used for milling the flour.

The mill was referred to in the Domesday Book as one of the mills in Cann. It was burnt down in 1954 but rebuilt in 1954/5. The overshot waterwheel is over 100 years old and still in good repair.

This mill produces hundreds of tons of flour per annum, which it sells mainly to wholefood shops and retail customers calling at the mill, but also to bakers and health food shops. The wholesale price for 70 lb is £6.50. The retail price for 70 lb is £7.00, for 28 lb, £3.00 and for 14 lb, £1.55 (1981 prices).

The wheat used comes from Hampshire, Dorset and Wiltshire, and is hard, high protein English grain. The mill produces stoneground wholemeal flour, 81% wholewheat flour and rye flour, organic when possible.

Cann Mills is not open to the general public, but is open to schools (by appointment). It is open to customers, of course.

DYFED
**Carmarthen**
THE MILL, White Mill, Carmarthen, Dyfed, Wales. Tel. Nantgaredig (025 788) 209.
*Owner:* Mrs. Frances Marjorie Lickley. The village takes its name from the mill after it was whitewashed many years ago.

This is a watermill, using French burrstones. Nowadays it is powered by diesel.

The exact volume of business is unknown although about 100 tons of wheat are milled each year. Wholemeal flour and 81% wholewheat flour are produced and sold to bakeries and private customers.

The mill is open to the public for business from 9.00 am—1.00 pm and 2.00—5.30 pm every day.

**Newcastle Emlyn**
FELIN GERI MILL, Cwm Cou, Newcastle Emlyn, Dyfed, Wales. Tel. Newcastle Emlyn (0239) 710810. *Owners:* Michael Heycock and Duncan Fitzwilliams.

The mill was bought in 1974 and restored in 1975. The current building dates back to 1604 and is believed to be on the site of a much earlier mill.

This watermill produces stoneground flour from British-grown high protein grain. Ten tons of stoneground wholemeal flour are produced in one week, making an output of over 4,000 sacks per

annum. They also produce unbleached white flour, semolina and bran. The mill supplies to bakeries and wholefood shops throughout Wales and also sells direct to customers.

The mill is open to visitors from Easter to October, 10.00 am—5.00 pm, seven days a week. It has its own bakery and the bread is sold to visitors. There is a café on the site, and also a water-powered nineteenth-century sawmill.

## ESSEX
### Chelmsford

CHELMER MILLS, W. & H. Marriage & Sons Ltd., New Street, Chelmsford, Essex. Tel. Chelmsford (0245) 354455. Owned by six Marriage directors.

It is a roller milling plant dating from 1899, with modern additions using French burr traditional horizontal millstones. The firm was founded in 1824, and produces 10,000 tons per annum. The mill sells to craftsman bakers and wholefood shops.

Wheat is bought from local Essex farmers and hard wheat is imported from Canada. They sell stoneground wholemeal, self-raising wholemeal, plain and self-raising 81% wholewheat, strong white, plain and self-raising, and wheat germ.

The mill is open to parties of visitors once a month, and details are available from the mill.

## GLOUCESTERSHIRE
### Dursley

COALEY MILL, Coaley, Dursley, Gloucestershire GL11 5DS. Tel. Cambridge (Glos.) (045 389) 376. *Owners:* Osman Michael Goring and family.

The mill dates from about 1700 although records of a mill there in the thirteenth century do exist. Osman Michael Goring and family bought it in 1962 and spent ten years restoring it, completely rebuilding it, including new foundations. They started operating it again in 1978 as a watermill with modern hydro-electric power, and it is now a full-time concern.

The mill now produces 2,000 sacks of flour per annum and this amount is increasing. It has a potential capacity of 10,000 sacks per annum or 24 tons a week.

They use their own home-grown wheat or local wheat bought from neighbouring farms, adding some Canadian wheat to improve the quality. Their

stoneground wholemeal flour is sold to private and trade customers, in large or small quantities.

The mill is open to visitors during working hours, but you should telephone first to confirm. You will find the mill four miles from the Slimbridge Wildfowl Trust, just off the A38.

## HAMPSHIRE
### Bordon

HEADLEY MILL, Bordon, Hampshire. Tel. Bordon (042 03) 2031/2. *Owner:* J. Ellis & Sons (Bordon) Ltd. The mill has been in the family since 1914.

Headley Mill is a watermill with a breast-shot wheel and four pairs of millstones.

The first record of a mill on the site was around AD 978 when it was owned by the King of Wessex, Earl Godwin. William the Conqueror acquired it in 1066 and gave it to Count Eustace III of Boulogne as spoils of war. It passed in turn to Matilda (Maud) of Boulogne and then to Stephen de Bois, who later married Matilda and became King Stephen. It did not remain long in the hands of the king, who exchanged it with the Bishop of Winchester for the Manor of Morden in Surrey. The mill remained in the hands of the church until 1899.

The wheat used is home-grown on the Headley Mill farm or purchased locally. The flour produced is wholemeal or 81% wholewheat. It is distributed to local shops and to health food shops within a 25 mile radius, but most is sold at the mill. It can be bought during normal shopping hours, except that the mill closes at 12.30 pm on Saturdays.

The mill can usually be viewed on Sunday afternoons in August, 2.00—5.00 pm. Tours for parties can be arranged throughout the year, by appointment. There is a small admission charge. The mill is situated in an area of historical interest and you can also visit Jane Austen's house at Alton and The Gilbert White Museum at Selborne.

### Southampton

BOTLEY MILLS, Botley Flour Milling Company Ltd., Botley, Southampton, Hants. Tel. Botley (048 92) 2202. Has been owned by the Appleby family since 1928.

There is a watermill in which a water turbine is used to drive the millstones that produce the stoneground wholemeal flour. There is also an electrically driven roller mill.

The Domesday Book of 1087 tells us that there were "2 mills worth 20 shillings" in Botley. This is the first record of any mills at Botley, and nothing more is known until 1307 when St. Elizabeth's College, Winchester, took possession, and monks may have operated the mill.

In 1536, Thomas Wriothesly, Earl of Southampton and later the Duke of Portland, owned the mill, and it was kept in the family until 1775. It is on record that in 1536, a Thomas Everad rented the mill consisting of "2 mills under one roof with stream for £15 per year". In 1770, or thereabouts, the present main building was built, together with the house, bolting mill, stables and hogsties.

The mill is now capable of producing about 10,000 tons of flour per annum, using various percentages of English wheat (soft) and Canadian wheat (hard). In addition to stoneground wholemeal flour it makes a very wide range of flour on the roller mill. These include 85 and 92% wholewheat, and white flours ranging from very soft to very strong. Besides delivering to bakers, pie manufacturers and caterers over a very wide area, the mill will deliver 12 kg (26½ lb) or 32 kg (70 lb) packs to the housewife or small user on a C.O.D. basis, within a radius of about 30 miles.

Mill visits by organised parties have been suspended temporarily, because of a serious fire in the animal feed mill, but it is hoped to recommence this facility in 1983.

## HEREFORD & WORCESTERSHIRE
### Bromsgrove

DANZEY GREEN WINDMILL at Avoncroft Museum of Buildings, Stoke Heath, near Bromsgrove, Hereford & Worcestershire. Tel. Bromsgrove (0527) 31886 and 31363.

Avoncroft Museum is an open-air museum of historic buildings. The windmill was originally built at Danzey Green in Warwickshire in about 1825. It was left to decay towards the end of the nineteenth century. In 1969, it was dismantled and rebuilt at Avoncroft where it was set to work again in 1976. It is the only working windmill in the West Midlands region.

This is a post windmill driving French burrstones. Wheat from local farmers is milled to produce up to 200 sacks (25 tons) of stoneground wholemeal flour each year. This is sold to visitors

at the museum: 1.6 lb costs 33p, 3.3 lb—55p, 28 lb—£3.50, 56 lb—£6.50 and 112 lb—£12.00 (1981 prices). The museum is open daily from March to November, 10.30 am—5.30 pm. Flour can be bought from the museum office in the winter. Visitors are very welcome and there is always a guide to show them round the mill.

### Tenbury

NEWNHAM MILL, Newnham Bridge, near Tenbury, Hereford & Worcestershire. Tel. Newnham Bridge (058 479) 445. *Owner:* Dr. R. Lear, the ownership having passed into his hands from the Newnham Estate in 1972.

It has an undershot 14-foot water-wheel which drives 3 pairs of 4-foot French burrstones.

The mill dates from around 1700. An iron water-wheel was installed in 1837. Restoration work at the mill began in 1976. They are still only using one of the three pairs of stones, but it is hoped that the situation will improve shortly.

Wheat is bought from a local corn factor. The mill produces half a ton of stoneground wholemeal flour each week, which it sells to bakers, wholefood shops, grocers and private customers. Price varies according to quantity.

The mill is open to the public from Easter to

September: Saturdays, afternoons only; Sundays and Bank holidays, mornings and afternoons. Flour is for sale at the mill all the year round. Telephone in advance to make sure that someone is at the mill.

## HUMBERSIDE
### Driffield
SOUTHBURN MILL, Southburn Farm, Driffield, North Humberside YO25 9ED. Tel. Driffield (0377) 89264. *Owner:* John Sykes Rymer, who runs it as part of his farming business.

Wheat is grown on the farm. It is milled with stones made of hard Derbyshire grit-stone. There are two mills producing 20 tons of wholemeal flour per annum which is sold to wholefood shops within a 30 mile radius.

The mill is open to visitors by appointment only, and on special days when the mills are operated by the farm steam engine.

## ISLE OF WIGHT
### Newbridge
LOWER CALBOURNE MILL, Newbridge, near Yarmouth, Isle of Wight PO41 OTZ. Tel. Calbourne (098 378) 228. *Owner:* John Robin Pretty, who bought the mill in 1967 and restored it to use in 1973. He now runs a company based on the mill, called Millers Damsel Enterprises Ltd.

Lower Calbourne Mill is a watermill operated by a water turbine, with an oil engine to supplement power when necessary.

The mill was mentioned in the Domesday Book. It thrived during the Napoleonic Wars when troops were based on the Isle of Wight. Most of the machinery, including the turbine, was installed after a fire in the mid-1890s destroyed some buildings. The Bake House adjoining the mill has a wood-fired brick oven, fuelled by faggots from the local forest, believed to be the only one of its kind left in England. Another unique feature is the dough mixer, operated by water power. It is hoped to restore the brewery that used to operate at the mill one day.

The mill buys wheat from the local farmers' co-operative. It produces 150 tons of stoneground wholemeal flour per annum (the equivalent of 1,200 sacks), which is sold to bakeries and wholefood shops. The flour costs 48p for a 1½ kg (3.3 lb)

bag, and £7.50 for a 32 kg (70 lb) bag ex mill (1981 prices). The mill's own bakery uses the flour to produce bread and a range of speciality biscuits, for sale on the island. It is hoped to extend the sale of these products to the mainland.

The mill is open to visitors by prior arrangement only. Soon guided tours for 6 to 8 people, with refreshments, should be available. The mill house can be let as holiday accommodation at certain times of the year. The Upper Mill, a mile away (tel. Calbourne (098 378) 227) is open to the public from Easter to October, and although it is not in operation, it is still of interest and sells the Lower Mill's flour and bread.

## KENT
### Ashford
SWANTON MILL, Mersham, Ashford, Kent. Tel. Aldington (023 372) 223 or 01-937 0931. *Owner:* Mrs. G. Christiansen, who restored it after it had been left derelict.

The present mill stands on the site recorded in the Domesday Book. It is part sixteenth century, with seventeenth and nineteenth century additions.

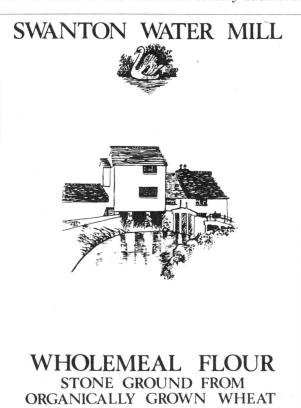

Swanton Mill is a watermill, producing wholemeal flour from organically grown wheat. The wheat is home-grown. The flour is sold to health food outlets, the local village shop and visitors.

The mill is open to visitors from April to October at week-ends from 3.00—6.00 pm. Visitors can watch the mill working, visit an exhibition of milling, and enjoy the large garden, water garden and nature reserve.

## LINCOLNSHIRE
### Alford
ALFORD FIVE SAILED MILL, East Street, Alford, Lincolnshire. *Owned by* Lincolnshire County Council, County Offices, Lincoln.

As you might guess from the name, this is a windmill. It was built in 1813 by the millwright Sam Oxley. It produces stoneground wholemeal flour which is sold to a few local customers and to visitors. Price varies according to quantity, but is about 12p per lb (1981 price).

The mill is open to the public on Bank holidays, and on the third Saturday of the month during July, August and September. The mill is operated on open days, weather conditions permitting. Visits by school parties can be arranged. All enquiries should be made to: Mr. C.F.L. Banks, "Four Winds", North Cliff Road, Kirton Lindsey, Gainsborough, Lincs. DN21 4NH. Tel. Kirton Lindsey (0652) 648382. Please enclose SAE for leaflet and information.

## MERSEYSIDE
### Liverpool
SOUTH END MILLS, Liverpool, Merseyside. Tel. Liverpool (051) 7091836. *Owner:* Wilson King Ltd.

The mill is run by an independent flour milling company and produces white flour. The company has built another mill in Warrington, Lancs., to respond to the growing demand for wholemeal bread and flour: it's called Cobbett's after William Cobbett who said in 1818: "We were a nation famed throughout the world for the plenty and solid quantity of our food."

*Cobbett's* wholemeal flour is available in 32 kg (70 lb) bags from South End Mills. It can be bought in 1.5 kg (3.3 lb) bags from health food shops in Merseyside, Lancashire, Greater Manchester, Cheshire and Derbyshire.

## NORFOLK
### East Dereham
THE "HOFELS" MILL, Borrow Hall Farm, Dumpling Green, East Dereham, Norfolk. Tel. Coney Weston (035 921) 441. *Owners:* Mr. and Mrs. David Backhouse of Coney Weston Hall, Bury St. Edmunds, Suffolk. Borrow Hall is the birthplace of George Borrow, the eminent author, whose books include *Lavengro* and *Romany Rye*.

A plate mill in stainless steel, but with grooves like a stone burr, is mainly used. There is also a hammer mill, which mills at a very low heat. *Hofels* flour is made from home-grown wheat only and is organic wholemeal. They sell to wholefood and health food shops and to department stores.

The mill and farm are open, by appointment, all the year round. The owners feel that it is important to show people how wheat is grown and milled.

The family also runs a 50-year-old wholefood company, *Hofels Pure Foods* of Woolpit, Suffolk. Details of their organically grown produce and recipes can be obtained free if you send a 9 in by 4 in SAE to the owners.

## NOTTINGHAMSHIRE
### Retford
NORTH LEVERTON WINDMILL, North Leverton, Retford, Nottinghamshire DN22 OBA. Tel. Gainsborough (0427) 880662. *Owned by* the North Leverton Windmill Company, and shareholders.

*NORTH LEVERTON WINDMILL*
*WHOLE MEAL FLOUR*
*1½ lb.*

*PIMHILL*
*STONEGROUND ORGANICALLY GROWN WHOLEWHEAT FLOUR*
*S. Mayall & Son*
*LEA HALL*
*HARMER HILL*
*SHREWSBURY*
*SHROPSHIRE*

Company secretary, R. Gray Esq. (Tel. Gainsborough 880200).

This windmill dates from 1813, when it was known as the Subscription Mill, because it was built by the village and the committee was elected from shareholders or subscribers.

Locally grown wheat is now stoneground at the mill and wholemeal flour, cracked wheat and bran are sold to visitors to the mill. The mill is also used for grinding up animal feed for local farmers, mainly during the winter months.

The mill is open to visitors whenever it is working and often on Saturdays from 10.00 am — 5.00 pm and Sundays 2.00 — 5.00 pm. It is opened by "The Friends of the Windmill" on Bank holidays. Schools and other parties are welcome. Apply to Mr. Gray at the telephone number above or write c/o The Farm, North Leverton, Retford, Notts.

SHROPSHIRE
**Shrewsbury**
PIMHILL MILL, Lea Hall, Harmer Hill, Shrewsbury, Shropshire SY4 3DY. Tel. Bomere Heath (0939) 290342. *Owner:* S. Mayall & Son.

It is now run by Mr. R. Mayall and his daughter.

The mill stonegrinds local home-grown wheat from Shropshire and Staffordshire, with additional organic wheat from elsewhere in the country if necessary. It produces 500 tons of flour per annum and 50 tons of oat products.

Sales are made to bakeries, wholefood shops and restaurants. A range of flour is sold, including wholemeal (plain and self-raising); 85% wholewheat (plain and self-raising); and rye. Various wheat and oat products are also available. All the products can be bought in small or bulk sizes.

The mill is open to customers Monday to Friday, 8.00 am — 5.00 pm. You should make an appointment if you want to see how the mill works.

## SOMERSET
### Crewkerne

CLAPTON MILL, Lockyer & Son, Crewkerne, Somerset TA18 8PX. Tel. Crewkerne (0460) 73124. *Owner:* Mr. C.G. Lockyer. The mill has been in his family for four generations.

Four mills are mentioned at Crewkerne in the Domesday Book and one of them may have been the original Clapton Mill. The first owners included Walter Le Dispenser, Baldwin de Clopton, Avice de la Barre and Walter Boce.

Clapton Mill is a watermill, producing stoneground wholemeal and 80% wholewheat flour which is sold to bakeries, wholefood shops and local customers.

The mill is open to visitors by special arrangement only.

## SUFFOLK
### Walsham-le-Willows

WALSHAM MILL, Wattisfield Road, Walsham-le-Willows, near Bury St. Edmunds, Suffolk. Tel. Walsham-le-Willows (035 98) 679. *Owners:* Walsham Mills Ltd. The mill was bought in 1975 by Michael Cooper (the managing director and majority shareholder) who runs it with three other directors.

Walsham Mill is a stoneground electric mill. There has been a mill on the site since 1577, but the old windmill is now used as offices. The modern mill dates from 1949 and 1954.

The mill produces about 320 sacks (40 tons) a week, which is sold to bakeries, health food shops, grocery shops, supermarkets and restaurants. Wheat, including some organic wheat, is bought locally in East Anglia. Their own flour is stoneground wholemeal flour, but they also sell other flours produced by a different miller, as well as wheat flakes and porridge oats. Flour prices vary,

for example, 3.3 lb is 50p, a 70.5 lb sack is £7.00 (1981 prices).

The mill is open to visitors by arrangement. Apply, in writing, to Michael Cooper.

## SUSSEX
### Bognor Regis

ELBRIDGE ORGANIC FARM MILL, Chichester Road, near Bognor Regis, West Sussex. Tel. Bognor Regis (0243) 822914. *Owner:* Geoffrey Alan Cobham.

Wheat is grown organically on the farm. It is stoneground in the electrically-powered mill which uses vertical stones. The mill produces 950 tons of stoneground wholemeal flour per annum, which is sold to bakeries, wholefood shops and in the farm shop.

Visitors are welcome, but large parties should

ELBRIDGE ORGANIC FARM

The soil must live if it is to produce healthy living food; that is why we are taking great care of it at Elbridge. No straw is burnt, most of it is used by the dairy herd and the remainder is chopped up and spread on the fields at harvest time where the soil soon absorbs it.

The five year pasture leys further enrich the land making chemical fertilizers unnecessary. Instead, our 130 Ayrshires provide the manure.

Our stone-ground flour from this land makes healthy bread of fine flavour.

Come and see us at work!

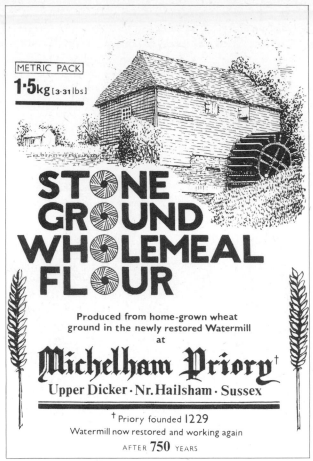

arrrange their visit with Mr. Boxall (telephone number as above). In addition to organic wholemeal flour, visitors can buy home-reared beef, free-range eggs (in the summer), and vegetables, when in season, from the farm shop.

### Hailsham
MICHELHAM PRIORY MILL, Upper Dicker, near Hailsham, East Sussex. Tel. Hailsham (0323) 844224. *Owners:* Sussex Archaeological Society, to whom the entire property including the mill was donated in 1960.

The mill is water-driven and uses French burr-stones. The first record of the mill dates back to 1434 when the Prior of Michelham paid 10 shillings to Battle Abbey for water for his mill. A drawing of the mill by a local carpenter exists, dated 1667.

Using local wheat from the adjacent farm, the mill produces 15 tons of stoneground, wholemeal flour per annum, the equivalent of 120 sacks. The mill is in operation from Easter to mid-October.

Visitors are welcome on any day from Good Friday to the third Sunday in October. Opening hours are 11.00 am—1.00 pm and 2.00—5.30 pm, and there is a small admission charge. Milling takes place on Wednesday afternoons and one or two other times during the week, depending on stock, and water availability. A shop in the grounds sells the wholemeal flour produced in the mill and booklets and other literature about watermills. There is also a museum which exhibits old mill tools and other articles connected with milling.

### Horsham
KINGS MILL, Shipley, Horsham, West Sussex. *Owner:* Mr. Philip Jebb, 1 Upper Butts, Brentford, Middlesex.

Kings Mill is a windmill (a smock mill), that was built in 1879 and owned by the writer Hilaire Belloc from 1904 to 1952. It is now owned by his grandson. It is not used commercially.

You can visit from May to October, when it is open for the first week-end in each month, from

2.30—5.30 pm. Arrangements can be made for private parties by writing to Mrs. A.E. Crowther, 13 Church Close, Shipley, Horsham, West Sussex.

## WARWICKSHIRE
**Alcester**
GREAT ALNE MILLS, Great Alne, near Alcester, Warwickshire. Tel. Great Alne (078 981) 341. *Owners:* Mr. and Mrs. O.J. Gray and Sons.

The mill dates from around AD 806 and has been in constant use, apart from a break from 1967 to 1978 when it was restored by the present owners. It is the only remaining mill in working order of 14 mills on the River Alne.

This is a watermill with a turbine driving two pairs of stones, producing 100 tons of flour in its first year of trading, 1979. The flour is milled traditionally from a mixture of local and imported wheat. They produce organic wholemeal flour which is sold to bakers, health food shops and individual customers.

The mill is open to visitors from April to October at week-ends and on Bank holidays, from 2.00—5.00 pm. Visitors can buy tea, with bread and cakes made from the flour produced at the mill, between 3.00 and 5.30 pm.

# DOVES FARM
## NATURAL FOODS

## WILTSHIRE
**Marlborough**
DOVES FARM MILL, Doves Farm, Ham, Marlborough, Wiltshire SN8 3QR. Tel. Inkpen (04884) 374. *Owners:* Michael and Clare Marriage, who started the mill in 1978 in an old tythe barn.

Grain is grown on the farm, and the methods of cultivation meet with the approval of The Soil Association Organic Standards Committee.

They produce many kinds of flour including organic, stoneground wholemeal and rye flour in the electrically powered mill, selling 600 tons each year to wholefood shops and bakeries.

The mill is not open to visitors.

**Marlborough**
WILTON MILL, c/o Midden Hollow, Wilton, Marlborough, Wiltshire. Tel. Marlborough (0672) 870268. *Owners:* Wiltshire County Council, who bought it derelict in 1971 and restored it.

The windmill produces 5,000 lb stoneground wholemeal flour every year, from wheat supplied by a local farmer. This flour is sold to visitors to the mill at about 55p per 1.5 kg or 3.3 lb (1981 prices).

You can visit from Easter Sunday to the last Sunday in September on Sundays and Bank holidays from 2.00—5.00 pm. Visiting at other times is by special arrangement only. Volunteer millers and guides are welcome.

## NORTH YORKSHIRE
### Skipton
HIGH CORN MILLS, George Leatt Industrial and Folk Museum, Skipton, North Yorkshire. Tel. Skipton (0756) 2883. *Owned by* George Leatt since 1964.

There are records of a mill on the site in the twelfth century when tithes were paid. It was owned for many years by the Skipton Castle Estate, dating back to the early Normans and then by other families subsequently.

This mill is a watermill producing stoneground flour from English grain. It produces a rough-

milled wholemeal and a granary flour, which it sells to bakers and to visitors.

Visitors are welcome at the mill which is open most days around midday, except for a period in winter. The mill and museum are usually open on Bank holidays, but you should check first. Parties can visit by arrangement. Write with full details and SAE to the owners. The admission fee is 20p for adults and 10p for children (1981 prices). Parties cannot be accepted before 2.00 pm and after 7.00 pm.

## SOUTH YORKSHIRE
### Barnsley
WORSBROUGH MILL MUSEUM, Worsbrough, Barnsley, South Yorkshire. Tel. Barnsley (0226) 203961. *Owners:* South Yorkshire County Council.

A watermill and a power mill operate on this site and both use millstones. The watermill dates from the early seventeenth century although there are records of a mill at Worsbrough from 1086. The engine-driven mill was built alongside the watermill in about 1843. It was formerly steam-driven and is now powered by a 1911 hot-bulb oil engine.

They use cleaned and blended wheat which is bought commercially. In 1981, 4 tons of wheat were milled into wholemeal flour and sold in the Mill Museum Shop in 1 kg (2¼ lb) cloth bags, at 40p per kg (1981 prices).

Worsbrough Mill Museum is open every week throughout the year from Wednesday to Sunday from 10.00 am—6.00 pm or dusk, whichever is earlier. Special events and exhibitions about milling, agriculture and local history are held at certain times each year and the museum has a growing reference collection of books and artefacts about the history and development of corn milling.

WEST YORKSHIRE
**Castleford**
ALLINSON QUEENS MILLS, Queens Mills, Aire Street, Castleford, West Yorkshire WF10 1JW. Tel. Castleford (0977) 556277. *Owners:* Booker Health Foods Ltd. who bought the mill from Allinson in 1970.

This mill has a large output—160,000 sacks of stoneground flour per annum, the equivalent of 20,000 tons. Both imported and home-grown wheat is used. They sell stoneground flour only, mainly wholemeal but also some 81% wholewheat at £8.55 per 32 kg (70 lb), 58p per 1.5 kg (3.3 lb) (1981 prices). This flour is sold to bakeries, grocers, wholesalers, health food shops and supermarkets.

The mill is open to individuals only. It is the biggest mill in the world milling stoneground flour.

**Thorner**
THORNER MILL, Elm Tree House, Main Street, Thorner, Leeds, W. Yorkshire LS14 3DX. Tel. Leeds (0532) 892629. *Owners:* Edwin Vero England and Andrew Timothy England, a father and son partnership.

Wheat is bought from the Organic Farmers and Growers Ltd., Suffolk, and milled into stoneground wholemeal flour. A small amount of rye is also milled. They produce 2 to 3 tons of flour each week which they sell to bakeries and wholefood shops.

The mill is open to the public only by special arrangement.

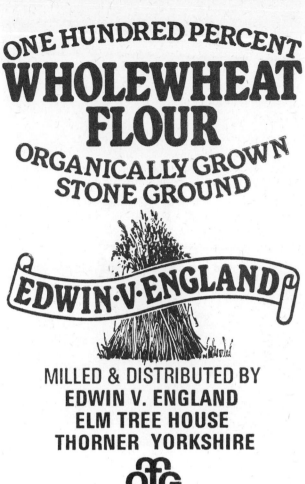

ONE HUNDRED PERCENT WHOLEWHEAT FLOUR ORGANICALLY GROWN STONE GROUND

EDWIN·V·ENGLAND

MILLED & DISTRIBUTED BY
EDWIN V. ENGLAND
ELM TREE HOUSE
THORNER YORKSHIRE

OFG

THE SYMBOL ON THE FRONT OF THIS BAG
IS THE ORGANIC FARMERS & GROWERS, MARK OF QUALITY
IT IS GENUINELY 100% WHOLE WHEAT
WITH NO ADDITIVES OR EXTRACTION.

# Retail Outlets Selling Wholemeal Flour

Wholemeal flour and flour of between 80 and 90% extraction can be bought in shops all over the country. In our survey, we discovered major supermarkets who supplied it as well as smaller shops. Here is a list of the supermarkets stocking this flour at the time of printing, followed by a list of the shops in one of the country's biggest health food chains, Holland & Barrett, and finally a directory, divided into counties, of other shops where you should be able to find good flour for making bread. Millers supplying these outlets are printed in italic.

## SUPERMARKETS

Asda—sells wholemeal and 85% wholewheat flour.

Bishops—sells wholemeal and 85-90% wholewheat flour.

Booth's—sells wholemeal flour.

Budgens—sells wholemeal and 81% wholewheat flour.

Fine Fare—sells wholemeal and 85-90% wholewheat flour.

International—sells wholemeal and 85% wholewheat flour.

Presto—sells wholemeal and 85% wholewheat flour.

Safeways—sells wholemeal and 85-90% wholewheat flour.

Sainsbury's—sells wholemeal flour.

Tesco—sells wholemeal flour.

Waitrose—sells wholemeal and 85-90% wholewheat flour.

Woolworth (and Woolco)—sell wholemeal and 85% wholewheat flour.

## HOLLAND & BARRETT

Here is a list of Holland & Barrett shops which sell wholemeal flour and 81 and 85% wholewheat flour (at the time of our survey). Our list is arranged according to town or, in the case of London, by street or region.

Amersham, 100 Sycamore Rd., Bucks.
Baker Street, 78 Baker St., London W1.
Basildon, Unit 8A, Eastgate, Essex.
Basingstoke, 15 Wote St., Hants.
Bath, 6 Cheap St., Avon.
Bedford, 10 Horne Lane, Harpur Centre, Beds.
Bingley, 6 Myrtle Walk, W. Yorks.
Birmingham, 20 The Priory Queensway, W. Midlands.
Bishop's Stortford, 12A South St., Herts.
Blackburn, 28 Lords Square, Lancs.
Bloomsbury, Unit 36, Brunswick Shopping Centre, London WC1.
Bootle, 10 The Palatine, New Strand Shopping Centre, Merseyside.
Bournemouth, 19 Criterion Arcade, Dorset.
Brent Cross, Unit W16, Brent Cross Shopping Centre, London N4.
Brentwood, 5 High St., Essex.
Brighton, Churchill Square, Western Rd., E. Sussex.
Bristol, 19 Broadweir, Avon.
Bromley, 56 High St., Kent.
Burgess Hill, 71 Church Rd., W. Sussex.
Bury, 14 Union Arcade, Lancs.
Camberley, 19 Grace Reynolds Walk, Surrey.
Camden, 86 High St., London NW1.
Cardiff, 11 High St., S. Glamorgan.
Catford, 33 Winslade Way, London SE6.
Chelmsford, 3 Exchange Way, Essex.
Chichester, 13 East St., W. Sussex.
Chiswick, 416 High Rd., London W4.
Coventry, 6 City Arcade, W. Midlands.
Coventry, 75 Corporation St., Warks.
Crawley, 3 Parkside, W. Sussex.
Crewe, 64 Market St., Cheshire.
Croydon, 100 High St., Surrey.
Croydon, 1088 The Mall, Whitgift Centre, Surrey.
Derby, 8 St. Peter's Way, Derbyshire.
Doncaster, Unit 23, Arndale Centre, S. Yorks.
Dorking, 185 High St., Surrey.
Dudley, 6/8 Fountain Arcade, W. Midlands.
Ealing, 6 Ealing Broadway, London W5.
Eastcote, 151 Field End Rd., Middx.
Edgware, 14 The Promenade, Middx.
Edmonton Green, 7 North Mall, London N9.
Epsom, 12 King Shade Walk, Surrey.
Fareham, 92 West St., Hants.
Farnham, 5A West St., Surrey.
Fulham, 220 Fulham Rd., London SW10.
Gloucester, 52 Kings Walk, Kings Square, Glos.
Golders Green, 81 Golders Green, London NW11.
Goodge Street, 19 Goodge St., London W1.
Gosport, 113A Stoke Rd., Hants.
Grimsby, 88 Victoria St., Humberside.
Guildford, Unit 3, Friary Centre, Surrey.
Hammersmith, 1-5 Kings Mall, London W6.
Harborne, 99A High St., Birmingham, W. Midlands.
Harlow, 12A Terminus St., Essex.
Harrogate, 1A James St., N. Yorks.
Harrow, 22/24 College Rd., Middx.
Hartlepool, 125 Middleton Grange Shopping Centre, Cleveland.
Hemel Hempstead, 16 Bridge St., Herts.
Hereford, 24 Eign Gate, Hereford & Worcs.
High Wycombe, 6 The Arcade, Octagon Precinct, Bucks.
Hitchin, 94 Hermitage Rd., Herts.
Holloway Road, 452 Holloway Rd., London N7.
Horsham, 23 Freshwater Parade, W. Sussex.
Hove, 31 George St., E. Sussex.
Huddersfield, 95 New St., W. Yorks.
Hull (Jefferson Health Food Stores), 62 Bond St., Humberside.
Ilford, 3 Centre Way, High Rd., Essex.
Ipswich, 14 Dial Lane, Suffolk.
Ipswich, 24 Westgate St., Suffolk.
Kenilworth, 44 The Square, Warks.
Kensington Church Street. 139 Kensington Church St., London W8.

Kensington High Street, Barkers, 63 Kensington High St., London W8.

Kensington High Street, 260 Kensington High St., London W8.

Kettering, 54 Gold St., Northants.

Kidderminster, 8 King Charles Square, The Swan Centre, Hereford & Worcs.

King's Heath, 33 Alcester Rd. South, Birmingham, W. Midlands.

King's Lynn, 13 St. Dominic Square, Norfolk.

Kingston, 4 Fife Rd., Surrey.

Leamington Spa, 55 Warwick St., Warks.

Leeds, 11 Arndale Centre Crossgates, W. Yorks.

Leeds, Bond St. Centre, W. Yorks.

Leicester, 33 Horsefair St., Leics.

Liverpool, c/o Owen Owen Ltd., Clayton Square, Merseyside.

Liverpool, 17 Whitechapel, Merseyside.

Loughton, 285 High Rd., Essex.

Luton, 53 Wellington St., Beds.

Maidenhead, 122 High St., Berks.

Manchester, Unit 122, Market Way/Upper Mall Arndale Centre, Greater Manchester.

Marble Arch, 62 Edgware Rd., London W2.

Middleton, Unit F10, Arndale Centre, Manchester, Greater Manchester.

Milton Keynes, 26 Midsummer Arcade Central, Milton Keynes Shopping Area, Bucks.

Muswell Hill, 121 Muswell Hill Rd., London N10.

Newcastle-on-Tyne, 11 Bigg Market, Tyne & Wear.

Northampton, 4 Peacock Way, Northants.

Northfield, 22 Grosvenor Shopping Centre, Birmingham 31, W. Midlands.

Oxford, 3 King Edward St., Oxon.

Oxford Street, Unit C12, West One Centre, London W1.

Palmer's Green, 332 Green Lane, London N13.

Pimlico, 10 Warwick Way, London SW1.

Poole, 14 Kingsland Crescent, Dorset.

Portsmouth, 126 London Rd., Hants.

Purley, 2 Brighton Rd., Surrey.

Putney, 28 High St., London SW15.

Redditch, 13 Royal Square, Hereford & Worcs.

Reigate, 68 High St., Surrey.

Richmond, 46 George St., Surrey.

Romford, 21 Laurie Walk, Essex.

Rotherham, 9 Eastwood Lane, S. Yorks.

Ruislip, 22 High St., Middx.

St. Albans, 13 French Row, Herts.

St. John's Wood, 55 St. John's Wood High St., London NW7.

Shepherd's Bush, 122 Shepherd's Bush Centre, London W12.

Shrewsbury, 3 The Square, Shrops.

Slough, 269 High St., Berks.

Solihull, 14 Drury Lane, W. Midlands.

Southampton, c/o Owen Owen Ltd., 173 High St., Hants.

Southampton, 176 Portswood Rd., Hants.

Southampton, 4 Pound Tree Rd., Hants.

Southport, Unit 12, Station Arcade, Merseyside.

Southsea, 63 Osbourne Rd., Hants.

Stafford, 12 St. Mary's Gate, Staffs.

Staines, Unit 29, Elmsleigh Centre, Surrey.

Stevenage, 19A Town Square, Herts.

Stourbridge, 59 High St., W. Midlands.

Stratford, 19 Rother St., Warks.

Streatham, 110 High Rd., London SW16.

Sunderland, 39 Blandford St., W. Midlands.

Sutton, 213 High St., Surrey.

Sutton Coldfield, 20 Birmingham Rd., W. Midlands.

Swiss Cottage, 14 Northways Parade, London NW3.

Temple, 17 Temple Fortune Parade, London NW11.

Tunbridge Wells, 5 Monson Rd., Kent.

Twickenham, 25 Heath Rd., Middx.

Urmston, 30 Moorfield Walk, Manchester, Greater Manchester.

Uxbridge, 5 Pantile Walk, Middx.

Wallasey, 9 Townfield Way, Merseyside.

Walsall, 4 Park St. Arcade, W. Midlands.

Walton, 23 The Centre, Surrey.

Wandsworth, 5 The Arndale Centre, London SW18.

Watford, 2 Clarendon Rd., Herts.

Welwyn Garden City, 36 Fretherne Rd., Herts.

Wembley, Unit 21, Central Square, High Rd., Middx.

West Bromwich, 43 The Mall, 3 Sandwell Shopping Centre, W. Midlands.

Wimbledon, 68 The Broadway, London SW19.

Winchester, 13 The Square, Hants.

Windsor, 29 St. Leonards Rd., Berks.

Woking, 11 Church Path, Surrey.

Wolverhampton, 13 Queens Arcade, Mander Centre, W. Midlands.

Worcester, 22 Mealcheapen St., Hereford & Worcs.

# RETAIL OUTLETS

## AVON

### Avonmouth

**Nurdin & Peacock (Cash & Carry) Ltd.**, Avonmouth Way. *Priston Mill.*

### Bath

**Bartletts & Sons (Butchers)**, Green St. *Priston Mill.*

**The Butter Pat**, 18 Upper Borough Walls. *Priston Mill.*

**Dillons Bakery**, Oldfield Park. Tel. Bath (0225) 25927. *Priston Mill.*

**Harvest**, 37 Walcot St. *Cann Mills.*

**Harvest Natural Foods**, Widcombe Hill. *Pimhill Mill.*

**Health Foods**, 6 Green St. *Pimhill Mill.*

**Homebake**, 3 Chelsea Rd. Tel. Bath (0225) 21702. *Priston Mill.*

**St. Kildas Bakery**, St. Kildas Rd., Oldfield Park. Tel. Bath (0225) 21900. *Priston Mill.*

### Bristol

**Bushells**, St. Nicholas Market. Tel. Bristol (0272) 615820. *Pimhill Mill.*

**Carrefour Delicatessen**, Patchway. *The "Hofels" Mill.*

**Foda**, 224 Cheltenham Rd. *Cann Mills.*

**Foda**, Sandy Park Rd. *Cann Mills.*

**Gateway Foodmarket Ltd.**, Cater Rd., Bishopsworth. Tel. Bristol (0272) 640500. *Priston Mill.*

**Grainstore**, 78-82 Bedminster Parade, Bedminster. *Cann Mills.*

**Grainstore**, 73 North St., Bedminster. *Cann Mills.*

**Grainstore**, 6 Cotham Hill, Cotham. *Cann Mills.*

**Grainstore**, 109 Regent St., Kingswood. *Cann Mills.*

**Grainstore**, 13 Broadwalk, Knowle. *Cann Mills*

**Grainstore**, 25 North View, Westbury Park. *Cann Mills.*

**Moores Health Foods**, 308 Lodge Causeway, Fishponds. *Pimhill Mill.*

**The Salad Kitchen Ltd.**, 18 Park Row. Tel. Bristol (0272) 24539. *Priston Mill.*

**Stoneground**, The Mall, Clifton. *Cann Mills.*

### Chew Magna

**Amors Stores.** *Priston Mill.*

Chipping Sodbury
**Mister Snodgrass,** 29 High St. Tel. Chipping Sodbury (0454) 313621. *Priston Mill.*

Farmborough
**A. Maisey & Son, The Bakery.** *Priston Mill.*

Keynsham
**Peter the Baker,** 8 Charlton Rd. Tel. Keynsham (027 56) 5740. *Priston Mill.*

Saltford
**The Cake Shop.** *Priston Mill.*

## BEDFORDSHIRE
Dunstable
**Ms. Penny,** 131 High St. *W. & H. Marriage & Sons.*

Luton
**Europa Delicatessen,** 166 Dunstable Rd. *W. & H. Marriage & Sons.*

## BUCKINGHAMSHIRE
Great Missenden
**Wheatsheaf,** 59C High St. Tel. Great Missenden (02406) 2655. *Pimhill Mill.*

## CAMBRIDGESHIRE
Cambridge
**Health Food Stores,** 3 Rose Crescent. *W. & H. Marriage & Sons.*

## CHESHIRE
Chester
**Granary Wholefoods,** 108 Northgate St. Tel. Chester (0244) 318553. *Pimhill Mill.*

Northwich
**The Happy Nut House,** 20 Market Way. *South End Mills.*

Warrington
**G. Dominik,** Unit 67, New Market. Tel. Warrington (0925) 32283. *Thorner Mill.*
The Happy Nut House, 69 Bridge St. *South End Mills.*

## CLEVELAND
Middlesbrough
**Impulse Wholefoods,** 47 Roman Rd., Linthorpe. Tel. Middlesbrough (0642) 826561. *Thorner Mill.*

## CORNWALL
Bodmin
**Homely Foods,** 1 Lower Bore St. *Cann Mills.*

Falmouth
**The Granary,** High St. *Cann Mills.*

Penzance
**The Granary,** 39A Causeway Head. *Cann Mills.*
**Richard's Health Food Store,** Bread St. Tel. Penzance (0736) 2828. *Pimhill Mill.*

Redruth
**Nature's Store Ltd.,** Paul Croft, Cardrew Industrial Estate. *W. & H. Marriage & Sons.*

Tintagel
**Vital Vittals,** Bossiney Rd. *Cann Mills.*

Truro
**The Granary,** Newham Rd. *Cann Mills.*
**The Granary,** 36 St. Austell St. *Cann Mills.*

Wadebridge
**The Wholefood Shop,** Piggy Lane. *Cann Mills.*

## CUMBRIA
Ambleside
**Harvest,** Compton Rd. Tel. Ambleside (096 63) 3151. *The Watermill.*
**Kirkstone Galleries,** Skelwith Bridge. Tel. Ambleside (096 63) 3296. *The Watermill.*

Barrow-in-Furness
**Furness Health Food Stores,** 58 Crellin St. Tel. B.-in-F. (0229) 25834. *Muncaster Mill.*
**H. Nuttall,** 103 Rawlinson St. Tel. B.-in-F. (0229) 22966. *Muncaster Mill.*

Brampton
**Harrisons Grocers,** 45 Front St. Tel. Brampton (069 77) 2422. *The Watermill.*

Carlisle
**Baecko's Delicatessen,** Rosemary Lane, English St. Tel. Carlisle (0228) 25683. *The Watermill.*
**Health Food Centre,** 7 Warwick Rd. Tel. Carlisle (0228) 25228. *The Watermill.*
**Patersons Shop,** 25 Edwardes St. Tel. Carlisle (0228) 24410. *The Watermill.*
**Robinsons VG Stores,** 53 Scotland Rd., Stanwick. Tel. Carlisle (0228) 27808. *The Watermill.*

Cartmel
**Cartmel Post Office.** Tel. Cartmel (044 854) 201. *The Watermill.*

Cockermouth
**The Granary,** Market Place. Tel. Cockermouth (0900) 822633. *Muncaster Mill.*

Grange-over-Sands
**The Dairy,** Kents Bank Rd. Tel. G.-o-S. (044 84) 2936. *Muncaster Mill.*
**Kents Bank Post Office.** Tel. G.-o-S. (044 84) 3112. *The Watermill.*

Grasmere
**Dixons Bakery.** Tel. Grasmere (096 65) 264. *The Watermill.*

Kendal
**Bean & Grain (A.E. Design),** Waterside. Tel. Kendal (0539) 21001. *The Watermill.*
**Booths.** Tel. Kendal (0539) 23706. *The Watermill.*

Keswick
**Horsburgh's,** 5 Bank St. Tel. Keswick (0596) 74071. *Muncaster Mill.*

Kirkby Stephen
**The Beehive.** Tel. Kirkby Stephen (0930) 71436. *The Watermill.*

Penrith
**Bluebell Market,** Bluebell Lane. Tel. Penrith (0768) 66660. *The Watermill.*
**J. & J. Graham,** Market Square. *The Watermill.*
**Village Bakery Foodshop,** Angel Lane. Tel.Penrith (0768) 62377. *The Watermill.*

Seascale
**T.F. Barnes & Son,** 1 South Parade. Tel. Seascale (094 02) 256. *Muncaster Mill.*

Ulverston
**Furness Health Food Stores.** Tel. Ulverston (0229) 53394. *Muncaster Mill and The Watermill.*

Wigton
**Manns,** 12 West St. Tel. Wigton (096 54) 3335. *The Watermill.*

## DERBYSHIRE

Buxton
**Lembas,** 5 Bridge St. Tel. Buxton (0298) 2343.
*Thorner Mill.*

Chesterfield
**Armadib Wholefoods Community Supplies,** New Covered
Market. *Thorner Mill.*
**The Happy Nut House,** 19 Glumangate. *South End Mills.*

## DEVON

Ashburton
**The Ark,** 38 East St. *Cann Mills.*

Axminster
**Health Food Shop,** Lyme Rd. *Lockyer & Son.*

Barnstaple
**Sunfood,** 5 Bear St. Tel. Barnstaple (0271) 3476.
*Pimhill Mill.*

Crediton
**Windmill Foods,** P.T. Janion, March Lane, Lords Meadow
Industrial Estate. Tel. Crediton (036 32) 430516.
*W. & H. Marriage & Sons.*

Exeter
**Messrs. French,** Hennock Rd. *Lockyer & Son.*
**Southern Health Foods (Head Office),** Vitality House,
Exhibition Way. Tel. Exeter (0392) 68897. *Pimhill Mill.*

Newton Abbot
**Market Health Foods,** Newton Abbot Market. *Cann Mills.*

Plymouth
**Beggar's Banquet,** 58A Regent St. Tel. Plymouth (0752)
28449. *Pimhill Mill.*
**Rikard Wanes,** 47 Mayflower St. *The "Hofels" Mill.*

Seaton
**Golden Hamper,** 21 Queen St. *Lockyer & Son.*

Totnes
**Sacks,** 80 High St. *Cann Mills.*

## DORSET

Beaminster
**Drimpton Post Office,** Drimpton. *Lockyer & Son.*
**Pines Ltd.** *Lockyer & Son.*

Blandford
**Blandford Wholefoods,** 7 Georgian Way. *Cann Mills.*
**Wholefoods,** 39/41 Salisbury St. *Cann Mills.*

Bournemouth
**Earth Foods,** 250 Old Christchurch Rd. *Cann Mills.*
**Earth Foods,** 113 Commercial Rd., Parkstone. *Cann Mills.*
**Gerard House Health Foods,** 736 Christchurch Rd.,
Boscombe. *Cann Mills.*
**Kinson Homebrew & Health Foods,** 1434 Wimborne Rd.,
Kinson. *Lockyer & Son.*
**Vitality Fare,** 119 Commercial Rd., Lower Parkstone.
*Cann Mills.*

Bradford Abbas
**Sherton Mill.** *Lockyer & Son.*

Bridport
**Bridport Health Shop,** West St. *Lockyer & Son.*
**Hussey & Son (Bakers),** East St. *Lockyer & Son.*
**Moores & Son,** Morecombelake. *Lockyer & Son.*

Dorchester
**Cornucopia,** 34A High West St. *Cann Mills.*
**Dorchester Health Food,** Trinity Rd. *Lockyer & Son.*
**Down to Earth,** 18 Princes St. *Lockyer & Son and
Cann Mills.*

Ferndown
**Tudormere,** Ringwood Rd. *Cann Mills.*

Gillingham
**Smiths Bakery.** *Cann Mills.*

Shaftesbury
**Anstee,** High St. *Cann Mills.*
**Mr. Anstey (Baker),** Angel Square. *Lockyer & Son.*
**Clares,** 14 Bell St. *Cann Mills.*

Sherborne
**Food for Thought,** Trendle St. *Lockyer & Son and
Cann Mills.*

South Bourne
**Earth Foods,** 75 Southbourne Grove. *Cann Mills.*

Thorncombe
**Thorncombe Post Office.** *Lockyer & Son.*

Wareham
**Purbeck Wholefoods,** 17 West St. *Cann Mills.*

Weymouth
**Health Food Stores,** 29 Middle St. *Lockyer & Son.*

Wimborne
**Health Food Stores,** 6A Leigh Rd. *Lockyer & Son.*
**Holt Stores,** Holt. *Lockyer & Son.*
**Spill the Beans,** 7 West St. *Cann Mills.*

## DURHAM

Darlington
**Atom Co-op Ltd. ("The Green Shop"),** 18A Larchfield St.
*Pimhill Mill.*

Durham
**Maggie's Farm,** 1 Allergate Terrace. Tel. Durham (0385)
45013. *The Watermill.*

## ESSEX

Abridge
**Mr. Beck,** Market Sq. *W. & H. Marriage & Son.*

Billericay
**General Stores,** Mr. Banks, Tye Common Rd. *W. & H.
Marriage & Sons.*
**N. A. Kassam,** 2 Bridge Parade, Perry St. *W. & H.
Marriage & Sons.*
**Queens Park Stores,** Mr. Shopland, 111 Perry St. *W. & H.
Marriage & Sons.*

Braintree
**J. Bowtell,** 31 Bank St. *W. & H. Marriage & Sons.*

Brentwood
**W. Shopland,** 259 Ongar Rd. *W. & H. Marriage & Sons.*
**Smith Brothers,** Crescent Rd. *W. & H. Marriage & Sons.*

Burnham-on-Crouch
**Norman's Self-Service,** 40 High St. *Walsham Mill.*

Chelmsford
**Mr. Jaggo,** Post Office Stores, Good Easter. *W. & H.
Marriage & Sons.*

Chingford
**Chasney,** 134-138 Station Rd. *W. & H. Marriage & Sons
and Walsham Mill.*

Clacton-on-Sea
**Health Food Centre,** 18 Orwell Rd. *Walsham Mill.*

Colchester
**Beaumonts Health Stores,** Pelmans Lane. *W. & H.
Marriage & Sons.*

**Bures Post Office,** Bures. *Walsham Mill.*

**Colchester Cooperative Society,** P.O. Box 4, Victoria Place, Eld Lane. *Walsham Mill.*
**Gourmet Delicatessen,** Eld Lane. *Walsham Mill.*
**H. Gunton,** 81-83 Crouch St. *W. & H. Marriage & Sons.*
**Harvest Natural Food,** St. John St. *Walsham Mill.*
**T. & B. Motts Ltd.,** 55-61 Mersea Rd. *Walsham Mill.*
**Mr. C.Parker,** 25 North Station Rd. *W. & H. Marriage & Sons.*

Galleywood
**Bakery,** Mr. Stuart, The Street. *W. & H. Marriage & Sons.*

Great Dunmow
**Terracorra,** 69B High St. *Walsham Mill.*

Hainault
**S. Arphanos,** 368 Manford Way. *W. & H. Marriage & Sons.*

Halstead
**Doubledays,** 1 Market Hill. *Walsham Mill.*
**B. & A. Fruiterer,** 3 The Centre. *Walsham Mill.*

Hornchurch
**Health Stores,** 37A High St. *W. & H. Marriage & Sons.*

Ilford
**Health Food Co.,** 235 Cranbrook Rd. *W. & H. Marriage & Sons.*

Leigh-on-Sea
**Beach Stores,** 3 Beach Ave. *W. & H. Marriage & Sons.*
**Brewer & Sons,** 48 Leigh Rd. *Walsham Mill.*
**Green's Health Food Stores,** 37 Rectory Grove. Tel. Southend (0702) 75338. *Walsham Mill and W. & H. Marriage & Sons.*

Maldon
**Matthews Ltd.,** 69 High St. *Walsham Mill.*

Manningtree
**Lawford Stores,** Lawford. *Walsham Mill.*

Manor Park
**Mrs Bakler,** 690 Manor Park High Rd. *W. & H. Marriage & Sons.*

Ongar
**The Dairies,** Mrs. Shepperd, High St. *W. & H. Marriage & Sons.*

Rayleigh
**Natra Foods,** 11 High St. *W. & H. Marriage & Sons.*

Saffron Walden
**The Brewhouse, Traditional & Health Foods,** Brick House, Wicken Bonhunt. Tel. Saffron Walden (0799) 40348. *Pimhill Mill and Walsham Mill.*
**H. J. Chisnall,** Market Hill. *W. & H. Marriage & Sons.*
**Nuts in May,** 32 Kings St. *Walsham Mill and W. & H. Marriage & Sons.*
**J.F. Penning,** 1 Market Sq. *Walsham Mill.*

Southend-on-Sea
**Howdens,** 17/19 Southchurch Rd. *W. & H. Marriage & Sons.*

Springfield
**J. Lawrie,** Byron Rd. *W. & H. Marriage & Sons.*

Stock
**R. & J. Sale,** High St. *W. & H. Marriage & Sons.*

Thaxted
**Mr. Prior,** High St. *W. & H. Marriage & Sons.*

Upminster
**Norton and Reeves,** 28 Station Rd. *Walsham Mill.*

Westcliff-on-Sea
**Natural Wholefoods,** R. & A. Roughton, 80 Westminster Drive. *W. & H. Marriage & Sons.*
**S. & B. Foodstore.** *Walsham Mill.*

West Mersea
**Country Fare,** Yorick Rd. *Walsham Mill.*

Witham
**Mr. Larman,** 48 Church St. *W. & H. Marriage & Sons.*

Wivenhoe
**The Delicatessen,** High St. *Walsham Mill.*

## GLOUCESTERSHIRE
Charlton Kings
**Leonards Supermarkets,** 229 London Rd. *Coaley Mill and The "Hofels" Mill.*

Cheltenham
**Barleycorn,** 317 High St. Tel. Cheltenham (0242) 41070. *Pimhill Mill.*
**Bath Road Wholefoods,** 133 Bath Rd. Tel. Cheltenham (0242) 54150. *Pimhill Mill.*

Cirencester
**Great Western Bakery.** *Coaley Mill.*
**Great Western Health Foods.** *Coaley Mill.*

Dursley
**Moons,** Parsonage St. *Coaley Mill.*

Gloucester
**Health & Beauty,** 19 St. John's Lane. Tel. Gloucester (0452) 24501. *Coaley Mill.*

North Nibley
**Davies Stores,** *Coaley Mill.*

Stroud
**B.J. Boon Ltd. (Cash & Carry),** Slad Rd. *Priston Mill.*
**Sunshine Health Stores,** 25 Church St. Tel. Stroud (045 36) 3923. *Pimhill Mill.*

Wotton-under-Edge
**Beanstalk,** 6 Bear St. Tel. W.-u-E. (045 385) 3325. *Coaley Mill and Cann Mills.*
**Cotswold Health Products,** 9 Church St. Tel. W.-u-E. (045 385) 3694. *Coaley Mill.*

## GREATER MANCHESTER
Altrincham
**Health Food Centre,** 41 Oxford Rd. *Pimhill Mill.*

Manchester
**Country Life Wholefoods,** 9 South King St. Tel. Manchester (061) 834 5923. *South End Mills.*
**On the Eighth Day,** 111 Oxford Rd. Tel. Manchester (061) 273 4878. *The Watermill.*
**The Happy Nut House,** 121 Oldham St. Tel. Manchester (061) 832 8791. *South End Mills.*

Salford
**The Happy Nut House,** 29 Brierhill Way. Tel. Manchester (061) 737 8811. *South End Mills.*

Stockport
**The Happy Nut House,** 97/99 Princes St. Tel. Manchester (061) 480 2314. *South End Mills.*

## HAMPSHIRE
Alton
**Rose & Sons,** 23 Market St. *Headley Mill.*

Fleet
**Fleet Garden & Pet Centre,** 323 Fleet Rd. *Headley Mill.*

Fordingbridge
**Country Fayre,** *Cann Mills.*

Lymington
**Gerard House Health Foods,** St. Thomas St.
  Tel. Lymington (0590) 72901. *Lower Calbourne Mill.*

New Milton
**Scoltocks,** Station Rd. *Cann Mills.*

Petersfield
**Bran Tub,** The Square. *Elbridge Organic Farm Mill.*

Ringwood
**Scoltocks,** 22 Lynes Lane. *Cann Mills.*

Romsey
**Peppercorn Natural Foods.** *Cann Mills.*

Southampton
**Danaan,** 6, Onslow Rd., Newtown. *Cann Mills.*

Winchester
**Wholefoods,** Kingswalk Market. *Cann Mills.*

## HEREFORD & WORCESTERSHIRE
Evesham
**Gateway Cake Shop,** 7 Market Place. *Great Alne Mills.*

Inkberrow
**J.L. Savage & Sons Ltd.,** The Bakery. *Great Alne Mills.*

Kington
**Spreadeagle Health Foods,** 5 Church St. *Pimhill Mill.*

Leominster
**Nitty Gritty Grain Shop,** 9 School Lane. *Pimhill Mill.*

## HERTFORDSHIRE
Boreham Wood
**Riches & Sons,** 132 Shenley Rd. *W. & H. Marriage & Sons.*

Bushey
**Start Living,** High St. *W. & H. Marriage & Sons.*

Harpenden
**Wavy Line,** 2 Grove Rd. *W. & H. Marriage & Sons.*

Hemel Hempstead
**H.R. Bird,** 252 Marlowes. *W. & H. Marriage & Sons.*

## HUMBERSIDE
Beverley
**G. Jack & Son Ltd.,** 6 Wednesday Market. Tel. Hull (0482)
  882 437. *Southburn Mill.*

Driffield
**Driffield Health Food Shop,** Middle St. South. *Southburn
  Mill.*

Hull
**Hull Foods,** 21 Princes Ave. *Southburn Mill.*

## ISLE OF WIGHT
Cowes
**Blacktons (Cowes) Ltd.,** High St. Tel. Cowes (0983)
  293011. *Lower Calbourne Mill.*
**Harbow Food & Wine Stores,** Birmingham Rd. Tel. Cowes
  (0983) 293471. *Lower Calbourne Mill.*

Freshwater
**Millers Damsel Real Bread Shop,** Avenue Rd.
  Tel. Freshwater (098 383) 2516. *Lower Calbourne Mill.*

Newport
**Newport Health Food Centre.** The Square. Tel. Newport
  (0983) 522121. *Lower Calbourne Mill.*
**Ralph Health Foods,** Upper St. James St. Tel. Newport
  (0983) 522353. *Lower Calbourne Mill.*

Ryde
**Health Food Stores,** High St. Tel. Ryde (0983) 962055.
  *Lower Calbourne Mill.*

Shanklin
**Newham Brothers,** High St. Tel. Shanklin (098 386)
  2122. *Lower Calbourne Mill.*

Yafford
**Yafford Mill.** Tel. Brighstone (0983) 740. *Lower Calbourne
  Mill.*

Yarmouth
**C.F. Hopkins,** High St. Tel. Yarmouth (0983) 760347.
  *Lower Calbourne Mill.*

## KENT
Aldington
**B.J. & S.A. Ash,** Post Office Stores. Tel. Aldington
  (023 372) 246. *Swanton Mill.*

Beckenham
**Herb of Grace,** High St. *W. & H. Marriage & Sons.*

Bexley
**Mr. Westerns,** 16 High St. *W. & H. Marriage & Sons.*

Bromley
**Bromley Health Centre,** 54 Widmore Rd. *W. & H. Marriage
  & Sons.*
**Health Foods,** 56 High St. *W. & H. Marriage & Sons.*

Canterbury
**Oasis Wholefood,** 24 Palace St. Tel. Canterbury (0227)
  63941. *Pimhill Mill.*

Chilham
**Brown's Kitchen Shop,** High St. *Pimhill Mill.*

Dartford
**Food for Living,** Lowfield St. *W. & H. Marriage & Sons.*

Hythe
**Hardy's,** 156B High St. Tel. Hythe (0303) 67005. *Swanton
  Mill.*

West Wickham
**Health Foods,** 7 Beckenham Rd. *W. & H. Marriage & Sons.*

## LANCASHIRE
Blackpool
**Circle Health Food Centre,** 311 Dickson Rd. *Pimhill Mill.*

Lancaster
**Community Supplies,** 78A Penny St. Tel. Lancaster (0524)
  63021. *The Watermill.*
**Spice of Life,** 5 Marine Drive, Hest Bank. *Pimhill Mill.*

Rochdale
**The Happy Nut House,** 72/74 Yorkshire St. *South End
  Mills.*

## LEICESTERSHIRE
Coalville
**The Bakery,** Forest Rd. *Pimhill Mill.*

Desford
**Mrs. Rose,** Forest Field, Leicester Lane. Tel. Desford
  (045 57) 2294. *Pimhill Mill.*

Leicester
**Downey's Health Food Centre,** 143 Evington Rd.
  Tel. Leicester (0533) 736108. *Pimhill Mill.*
**Whole Meal,** 158 Queens Rd., Clarendon Park.
  Tel. Leicester (0533) 703617. *Pimhill Mill.*

Loughborough
**Caldwell's Bakery**, Swan St. Tel. Loughborough (0509) 212015. *Great Alne Mills.*
**Combine Wholefood Collective**, 7/7A Leicester Rd. Tel. Loughborough (0509) 213865. *Pimhill Mill.*
**S. & R. Coombes**, The Coneries. Tel. Loughborough (0509) 63297. *Great Alne Mills.*

Market Harborough
**Nuts & Co.**, 3 Coventry Rd. *Pimhill Mill.*

Quorn
**Waverley's of Quorn**, 1 & 3 Leicester Rd. Tel. Loughborough (0509) 42559. *Great Alne Mills.*

## LINCOLNSHIRE
Scunthorpe
**Healthfood Store**, 11 Oswald Rd. *Pimhill Mill.*

## LONDON
**Aurora**, 22 Bristol Gardens, W9. *The "Hofels" Mill.*
**Baldwins**, Walworth Rd., SE17. *Doves Farm Mill.*
**Bon Appetit**, 299A Lavender Hill, SW11. *W. & H. Marriage & Sons.*
**Bread and Roses**, Upper St., N1. *Doves Farm Mill.*
**Bridge to Health**, 25C Bridge Rd., Wembley, Middx. *W. & H. Marriage & Sons.*
**Chalk Farm Nutrition Centre**, 40 Chalk Farm Rd., NW1. *Doves Farm Mill and Foelas Watermill.*
**City Wholefoods**, 73 Queen Victoria St., EC4. *W. & H. Marriage & Sons.*
**Cornucopia**, 64 St. Mary's Rd., Ealing, W5. Tel. London (01) 579 9431. *Pimhill Mill; The "Hofels" Mill; and Doves Farm Mill.*
**Cory Bros.**, 166-168 High Rd. East, Finchley, N2. *Walsham Mill.*
**Crank's Health Store**, Marshall St., W1. Tel. London (01) 437 2915. *Foelas Watermill; Pimhill Mill; Swanton Mill; and Walsham Mill.*
**Crunch Foods**, 61 Marsh Rd., Pinner, Middx. *W. & H. Marriage & Sons.*
**Eden Health Foods**, Ascot Parade, Clapham Park Rd., SW4. *Doves Farm Mill.*
**Edwin T. Baker**, 76 Caledonian Rd., N1. *W. & H. Marriage & Sons.*
**Elizabeth David**, 46 Bourne St., SW1. *W. & H. Marriage & Sons.*
**Eltham Health Foods**, 112A Westmount Rd., Eltham, SE9. *W. & H. Marriage & Sons.*
**Falcon Herbal and Health Foods**, 120 Northcote Rd., SW11. *W. & H. Marriage & Sons.*
**Food for Health**, Blackfriars Lane, EC1. *Doves Farm Mill.*
**Gate Delicatessen**, 343 Archway Rd., Highgate, N6. *W. & H. Marriage & Sons.*
**Golden Orient**, Shorts Gardens, WC2. *Doves Farm Mill.*
**The Granary**, Highgate Village, N6. *Foelas Watermill.*
**Haelon Centre**, 39 Park Rd., Hornsey, N8. *W. & H. Marriage & Sons.*
**Harrods**, Knightsbridge, SW1. *The "Hofels" Mill and W. & H. Marriage & Sons.*
**Health and Beauty**, 42 High St., Southgate, N14. *W. & H. Marriage & Sons.*
**Health Centre**, 74 High St., Wimbledon, SW19. *W. & H. Marriage & Sons.*
**Health Foods**, 1 Cuckoo Hill, Pinner Green, Middx. *W. & H. Marriage & Sons.*
**Health Foods**, 767 Fulham Rd., SW6. *W. & H. Marriage & Sons.*

**Health Foods**, Hansworth Rd., Hounslow, Middx. *W. & H. Marriage & Sons.*
**Healthways**, 36A The Broadway, Mill Hill, NW7. Tel. London (01) 959 0771. *Pimhill Mill and W. & H. Marriage & Sons.*
**James John Health Foods**, 211 Upper Tooting Rd., SW17. *W. & H. Marriage & Sons.*
**Jappie Delicatessen**, 79 Dulwich Village, SE21. *W. & H. Marriage & Sons.*
**Justin de Blank Ltd.**, 42 Elizabeth St., SW1. *Walsham Mill.*
**Lima Shop**, 59 Station Rd., Winchmore Hill, N21. *W. & H. Marriage & Sons.*
**Linkers**, 86-90 High St., Clapham, SW4. *W. & H. Marriage & Sons.*
**Naturally**, Earlsfield Rd., SW16. *Elbridge Organic Farm Mill.*
**Nature's Larder**, 340 Norwood Rd., South Norwood, SW27. *W. & H. Marriage & Sons.*
**Neals Yard**, Neals Yard, WC2. *Doves Farm Mill.*
**Phoebus Natural Foods**, Willesden Lane, NW6. *Doves Farm Mill.*
**Selfridges**, Oxford St., W1. Tel. London (01) 629 1234. *Foelas Watermill.*
**Tates Health Foods**, 613 Forest Rd., Walthamstow, E17. *W. & H. Marriage & Sons.*
**Towards Jupiter**, 191 Mare St., E8. *Walsham Mill.*
**Unicorn Wholefoods**, Boston Rd., W7. *Doves Farm Mill.*
**Vanns Health Foods**, 28 Kirkdale Rd., Leytonstone, E11. *W. & H. Marriage & Sons.*
**Village Health Foods**, Belsize Village, NW3. *Foelas Watermill.*
**West Ealing Health Stores**, Leeland Rd., W13. *Doves Farm Mill.*
**Wholefood**, 112 Baker St., W1. Tel. London (01) 935 3924. *Pimhill Mill.*
**Wilkins**, 56 Marsham St., SW1. *W. & H. Marriage & Sons.*
**Wilkins Natural Foods**, Marshall St., W1. *Foelas Watermill.*

## MERSEYSIDE
Birkenhead
**The Happy Nut House**, 13 Princes Pavement, Grange Rd., Shopping Precinct. *South End Mills.*

Liverpool
**The Happy Nut House**, 27 Warbeck Moor. *South End Mills.*
**The Happy Nut House**, 48/50 Whitechapel. *South End Mills.*

St. Helens
**Country Life Wholefoods**, 19 Barrow St. *South End Mills.*

Wallesey
**Crown Park Pkg. Co. Ltd.**, 41 Leasowe Rd. *Felin Isaf Mill.*

## NORFOLK
Aylsham
**Harveys**, Red Lion St. *Walsham Mill.*

Cromer
**The Cromer Kitchen**, 3 Church St. *Walsham Mill.*

Diss
**The Bob Shop**, Rickenhall. *Walsham Mill.*
**Mr. Lloyd**, 146 Victoria Rd. *Walsham Mill.*
**The Natural Food Shop**, Norfolk House, St. Nicholas St. *Pimhill Mill.*

Holt
**Gibbs**, 37 Bull St. *Walsham Mill.*

Norwich
**John Copeman & Sons Ltd. (Mace)**, Drayton Rd. *Walsham Mill.*
**The Mecca**, 5 Orford Hill. *Walsham Mill.*
**Rainbow**, 16 Dove St. *Walsham Mill.*
**Renaissance Pure Foods**, 4 St. Benedict St. Tel. Norwich (0603) 25686. *Pimhill Mill.*

Oulton
**Ardley**, 1 Golden Court, Bridge Rd, Oulton Broad. *Walsham Mill.*

Stalham
**Mr. Meek**, High St. *Walsham Mill.*

Thetford
**Post Office Stores**, Great Hockhorn. *Walsham Mill.*

## NORTHAMPTONSHIRE
Northampton
**Tony Back (Grocer)**, 12 St. Giles Square. Tel. Northampton (0604) 36558. *Pimhill Mill.*

## NORTHUMBERLAND
Corbridge
**Corbridge Larger**, Town Hall. Tel. Corbridge (043 471) 471. *The Watermill.*

Hexham
**Country Kitchen**, Market St. Tel. Hexham (0434) 603835. *The Watermill.*
**Robbs**. Tel. Hexham (0434) 602151. *The Watermill.*
**Seasons**, 11 Hencotes. Tel. Hexham (0434) 605639. *Pimhill Mill.*

## NOTTINGHAMSHIRE
Nottingham
**Onroboros Wholefoods**, 37A Mansfield Rd. Tel. Nottingham (0602) 49016. *Pimhill Mill.*

## OXFORDSHIRE
Banbury
**Geronimo**, Butchers Row. Tel. Banbury (0295) 53352. *Great Alne Mills.*

Oxford
**Oxford Swindon Co-op**, 21 The Square. *The "Hofels" Mill.*
**Wholefoods**, 6 Suffolk House, Summertown. *Pimhill Mill.*

## SCOTLAND
*FIFE*
St. Andrews
**Lemnos Wholefoods**, 183 South St. *Pimhill Mill.*

*GRAMPIAN*
Aberdeen
**Ambrosia Wholefoods**, 165 King St. *Pimhill Mill.*

*HIGHLAND*
Garve
**Scorriag Supplies**, Dundonnell. *Pimhill Mill.*

Thurso
**Health Food Centre**, 5 Princes St. *Pimhill Mill.*

*LOTHIAN*
Edinburgh
**Good Food (Edinburgh)**, 255 Morningside Rd. Tel. Edinburgh (031) 447 3020. *Pimhill Mill.*
**J.M. Henderson**, 92 Hanover St. Tel. Edinburgh (031) 225 6695. *Pimhill Mill.*

*STRATHCLYDE*
Ayr
**McWhirter**, 8 Cathcart St. *Pimhill Mill.*

Glasgow
**Forest & Niven**, 73 St. Vincent St. *The "Hofels" Mill.*

## SHROPSHIRE
Bridgnorth
**Acorn Natural Foods**, 64 St. Mary's St. Tel. Bridgnorth (074 62) 61896. *Pimhill Mill.*

Ellesmere
**Beanstalk Natural Foods**, 6 Scotland St. *Pimhill Mill.*
**Vermenlen**, 6 Cross St. *Pimhill Mill.*

Ludlow
**Broad Bean**, 60 Broad St. Tel. Ludlow (0584) 4239. *Pimhill Mill.*
**Earthworks**, 22 Cove St. Tel. Ludlow (0584) 2010. *Pimhill Mill.*

Oswestry
**Honeysuckle**, 53 Church St. Tel. Oswestry (0691) 3125. *Pimhill Mill.*

Shrewsbury
**Crabapple**, 16 St. Mary's St. Tel. Shrewsbury (0743) 64559. *Pimhill Mill.*
**Healthway Stores**, Riverside Shopping Centre, Smithfield Rd. Tel. Shrewsbury (0743) 4523. *Pimhill Mill.*
**Henry Lee & Co.** The Square. Tel. Shrewsbury (0743) 62606. *Pimhill Mill.*
**Sugar 'n' Spice**, High St. *Pimhill Mill.*

Wem
**Wem Wholefoods**, Noble St. Tel. Wem (0939) 32321. *Pimhill Mill.*

## SOMERSET
Bridgwater
**Bridgwater Health Shop.** *Lockyer & Son.*

Crewkerne
**Seaton-Thurgur Ltd.**, Middle Path. *Lockyer & Son.*

Frome
**John's Bakery**, 5 Badcox. Tel. Frome (0373) 3703. *Lockyer & Son.*
**Maid Marion Foodstore**, Locks Hill. Tel. Frome (0373) 2828. *Priston Mill.*
**The Wholefood Shop**, 17 St. Catherine St. *Cann Mills.*

Hinton-St.-George
**Mr. Garnham.** *Lockyer & Son.*

Ilton
**F.E.R. Hayman & Son**, The Bakery. Tel. Ilminster (046 05) 2704. *Lockyer & Son.*

Langport
**The Country Stores.** *Lockyer & Son.*

Merriott
**Broadway Stores.** *Lockyer & Son.*

Norton-sub-Hambdon
**Spar Store.** *Lockyer & Son.*

Othery
**M.N. Maisey, The Bakery.** *Priston Mill.*

Parbrook
**Parbrook Post Office.** *Lockyer & Son.*

Radstock
**L. & F. Jones Ltd. (Cash & Carry)**, Frome Rd. Tel. Radstock (0761) 32781. *Priston Mill.*

Shepton Mallet
**Sunshine Healthfoods,** 8 Commercial Rd. *Lockyer & Son and Cann Mills.*

Street
**Puddy (Mark) Ltd., The Bakery,** 102 High St. Tel. Street (0458) 43643. *Priston Mill.*

Wedmore
**Chas Binning Bakers.** Tel. Wedmore (0934) 712261. *Lockyer & Son.*

Wells
**The Good Earth,** Priory Rd. *Cann Mills.*

Weston-super-Mare
**Sunflower,** 67B Orchard St. *Cann Mills.*

Yeovil
**Ceres Natural Foods,** 42 Princes St. *Lockyer & Son.*

## STAFFORDSHIRE
Burton-on-Trent
**The Happy Nut House,** 3 St. Modwens Walk. *South End Mills.*

Newcastle under Lyme
**Kermase,** 64 Liverpool Rd. *Pimhill Mill.*

Tamworth in Arden
**Grape & Grain,** 25 Lower Gun Gate. Tel. Tamworth (0827) 62133. *Great Alne Mills.*

## SUFFOLK
Beccles
**Mrs. Dowding,** 4 Hungate. *Walsham Mill.*

Brantham
**G. R. & A. Bridger (Spar),** The Pippins. *Walsham Mill.*

Bury St. Edmunds
**Health Foods,** 9 The Traverse. *W. & H. Marriage & Sons.*
**P.A. Lay (Spar Food),** Cadogan Rd. *Walsham Mill.*
**Marpa Health Foods,** 22 St. John's St. *Walsham Mill.*
**Mrs. Pratt,** Norwich Ales Stores, Badwell Ash. *Walsham Mill.*
**Ridleys,** 35 Abbeygate St. *Walsham Mill.*
**Savory & Moore (Chemists),** Abbeygate St. *W. & H. Marriage & Sons.*
**Woolpit Bakery,** Woolpit. *Walsham Mill.*
**Wyverstone Post Office,** Wyverstone. *Walsham Mill.*
**K.J. & V.W. Youngs,** 1 Stamford Court. *Walsham Mill.*

Capel St. Mary
**Margaret's,** 27 The Street. *Walsham Mill.*

Diss
**Mr. Lloyd,** 146 Victoria Rd. *Walsham Mill.*

Earl Soham
**Mr. Ashwell,** The Bakery. *Walsham Mill.*

Glensford
**W.T. Argent & Son,** The Green. *Walsham Mill.*

Hadleigh
**The Bakery,** 34 High St. *W. & H. Marriage & Sons.*
**Hadleigh Health Foods.** *Walsham Mill.*
**Stonehouse Corner Dairy,** 11 High St. *W. & H. Marriage & Sons.*
**Sunflower,** 101 High St. *Pimhill Mill and Walsham Mill.*

Halesworth
**Mrs. Haughton,** Betacea Gardens, Bramfield. *Walsham Mill.*

Haverhill
**Ellis Home Bakery,** 27 Queen St. *Walsham Mill.*

**Wiggons Wholefoods,** Wiggons Farm, Helione Bumpstead. Tel. Steeple Bumpstead (044 084) 237. *Pimhill Mill.*

Ipswich
**Alliance Stores,** 310 Nacton Rd. *Walsham Mill.*
**Barkers Mace Shop,** 111 Cliff Rd. *Walsham Mill.*
**Bixley Stores,** 2 Bixley Rd. *Walsham Mill.*
**Orwell Stores,** Nacton. *W. & H. Marriage & Sons.*
**Oxborrows,** Felixstowe Rd. *Walsham Mill.*
**Ridleys,** Dial Lane. *Walsham Mill.*
**Spar Food Shop,** Bramford. *Walsham Mill.*

Kesgrave
**The Mini Stores.** *Walsham Mill.*

Kessingland
**Jekells,** High St. *Walsham Mill.*

Lowestoft
**Elmers Mace Market.** 61 Edmonton Rd. *Walsham Mill.*
**Food for Thought,** High St. *Walsham Mill.*
**Oregano,** 88 High St. *Walsham Mill.*
**Phoebe's Pantry,** 124 Bevan St. *Walsham Mill.*
**Waveney Cooperative,** 41 London Rd. North. *Walsham Mill.*

Mildenhall
**Barleycorn,** 20 Market Place. *Walsham Mill.*

Needham Market
**Mr. Parsons,** 40 High St. *Walsham Mill.*

Newmarket
**Mrs. Waddilove (Greenstage Ltd.),** 1 The Rookery. *Walsham Mill.*

Saxmundham
**Saffrons,** Market Place. *Walsham Mill.*

Southwold
**Nutters,** 11 Cast St. *Walsham Mill.*

St. Andrews
**Beechwood Stores,** Woodbridge Rd., Rushmere. *Walsham Mill.*

Stowmarket
**Better Foods,** Bury St. *Walsham Mill.*

Sudbury
**E. W. King & Son,** Market Hill. *Walsham Mill.*

Walsham-le-Willows
**Rolfe the Butchers,** The Street. *Walsham Mill.*
**The Village Stores (Mace),** The Street. *Walsham Mill.*

Woodbridge
**The Cake Shop,** The Thorofare. *Walsham Mill.*
**Henry's Delicatessen,** 1 The Thorofare. *W. & H. Marriage & Sons.*
**Loaves and Fishes,** 52 The Thorofare. *Walsham Mill.*

Yoxford
**Natural Choice,** The Street. *Walsham Mill.*

## SURREY
Banstead
**Variety Fare,** 125 High St. *W. & H. Marriage & Sons.*

Cheam
**Cheam Village Health Foods,** 60 The Broadway. *W. & H. Marriage & Sons.*

Cobham
**The Wholefood Centre,** 35 Oakdene Parade. Tel. Cobham (093 26) 4553. *Great Alne Mills.*

Croydon
**Friends Foods,** St. Michael's Rd. *Doves Farm Mill.*

Farnham
**Rose & Company,** 5 Cambridge Place. *Headley Mill.*

Guildford
**Crank's Health Shop,** 35 Castle St. *Pimhill Mill.*

Kingston-on-Thames
**Burn's Bakery.** *Elbridge Organic Farm Mill.*

Leatherhead
**Leatherhead Wholefoods,** 34 High St. *W. & H. Marriage & Sons.*

Wallington
**Health Foods,** Mr. Noah, 4 South Parade, Stafford Rd. *W. & H. Marriage & Sons.*

Worcester Park
**Health Foods,** Cheam Common Rd. *W. & H. Marriage & Sons.*

## SUSSEX
Barnham
**Holt's Bakery,** Lake Lane. Tel. Yapton (0243) 352088. *Elbridge Organic Farm Mill.*

Bexhill-on-Sea
**Nature's Way,** Head Office, 1 Clifford Rd. Tel. Bexhill-on-Sea (0424) 222125. *Elbridge Organic Farm Mill.*

Brighton
**Infinity Foods,** 25 North St. Tel. Brighton (0273) 603563. *Elbridge Organic Farm Mill.*
**Simple Supplies,** 11 George St. Tel. Brighton (0273) 694600. *Pimhill Mill.*

Chichester
**Bean Feast,** 256 Southgate. Tel. Chichester (0243) 783823. *Elbridge Organic Farm Mill.*

Claygate
**Studio Cake Shop.** *Elbridge Organic Farm Mill.*

Forest Row
**Ashdown Store,** The Square. *The "Hofels" Mill.*
**The Seasons,** Lewes Rd. Tel. Forest Row (034 282) 2931. *Pimhill Mill.*

Horsham
**Simple Living,** East St. *Elbridge Organic Farm Mill.*

Pulborough
**Mace.** *Elbridge Organic Farm Mill.*

Seaford
**Health Store,** 14 Place Lane. *Pimhill Mill.*

## TYNE & WEAR
Newcastle-on-Tyne
**Cinnamon,** 21 Leazes Park Rd. Tel. Newcastle (0632) 26268. *The Watermill.*
**Mandala Wholefoods,** 43 Manor House Rd., Jesmond. *Pimhill Mill and The Watermill.*

## WALES
*CLWYD*
Colwyn Bay
**Colwyn Bay Health Foods,** 38 Seaview Rd. Tel. Colwyn Bay (0492) 30895. *Felin Isaf Mill.*
**Compton Stores,** Capel St., Abergele. Tel. Abergele (0745) 822067. *Felin Isaf Mill.*
**Corner Cupboard,** Wynnstay Rd. Tel. Colwyn Bay (0492) 2760. *Felin Isaf Mill.*
**Country Kitchen,** 26 Seaview Rd. Tel. Colwyn Bay (0492) 33329. *Felin Isaf Mill.*

**Tudor Bakeries,** Grove Park. Tel. Colwyn Bay (0492) 2585. *Felin Isaf Mill.*

Denbigh
**Larson's Delicatessen,** Love Lane. Tel. Denbigh (074 571) 712511. *Felin Isaf Mill.*

Penrhyn Bay
**Penrhyn Bay Stores,** Llandudno Rd. *Felin Isaf Mill.*

Prestatyn
**Sarah's Delicatessen.** *Felin Isaf Mill.*

*DYFED*
Aberystwyth
**Maeth-y-Meysydd (The Wholefood Shop),** 11 Lon-Rhosmari. *Pimhill Mill.*

Carmarthen
**Aardvark Wholefoods,** 2 Mansel St. Tel. Carmarthen (0267) 32497. *Pimhill Mill.*

Lampeter
**Mulberry Bush,** 2 Bridge St. Tel. Lampeter (0570) 46380. *Pimhill Mill.*

Newport
**Wholefoods of Newport,** Market St. *Pimhill Mill.*

*GWENT*
Newport
**Sansom's (Newport) Ltd. (Bakers),** Adelaide St. Tel. Newport (0633) 855424. *Priston Mill.*
**R.G. Thompson: Newport Provisions,** Stalls 50/51. *Pimhill Mill.*

*GWYNEDD*
Bangor
**Sandwich Box,** 103 High St. *Felin Isaf Mill.*

Betws-y-Coed
**Anna Davies,** Welsh Wool Shop. *Felin Isaf Mill.*

Caernarfon
**Caernarfon Country Kitchen,** Plas Llan Faglan. Tel. Caernarfon (0286) 3163. *Felin Isaf Mill.*

Conwy
**P.A. Roberts,** Pharmacy, 12 Castle St. Tel. Conwy (049 263) 2453. *Felin Isaf Mill.*

Deganwy
**Anchor Cafe,** Station Rd. Tel. Deganwy (0492) 83133. *Felin Isaf Mill.*

Dolgarrog
**Post Office.** Tel. Dolgarrog (049 269) 969239. *Felin Isaf Mill.*

Llandudno
**Dunphys Stores,** 31 Mostyn Ave. Tel. Llandudno (0492) 77174. *Felin Isaf Mill.*
**Health Food Store,** Gloddaeth Ave. *Felin Isaf Mill.*
**Mawdsley's Home Bakery Ltd.,** 39 Mostyn Ave. *Felin Isaf Mill.*
**Sumners Ltd.,** Mostyn St. *Felin Isaf Mill.*

Llandudno Junction
**A. Hughes,** 173 Conwy Rd. *Felin Isaf Mill.*

Llanfairfechan
**Spar Foodmarket,** Village Rd. *Felin Isaf Mill.*

Llanrhos
**Post Office & Corner Stores,** Maes-y-Castell. *Felin Isaf Mill.*

Llanrwst
**Comet Bakers,** Station Rd. Tel. Llanrwst (0492) 640298. *Felin Isaf Mill.*

Penmaenmawr
**The Granary,** Westminster Building. *Felin Isaf Mill.*

Trefriw
**Mace Stores.** Tel. Llanrwst (0492) 640734. *Felin Isaf Mill.*

*POWYS*
Llandrindod Wells
**Vans Good Food Shop,** Clovelly, High St. *Pimhill Mill.*

*SOUTH GLAMORGAN*
Cardiff
**Beans 'n' Erbs,** 171A Kings Rd., Canton. *Pimhill Mill.*
**The Wholefood Shop,** 1A & 1B Fitzroy St., Cathays.
 Tel. Cardiff (0222) 395388. *Pimhill Mill.*

*WEST GLAMORGAN*
Neath
**Neath Health Foods,** Market Hall. *Pimhill Mill.*

WARWICKSHIRE
Alcester
**Buntings Delicatessen,** 5 High St. Tel. Alcester (078 971)
 2133. *Great Alne Mills.*
**Whitehead's Home Baker,** 67 High St. Tel. Alcester
 (078 971) 2647. *Great Alne Mills.*

Rugby
**Wholefood Shop,** 24 Little Church St. *Pimhill Mill.*

Warwick
**Sesame Seed,** Smith St. Tel. Warwick (0926) 499890.
 *Great Alne Mills.*

WEST MIDLANDS
Birmingham
**Cottage Stores,** The Green, King's Norton. *Great Alne
 Mills.*
**The Country Bakehouse,** The Bullring. *Pimhill Mill.*
**The Country Baker,** Grosvenor Centre, Northfield.
 *Pimhill Mill.*
**A. Hirons Ltd.,** 10 The Green, King's Norton.
 Tel. Birmingham (021) 458 2702. *Great Alne Mills.*
**Lukers Bakery,** 21 Woodbridge Rd., Moseley.
 Tel. Birmingham (021) 449 0229. *Great Alne Mills.*
**Sage Wholefoods,** 148 Alcester Rd., Moseley.
 Tel. Birmingham (021) 449 7921. *Pimhill Mill.*
**Sunrise World Shop,** 247 Dudley Rd., Winson Green.
 Tel. Birmingham (021) 454 0435. *Pimhill Mill.*

Castle Bromwich
**Copperfields,** 346/8 Bradford Rd. Tel. Birmingham (021)
 454 7921. *Pimhill Mill.*

Coventry
**Drop in the Ocean,** 74 Walls Graves Rd. Tel. Coventry
 (0203) 459936. *Great Alne Mills.*

Earlswood
**Wedges Bakery,** 495 School Rd., Hockley Heath.
 Tel. Earlswood (056 46) 2542. *Great Alne Mills.*

Halesowen
**Phillips Bakehouse,** 34 The Precinct. *Pimhill Mill.*

Knowle
**The Bay Tree,** High St. Tel. Knowle (056 45) 79240.
 *Great Alne Mills.*
**Curtis's Bakery,** 1701 High St. Tel. Knowle (056 45) 2124.
 *Great Alne Mills.*

Solihull
**Rima Patisseries/The Upper Crust Bakery,** 54 Dury Lane.
 Tel. Birmingham (021) 405 7963. *Great Alne Mills.*

Stourbridge
**Uhuru,** 121 Hagley Rd. *Pimhill Mill.*

Sutton Coldfield
**Grape & Grain,** 6 Carlton House, Mere Green Rd.
 Tel. Birmingham (021) 308 7020. *Great Alne Mills.*

Wolverhampton
**Bran Tub,** 5 High St., Albrighton. *Pimhill Mill.*

WILTSHIRE
Salisbury
**Sunrize,** Fisherton St. *Cann Mills.*

Tisbury
**Ellis & Ricketts,** The Square. *Cann Mills.*

NORTH YORKSHIRE
Grassington
**Craven Wholefoods.** *Thorner Mill.*

Harrogate
**The Natural Way,** 81 Leeds Rd. *Thorner Mill.*
**Stoneground,** 64 Station Parade. Tel. Harrogate (0423)
 6522. *Thorner Mill.*
**Wrays (Harrogate) Ltd.,** 79 Station Parade. *Pimhill Mill.*

Knaresborough
**Farm Dairy,** Market Square. Tel. Harrogate (0423) 867185.
 *Thorner Mill.*
**Natural Choice,** Gracious St. *Great Alne Mills.*

Malton
**Williamsons,** 13 Newbiggin. Tel. Malton (0653) 3423.
 *Southburn Mill.*

Market Weighton
**The Buttered Bun,** 38 High St. Tel. Market Weighton
 (069 62) 2376. *Southburn Mill.*
**Southgate Stores,** Southgate. Tel. Market Weighton
 (069 62) 3217. *Southburn Mill.*

Northallerton
**Lewis & Coopr Ltd.,** Main St. Tel. Northallerton (0609)
 3776. *Thorner Mill.*

Pateley Bridge
**Ellisons,** High St. Tel. Harrogate (0423) 711247. *Thorner
 Mill.*

Ripon
**The Warehouse,** Unicorn Yard, Kirkgate. Tel. Ripon (0765)
 4665. *The Watermill.*

York
**York Wholefood,** 98 Micklegate. Tel. York (0904) 56804.
 *Pimhill Mill and Southburn Mill.*

SOUTH YORKSHIRE
Rotherham
**Story's Health Foods,** 26 Wellgate. Tel. Rotherham (0709)
 77885. *Thorner Mill.*

Sheffield
**Down to Earth,** 406 Sharrowvale Rd. Tel. Sheffield (0742)
 685220. *Pimhill Mill.*

WEST YORKSHIRE
Bingley
**Fodder Wholefoods,** 2 Norfolk St. Tel. Bradford (0274)
 560790. *Pimhill Mill and Thorner Mill.*

Boston Spa
**Maid Marion Stores,** 164 High St. Tel. Boston Spa (0937)
 842864. *Thorner Mill.*

**Rider's,** 179 High St. Tel. Boston Spa (0937) 842527. *Thorner Mill.*

Bradford
**Great Life Wholefood Co-op,** 78 Morley St. *Pimhill Mill and Thorner Mill.*

Guiseley
**Dibb & Son.** Tel. Guiseley (0943) 72665. *Thorner Mill.*

Haworth
**Harvest,** Victoria Rd. Tel. Haworth (0535) 4371. *Thorner Mill.*

Hebden Bridge
**Aurora Foods,** 54 Market St. *Pimhill Mill.*

Huddersfield
**Country Store,** 12 Towngate, Holmfirth. Tel. Holmfirth (048 489) 6204. *Pimhill Mill.*
**Peace Works,** 58 Wakefield Rd., Aspley. Tel. Huddersfield (0484) 23915. *Pimhill Mill.*

Leeds
**Beano,** 86 Kirkgate. Tel. Leeds (0532) 35737. *Thorner Mill.*
**Coffee Shop,** 71 Street Lane. Tel. Leeds (0532) 662457. *Thorner Mill.*
**Curtis Health Food Stores Ltd.,** 4 Fish St. Tel. Leeds (0532) 457948. *Thorner Mill.*

**Grasscock & Son,** 31 Otley Rd. Tel. Leeds (0532) 751341. *Thorner Mill.*
**Leeds Wholefoods Ltd.,** 182 Woodhouse Lane. Tel. Leeds (0532) 35018. *Thorner Mill.*
**Mace Stores,** Main St., Thorner. Tel. Leeds (0532) 892404. *Thorner Mill.*
**H. Moorhouse & Son Ltd.,** 72 Otley Rd. Tel. Leeds (0532) 751130. *Thorner Mill.*
**West Yorkshire Health Stores,** 20 Eastgate. Tel. Leeds (0532) 451095. *Thorner Mill.*

Ossett
**Funny Foods,** 82 Station Rd. Tel. Ossett (0924) 273255. *Thorner Mill.*

Otley
**Dodgshons.** Tel. Otley (0943) 463231. *Thorner Mill.*
**Health Stores,** 28-30 Gay Lane. *Pimhill Mill.*
**Stephen H. Smith,** Pool Rd. Tel. Otley (0943) 12195. *Thorner Mill.*

Wetherby
**Provender,** 1A Church St. Tel. Wetherby (0937) 64051. *Thorner Mill.*
**Wholefoods,** 2 Westgate. Tel. Wetherby (0937) 64358. *Thorner Mill.*

# BIBLIOGRAPHY

The authors would like to acknowledge the following books which have been a source of encouragement and information.

Bailey, Adrian. *The Blessings of Bread*. Paddington Press, 1975.

Bateman, Michael; Conran, Caroline; Gillie, Oliver. *The Sunday Times Guide to the World's Best Food*. Hutchinson, 1981.

Brown, Edward Espe. *The Tassajara Bread Book*. Shambhala Publications, Boulder, Colorado, USA, 1970.

David, Elizabeth. *English Bread and Yeast Cookery*. Allen Lane, 1977.

Davidson, Sir Stanley; Passmore, R.; Brock, J.F.; Truswell, A.S. *Human Nutrition and Dietetics*. Churchill Livingstone, 1969.

Drummond, J.C., Wilbraham, Anne. *The Englishman's Food*. Jonathan Cape, 1957.

*Farmhouse Cookery*. Reader's Digest, 1980.

Floris, Maria. *Bakery*. Wine and Food Society, 1968.

Grant, Doris. *Your Daily Bread*. Faber, 1944.

Grant, Doris. *Your Daily Food*. Faber, 1973.

Hanneman, L.J. *Bakery. Bread and Fermented Goods*. Heinemann, 1980.

London, Mel. *Bread Winners*. Rodale Press Inc., USA, 1979.

*Manual of Nutrition*. Ministry of Agriculture, Fisheries and Food, 1976.

Maisner, Heather (ed.). *Country Cooking*. Marshall Cavendish, 1978.

Mellanby, Dr. Kenneth. *Can Britain Feed Itself?* Merlin, 1975.

Norman, Ursel. *Use Your Loaf*. Collins, 1974.

*Our Daily Bread*. British Society for Social Responsibility in Science, 1978.

*Scientific Tables*. Geigy Pharmaceuticals, 1970.

Scurfield, George and Cecilia. *Home Baked*. Faber, 1956.

Seymour, John and Sally. *Self-Sufficiency*. Faber, 1973.

Stobart, Tom. *The Cook's Encyclopaedia*. Batsford, 1980.

Technology Assessment Consumerism Centre. *Bread, the TACC Report*. Intermediate Publishing, 1974.

Williams, A. (ed.). *Breadmaking: The Modern Revolution*. Hutchinson, 1975.

Wilson, C. Anne. *Food and Drink in Britain*. Constable, 1973.

# INDEX

Acetic acid 33
Adams, Ronnie 125
Adamson, Doreen, recipes of 150
Agricultural Development Advisory Service 21, 31
Alford Five Sailed Mill 313
Allied Bakeries Ltd. 33, 43, 125
Allinson's flour 118
Allinson Millers 249
Allinson Millers, recipes of 250-251
Alpha amylase activity 39
Andrews, Molly, recipes of 145
Aniseed 302
Antibiotic, natural 66
Ascorbic acid 42
Asher, Jane, recipes of 272
Associated British Food Ltd. 39, 51
"Avadex" 31

Baguettes 42
Bailey, Adrian 206
Bailey, Adrian, recipes of 207-217
Bake, how to 284
Baking, pre-heat oven 288
—quantities for 294
—steam in 289
—times 289
Baker's yeast 297
Bamboo Grove 172
Barley flour 51, 296
Barms 253, 297, 298
—use of 125
Batter 297
"Bayleton" 31

Bean growing 20
Beard, James 158
Beer, used in break-making 297
"Benlate" 31
Binns, Brian 125
—recipes of 126-135
Boby wheat cleaner 26
Botley Mills 310
Boxer, Arabella 222
—recipes of 222-224
Braiseworth Hall Farm 31
Bran, extraction 19, 42
—importance in diet 45
—Vitamin B1 in 66
Bran and leaven 253
Bread, baking, frequency of 50
—future of better 51
—history of 10-15
—left-over recipes for 273
—microwave cooking of 97
—mineral content of 41
—nutritional content of 41
—plant-baked 59
—quick 158
—technology 39
—types of 33
—vitamin content of 41
British Baking Industries Research Association 14
British Flour Millers Research Association 14
"Britox" 31
Brown bread, experiments with rats 42
Brown, Edward Espe 172

Brown, W. & G. 237
Buckwheat flour 296
Burkitt, Dr. Denis 44, 45, 46
Butter 300
—melted 301
Buttermilk 299
Butylated hydroxytoluene 83

Calcium 119
CAMREB 15
Cann Mills 308
Caraway seeds 301
Carbohydrates, metabolism of 66
Cartland, Barbara 266
—recipes of 266-267
Celery seeds 302
Ceres bakery 252
Chalice Wholemeal Bakery 172
—recipes of 173-175
Chalk 66
Chelmer Mills 310
Chlortoluron 31
Chorleywood Bread-making Process (CBP) 15, 39
Clapton Mill 315
Cleave, Surgeon-Captain Peter 15, 44, 45, 46
Clover 20
Coaley Mill 310
Codex Alimentarius 43
Cooling bread after cooking 289
COMA report 118
Conran, Caroline 59
—recipes of 60-64

| | |
|---|---|
| Coombes, Margaret | 96 |
| Cornflour glaze | 300 |
| Cornmeal | 296 |
| Corn-mill, rotary | 11 |
| Coronary disease | 45 |
| Cranks Health Foods | 97, 256 |
| —recipes of | 257 |
| Crop rotation | 20 |
| Cumin seeds | 302 |
| "Cycocel" | 31 |
| | |
| Danzey Green Windmill | 311 |
| David, Elizabeth | 40, 50, 51 |
| —recipes of | 52-54 |
| Davidson, Alan | 83 |
| De Blank, Justin | 23, 96 |
| —bakery | 33 |
| Decorating | 288 |
| Deighton, Len | 259 |
| —recipes of | 259-260 |
| "Delsene M" | 31 |
| Diabetes | 45 |
| Dough, fast | 37 |
| —hook, Kenwood Chef | 55 |
| —keeping it warm | 286 |
| —knocking back | 288 |
| —mixer | 39 |
| —mixer, fast | 33 |
| —mixer, Tweedy fast | 39 |
| —rising of | 287 |
| Doves Farm Mill | 317 |
| Downfield Mill | 25, 306 |
| Duff, Gail | 97  98, 106 |
| | |
| EEC Intervention tests | 43 |
| Egg, beaten whole as a glaze | 300 |
| —white, beaten as a glaze | 301 |
| —yolk, beaten as a glaze | 301 |
| Elbridge Organic Farm Mill | 315 |
| Equipment for baking | 302 |
| Evans, Beverley, recipe of | 157 |
| | |
| Federation of Wholesale and Multiple Bakers | 14 |
| Felin Geri Mill | 309 |
| Felin Isaf Mill | 306 |
| Ferment | 297 |
| Fermentation, process of | 40, 125 |
| Fertilisers | 20 |
| —phosphate | 31 |
| —yield ratio | 29 |
| Fibre, absence of in diet | 45 |
| —importance of in diet | 46 |
| Fitzbilly Chelsea buns | 55 |
| FitzGibbon, Theodora | 218 |
| —recipes of | 219-221 |
| Flatford Mill | 23 |
| Flour | 290 |
| —baking test of | 43 |
| —barley | 51, 296 |
| —brown | 294 |
| —buckwheat | 296 |
| —Graham | 294 |
| —Granary | 294 |
| —Hofel's | 172 |
| —machinability tests of | 43 |
| —maize | 296 |
| —mineral content of | 292 |
| —nutritional content of | 292 |
| —rye | 51, 294 |
| —stoneground | 22, 23, 74, 290 |
| —strong white | 33 |
| —vitamin content of | 293 |
| —wheatmeal | 294 |
| —white | 294 |
| —white, soft and hard | 294 |
| —white, unbleached | 294 |
| —wholemeal | 19, 33, 51, 290 |
| —wholewheat 85% and 81% | 290 |
| Flour Milling and Baking Research Association | 24, 39, 43, 65 |
| Food labelling | 43 |
| Foelas Watermill | 307 |
| Freeman, Bobby | 190 |
| —recipes of | 191-197 |
| Freezing of bread | 289 |
| Freud, Clement, recipes of | 258 |
| Froud, Nina | 108 |
| —recipes of | 109-117 |
| Fruit juice, used in bread-making | 299 |
| Fungicides | 19, 20, 31 |
| | |
| Gallstones | 45 |
| Garboldisham mill | 19 |
| Glazes and finishes | 300 |
| —experimental | 301 |
| Gluten | 34 |
| Godwin, Fay | 270 |
| —recipes of | 270-271 |
| Good Housekeeping Institute, The | 96 |
| Graham flour | 294 |
| Grain, alpha amylase content of | 30 |
| —mature | 27 |
| —storing time of | 19 |
| Granary baps | 33 |
| —brand | 51 |
| —flour | 294 |
| —loaves | 33 |
| Grant, Betty | 151 |
| —recipes of | 151-153 |
| Grant, Doris | 14, 21, 65 |
| —recipes of | 67-73 |
| Great Alne Mills | 317 |
| Grigson, Jane | 55 |
| —recipes of | 55-58 |
| Grodzinski Bakeries | 182 |
| —recipes of | 184-189 |
| | |
| Hagberg falling number test | 30 |
| Hall, Stuart | 268 |
| —recipes of | 268-269 |
| Hanbury-Tenison, Marika | 225 |
| —recipes of | 226-227 |
| Harrop, Renny | 96 |
| —recipes | 97-107 |
| Hazan, Marcella | 64 |
| Headley Mill | 310 |
| Herbicides, residue in crops | 43 |
| —use of | 31 |
| Heron Corn Mill | 307 |
| "Hi-Bran" | 51 |
| High Corn Mills | 318 |
| "Hofel's" Mill, The | 313 |
| Holme Mills | 245, 305 |
| Horsfield's mill | 191 |
| —stoneground rye meal | 52 |
| | |
| Insecticides | 19, 20 |
| Iron | 66 |
| | |
| Johnson, Maria | 83 |
| —recipes of | 84-95 |
| Jordan's Millers | 245 |
| —recipes of | 246-248 |
| Juggernaut stonemill | 26 |
| | |
| Kaiser rolls | 125 |
| King's Mill | 316 |
| Kneading | 286 |
| | |
| Laboratory anaylsis | 23 |
| —tests | 43 |
| Lactic acid | 252 |
| Lard | 300 |
| Leaven, natural | 252, 253, 297, 298 |
| Lima Bakery | 252 |
| Liquids used in baking | 298 |
| Long, Alan | 236 |
| —recipes | 237-244 |
| Lower Calbourne Mill | 312 |
| | |
| Maize flour | 296 |
| Malt | 300 |
| Margarine | 300 |
| Maschler, Fay | 262 |
| —recipes of | 263 |
| May, A.D. | 276 |
| Mayall, Sam, stoneground wholemeal flour | 147 |
| Metoxuron | 31 |
| Michelham Priory Mill | 316 |
| Milk | 299 |
| —as a glaze | 300 |
| —rolls, recipe for | 34 |
| Mill, The (Over, Cambs.) | 305 |
| Mill, The (Carmarthen, Dyfed) | 309 |
| Millet | 296 |
| Millstones | 24 |
| Mineral content of flours | 292 |
| Minerals contained in bread | 41 |
| Moghul bread | 59 |
| Molasses | 300 |
| Morrison, Dinah | 176 |
| —recipes of | 177-181 |
| Morrison, George | 218 |
| Mosimann, Anton | 230 |
| —recipes of | 232-235 |
| Muffins, over-bottom | 125 |
| Muncaster mill | 24, 25, 307 |
| Myco-toxins | 43 |
| | |
| Nash, Shirley | 148 |
| —recipes of | 148-149 |
| National Institute of Agricultural Botanists | 30 |
| National Seed Development Organisation | 31 |
| National Society of Health | 266 |

Natural Food Company 249
Natural foods, information sources 119
Newnham Mill 311
Niacin 66
Nitrates 31
Nitrogen fertiliser 31
Norman, Ursel 198
—recipes of 198-205
North Leverton Windmill 313
Nutrition 43
Nutritional content of bread 41
—content of flour 292

Oats 296
Oatmeal 296
Odell, Olive 136
—recipes of 137-141
Oil as glaze 301
Oils and fats 300
Old Corn Mill, The 308
Oldham, Margaret 146
—recipes of 146-147
Organic Farmers and Growers 19
Organic farming 19
—stoneground wholemeal flour 23
—stoneground wholemeal flour, consumer tests 119
Ortiz, Elisabeth Lambert 158
—recipes 160-171
Ovens 33

Pakenham Mill 23
Pearl barley 296
Peptic ulcers 45
Pesticides, accumulation in wheat 43
—testing of 42
Phytic acid 119
Piles 45
Pimhill Mill 314
Plant Breeding Institute 29, 30
Polunin, Miriam 118
—recipes of 120-124
Poppy seeds 301
Post windmill 24, 25
Potassium bromate 118
Prewett's rye flour 52
Priston Mill 305
Protein content of bread 29, 42

Rank Hovis McDougall Ltd. 39, 51
Reynard, John 172
Roden, Claudia 228
—recipes of 228-229
"Rogor" insecticide 31
Rojé, Judy 155
—recipes of 155-156
Rolls, Kaiser 125
Rolls, milk, recipe for 34
Ronay, Barbara, recipes of 261
"Rope" fungus 33
Royal Institute of Public Health and Hygiene 40
Rye flour 51, 294
Rye, non-retention in bread 40

Sadler, Mabel 142

—recipes of 142-145
Salt, sea 33
—use of in bread 299
—water 301
Sams, Craig 252
—recipes of 254-255
Sayer's Confectioners Ltd. 125
Schumaker, Dr. Otto 19
Scurfield, George and Cecilia 74
—recipes of 75-82
Seed Wholefood restaurant 252
Seeds and garnishes 301
Self-sufficiency 264
Sesame seeds 301
Seymour, John 264
Soil Association, The 19
Sour black bread 108
—milk 299
Sourdough breads 40, 42, 252, 253
—starter 297
Southburn Mill 312
South End Mills 313
Southern Oil Company 125
Soya bean paste 108
—flour 297
Spencer, Bill 125
Spillers Ltd. 33, 39
Springhill Farm Mill 305
Steel roller milling 290
Stoneground flour 22
—storage of 290
Stonegrinding 290
Storing of bread 289
Sugar, refined 45
"Sun Bran" loaf 51
Sunflower seeds 302
Sunday Times One-day Real Bread Conference 40
Swanton Mill 312
Sweeteners 299
Syrup as glaze 301

Tea, used in bread-making 299
Thorner Mill 319
Tofu 108
Townsend, Yvonne, recipe of 156
Traeger, Tessa 265
Treacle, black 300
"Tribunil" herbicide 31
Trowell, Rev. Dr. Hugh 44, 46
Turog 125
Tweedy fast dough mixer 39

Varicose veins 45
Vegetarian Society 15, 236
Vegetable oils 300
Vickery, Dr. Kenneth 40
Vitamin B complex 65, 66
Vitamin C 42
—addition to dough 118, 287
—content of bread 41
—content of flours 293

Walsham Mill 23, 24, 26, 27, 315
—flour from 33
Water, in dough-making 298

Waterfield, Harold 125
Watermill, The 307
Webster, Frank 125
Weeds 20
Wheat 20
Wheat, Canadian 40
—Canadian, Red Western spring 245
Wheat cleaning machine 22
Wheat, cracked 302
Wheat, diseases of 30
Wheat germ 296
—extraction of 19
—Vitamin B1 in 66
Wheat growing, without fertilisers or pesticides 18
Wheat, kibbled 302
Wheat, organic 23
Wheat, tonnage of 29
Wheat, varieties of
—Avalon 30, 31
—Bounty 29, 30, 31, 43
—Bouquet 24
—Browick 29
—Cappelle 23, 30
—Durin 30
—Flinor 24
—Hobbit 30
—Holdfast 30
—Huntsman 30
—Hustler 31
—Maris Freeman 24
—Maris Huntsman 30, 43
—Maris Widgeon 21, 24, 30
—Red Fife 29
—Sappo 24
—Sicco 24
—Timmo 24
—Waggoner 24
—White Fife 30
—Yeoman 29
White bread 42
—additives 65
—experiments with rats 42
—milling destroys vitamins and minerals 65
—sliced 51
—with added bran 47
White flour 45, 294
—V natural wholemeal flour 19
"White 'N' Bran" 51
Wholemeal bread 21, 27, 45, 46, 47, 51, 59, 237, 249, 262
—dough 33
—expensive v white 42
—experiments with rats 42
—good plant-baked 42
—not well-risen 42
Wholemeal flour 19, 33, 51
—stoneground 23, 74, 290
Williams, Leslie 125
Williams, Peggy, recipe of 154
Wilton Mill 317
Windmill Post, Chillenden 23
Women's Institute, The 136, 142
Workers' Educational Association 146
Worsbrough Mill 318

Yeast 297
—bringing to life 297
—dried 298
—*Harvest Gold Fermipan* 55
—kinds of 297
—storing fresh 297
Yoghurt 299

Z-blade Morton mixer 39
Zen Centre 172

# RECIPE TITLE INDEX

Ale buns 238
Aphrodisiac milk bread 268
Apple bread 149
Apple muffins **120**, 138
Apple scones, wholemeal **232**, 248
Apricot and hazelnut loaf **120**, 140
Apricot bread **88**, 211
Arab peasant bread 228
Arepas 159, 166
Artologanos 215

Bagels 113
Bagels, wholemeal 122
Bakestone bread 191
Ballymaloe brown bread 263
Banana bread 161, **201**, 234
Baps 148
Baps, Cranks' cheese 257
Baps, rosemary 101
Baps, Scotch 66, 72
Bara Brith 157
Bara Brith, wholemeal 194, **216**
Barbecued bread 274
Barley bread 196
Barley bread, mild 54, **216**
Barley bread on the bakestone 191
Barley bread, wholemeal 270
Barm brack, Irish 40
Basic bread 265
Basic wheat germ brown
    bread 205, **273**
Bastable bread 137
Bath buns **105**, 130
Belgian loaf 97
Biscottes **105**, **217**
Black bread 204
Blini 108, 109, **200**
Boija 160
Bolillos 168
Boston brown bread 212, **216**
Boxty bread 220, **233**
Bran loaf, Irish **233**, 242
Bran-plus loaf 68
Bread and butter pudding, cheesy 274
Bread and butter pudding,
    Mr. A.D. May's 276
Bread pudding 277
Bread pudding, spicy 276
Bread rolls 233
Bread sauce 273
Bread sippets 273
Bread sticks 224
Bread stuffed with split peas 165

Bread, sun and planet 90, **105**
Brioche/savarin **232**, 260
Brioches 232
Brown bread, Ballymaloe 263
Brown bread, basic wheat
    germ 205, **273**
Brown bread, Boston 212, **216**
Brown bread, quick 144
Brown bread, steamed 192
Brown turban loaf 93, **105**
Buckwheat and buttermilk
    waffles **129**, 180
Bulgarian Easter loaf 84, 94
Bulkalech 182, 186
Buns, ale 238
Buns, Bath 130
Buns, butter 132
Buns, curd cheese 184
Buns, farthing 134, **217**
Buns, hot cross 177
Buns, lemon Chelsea 155
Buns, pumpkin 162
Buns, spice 79
Butter buns 132
Buttermilk rolls 203

Cake, dough **121**, 156
Cake, fruit, made with yeast 124
Cake, lardy **121**, 152
Cake, milk steam 76
Cake, Polish 112
Cake, Russian Easter 110
Cake, walnut hearth 170
Cake, yeast (Gugelhupf) 80
Cake, yeast, Mrs. Beeton's 82
Calabrian pizza 63, **88**
Cappodocia 214
Carrot and walnut loaf, golden 100, **112**
Cereal bread, special four **232**, 239
Chappatis 61, **200**
Cheese and herb plait **128**, 148
Cheese baps, Cranks' 257
Cheese bread 86
Cheese buns, curd 184
Cheese plaits 150
Cheese pull-aparts 103
Cheese scones, Cheshire 269
Cheesy bread and butter pudding 274
Chelsea buns, lemon 155
Cheshire cheese scones 269
Chicago pumpernickel 204, **216**
Chinese dumplings 116
Cholla 60, 109, 186
Christmas bread 138
Christmas loaf 133
Christmas pudding, light 277
Cinnamon rolls 173
Clapbread 100
Coconut bread 164, **200**
Coconut clusters 102, **120**
Coconut corn bread 160
Corn bread 216, 241
Corn bread, coconut 160
Corn bread, Paraguayan 168
Corn bread, sweet 167
Corn muffins 214

Cornish splits **121**, 144
Cotswold loaf 104
Cottage loaf 201, **216**
Coulibiac 114
Cretan olive and onion bread 57, **88**
Croissants, granary 123
Croissants, wholemeal 106
Crumpets **120**, **129**, 238
Cumin and poppy seed rolls 226, **233**

Dal Puri 165, **200**
Danish ring 188
Date loaf 69, **129**
Date, pecan and orange bread 210
Dee dee cake 94, **105**
Dough cake **121**, 156
Doughnuts **129**, 154
Dumplings, Chinese 116
Dutch honey bread 213

Easter cake, Russian 110
Easter loaf, Bulgarian 84, 94
Eggy bread 273
Everyday bread 120
Everyday loaf 261

Farl, wholemeal **120**, 135
Farmhouse plait 98, **112**
Farthing buns 134, **217**
Floats 160, **200**
Flowerpot loaves 98, **272**
Focaccia Con La Salvia 59, 64, **88**
Fouace 170, **256**
Four-cereal bread, special **232**, 239
French loaf, savoury 152
French toast 273
Fried crispy bread 160
Fruit cake with yeast 124
Fruit loaf, yeasted 220
Fruit or vegetable filled loaves **88**, 174
Fruit pan 220
Fruity tea bread 251

Golden carrot and walnut loaf 100, **112**
Granary bread 156
Granary bread, walnut 56
Granary croissants 123
Granary loaf, walnut and onion 180
Grant loaf, the 65, 67
Grapenut, Weetabix, wholemeal
    loaf **257**, 258
Grissini 209
Gugelhupf 80, **104**

Hairy bread **120**, 121
Hazlenut and apricot loaf **120**, 140
Hazlenut brioche loaf 58
Herb and cheese plait **128**, 148
Herb bread **105**, 131
High protein-low calorie bread 240
Honey bread, Dutch 213

Irish barm brack 140
Irish bran loaf **233**, 242

Kolatschen 80, **104**

Kozounak, wholemeal 84, 94
Kulich 84, 110, **113**

Lahma Bi Ajeen 229, **232**
Lardy cake **121**, 152, 159
Leaven bread, natural 255
Lemon Chelsea buns 155
Lincolnshire plum bread 145
Loaf, double plaited 178

Maize and millet bread **232**, 244
Malt bread, quick 139
Maslin bread 192, **216**
Melitutes 216
Mexican bread rolls 168
Mild barley bread 54, **216**
Milk bread, aphrodisiac 268
Milk steam cake 76
Millet and maize bread **232**, 244
Monastery oat bread 200, **256**
Mrs. Beeton's yeast cake 82
Muesli loaf 207, **232**
Muffins, apple **120**, 138
Muffins, corn 214

Naan 59, 62, **200**
Natural leaven bread 255
No-quantity bread 264
Nutritional loaf 240

Oat bread 89, 143
Oat bread, monastery 200, **256**
Oat cakes, Welsh 195, **273**
Oak cakes, Yorkshire 181
Oatmeal bread 75, 100, 247
Oatmeal rye, country style 202, **216**
Olive and onion bread, Cretan 57, **88**
Onion and walnut loaf **128**, 180
Onion bread 227
Onion bread, wholemeal 222
Orange, date and pecan bread 210
Oven wholemeal flatties 73, **88**

Pain perdu 275
Panbread, wholemeal 88, **105**
Pancakes, wholemeal 248
Pancakes, yeast 109
Paraguayan corn bread 168
Parker House rolls **216**, 217
Pecan, date and orange bread 210
Pie, Russian 114
Pie, yeast raised 117
Pikelets **120**, 129
Pitta bread 60, 109
Pitta bread, wholemeal 179
Pizza 198
Pizza, Calabrian 63, **88**
Pizza, wholemeal 146
Planc bread 193
Platzels 185
Plum bread, Lincolnshire 145
Pogacha/Pogača 92, **105**
Polish cake 112
Poppy seed roll **105**, 112
Poppy seed rolls, cumin and 226, **233**
Potato bread 237, 271

Potato bread, Irish 220
Potato rolls 223
Potato scones 141, **272**
Printer's pudding 275
Protein, high, low calorie bread 240
Pumpernickel, Chicago 204, **216**
Pumpkin buns 162

Raisin and walnut bread 234
Raisin bread 220
Raisin loaf 68
Raisin scones, Ruth's 72, **272**
Raisin, soya rice bread 242
Rice bread 53, **88**, 210, 243
Rice raisin soya bread 242
Rolls, bread 233
Rolls, buttermilk 203
Rolls, cinnamon 173
Rolls, cumin and poppy seed 226, **233**
Rolls, Jewish crusty (Platzels) 185
Rolls, Mexican bread 168
Rolls, Parker House **216**, 217
Rolls, potato 223
Rolls, wedding 182, 186
Rolls, wholemeal (Bagels) 122
Rosemary baps 101, **112**
Roti 162, **200**
Rum Baba 189, **201**
Russian Easter cake 110
Russian pie 114
Ruth's raisin scones 72, **272**
Rye bread 89, 126, 196, **216**
Rye bread, sour 78
Rye loaf, easy 52

Sally Lunn loaf 127
Savoury French loaf 152
Savoury walnut bread 102
Scones 70
Scones, Cheshire cheese 269
Scones, potato 141, **272**
Scones, Ruth's raisin 72, **272**
Scones, sultana 71
Scones, wholemeal 70
Scones, wholemeal apple **232**, 248
Scotch baps 66, 72
Semolina bread 159, 171
Slavonic ritual bread 92
Soda bread **120**, 219
Soda or bastable bread 136, 137
Sopa Paraguaya 168, **200**
Sour rye bread 78
Sourdough bread **128**, 147, 254-5, **256**
Sourdough starter 254
Southern spoonbread 212
Soya rice raisin bread 242
Spice buns 79
Spicy bread pudding 276
Sultana scones 71
Summer pudding 274
Sun and planet 90, **105**
Swedish tea ring 208, **217**
Sweet corn bread 167, **201**

Tea brack **120**, 221
Tea bread 102

Tea bread, fruity 251
Tea bread, Swedish 208
Tea cakes, Yorkshire **120**, 128
Toast, French 273
Tomato bread 88, 142
Torriga 275
Tortillas 159, 166
Tortillas, wheat 167
Toutmanik 86, **105**

Unleavened bread 228

Vegetable or fruit filled loaves 88, 174
Vienna bread 77

Waffles, buckwheat and
  buttermilk **129**, 180
Walnut and carrot loaf,
  golden 100, **112**
Walnut and onion loaf **128**, 180
Walnut and raisin bread 234
Walnut bread, savoury 102
Walnut granary bread 56
Walnut hearth cake 170
Wedding rolls 182, 186
Weetabix, wholemeal and grapenut
  loaf **257**, 258
Wheat germ brown bread,
  basic 205, **273**
Wheat germ loaf 246
Wheat tortillas 167
White bread, quick almost 84
Wholemeal apple scones **232**, 248
Wholemeal bagels 122
Wholemeal Bara Brith 194, **216**
Wholemeal barley loaf 270
Wholemeal bread 151, **257**
Wholemeal bread, basic 250
Wholemeal bread, mixed **257**, 259
Wholemeal bread, nutritional 266
Wholemeal bread with eggs 267
Wholemeal croissants 106
Wholemeal farl **120**, 135
Wholemeal flatties, oven 73, **88**
Wholemeal loaf, Cotswold 104
Wholemeal onion bread 222
Wholemeal panbread 88, **105**
Wholemeal pancakes 248
Wholemeal pitta bread 179
Wholemeal pizza 146
Wholemeal scones 70
Wholemeal sourdough bread **128**, 147
Wholemeal, Weetabix and grapenut
  loaf **257**, 258

Yeast cake (Gugelhupf) 81
Yeast cake, Mrs. Beeton's 82
Yeast fruit cake 124
Yeast pancakes (Blini) 109
Yeast raised pie 117
Yeasted fruit loaf 220
Yoghurt bread **257**, 272
Yorkshire oat cakes 181
Yorkshire tea cakes **120**, 128

Zopf **232**, 235